COGNITIVE ANALYTIC THERAPY
FOR ADULT SURVIVORS OF CHILDHOOD ABUSE

COGNITIVE ANALYTIC THERAPY FOR ADULT SURVIVORS OF CHILDHOOD ABUSE

Approaches to Treatment and Case Management

PHILIP H. POLLOCK

MV Psychology Consultancy, Belfast
Down Lisburn Trust, Northern Ireland

With specialist contributions from

Sue Llewelyn
Oxford University, UK

Sue Clarke
Dorset Healthcare Trust, UK

Teresa Hagan and Kath Gregory
Community Health, Sheffield, UK

Mark Stowell-Smith
Knowsley and St Helens Hospital Trust, UK

Michael Göpfert
Webb House Therapeutic Community, Crewe, UK

Susan Mitzman
North Mersey Community NHS Trust, UK

Martin Bamber
York NHS Trust, University of Teesside, UK

JOHN WILEY & SONS, LTD
Chichester · New York · Weinheim · Brisbane · Singapore · Toronto

Other Wiley Editorial Offices

John Wiley & Sons, Inc., 605 Third Avenue,
New York, NY 10158-0012, USA

WILEY-VCH GmbH, Pappelallee 3,
D-69469 Weinheim, Germany

John Wiley Australia Ltd, 33 Park Road, Milton,
Queensland 4064, Australia

John Wiley & Sons (Asia) Pte Ltd, 2 Clementi Loop #02-01,
Jin Xing Distripark, Singapore 129809

John Wiley & Sons (Canada) Ltd, 22 Worcester Road,
Rexdale, Ontario M9W 1L1, Canada

British Library Cataloguing-in-Publication Data

Pollock, Philip, 1968–
    Cognitive analytic therapy for adult survivors of childhood abuse : approaches to
    treatment and case management / Philip H. Pollock ; with specialist contributions by
    Sue Llewelyn . . . [et al.].
        p. cm.
    Includes bibliographical references and index.
    ISBN 0-471-49160-8—ISBN 0-471-49159-4 (pbk)
    1. Adult child abuse victims—Mental health. 2. Cognitive-analytic therapy. I.
    Llewelyn, Susan P. II. Title.
    RC569.5.C55 .P65 2001
    616.85'82230651—dc21

                                                                    2001024249

British Library Cataloguing in Publication Data

A catalogue record for this book is available from the British Library

ISBN 0-471 49160-8 (cased)
ISBN 0-471-49159-4 (paper)

Typeset in 10/12pt Times by Dorwyn Ltd, Rowlands Castle, Hants
Printed and bound in Great Britain by Biddles Ltd, Guildford and King's Lynn
This book is printed on acid-free paper responsibly manufactured from sustainable
forestry, in which at least two trees are planted for each one used for paper production.

Til ma faither Hugh an ma mither Sarah Ann
Fur thair minefu bield o ma rairin

To Amy and Conor, proof of God's work

Contents

List of figures and tables

About the author

Dr Philip H. Pollock BSc (Hons), MSc, CPsychol, PhD, AFBPsS trained at the Queens University of Belfast, University of Newcastle upon Tyne and Durham University, qualifying as a clinical psychologist in 1992. Presently, he holds the posts of Consultant Clinical Psychologist and Head of Adult Mental Health with the Down Lisburn Trust based at the Downshire Hospital in Downpatrick, Northern Ireland. He is also the founder and lead clinical manager of M.V. Psychology Consultancy, a forensic private practice based in Belfast serving numerous organisations across the UK and with links to the USA. He has published widely in the fields of forensic, child and adult mental health, with a particular interest in applying Cognitive Analytic Therapy (CAT) for a variety of psychological difficulties and disorders. He has provided training in CAT for several professions and is currently leading a research-based study investigating the relative efficacy of CAT compared to other psychotherapies for adult survivors of childhood abuse who commit abuse against others in adulthood.

Dr Pollock can be contacted at the Department of Clinical Psychology, Downshire Hospital, Ardglass Road, Downpatrick, County Down, BT30 6RA, Northern Ireland, e-mail Philip_Pollock@DLTrust.n-i.nhs.uk.

List of contributors

Dr Susan Llewelyn is the Course Director of Clinical Psychology Training in the Oxford Region. She has special interests in the psychotherapy process and outcome and in the development of therapies for abuse survivors. She is a CAT practitioner and supervisor and has published widely on CAT, sexual abuse, women's psychological issues and psychotherapy.

Dr Sue Clarke is a Consultant Clinical Psychologist and holds a PhD in psychology from the University of Southampton. She currently works for Dorset Healthcare Trust as the head of a specialist service for people with personality disorders, many of whom have experienced childhood neglect or trauma. She is an experienced CAT psychotherapist and trainer, her interest in this approach originating from clinical and research work with people suffering the long-term effects of childhood trauma and neglect. Her recent research publications are concerned with the psychological process underlying complex problems (e.g., revictimisation) and the systematic evaluation of treatment.

Dr Teresa Hagan is a Clinical Psychologist working in a Community Mental Health Team with a lead role in research and development in the Mental Health Directorate. She has published work on users' views of health care and she has a special interest in community and social psychology. She is a CAT practitioner and initiated a group-based service for survivors of childhood sexual abuse.

Kath Gregory is a retired Community Mental Health Nurse with many years of experience working in mental health care and she was also involved in the initiation of the Women's Therapy Service in Sheffield.

Dr Mark Stowell-Smith is a psychotherapist working in the Psychological Therapy Service in the Knowsley and St Helens Hospital Trust.

Dr Michael Göpfert has a background in Nursing, Child and Adolescent Psychiatry, Adult Psychiatry and Psychotherapy. He is an integrative psychotherapist and a family therapy and psychotherapy trainer. He also has an interest in CAT and interpersonal cognitive and behavioural psychotherapies. He has researched in the area of neurolinguistics, psychosomatics and parental psychiatric disorders. Recent publications cover CAT, family therapy and families with a parent who is a user of mental health services. He works as a psychotherapist specialising in the treatment of people with severe personality disorders.

Susan Mitzman is a Consultant Clinical Psychologist and head of the Adult Eating Disorder Service in the North Mersey Community NHS Trust. She is also a CAT accredited practitioner, trainer and supervisor.

Dr Martin Bamber is currently working as a Consultant Clinical Psychologist managing the York Cognitive and Behavioural Therapies Centre, which is a part of York NHS Trust. He is also Assistant Director of the Teesside Doctoral Training Programme in Clinical Psychology. His interests lie in the field of psychoneuroimmunology, promoting the biopsychosocial model of health and the development of new cognitive-behavioural techniques which can be incorporated into everyday therapeutic clinical practices.

Foreword

It is a great personal pleasure to recommend this book, both as a valuable addition to the literature on childhood abuse and as a systematic extension of CAT practice. CAT took shape about twenty years ago as a time-limited model of integrated individual psychotherapy; in the intervening years its theory has become increasingly defined and differentiated from the original cognitive and psychoanalytic sources. Its practice has been enriched by the contributions of many people from many different professional backgrounds; its theory has increasingly emphasised the need for a dialogic rather than monadic understanding of human personality development and of psychotherapy. Its research base has expanded through naturalistic studies and some small-scale controlled studies. More recently, its application to particular patient groups and in particular settings has been reported. This book is a continuation of this evolution; all the various contributors have drawn on their experience of working in other modes and have shown how these may contribute to practice within a CAT framework, and many of them have backed up their clinical work with related research. The literature related to the book's topic has been thoroughly reviewed.

The basic 'techniques' of CAT involve an early collaborative reformulation of a patient's difficulties in the form of a narrative reconstruction (there are many good examples of these often moving letters in the text) and written and diagrammatic descriptions of problems and the procedures which maintain them. The formation and use of these techniques provide patients with a new basis for self-reflection and integration and give therapists clear, individual understandings which enable them to enter into safe (non-collusive), but intense therapeutic relationships. These methods address the person, not the symptom, behaviour, faulty belief or unconscious conflict. This makes it a particularly appropriate intervention for the survivors of childhood abuse who suffer from a wide variety of symptoms, but whose underlying damage is to their sense of self and, often, to the structure of their self processes.

Survivors have no reason to trust others and have often established ways of avoiding closeness, which may involve being hostile or emotionally unavailable. The non-judgemental process of reformulation, the focus on the person's individual, persistent procedures (which may enable, but never insists on, traumatic memories being thought and talked about) and their recognition and non-reinforcement in the therapy relationship, whether individual or group, provide an example of a respecting relationship which can be internalised. The diagrammatic mapping of the partial dissociation into separate self-states which commonly follow abuse enables the confusion which is experienced by many survivors and which is often induced in the therapist to be understood, so that a sense of wholeness and of control over one's life can be established.

Within this framework, a wide range of particular approaches may be usefully employed, as is evident in the work of all of the contributors to this book. Some, like the use of 'power mapping' and 'lessons learned' diagrams, are extensions of the existing reformulation methods, which deserve to find their way into basic CAT techniques. Others open up the questions which further research may clarify, such as the different forms of group therapy proposed. Pollock's modestly presented, naturalistic, carefully measured outcome study of 37 adult survivors establishes that here, as in other areas, more elaborate and controlled studies are clearly justified; unfortunately there is no guarantee that research funding will be available.

Meanwhile, one main achievement of the book is that it conveys, in relation to painful and degrading human experiences, the human resourcefulness of both survivors and their therapists.

ANTHONY RYLE
Italy, June 2000

Preface

The horror and aftermath of abusive experiences during childhood are difficult to verbalise faithfully. Listening to the narrative accounts of survivors can be harrowing and touching. A moving illustration can be found in the depiction of fictional lawyer Jake Brigance in John Grisham's book *A Time to Kill* who, when making his closing arguments to the jury during a case where a father, Carl Lee, is tried for killing his daughter's rapists, captures the plight of both victim and family alike:

> He had a daughter, the only one he would ever have. She was four, almost five, and his world revolved around her. She was special; she was a little girl, and it was up to him to protect her. There was a bond there, something he could not explain. He talked about little girls. Carl Lee had a daughter. Her name was Tonya. She's a beautiful little girl, ten years old. He talked about rape for a while . . . every hour of every day, the victim thinks of the rape and asks herself a thousand questions. She relives it, step by step, minute by minute, and it hurts just as bad . . . Perhaps the most horrible crime of all is the violent rape of a child . . . suppose you're a parent. Imagine yourself trying to explain to your child why she was raped. Imagine yourself trying to explain why she cannot bear children . . . He wanted to leave them with one thought. Picture this if they could. When she was lying there, beaten, bloodied, legs spread and tied to trees, she looked into the woods around her. Semiconscious and hallucinating, she saw someone running towards her. It was her daddy, running desperately to save her. In her dreams she saw him when she needed him the most. She cried out to him, and he disappeared . . . Suppose your ten-year-old daughter is raped, and you're a Vietnam vet, very familiar with an M-16, and you get your hands on one while your daughter is lying in hospital fighting for her life. Suppose the rapist is caught, and six days later you manage to manoeuvre to within five feet of him as he leaves court . . . What do you do? (pp. 699–701, *A Time to Kill* © John Grisham, 1989, published by Hutchinson)

As therapists, the fantasies we often harbour about helping an adult survivor who has been severely abused in childhood range from the wish to assume the actual pain experienced, to rescue or save the survivor, and to wreak revenge on the perpetrator. These fantasies can induce us to act protectively, stretching our resources, extending one's own psychological boundaries of experience when listening to the unspeakable anguish of indescribable experiences. Ultimately, we come to acknowledge the crassness and cruelty of human nature—a disappointing and humbling insight. The role we attempt to play for sufferers of abuse demands us to be touched by the reality of events which we are powerless to change or to undo: the deed is done. The care we try to give must be sensitive and thoughtful in its delivery to avoid causing retraumatisation and additional distress for the survivor whose bravery in placing his/her distress in our hands is always genuinely and honestly invested. They deserve our best efforts and careful practice. With experience, our own omnipotent fantasies of rescue and undoing become tempered, but a therapist's bravery must match that of the survivor.

A number of years ago, I naïvely harboured fantasies of dissolving away the facts and pain of childhood abuse when, on a daily basis, I listened to both sides of the dark scenario of trauma. Working with survivors and perpetrators portrayed a balanced yet tragic picture of human degradation and disrespect. It is easy to become demoralised and deflated when undertaking this sort of work. For me, my idealised fantasies were inevitably disappointed but replaced by an admiration for the craft and creativity which survivors of abuse demonstrate as children or adolescents faced with the confusing mess that accompanies abuse. Rarely, in the beginning, do adult survivors have any appreciation of their resilience and resourcefulness that they have shown during childhood. For those of us whose lives have not been scarred by trauma, we can only imagine how survivors of abuse muster the courage to cope.

Cognitive Analytic Therapy (CAT) is a relatively young form of psychotherapy in comparison to others. Its application to the psychological problems which accompany childhood abuse and continue into adolescence and adulthood has produced promising results. Here, I present a description and illustration of CAT for adult survivors of childhood sexual, physical and/or psychological abuse. A psychotherapy of choice does not exist to help these clients. Currently, the evidence base for differing forms of psychotherapy is sparse for survivors of abuse. Whether CAT can enhance our clinical practice is open to debate. CAT features certain advantageous aspects in that it is a brief, client-centred and collaborative approach that encourages the adult survivor to acquire as much purchase as possible on their often marred lives. Similarly to all other therapies, CAT is not a panacea for a spoiled childhood, but it can be of significant benefit for adult survivors who have experienced a spectrum of childhood abuse.

Part I of the book progresses from a discussion of the complex interplay of factors which are involved in childhood abuse, and the unique and often idio-syncratic ways in which survivors cope with the trauma they experience (Chapter 1), to a basic description of CAT language and practice (Chapter 2). A CAT model of pathological developmental outcomes based on Ryle's Multiple Self-States Model of trauma is described in Chapter 3 and a review of treatment models for abuse (Chapter 4) follows. In Part II, a series of case illustrations of increasing pathological severity are reported (Chapters 5 and 6 by Susan Llewelyn and Sue Clarke and also Chapter 7). Chapter 8 considers how victimisation can colour the interactions between survivor and therapist within the helping relationship. The applications of CAT in group approaches are described in Chapter 9 by Teresa Hagan and by Mark Stowell-Smith, Michael Göpfert and Sue Mitzman in Chapter 10. Part III consists of the description of a case series outcome study (Chapter 11) which reports the findings of individual CAT for survivors, drawing tentative conclusions about the clinical efficacy of this form of intervention and suggestions for future research. Chapter 12 consists of an empirical research project which reports on the construction, development and clinical applications of the Personality Structure Questionnaire (PSQ), which is an important instrument for assess-ing the CAT model proposed. In the final chapter Martin Bamber provides an independent commentary on the contribution CAT makes to understanding of responses to childhood abuse in adulthood and its strengths and weak-nesses as a therapeutic approach.

I have chosen to concentrate on childhood abuse and trauma that includes sexual, physical and emotional abuse in various combinations. Empirical research has indicated that single forms of abuse in childhood are rarely evident in the majority of cases and that the family environment can greatly influence the developmental pathway shown by the survivor and the long-term effects of the abuse experienced. The survivor's own resilience and con-tribution to adjusting cannot be underestimated given the evidence that not every case of abuse results in a pathological outcome requiring professional assistance. To focus exclusively on one form of childhood abuse (e.g., incest) would, to my mind, be denying the reality of clinical practice with survivors and limit the generalisation of research findings. It is not uncommon for survivors of abuse to experience revictimisation (e.g., a survivor of childhood sexual abuse becoming raped while an adolescent). Therefore, the cases described portray a diverse array of abusive experiences. I have used the term 'survivor' rather than 'victim' throughout the book, although it must be stressed that many adults who have been abused in childhood have not contemplated the fact that they have been victimised and still conceive that they were contributors and participants in their own trauma. Movement towards perceiving oneself as a 'victim' often precedes the transition to becoming a 'survivor'. This process is illustrated using case examples.

I make no apologies for applying diagnostic statements within the CAT model presented and the illustrative cases. Communication of ideas between clinicians does not immediately imply that the person or individual is reduced in some way to a label. I would argue that, if diagnostic statements about patterns of psychopathology help clinicians to understand the patient's problems (I am not inferring that such language is used with the patient him/herself at any time), this means of describing psychological problems has reasonable value.

Similarly, it could be debated whether any psychotherapy should advocate a view that the survivor of abuse is defined by a given role ('victim', 'survivor', 'thriver' and 'aggressor') because it insinuates that the abuse is seated within the person and part of his/her personality. At first glance, it appears that CAT does focus upon these sorts of roles. I would hope that more rigorous reading would lead to an appreciation that CAT encourages the use of constructs of this type to convey the real experience of abuse for the survivor and its often persisting effects upon him/her. Drawings, metaphors, musical compositions, dramatic role-plays etc. are more helpful to depict states of being experienced by survivors of childhood abuse and our lexicon of words fails their description of suffering dismally. It must be accepted that the verbal vehicle which forms a significant part of therapy is not enough in some cases and striving to develop an adequate system of description is a difficult task for any psychotherapy.

In writing this book about applying CAT for survivors of childhood abuse, my intention was to illustrate a way of thinking about and conceptualising the difficulties these survivors experience. CAT is not the 'Holy Grail' of psychotherapies. It has its strengths and limitations, like any other method of helping. My hope is that the reader will reflect upon its usefulness in addressing survivors' psychological problems and decide whether it will enhance his/her capability to help these clients to rid themselves of emotional pain which has usually continued for too long already before they enter our consulting rooms.

Several details have been altered to protect the identities of survivors used in each of the case illustrations described throughout the book.

PHILIP H. POLLOCK
Belfast, July 1999

Acknowledgements

The following people deserve mention and thanks for the help and assistance they have provided during the writing of the book. My thanks to Dr Tony Ryle for his encouragement and guidance. I have always appreciated his willingness to listen and found our discussions to be stimulating and thought provoking.

The editorial team at John Wiley & Sons for their patience and advice. I would also like to extend my appreciation to the contributors to the book, who are busy clinicians with lives of their own—many thanks for your help.

Most of all, to the survivors who work so hard to achieve a sense of themselves as worthy and of value during therapy.

Part I

CAT reformulation of traumatic experiences in childhood

CHAPTER 1

Conceptualising the developmental outcomes of abuse

> At the highest with dull malice reaches,
> As slugs pollute the fairest peaches,
> Envy defames as Harpyes vile,
> Devours the fruit they first defile.
> (P. Delaney, 1792; cited in J.H. Burke, 1988)

Putting abuse into words

The abuse of a child violates one of our most cardinal and fundamental tenets of society. Such acts can extend from aggressive defilement and entrapment during sexual abuse to pernicious insults during psychological abuse to brutal bombardment through physical harm. Often, differing forms of abuse are amalgamated into one by the perpetrator. The harm inflicted can take a plethora of forms. Perpetrators of abuse operate along a spectrum of behaviours displaying, at one end, violent degradation (as depicted in Delaney's poetic description above) to exploitation under the pretence of tenderness, emotional need and affection at the other (illustrated by Vladimir Nabokov's *Lolita*). The impact upon the child can show unlimited diversity matching the range in manner and types of abuse exhibited by perpetrators. It must be appreciated that how the perpetrator behaves, the coping responses shown by the survivor and the context of the abusive experiences themselves will influence the developmental outcome for the child. There are many forms of abuse occurring in differing combinations and, similarly, unique patterns of coping are demonstrated by the child and, later, the adult survivor.

Abuse of whatever form induces states of mind in the child reflecting an unnatural type of imposed reality. When an adult survivor reminisces about a father's relentless and predatory sexual assaults and how she was recurrently being forced to assume a subordinated, defeated role, she may recall the experience to have caused states of dread and panic, feeling immobilised by these emotions and perceiving herself as a powerless receptacle for the perpetrator's perversion: a toy, an object or his prey. The perpetrator is remembered as demonic and merciless, the child as worthy only of being used for the perpetrator's indulgence. The impact of this contrived reality can persist unaltered long after the abuse has ended, potentially affecting every facet of the survivor's personality. Making sense of what the perpetrator created and its impact is a confusing task.

The profile of psychological dysfunction exhibited by a child is a reflection of attempts to cope with the impact of the perpetrator's imposed reality. In essence, the perpetrator defines a part of the survivor's reality, sometimes persisting into adulthood with respite only attained through the false solutions of symptoms. Each child possesses unique vulnerabilities, reactions and creative strategies for coping, and manages the imprint of abusive experiences differently. The child's contribution to surviving can differ extensively, dependent upon a complex interplay of factors, and the uniqueness of each child's pattern must be appreciated.

Adequately verbalising the effects of abuse can be a disappointing endeavour for the survivor and may fail to capture the true substance of those experiences. van der Kolk (1988) suggested that 'traumatic experiences will be stored in memory, but the somatosensory elements may override linguistic representation' (p. 283). Abuse creates an imposed reality that is difficult, if not impossible, to make sense of. A survivor's description that he feels 'invaded', contaminated and corrupted by a 'malignancy' or 'cancer' can impose words onto physical experience, sensations and emotional trauma that is dissatisfying and incomplete. Often the description cannot be given words and other vehicles of expression are necessary. One survivor painted a portrait of himself, hunched and defeated with what he could only refer to as a 'shadow of sadness hovering over my shoulder'. Another survivor stated that she could not describe the cruelty she endured in a psychologically abusing childhood but brought with her to a therapy session a musical piece of discordant orchestral music, which she felt more accurately captured her sense of herself and her history. Our lexicon of words can appear bankrupt and facile in its attempt to crystallise abusive experiences into meaningful versions of the adult and once child's reality.

All forms of abuse constitute interpersonal events during which a relational unit is created between the perpetrator and survivor. In later years, the survivor's plight goes on. A survivor, whose therapy is described in Chapter 7 in this book, portrays the relentless reliving of the abuse she endured many years previously when she comments 'he appears out of the blue. He even says hello. I don't know where he lives. It's like a cat playing with a mouse. I'm just a mouse, frightened, in a panic, paralysed by fear, haunted by a living ghost. He has some sort of control over me, like an authority figure. I become instantly helpless'. Even a single incident trauma such as rape or physical assault can cause the survivor to harbour a sense that the perpetrator will return into the survivor's life and inflict further harm.

A totality of influences

Figures regarding the prevalence and incidence of different forms of childhood abuse are equivocal and affected by many factors, particularly methodological problems within the studies conducted. It has been estimated that female children are at most risk and retrospective reporting for community samples shows that up to 54% of girls and 18% of boys have experienced unwanted sexual contact with an adult before the age of 18 (Fleming, 1987; Gorey & Leslie, 1997). In clinical samples, prevalence rates tend to be much higher, with specific diagnostic groups demonstrating differential rates (Parry, 1999). For child sexual abuse, specifically, statistics are clouded by the definitions of abuse used and subsequent questions asked, the rate of responding, willingness to disclose the abuse (men being less disclosing) and the effects of memory impairment. In relation to poor recall or suppression of memories of abuse, Williams (1994) found that 38% of women, whose cases showed verifiable documented evidence of sexual abuse, declared that they had not experienced such a history. Interestingly, Elliott and Briere's retrospective study (1995) of a variety of trauma experiences showed that 42% of survivors reported amnesia for the abuse at some point in the case of general abuse and 20% of sexually abused survivors claimed complete lack of recall. This can be interpreted as reflecting an abused child's use of dissociation at the time of encoding the abusive events into memory resulting in fragmented, sensory, partial memories which are verbally inaccessible or successful avoidance of thinking about these events (Andrews, 1999). Rates of forgetting abusive experiences are startling, showing that an inability to recall documented abuse ranges from 16% to 38% (see DelMonte, 2000, for a review).

With respect to prevalence rates of abuse generally, the most relevant caveat is that it is also almost impossible to disaggregate the direct effects of one form of abuse from another. Only 5% of abuse cases involve a single form of mistreatment (Ney, Fung & Wickett, 1994), with a combination of physical neglect, physical abuse and verbal abuse having the most detrimental effect upon a child, indicating that 'a tangled web' (Ney et al., 1994, p. 711) of abuse and neglect is typically observed. In addition, a pathogenic family structure and environment can be the primary source of non-specific problems in development of the sexually abused child, rather than the abuse per se (Alexander & Lupfer, 1987; Nash et al., 1993; Alexander, 1992). The conclusion to be drawn, therefore, is that it is likely that each child's response will be idiosyncratic and unique, given the multitude of influences affecting trajectories towards psychological health or dysfunction. The entire spectrum of factors involved must be taken into account. Disentangling single influences and attributing causation to them denies an acknowledgement of the complexity inherent within these cases of abuse (Briere & Elliott, 1993).

Psychopathology and abuse

To state that abusive experiences in childhood are noxious to the development of good mental health is a given based on the empirical evidence available (Parry, 1999). Thirty-four to fifty-three percent of patients with a severe mental illness report childhood sexual or physical abuse (Ross, Anderson & Clarke, 1994), representing much higher rates of trauma than those cited for the general population (Mueser *et al.*, 1998). A meta-analysis of 26 published studies relating to outcomes conducted by Jumper (1995) indicated that, in general terms, child sexual abuse accounted for an important amount of single-factor variance in adult survivors' scores on measures of psychological symptomatology.

The environmental context in which the abuse occurs is also critical. Certain factors have been identified which affect the outcome of a child's response to trauma such as younger age at onset of the abuse (Courtois, 1979; Browne & Finkelhor, 1985). Beitchman *et al.* (1992) suggest also that abuse-specific variables (such as being abused by a father or stepfather), more forceful and violent abuse, more penetrative and invasive abuse (Sedney & Brooks, 1984) are associated with trauma-related symptoms. A rating of 'lasting harm' was related to longer duration and frequency of abuse (Mullen *et al.*, 1993). More recent research on the objective characteristics of sexual abuse has confirmed the importance of these factors showing that greater severity, duration and frequency of abuse are, in combination, associated with more severe psychopathology in adulthood (Lange *et al.*, 1999). For example, a number of risk factors have also been identified for vulnerability of sexual abuse. These include the presence of a non-biologically related father, parental disability or illness, a violent or conflicted relationship between parents, experiencing physical abuse (Mullen *et al.*, 1993, 1994), being separated or living apart from one's mother during childhood, social isolation (Finkelhor, 1994), growing up in a rural area and poor relationships with one's parents (Russell, 1986).

Fleming, Mullen and Bammer (1997) reported key risk factors for sexual abuse in young females, identifying a combination of five main predictors including experiencing physical abuse, having a mother who was mentally ill, being socially isolated, and lacking emotional support. The strongest predictor was the occurrence of physical abuse. Physical attack, emotional isolation, no access to a caring adult figure and an alcohol-dependent father predicted abuse perpetrated by a family member. For women abused outside the family, the predictors were physical attack, social isolation, an alcoholic mother and the mother's death. Therefore, the environment of most risk entails non-existent parental care, a lack of safety and protection and exposure to potential perpetrators.

The shorter-term effects of sexual abuse have been found, with the exception of sexualised behaviours, to be very similar to samples of children and adolescents seen in psychiatric settings (Beitchman *et al.*, 1991). These authors argue that the data does not lend support to a 'sexual abuse syndrome' which shows a specific course or outcome. Anxiety, depressive symptoms, inappropriate sexualised behaviours, nightmares, social withdrawal, sleeping difficulties, anger and aggression, delinquency, school adjustment problems and physical conditions have been described as reactions to childhood abuse. Other consequences such as HIV infection are tragic complications for abused children in modern society (Whitmire, Harlow, Quina & Morokoff, 1998).

In the longer term, the effects of sexual abuse include a diversity of difficulties (Beitchman *et al.*, 1992), including sexual disturbance and dysfunction, homosexuality, depression, revictimisation, anxiety, fear and suicide completion. Post-traumatic stress disorder (PTSD) symptoms such as re-experiencing the event (e.g., nightmares, flashbacks, recurrent enactment of traumatic themes during play), increased physiological arousal (e.g., irritability, poor concentration) and avoidance have been suggested to account for the disturbances occurring immediately in response to these experiences, these difficulties reverberating for years afterwards (McLeer *et al.*, 1988). The value of the PTSD model is disputed (Mullen *et al.*, 1993) because there is often little continuity between problems shown at the time of the abuse and later, with minimal association between PTSD symptoms and emerging problems throughout a survivor's development (Mullen *et al.*, 1994). Others argue that many survivors of child abuse do display a stable pattern of dysfunction, which persists into adolescence and later adulthood (Carlson, Furby, Armstrong & Schlaes, 1997). Any psychosocial model of victimisation must, therefore, account for discontinuity and continuity in symptomatology across an abused child's maturity to adulthood. It must also be accepted that changes in presentation will be observed within a single individual due to developmentally challenging tasks affecting his/her functioning. Of course, a spectrum of severity is inferred, with a proportion of survivors being asymptomatic (approximately 25%; Follette, Naugle & Follette, 1997), progressing to others who demonstrate severe psychopathology (Wilbur, 1984). It must also be recognised that approximately one-third of children abused do not progress to experiencing significant psychological problems later in life.

Inferring that direct linear pathways exist from childhood victimisation to adult psychopathology is an over-simplistic notion which is not supported by empirical evidence (Wachs, 1999). Childhood abuse must be considered to be a single potential influence amongst many which may be 'necessary but not sufficient' in itself to account for a survivor's presentation and difficulties. The array of influences which affect a child's response to abuse dictates that any useful psychological theory, formulation and therapy will be required to appreciate the idiosyncratic coupling of a perpetrator's behaviour, the survivor's coping responses and the nature and context of the abusive acts. The development, course and stability of psychological problems can vary across time and understanding the progression to adult psychopathology is a complex process. The effects of childhood abuse can range from minimal dysfunction to devastating psychopathology and each case must be located along this continuum of severity.

Continuity and discontinuity: the developmental pathway perspective

A complicated aggregate of influences operates to direct the pathway a child who has suffered childhood abuse will follow and a diversity of outcomes is possible. As stated by Mullen *et al.* (1994), 'abuse is not destiny' (p. 45). Some argue that childhood abuse has persisting and debilitating effects into adulthood (Carlson *et al.*, 1997), others that a child may be exposed to developmental experiences which compensate for the abuse, promoting positive adjustment and adaptation to the trauma. Two children sexually abused by the same perpetrator are likely to demonstrate unique and idiosyncratic reactions. Their eventual adjustment is also unlikely to be the same. To a certain extent, the fact that the perpetrator has introduced abuse into the survivor's life experiences means that some form of negative impact is likely, although this is not a given for every case. The perpetrator does not simply define the child as a 'victim' and the maturing survivor contributes greatly to his/her ultimate betterment or otherwise. Those who claim that sexual abuse results in an 'incest survivor syndrome' or a 'post-sexual assault syndrome' which is typical of all cases deny the influence of a multitude of factors and lifetime events which can affect the child's developmental trajectory over time and the continuum of severity in responses shown by survivors generally.

The patterns of psychological reactions to different forms and combinations of abuse in childhood are diverse and heterogeneous (Follette *et al.*, 1997). An idiographic approach is necessary which accepts the influence of developmental processes, the abusive environment in its totality and the child's unique response to this adversity (Downs, 1991). The trauma related to abuse in formative years may accumulate as time progresses and as the survivor matures into adulthood. Downs and Doueck (1991) proposed that a 'progressive accumulation' of events which interrupts tasks of development tends to result in an unfavourable outcome for the child. Early effects may impede later developmental tasks even though the actual abuse has ended with short- and longer-term effects modulated by the interplay of changing circumstances as time progresses, increasing maturity and the removal of environmental adversity (e.g., when the young adult leaves the family home). Often, behavioural symptoms related to abuse in childhood will change within the presentation of the same individual over time or 'developmental triggers' in, perhaps, later adolescence or adulthood may activate previously dormant memories of the abuse in later life (Gelinas, 1983). Developmental psychopathology represents the best avenue to integrating the commonalities and recurring patterns of psychological disturbance associated with abuse and allows the adoption of a perspective encouraging acknowledgement of each survivor's idiosyncratic responses.

Three specific points are made here which, hopefully, set the stage for the introduction of the Cognitive Analytic Therapy (CAT) model in Chapter 3. Firstly, a complex interplay of factors and influences is involved in childhood abuse and the child's developmental trajectory into adulthood can show a continuity or discontinuity (Sparracelli, 1994). The pathways to negative or positive outcomes are rarely linear. Secondly, the response of each child is idiosyncratic and unique and it is simplistic to infer that the perpetrator defines the personality of the victim given the contribution that each survivor brings to the process of coping and adapting to adversity. The more chronic, invasive and severe is the abuse, the more direct will be the potential impact of the perpetrator's actions. Thirdly, abuse is an interpersonal event and, similarly to the internalisation of nurturing interactions with significant others, the internalisation of the perpetrator, the version of reality he/she imposes and states of mind produced can continue to affect the survivor for many years after the termination of the episode of victimisation. Any clinical model of value must encompass these issues.

The work of Alexander (1992) and Cole and Putnam (1992) deserves particular attention to explain how long-term effects are expressed along the continua of both severity and progressive developmental maturity. A modified version of Cole and Putnam's conceptualisation, combining Alexander's suggestions, is shown in Figure 1.1, which describes symptomatic problems indicative of three areas of dysfunction.

The three areas of impact upon a survivor's personality functioning are seen within this model to include (1) *disturbances of the self*, (2) *affect dysregulation* and (3) *interpersonal/social problems*. This analysis allows an appreciation of the interaction between maturity across time, developmental tasks and the impact of abuse. These domains of difficulty in survivors' presentations afford us a framework for conceptualising the developmental pathways the individual survivor has pursued and also to estimate the severity of the impact upon the survivor's functioning throughout his/her development. As a distillation of many years of empirical research, focusing on these three aspects of personality functioning in the adult survivor organises one's thinking about formulation and intervention for effective help.

DISTURBANCE OF SELF

discontinuity in self-experience   sexual dysfunction
incoherence in identity   eating disorders
intense, unstable moods   dissociative symptoms
poor self-reflection/introspection   intimacy problems
low self-worth   psychosomatic problems
impaired reality testing   impulsivity/unpredictability
self-hatred/suicidal ideation   self-injury

AFFECT DYSREGULATION

depression   guilt/shame
anxiety states   self-blame
impulsive aggression   powerlessness
trauma symptoms
(re-experiencing/arousal)

INTERPERSONAL PROBLEMS

prostitution/promiscuity   delinquency/criminality
revictimisation   violent conduct
alcohol/substance misuse   marital difficulties
compulsions/addictions   social withdrawal/avoidance
academic/occupational underachievement

NB. All three domains can be linked within the same problem; e.g., self-hatred leads to depressed mood, managed through alcohol misuse; intimacy problems related to guilt/shame causing revictimisation

Figure 1.1   Domains of dysfunction in adulthood associated with a history of childhood abuse

The CAT model for trauma is presented in Chapter 3. The model focuses on the centrality of *identity disturbance* as a consequence of abuse as proposed by empirical research findings by Classen, Field, Atkinson and Spiegel (1998) and others. Disturbances of the self, affect dysregulation and interpersonal behaviour form the principal domains for conceptualising the plethora of effects upon the survivor's functioning. CAT is a relational model of pathology and it is well placed to describe the interpersonal facets of abuse. The interactions between perpetrator and survivor are conceptualised and the process whereby the survivor internalises cognitive–perceptual–emotional representations of the perpetrator and the meanings of the abuse is provided. CAT also attempts to explain why survivors continue to suffer from distress long after the actual episode of victimisation has ended. The model is not an attempt to explain why sexual, physical and psychological abuse occurs to some children. It does, however, strive to account for the patterns of psychopathology shown by survivors of abuse and provide a framework for understanding, breaking and revising these patterns through a joint discourse between therapist and survivor. The CAT model provides a clinical lexicon for describing the subjective experiences endured by the survivor. It presents a reformulation of the status of the survivor's identity disturbances and psychological functioning and an appreciation of the extent to which the 'relational unit' between perpetrator and survivor continues to cause distress.

CHAPTER 2

The language and practice of CAT: assessment and treatment procedures

CAT is best conceived as a time-limited, relational therapy, which, like many similar brands in psychotherapy, blends several different strands of theory and techniques into a new model. It is comparative to relational-based, brief psychoanalytic psychotherapies such as those by Luborsky, Horowitz, Weiss and Simpson, Strupp and Binder. To a greater or lesser extent, merger between psychoanalytic and cognitive-behavioural therapy models has been observable over recent years with differences blurring, uniqueness requiring explanation and similar techniques being attributed different names depending on theoretical terminology (Northcut & Heller, 1999). Within managed health care, the appraisal of clinical effectiveness and efficiency is at the forefront of service provision and justifying the benefit for a client's general well-being is difficult to operationalise, measure and account for (Spiegel, 1999). CAT emerged within this culture of rationalisation, management and accountability.

Messer and Warren (1995) reviewed the evidence base for the effectiveness of time-limited psychotherapies, concluding that they were of comparative benefit to any other psychotherapy. Referring to relational, time-limited therapies, they stated that they are similar in their perception that psychopathology is a reflection of recurring patterns of interpersonal behaviour which are maladaptive and require a 'two-person' process to achieve change. CAT fits this profile as a brief, structured, relational form of psychotherapy. Managed health care denies therapists the 'romantic' vision of psychotherapy described by Messer and Warren (1995), which proposes that during an unrestricted journey of exploration the truth and change will be discovered. Instead, the notion that psychotherapy should be like an uncharted voyage taken by two people (patient and therapist) does not serve our health care culture today.

The use of CAT has been reported with numerous clinical disorders including anorexia nervosa (Treasure *et al.*, 1994), deliberate self-harm

(Cowmeadow, 1994), poorly controlled insulin-dependent diabetes (Fosbury, 1994), in community mental health patients (Garyfallos *et al.*, 1993), border-line personality disorder (Ryle & Beard, 1993; Ryle, 1997; Golynkina & Ryle, 1999), substance abuse (Leighton, 1997) and more severely disturbed psychiatric patients (Dunn, 1994). Group treatment (Maple & Simpson, 1995) and individual approaches (Duignan & Mitzman, 1994) have both been described applying CAT with relatively successful outcomes. More recently, I have undertaken CAT with patients experiencing chronic pain conditions (Pollock, 1998a) and auditory hallucinations during brief psychotic episodes (Pollock, 1999). The diversity of conditions to which CAT is relevant is expanding as clinicians use their enterprise to treat different psychological and physical problems.

The language of CAT

For clients, it is of paramount importance that their problems are described to them in a clear, simple and portable form. CAT is described in an often dense and taxing language of terminology, concepts and technical processes but can be translated into simplistic ideas to the majority of those with average intelligence. As a theoretical model and psychotherapy modality, it has become refined over a 20-year period to date. CAT is an integrative model of psychopathology and therapy, which blends and revises several concepts from, in particular, psychoanalytic and object relations thinking. The theory synthesises features from personal construct theory (Kelly, 1955), cognitive-behavioural practice and object relations perspectives. A thorough account of the origins, history and features of CAT is provided in Ryle (1995a, 1997).

Basic concepts in CAT: the process of reformulation

The interaction between the therapist and client during a CAT therapy is founded on a model of learning, which describes how the client internalises portable, psychological 'tools' to achieve lasting change. Interpsychological processes occurring between parent and child become intrapsychological experience, captured in cognitive-affective structures which form the substance of the child's personality. This occurs during play, teaching skills and even during a parent's explanation of logic and cause–effect relationships in the real world. Differences between therapies can be traced to the level of inference and 'structures', which represent this internalisation. At the core of CAT theory is the idea that a child acquires and learns to convert interpersonal experiences into intrapsychological processes and structures (Wertsch, 1985). Learning in CAT is formulated as the internalisation of higher-order language and goal-directed action units referred to as *procedures* in CAT. A rudimentary description of this process of internalisation will be described here (readers interested in the theoretical underpinnings of these concepts should refer to Leiman, 1992, 1995, Leighton & Ryle, 1995 and Ryle, 1990).

In cognitive-behavioural therapy, cognitive schemata (early maladaptive schemata, assumptions, beliefs) are inferred; in psychoanalytic psychotherapy object and self-representations are described; in CAT the basic structures are referred to as *reciprocal role procedures* (RRPs). The transition from inter- to intrapsychological learning occurs between parent and child and similarly between therapist and patient in 'tool-mediated goal-directed' action (Ryle 1990):

1. The child's cognitive readiness (i.e., the patient is oriented to focus on the tasks of therapy).
2. The parent transfers agentic responsibility to the child (the therapist explicitly shares and facilitates the patient using the tools of therapy).
3. The adult facilitates the child to reflect on the task (the therapist focuses attention on the process and work of therapy).
4. The adult prescriptively directs the child about what to do (the therapist scaffolds the process of therapy and directs the patient).
5. The child incorporates and masters the relational, dyadic sequence in dialogic structure from outside to inside (the patient internalises the new learning and the internal voice of the therapist as an introject).

Emphasis is given, therefore, to the shared, collaborative, internalisation of learning, self-understanding and acquisition of language-based tools or skills. The capacity to reflect and observe oneself in relation to others (and the self) is developed through external learning becoming an internalised dialogue, which influences thinking, affects feeling and guides acting.

An overview of the CAT process: the three 'R's of therapy

CAT has three specific aims, termed the three 'R's of therapy, namely *reformulation* of the client's difficulties, his/her *recognition* of the harmful patterns of thinking, feeling and relating which cause and maintain these problems and their *revision*, through joint working by client and therapist, by learning new ways of thinking, feeling and behaving. Ryle (1990) describes how a child learns to internalise a parent's actions as a sign-mediated tool. The sequence enacted between parent or teacher and child is, in substance, a blueprint for the interaction sequence between therapist and client during CAT.

Reformulation stems from several varied sources including a comprehensive history of the client, psychological testing, and the therapist's 'naturalistic

REFORMULATION
- presenting complaints, personal history, semi-structured interviews
- Psychotherapy File, self-monitoring diaries, psychometric testing, repertory grids
- naturalistic observation of therapist–patient interactions, extraction of narrative themes from previous relationships, sequences and patterns of thinking, feeling and behaving
- presentation of Reformulation Letter, agreement about Target Problems (TPs) and underlying Target Problem Procedures (TPPs)
- joint construction, discussion and refinement of sequential diagram including identification and naming of prominent self-states and their RRPs

RECOGNITION
- recurrent use of diagram outside and within sessions to improve accuracy of reformulation
- review of themes within self-monitoring diaries
- ratings of recognition (and revision) for TPPs using TP Rating Chart
- agreement about between-session tasks ('homework')
- reference to transference and countertransference RRPs
- monitoring dilemmas, traps and snags

REVISION
- encouraging and practising new ways of thinking, feeling and behaving
- identifying 'exists' from TPs
- use of cognitive, experiential, behavioural and interpersonal techniques to achieve change
- use of transference–countertransference understanding to actively avoid collusion
- breaking patterns within dilemmas, traps and snags
- discussion of termination of therapy and 'Goodbye Letter'

Figure 2.1   The elements of reformulation, recognition and revision (the three 'R's)

observation' of how the client presents him/herself, communicates, interacts and describes the narrative episodes of his/her life experiences. Recurring patterns, their sources and maintenance are the essential materials of reformulation. Recognition of these patterns and the harmful procedures which cause them is not always achieved quickly in some treatment cases. On occasion, the client may have difficulty grasping the sequential pattern and its context. Clients often state the sense that they have 'gone around the same old circuit again' without being able to intervene successfully, experiencing psychological distress and dealing with it using symptomatic ways of coping. As self-observation crystallises, the client can be encouraged to break these patterns with the help and guidance of the therapist. In a joint venture, the client and therapist share the duties and quest towards a shared vision and outcome. What follows is an account of the process of 'scaffolding' therapy to achieve accurate, useful reformulation, facilitating recognition of problems and their revision. Sections will focus on the application of CAT to survivors of abuse specifically as well as other types of clients and problems.

Reciprocal role procedures

A *procedure* (Ryle, 1982) describes intentional acts or enactment of roles in relationships maintained by repetitive sequences of mental, behavioural and environmental processes. The sequence occurs as follows: (1) mental processes (perception, appraisal of knowledge, action planning, prediction; (2) the effective enactment of an action or role; (3) the consequences of the action or enactment, particularly the response of others, are evaluated; and (4) confirmation or revision of the aim or the means attempted to achieve this aim. The most important procedures within reformulation and therapy of the patient's difficulties are termed *reciprocal role procedures* (RRPs), which represent, theoretically, a direct incorporation of object relations concepts.

RRPs are the basis of early care-taking and care-receiving relationships, resulting in the child's acquisition of a *repertoire* of RRPs which are deployed to facilitate and manage self–other and self–self interactions. Therefore, the sequence consists of learning about how to relate to another person, these learned patterns of thinking, feeling and acting associated with socially derived meanings (e.g., language, symbols, signs; Leiman, 1995). Procedural learning, once acquired, is difficult to alter and revise (Crittenden, 1985) and represents the source of distress and symptoms maintained by a failure to recognise and revise the harmful outcomes of deploying unhelpful RRPs. When ways of acting in relationships do not achieve the aims intended, conflict is experienced as to how best to behave with others and these patterns often defy revision and are maintained despite their unhelpful complications.

RRPs are enacted in relationships on two levels—*self–other* transactions and *self–self* management—defined in terms of Ryle's Procedural Sequence Object Relations Model (PSORM; Ryle, 1995), where RRPs form the most basic units of mental development, organising interactions with others and representing repertoires of joint action sequences (Leiman, 1995). This model is a restatement of concepts such as object and self-representations and projective identification. Self–other (and vice versa other–self) relations are organised with the prediction of the other person's response being of paramount consideration. A person may enact or choose to act a certain role (which combines, action, affect, expectation and communication) with an implicit or explicit prediction that the interacting other will reciprocally enact an anticipated role in relation to oneself. With regard to abusive environments, the survivor may have acquired an RRP characterised by *crushed, submissive* in relation to *controlling/dominating*, and such an RRP may lead to different affects and behaviours depending upon which role is enacted by the survivor. Either role of the RRP can be enacted by the survivor and *induced* within the other person. A survivor may perceive others to be potentially abusing and controlling and behave in a manner which attempts to evoke his/her partner to be controlling etc. The other person is induced to collude with the reciprocal role of the RRP enacted. Self–self management can be observed when a survivor enacts an internalised RRP towards him/herself. The most maladaptive and dramatic occurs when an RRP of *controlling, neglecting-to-crushed, depleted* is demonstrated through a survivor's extreme over-control of food intake and neglectful starvation or *sadistic torturing-to-masochistic martyr* via self-injury with associated pleasure of relief. Quite simply stated, RRPs indicate the nature of intrapsychic and interpersonal relationships where any role can be enacted towards oneself or towards another.

Dilemmas, traps and snags

Neurotic or self-damaging ways of relating to oneself and others can be classified within three common patterns which cause harmful RRPs to fail to become revised (Ryle, 1979). *Dilemmas* are evident when the options for roles, choices or acts are restricted to falsely dichotomised alternatives, where both alternatives are unsatisfactory and self-confirming. *Traps* represent negative beliefs, which generate actions resulting in consequences, which confirm the original beliefs, similarly to the notion of cyclic, vicious circles. *Snags* occur when appropriate aims (e.g., to be in a rewarding relationship) are abandoned on the prediction (either rightly or wrongly) that their achievement will evoke negative consequences. Dilemmas, traps and snags are described in the Psychotherapy File and can be gleaned from a survivor's description of patterns of relating to oneself and others and the survivor's thinking, management of affect and predictions inherent in these patterns.

As an example, consider Jane, a 33-year-old woman who was seen in an alcohol rehabilitation centre. Her alcohol abuse had been detrimentally affecting her ability to care for her 18-month-old child, who had been placed in foster care. She had been encouraged to become a prostitute to sustain her father's own alcohol abuse and she felt this activity to be exploitative and a violation of her childhood. Jane had been raped and physically beaten when detained in a psychiatric hospital as an adolescent (due to depression and self-injury) and her last partner had engaged in drug dealing from her home, threatening her into prostitution and stealing from her to the point where she could not feed herself or her child. She drank excessively 'to block everything out, stop me thinking'.

A dominant RRP for Jane was *exploiting, abusing* in relation to *exploited, abused*. In Figure 2.2, the permutations of enactment of this RRP between self-to-other and self-to-self are shown. Her male partner enacted a similar role towards her that Jane's father did in the past: (a) *other to self*. On occasions, Jane would also perceive the therapist to be enacting this role towards her, treating her like an 'interesting subject, not treating me like a respected human being': (b) *other to self*. Jane would also be verbally abusive or sneering towards the therapist and mockingly demand letters to obtain disability allowances, rehousing etc.: (c) *self to other*. She would actively engage in prostitution or injure her arms and body, enacting the exploiting and abusing RRP towards herself in a self-management procedure: (d) *self to self*. Other CAT patterns of dilemmas, traps and snags in Jane's case are shown in Figure 2.2. A second dominant RRP for Jane was *contemptuous* in relation to *contemptible*. Emerging from this RRP was a dilemma (2) in which Jane felt herself 'between a rock and a hard place' restricted by two limited options of either acting superior, haughty, leading to her feeling unwanted and ostracised, with others treating her contemptuously, or submitting to and appeasing others, feeling weak, worthless and contemptible. Her relationships were spoilt by either way of behaving.

A trap (3) was observed whereby Jane would describe feeling worthless and emotionally depleted, causing a sense of depression and emptiness. To 'fill myself up', Jane would binge on sugary foods or alcohol for comfort which, inevitably, reinforced her feelings of self-disgust, unhappiness and emptiness in the longer term. A snag (4), termed a 'therapeutic snag' (Pollock & Kear-Colwell, 1994), existed in Jane's repertoire which destroyed any positive progress made in treatment. She had always considered herself to be unlucky, deserving of unhappiness, and she typically predicted bad outcomes in everyday life. Success was forbidden and confusing. When Jane did make positive steps (e.g., symptom relief, improvement in her outlook) she would sabotage or stagnate therapy by intensifying or exaggerating her problems to return to her previous state of distress.

Dilemmas, trap and snags may cause impasses within the therapeutic relationship (Horowitz & Marmar, 1985). For example, a client may act rebelliously when asked to keep a self-monitoring diary of thoughts and feelings, then feel criticised and resentful when the therapist enquires about problems doing so, increasing resentment and passive aggression (a CAT trap). A client's depression and pessimism may result in little effort, increasing a sense of failure and stagnation, the therapist's optimism and encouragement perceived as naive and lacking understanding of the client's state of mind.

The process of reformulation

CAT reformulation uses a number of methods to provide a succinct, portable reformulation of the survivor's difficulties. A clear and convincing rationale for a client's problems is vital to promote engagement and adherence to a therapeutic regime (Goldfried & Davison, 1976). The therapeutic 'frame' is generated within an atmosphere of active collaboration and empathy based on a joint construction of the client's problems. The initial work is exploratory,

(1) Projective identification
   e.g., dominant RRP (A_1) *exploiting, abusing* in relation to (A_2) *exploited, violated*

(a)   OTHER (A_1) *exploiting, abusing*   (male partner—stealing money, rape,
                                                          using her home for drug dealing)

              SELF (A_2) *exploited, violated*   (feeling used, taken for granted, a
                                                          'doormat')

(b)   OTHER (A_1) *exploiting, abusing*   (therapist perceived as being unfair, only
                                                          interested in her as subject)

      SELF (A_2) *exploited, violated*   (sensitivity to therapist's interaction,
                                                          behaviour towards her)

(c)   SELF (A_1) *exploiting, abusing*   (patient enacts exploiting, abusing role,
                                                          sneering at therapist's work, demanding
                                                          the therapist writes letters for disability
                                                          allowance, housing, etc.)

      OTHER (A_2) *exploited, violated*   (therapist senses being abused, therapy
                                                          process and therapist are demeaned)

(d)   SELF (A_1) *exploiting, abusing*   (prostitution, self-injury by lacerating arms
                                                          and body)

      SELF (A_2) *exploited, violated*

(2) Dilemma

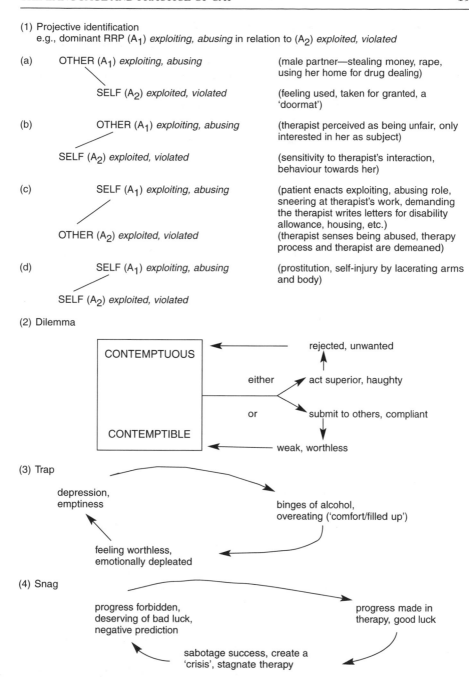

(3) Trap

(4) Snag

Figure 2.2   Reciprocal role procedures, dilemmas, traps and snags

encouraging the client to provide a subjective account of the difficulties experienced and, later, therapy becomes more targeted and structured, although the client's feedback is sought repeatedly (Kiesler, 1988). CAT therapies are time limited (typically 12–24 sessions)and focused, with an expectation that the client will participate actively in achieving change. Problems within the therapeutic relationship are addressed as naturalistic observations of 'interpersonal markers' (Safran, 1990) and any ruptures to the alliance are perceived as important illustrations of the client's ways of interacting and explored fully. Impasses to progress are treated similarly. The main methods of assessment to derive a CAT reformulation are described below.

The Psychotherapy File

Ryle (1990, 1995) created the Psychotherapy File (see Appendix 1) as a means of introducing the patient to the recurring self-defeating and circular patterns of thinking, feeling and acting which produce distress and symptoms. The patient is encouraged to keep a self-monitoring diary of mood changes, occurrence of symptoms, interpersonal conflict and self-management problems. These areas are agreed between therapist and patient and reviewed regularly to extract new and repeated themes or issues in the patient's daily life. Patients are often resistant to completing these diaries and Meichenbaum (1994) has detailed several reasons why patients experience difficulties doing so in cognitive therapy and other therapies generally. Reasons include passive-aggression and rebelliousness, a wish to avoid focusing upon the problems between sessions without direct availability of the therapist and an inability to grasp the use of the diaries to improve recognition of target problems. At the other extreme, obsessional patients become consumed by the task and produce reams of material with incredible amounts of detail. Thorough explanation and discussion, explaining the benefits of the data for the patient, should precede requesting the patient to keep a diary of any kind.

The patient is provided with a description of dilemmas, traps and snags in the File and a number of common patterns are included, the patient being asked to endorse the extent to which each pattern is relevant to him/her. Unique patterns of dilemmas, traps and snags can be interwoven into the File by the patient or therapist as they become apparent. A latter section of the File introduces unstable states of mind, mood variability and contrasting, conflicting and contradictory self-experiences. Again, the patient endorses the degree to which this occurs for him/her, and the Personality Structure Questionnaire (PSQ; see Chapter 12) can be used to probe these problems further. The Psychotherapy File is not a psychometric instrument, but does educate and focus the therapy process in CAT, advancing and explaining where problems may emerge for the patient.

The Reformulation Letter

Written 'letters' are used in CAT as a distinctive means of communicating the therapist's thoughts about the survivor's difficulties, their source and how they are maintained, and to explicitly agree the work to be undertaken. A *Reformulation Letter* is produced and presented to the survivor in the early stages of treatment (typically during session 4 or 5) and a *Goodbye Letter* is compiled towards the end of the therapy referring to the work completed to date, acknowledging termination issues and problems which still require attention and monitoring.

The Reformulation Letter helps to cement the therapeutic relationship, check the accuracy of the client's and therapist's perceptions of problems to be worked upon, and the derived problems to be targeted are written in the letter, which is shared with the client. The contents of the letter are drawn from several sources, including the client's narrative history of relationship episodes, events and how he/she coped, the observations of the therapist and any problems emerging from the Psychotherapy File or psychological testing (e.g., repertory grids, see below). A number of features should be evident in the letter, although each therapist will express the issues to be included in their own personal style, taking into consideration the client's personality and likely response to the letter. Points to include are as follows:

1. A succinct description of the relationship between the client's personal history and adversity, the emotional pain caused and the client's own subjective account of these experiences.
2. Following on from (1), a description of the means used by the client to survive, cope or manage the pain experienced. Helping the client to recognise the link between the psychological pain and feelings endured as a result of events and how he/she coped as best possible at that time promotes consideration as to how and why these patterns have become unhelpful and hard to break.
3. Focusing on specific target problems (TPs) which emerge from the reformulation and defining the target problem procedures (TPPs) underlying them encourage the client and therapist to concentrate on specific areas to be addressed. These are listed in the letter, prioritised by both therapist and client and named on a rating sheet to aid monitoring of the client's recognition and subsequent revision.

Explicit reference is made to how the procedures identified may affect the therapeutic relationship, particularly highlighting the expectations the client may have of the therapist (e.g., being an omnipotent saviour, 'a knight in shining armour') and placing these perceptions in a realistic light. Stating the 'holes in the road' where therapist and client may experience tension or stagnation can be useful—for example, articulating that the client may perceive the therapist as demanding or tyrannical leading to rebelliousness by the client.

Identifying self-states and producing the diagram

The notion that we have multiple working models of ourselves which explain our internal variations in thinking, feeling and acting is not a new one (Bretherton, 1985). CAT places an emphasis on identifying, recognising and addressing these recurring models or 'states of being', including them within a diagram called a *Sequential Diagrammatic Reformulation* (SDR) or a *Self-States Sequential Diagram* (SSSD). This diagram consists of the major distinct states of mind, the underlying RRPs, affective states and ways of thinking about oneself and others. It is generated with the client's collaboration and refined as therapy progresses.

The identification of distinct self-states, which anchor the patient's perceptions of self and others, is a pivotal exercise in CAT. A *self-state* appears as a recurring dominant RRP that permeates the patient's experiences. The concept of multiple self-states is not a new one within psychotherapy. Horowitz (1997) has described the need to define separate 'states of mind' within Configurational Analysis, typically labelled as *dreaded*, *desired* or *compromised*. These are named explicitly and the patient monitors the content and triggers for their recurrence, symptoms associated with them and the control of emotional regulation experienced (over-controlled, under-controlled). Movement between states can be experienced very abruptly or a *shimmering* is noted when a patient experiences changes between one state and another as such a transition is occurring. Similarly, Rowan (1990) proposed that we can identify 'subpersonalities' which function as semi-autonomous personalities. CAT differs from these conceptions of multiplicity of the self by explicitly cementing qualitatively contrasting and often contradictory states of mind within a relational framework.

For example, if a patient identified himself to be a 'greedy user' within heterosexual relationships (one RRP of a distinctive self-state), he may be quite capable of articulating that his control of emotion is excessive when in this state of mind, that he behaves in a manipulative, selfish and denigratory manner and that he perceives himself to be contemptuous and superior when interacting with females. This state could be defensive and employed to ameliorate feelings of worthlessness and weakness. It could also be an identification with a role that women have displayed towards him in the past, helping him to manage insults to his masculinity or distress related to, perhaps, a previous partner's infidelity. Alternatively, this patient may consider this state to best reflect how he wishes to perceive himself, therefore representing an idealised or desired state. CAT's use of RRPs directly infers that, although the patient's self-perception is identified first, the other person is, by definition, the essential reciprocal to the patient's procedures. If the patient described defines a recurrent state of mind to be a 'greedy user' then women are inferred to be perceived as, perhaps, 'expendable objects' (an RRP of *exploiting/contemptuous* in relation to *exploited/inferior*).

Defining the RRP and naming the self-state provides a structural anchor point to trace patterns which tend to emerge from and circle back to each self-state in sequences of thinking, feeling and acting. Movement within and between states can be tracked through *role reversal, response shifts* and *states switches* and symptomatic or avoidant procedures and dilemmas, traps and snags traced from one self-state to another.

Each state of mind is the named reciprocal pole of an RRP, the most basic for survivors of abuse being *abusing* (perhaps named, as in one case, the 'monster') and *victimised* (named, in the same case, the 'lost child'). The patient should be encouraged to label or name the states of mind and self-state using terminology and language which have personal meaning and the therapist should not impose a lexicon of descriptors onto these states. Once named, the *procedural loops* (cyclical patterns from one self-state to another; see Figure 2.3) of perceiving, feeling and behaving can be explored and shifts and switches within and between states monitored.

'Core pain', survival strategies and procedural loops

It is often advisable to start generating the diagram by focusing upon the patient's persisting and unresolved unmanageable feelings (referred to as *core pain*), the more or less adaptive methods that have been constructed to avoid or deal with these feelings (the *survival strategies* or *coping modes*) and the symptoms accompanying these coping strategies. Survivors of childhood abuse experience psychological pain directly attributable to the harm they endured, and describe perceptions and feelings of shame, worthlessness, powerlessness, guilt, debasement, self-hatred and rage. It is as if the abuse has left a putrid legacy, which cannot be contemplated, as an emptiness and sense of deprivation, which cannot be discounted. For the survivor, the residual pain from the trauma is often the most difficult to verbalise or even acknowledge. It is possible to improve the functioning of survivors who do not articulate or 'visit' the feelings surrounding the abuse and to address their difficulties on a surface level with some success (A. Ryle, personal communication). It has been argued (Brewin *et al.*, 1993) that the simple process of contemplating and verbalising the trauma within a safe and empathic environment or relationship is therapeutic in itself.

Survivors cope with their feelings and experiences using whatever means they can adopt. At times, these strategies are desperate yet vital in the short-

SELF-STATE/STATES OF MIND

RRP = *abusing-to-victimised* form distinct self-state: *'victimised'* and *'abusing'* states of mind with characteristic thoughts, feelings, perceptions and actions

RESPONSE SHIFT

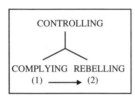

(1) → (2) an adolescent who behaved compliantly to a controlling parent shifts response, becoming rebellious and challenging

ROLE REVERSAL

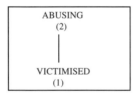

(1) → (2) victim rage expressed by attacking an abusing partner, the victim assuming an abusing role

STATE SWITCH

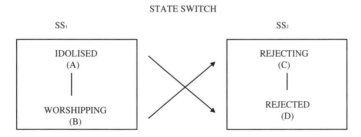

(A) ⟶ (D) an idolised partner is worshipped (SS1), then rejected (SS2) following disappointment, switching from one self-state to a different self-state

Figure 2.3   Self-states, states of mind. response shifts, role reversals and state switches in diagrams

term, but ultimately self-defeating and symptomatic when they become habitual. Assessment should encourage the survivor to adopt an uncritical stance towards the coping strategies developed during adversity, pointing out that despite these strategies' current hindrance or perpetuation of distress, they were invented or created at a time when maintaining any semblance of integrity to one's experience was challenged severely. The perception to promote is that the survivor applied whatever means possible to cope with unmanageable feelings and ideas, at a time when thoughts were invalidated, one's sense of reality was corrupted, confusion reigned and 'something' needed to be done to express or manage the situation and make sense of one's own experiences and events.

A survivor who becomes addicted to cocaine may do so because the drug provides a feeling of blissful fusion and the capacity to relate to others without anxiety. Excessive eating to obtain feelings of comfort and to distance the perpetrator by changing one's appearance is functional at that time. Concentrating on schoolwork or aesthetic activities such as art, music or writing are more adaptive coping strategies which allow a degree of release from emotional pain. Even radically submissive or desperate coping strategies are often the only apparent option for the survivor when abuse is prolonged and intrusive. Gilbert's (1992) model of subordination–domination in Social Rank theory views passivity, defeat and hopelessness depression to be functional because these behaviours allow the subordinated individual (the survivor) to 'live and fight another day'. The survivor's identity integrity is compromised accordingly to a severe degree in these chronic situations and, because the abuse is predictably habitual, the survivor learns to rely upon dramatic and maladaptive coping strategies. A detained 24-year-old female patient with a history of sexual and physical abuse by her stepfather would experience 'absences' when her stepfather visited the psychiatric ward, later reporting anaesthesia for acts of self-injury when he left. She described the 'absences' to be a form of 'opting out until he's finished', hurting herself being an enactment of the abuse she anticipated towards herself and expression of her self-hatred and submission to the perpetrator in a symbolic manner.

The *core state* or emotional pain created by childhood abuse or adversity is a pivotal starting point to assess when constructing the diagram. Survivors manage feelings of vulnerability and pain in a diversity of ways. Certain emotional states have been shown to be common consequences of childhood, including feelings of shame (Andrews, 1999), powerlessness (Finkelhor, 1987), guilt (Jehu *et al.*, 1988), worthlessness and poor self-image and hopelessness. The degree of self-loathing expressed by survivors of abuse is as startling as relative absence of anger and rage towards the perpetrator. When rage is acknowledged and validated by the therapist as appropriate and welcomed, survivors are prone to deny or deflect its significance. They are often afraid of the intensity of rage and hatred felt towards the perpetrator and the acts of abuse themselves, suppressing or converting these feelings into self-disgust for participating in the abuse, self-blame for being sexually provocative or other misattributions.

Guilt and shame are defined differently in the psychological literature and it is easy to use these terms interchangeably when working with survivors. Tangney, Wagner and Gramzow (1992; p. 469) described guilt to equate with remorse and regret concerning 'the bad thing that was done', whereas shame occurs when 'the object of concern is the entire self', the 'bad self' a reflection of the 'bad thing' with negative evaluation of oneself in entirety. Bodily shame, self-hatred, low self-worth and urges to punish oneself (through poor self-care, self-starvation or injury) can emanate from feelings of guilt and shame. Of course, the survivor of abuse, especially sexual abuse, may misconstrue that passivity during the abuse was indicative of consent to participation. These feelings can colour the rest of the survivor's life and the view of him/herself in relation to others, assuming the role of someone who is unworthy and deserving of punishment and misery, thereby maintaining a vicious cycle by means of CAT traps and snags.

Guilt is a difficult emotional response to address for many survivors and attributing blame correctly cannot be achieved by logical reasoning or simple discussion. Experiential techniques such as guided imagery and Gestalt exercises are required to help the survivor rationally allocate responsibility (Pollock & Kear-Colwell, 1994). Successful attribution of guilt can have its own complications whereby the survivor begins to report feelings of intense rage towards the perpetrator and homicidal thoughts. The fact that he/she has been mistreated and violated generates ideas of revenge and angry feelings, which require acknowledging and containment. Survivors may have demonstrated patterns of behaviour in which they have acted over-compliantly to appease and placate others because they fear that any expression of anger will be excessive and out of control, perhaps harming others (a CAT dilemma). Channelling the rage associated with these states of mind and development of skills to appropriately assert oneself are important goals to help the survivor achieve a balanced means of interacting with others (e.g., neither too compliant, inhibited and resentful nor aggressive and guilty).

Feelings of powerlessness and ineffectiveness require consideration also. Survivors of abuse often experience a pervading sense of resourcelessness, low self-worth and self-defeat. Access or the right to achieve a sense of competence and control in domains of life such as employment, loving relationships, finances etc. may be considered unattainable or undeserved. Empowering and enabling the survivor are key therapeutic tasks and a technique such as power mapping (see Chapter 8) represents a specific tool to promote these goals. Helping the survivor to verbally access and articulate the core emotional pain requires the therapist to be facilitative, patient and unobtrusive as the survivor disentangles the combination of difficult feelings the abuse evokes. Guided imagery techniques, which prompt retrieval of state-dependent memories and feelings, are helpful at this stage of the assessment. As described previously, procedures such as Imagery Rescripting and Reprocessing (Smucker *et al.*, 1996; Smucker and Dancu, 1999) can generate repressed or partially denied or dissociated states of mind and feelings which can be explored by therapist and survivor to formulate the central themes from nuclear scripts of abusive memories. On occasions, focusing upon traumatic memories and negative childhood experiences to trace the source and nature of an individual's unresolved residue of emotional pain can induce a profound deterioration in his/her mood and self-perception. A sense of sadness, loss, hopelessness and regret accompanies memories of childhood abuse and the meaning of this for the survivor must be acknowledged and explored.

As an example, a 64-year-old female patient who had only recently entered therapy, when asked to recount the nature of the relationship she had with her psychologically cruel father and disinterested and dismissing mother, recalled the impact of her parents' behaviour upon her as a child by stating 'I still fear for that little girl. She doesn't know what it's like to play, explore, try something new. I can see her watching as he [her father] killed the pet dog in the back garden. He took another thing she loved away. That little girl never knew she was being deprived of a loving, normal childhood. She didn't know anything else'. This woman's response following this description was significant. She became reclusive, her self-care deteriorated dramatically, her husband described her as lethargic and uncommunicative, and her attendance at a day centre ended without explanation. In a therapy session, she voiced her sense of confusion that it had taken so many years to realise that her parents' cruelty was so intentional and damaging. She stated that she cried continuously for hours when her husband went to work, sobbing for the childhood the 'little girl' had suffered and been denied. This was the first occasion she had contemplated that the 'little girl' was herself. She had always found it easier to disavow that she and the little girl were one and the same. Her depressive episodes over many years had been experienced as 'out of the blue' yet appeared to follow periods of intensive involvement as a volunteer caring for mistreated animals, a pursuit she felt passionate about. The risk of suicide increased markedly at this point in therapy for this woman. Helping her to understand how the cauldron of emotional pain had moulded her patterns of behaving throughout adulthood allowed her to assign responsibility and blame upon her parents and to think about integrating the adult part of herself with the 'hurt, lost, confused little girl'.

Projective identification: transference and countertransference in CAT

Kiesler (1988) stated that a therapist 'cannot not be pulled in by the patient' (p. 38) referring to the manifestations of transference and countertransference within the 'transitional game' that form as the therapeutic dyad interact. Any ruptures to the alliance must be conceptualised and impasses or stagnation in progress addressed. The therapist is required to undertake a task of internal observation regarding his/her own thinking, emotional reactions and perceptions of the client. Collusion with a client's self-perpetuating patterns of RRPs, dilemmas, traps and snags leads to stagnation and 'drop-out' from therapy and reinforces the client's unhelpful ways of thinking, acting, feeling and relating.

Projective identification is an important process (Ogden, 1983, Sandler, 1976) which underpins transference and countertransference responses during therapy and its conceptualisation within the CAT model is an important facet of clinical practice. Essentially, within relationships, the dyad is composed of a *projector* and a *recipient*. The projector enacts a certain role of an RRP and the recipient is anticipated or induced (often in an implicit, controlling manner) to enact the reciprocal affecting interpersonal activities and communication about internal affects and expectations in relationships. The naturalistic observation of the therapeutic alliance allows the therapist to gain a sense of the survivor's history, its impact and how the affect associated with these adversities are active and influential.

Ryle (1997) has specified a number of specific forms of transference and CT which occur between therapist and patient and how these responses can be used to improve the planning of treatment and its forms explicitly. Inducement of the therapist to assume a given role, the affect associated with it and analysis of the origin of the underlying RRP is a vital task of therapy. Patients with greater fragmentation and identity disturbances often exert strong pressure upon others in general life and the therapist to collude by assuming the reciprocal role. If the patient's repertoire of RRPs is narrow, inflexible and restricted, the pressure to collude can be intense and controlling for the therapist (projection of a reciprocal role and a 'pull' to identify and reciprocate by the therapist as recipient). Collusion evidently reinforces the harmful, maladaptive RRP and maintains the fragmented structure of the patient's personality. Because the vast majority of RRPs are enacted automatically and implicitly learnt, repetitive patterns of damaging interpersonal procedures continue if they are not recognised and addressed. Ryle described a number of different forms of transference and countertransference within the CAT model. These include the following:

1. An *identifying transference* occurs when a patient seeks to imitate, or become similar in role, manner or physically to the therapist, akin to a mirroring transference. This may be observed by a change in the patient's physical appearance, use of language, attitudes and opinions, and mannerisms. To some extent, a loss of normal separateness and differentiation is likely to occur with this form of relating.

2. A *reciprocating transference* represents a patient's attempts to induce the therapist to assume the reciprocal role of a given RRP. The patient's switching between these transference patterns and their underlying RRPs must be recognised, tracked and included within the SSSD.

Regarding CT patterns, Ryle (1997) proposed differing forms including *personal*, and two types of elicited (*identifying* and *reciprocating*) CT. *Personal CT* is a feature of the therapist's own history, repertoire of experiences and RRPs, conflicts and early unresolved issues. Knowledge of the nature and meaning of these CT reactions is vital to avoid becoming crippled or overwhelmed by the patient's current influence.

Elicited CTs are of diagnostic value for the therapist. An *identifying CT* is indicative of empathic understanding, the therapist experiencing the role, state of mind and emotional responses of the patient, similar to the affective attunement of parent and child. The role and state of mind evoked in the therapist may represent a defensive or avoidant manoeuvre, which requires examination to discern the underlying state or role defended against. A reciprocating CT occurs when a therapist experiences him/herself drawn into or induced to assume a reciprocal role of a given RRP, the other pole enacted by the patient. This is, essentially, a signal to the therapist that he/she has become part of a projective identification relation with a dominant RRP functioning.

These CTs are diagnostic to the extent that they permit the therapist to directly witness and experience RRPs of the patient. A particular skill is the therapist's ability to track the patient's switches, reversals and transitions within dominant RRPs and between different self-states. If this is not achieved, the interaction between therapist and patient can be experienced as confused and unpredictable, and provoke anxiety for the therapist and a lack of containment for the patient.

Transference patterns with survivors of abuse

Psychotherapy with survivors of childhood abuse can be a stormy and challenging encounter for therapist and patient alike. Entering the therapeutic relationship can be a precarious and frightening undertaking. The survivor carries into this situation unique expectations, predictions, fears and needs which colour the interaction between the therapist–survivor dyad. Two individuals, each with potentially strong affects, contribute to creating a new relational bond and a new history together (Meissner, 1980; Ogden, 1983). The survivor is often ambivalent and reticent about engaging entirely in the therapeutic relationship and driven by the burden of prolonged self-defeating patterns and distressing symptoms. The construction of a therapeutic frame encouraged by the therapist, with its suggestion of safety, empathy and absorption of the survivor's distress and suffering, requires sensitive, tactful and diligent tracking of the interaction between therapist and survivor. Eltz, Shirk and Sarlin (1995) stated that initial alliance difficulties are common when abuse survivors enter therapy and, as pointed out by Clarke and Llewelyn (1994) and Price (1994), trauma lies at the core of the survivor's personality, colouring interactional patterns in adult relationships.

In certain respects the risk of dependency upon the helping professional evokes the expression of internalised relations and the difficulties associated with them. An analysis of transference, CT, and other dysfunctional patterns of relating and symptoms, which accompany potentially intense interactions in CAT terms, is of value here prior to illustration through treatment cases. Structuring the therapy format needs particular attention due to the subtle appearance of violations and confusion regarding boundaries, both physical and functional. Many survivors, especially where a history of incest is evident (Price, 1992), find difficulty in adhering to arrangements regarding boundaries openly agreed about times, physical contact and propriety. The expectation that boundaries will be violated is understandable and a predictable fear for the survivor.

Often, the survivor may test the therapist by requesting or attempting physical contact (e.g., hugging, touching non-intimately) with the therapist. The survivor places him/herself at real risk if the therapist actively takes such an opportunity. The issue of control over times of appointments, the pace of therapy and topics discussed can be contentious for the survivor. The survivor may, within a potential imbalance of power in the therapeutic relationship, stubbornly defend any degree of control over the work undertaken, to the point where he/she may appear grandiose ('special') and competitive with other patients whom he/she fantasises are stealing the therapist's care and attention. The extent of the survivor's misery and suffering can overwhelm the therapist who experiences helplessness, feeling deskilled and impotent to save or rescue the survivor from the continuous torment and crises he/she presents with. Inquiries about the survivor's inner experience, thoughts and feelings can appear intrusive, stabbing and invasive for therapist and survivor alike, the former feeling guilty and cruel, the latter treated insensitively and empathically failed.

Most importantly, the survivor is likely to experience the therapeutic situation as a vehicle for the potential re-enactment of the abuse, questioning whether the therapist will become a perpetrator also (Josephs, 1992). A number of transference and CT patterns emerge with adult survivors. They include an enactment of the originally abusive relationship, fantasies that the survivor will be ideally cared for and that blissful symbiosis will occur with an omnipotent, protective and rescuing therapist, or that realistic safety will be provided for the survivor to recognise and repair and master the traumatic experiences from the past. Survivors often display these transference patterns in sequence with others also. Hedges (1999) refers to 'terrifying transferences' occurring with survivors of trauma in which a process of 'trauma recreation' tests both the therapist's empathic capacity and resilience as the survivor moves through a re-experiencing of the physical and psychological pain associated with re-visiting the abuse itself. The survivor may accuse the therapist of being directly responsible for the emotional pain felt.

The internal world of the survivor may be polarised into a narrow, restricted and distorted repertoire of relations in which the abuser–victim relationship is pervasive (Pollock & Kear-Colwell, 1994; Price, 1994; Pollock, 1996, 1997, 1998). Such a rigid and narrow means of relating can promote a re-enactment or compulsion to repeat the trauma (van der Kolk, 1988), the survivor's expectations and predictions about the therapist's behaviour incorporated through this template (Price, 1993). Other forms of potentially more flexible and adaptive ways of relating are limited and unavailable. For some survivors, the perpetrator may be idealised in a form of 'traumatic bonding' (Dutton & Painter, 1981).

Intermittent indulgence and care interspersed with exploitation and harm reinforce idealisation of the perpetrator because an abusive relationship may feel, essentially, better than none. The survivor may cope with the abuse by idealising the perpetrator and concurrently devaluing him/herself, splitting people into a dichotomous version of the world as either perfect or evil (the concept of 'splitting'; Grotstein, 1981). The survivor makes sense of this configuration by owning the badness of the abuse, denying the same of the perpetrator. Perpetrators of abuse who oscillate between complimenting the victim and haranguing him/her alternately create this splitting of versions of reality encouraging internalisation of devaluation and creating self-blame, guilt and self-hatred for the horror of the acts. The dependency upon connectedness with significant others (especially parents) sets the stage for such distorted manoeuvres to protect the image held of the perpetrator by the survivor (Heineman, 1998). The therapist, if idealised initially, may become swiftly devalued and denigrated as therapy progresses when ideal care is not forthcoming or, alternatively, the survivor may consider him/herself unworthy and undeserving of effort and attention, uncomfortable with the role assigned by the process of helping.

Oscillation may occur within the therapeutic relationship where the therapist is perceived as idealised, the survivor anticipating an all-consuming symbiotic merger and fusion with a perfect carer, angry rebellion and rage when disappointed and perception of the therapist ultimately as exploitative and abusing. Tracking the sequential path transference themes take is vital to adequate containment and undertaking of the survivor's experiences.

The therapist may be confused by a survivor's triumphant enactment of an abusing role towards him/her when unconditional helping is the objective sought. The survivor may identify with the abusing role (Pollock, 1994) and mock, deride and humiliate the therapist for his/her incompetence, stupidity and inability to understand. Expressions of hostility and aggression in this context differ greatly from the survivor's enactment of rage, which accompanied becoming, or experiencing awareness that he/she was selfishly used to meet the needs of the perpetrator. The therapist's response to victim rage is typically encouraging and considered appropriate.

Extending from these enactments by the survivor are observable complications within relationships, evident as procedural dilemmas (Ryle, 1979). Survivors may decide to meet their emotional needs by entering relationships with the expectation that seeking intimacy risks revictimisation (van der Kolk, 1988), becoming dependent and controlled. Avoiding relationships leads to a differing unsatisfactory outcome where emotional needs are unmet, and isolation and loneliness are experienced (Pollock, 1996). To some extent, this pattern reflects the unique conflict about attachments for survivors of abuse. Revictimisation appears, in part, to stem from the unchanged nature of the RRPs at the core of the survivor's personality, emerging within the therapy situation. The therapist is afforded an opportunity within this process of providing a corrective emotional experience for the survivor and an adaptive, non-colluding 'analytic introject' (Meissner, 1981) representing a new, central RRP for relating.

Sexuality can become a prominent part of the transference with sexually abused patients. An erotic transference may emerge with sexual overtones evident in the survivor's manner of relating to the therapist as subtle confusion with sexuality and attachment. The survivor may act seductively, inducing reciprocation from the therapist, this pattern indicative of the survivor's prominent way of relating to others, a relic of the abusive experiences and the perpetrator's grooming of his victim into this learned behaviour. Secrecy can become a feature of the therapeutic relationship whereby promises are required if information (e.g., secrets) is made known from the survivor. Rewarding a secretive exchange during disclosure must be avoided and confidentiality within therapy must not be distorted to become similar to the perpetrator's version of reality imposed upon the survivor. Some survivors may have been rewarded by praise, attention or in material ways, a 'special' privileged relationship with the perpetrator. The therapist must resist collusion and verbalise the re-enactment of this pattern to the survivor. Confidentiality may be uneasy for a survivor who has been threatened to maintain secrecy and told that disclosure will violate the 'agreement' between perpetrator and survivor (e.g., threat of being killed, cause the break-up of a family). The therapist must encourage disclosure in a climate of confidentiality entirely different from the perpetrator, who may have maintained secrecy through threats, bribery or other means.

Repertory grids in CAT

Forms of repertory grid (Kelly, 1955; Ryle, 1979) are methods of assessment that have been historically used as part of CAT reformulations. A repertory grid produces a graphical representation (based on the statistical method of factor analysis) of how the individual uses descriptors to construe or understand his/her relational world. *Elements* are derived by asking the individual to name significant entities (e.g., people, roles, things and aspects of the self) and to describe how they relate to each other using descriptors (e.g., adjectives, properties), termed *constructs*. Survivors of childhood abuse frequently report, as elements, significant people to be the perpetrator, parents, or partner, and roles to be scapegoat, victim, accessory for sex, 'doormat' or 'object'. Aspects of the self include *victim* self, *ideal* self, *past* self, *dreaded* self, *survivor* self and *abusing* self. Elements used can be spontaneously elicited from the survivor or imposed by the therapist to tap certain relationships between them (e.g., *person who feels guilty, victim self, perpetrator, person who should feel guilty*). Elements are derived first.

Constructs are elicited by presenting three random elements and asking the survivor to choose a descriptor, which is common to two elements and different for the third. Constructs are bipolar (e.g., *hopeful–hopeless, loving–hating*) and those typically elicited from survivors of childhood abuse include *trusting–betraying, abusing–caring, controlling–accepting*. When a list of constructs is obtained, each element is rated on each construct using a five- or seven-point Likert scale (1 = not at all to 7 = extremely like). This produces a matrix of scores for each element on each construct. The matrix grid is then subjected to principal components factor analysis (for example, the Flexigrid program of Tschudi, 1989). A survivor's repertory grid is shown in Figure 2.4. The grid shows that two axes are evident.

Axis 1 (termed component 1) includes constructs *hopeful–hopeless, trustworthy–untrustworthy* and *painless, tolerating–dangerous, vulnerable*. Axis 2 (component 2) is formed of *regressing–growing, smothering–actualising* and *controlling–freeing*. Elements are spread across the grid space; for example, this survivor's child self was construed as hopeless, her boyfriend as manipulative, her father as a dangerous and painful person and her ideal self as growing and free. It is worth pointing out that the survivor's child self, perpetrator and abused self are close in the grid space and therefore construed similarly.

Repertory grids help the reformulation process by creating a visual picture of a survivor's ways of understanding the self and relationships—matters that are often difficult to verbalise. Elicited constructs can provide the therapist with hints about how the survivor may describe his/her core relational repertoire. For example, the constructs *controlling–controlled* and *rejecting–rejected* may represent a central RRP within a prominent self-state (see Pollock & Kear-Colwell, 1994) and this insight can help generate the SSSD. A different type of repertory grid (the States Grid) is described in Chapter 3.

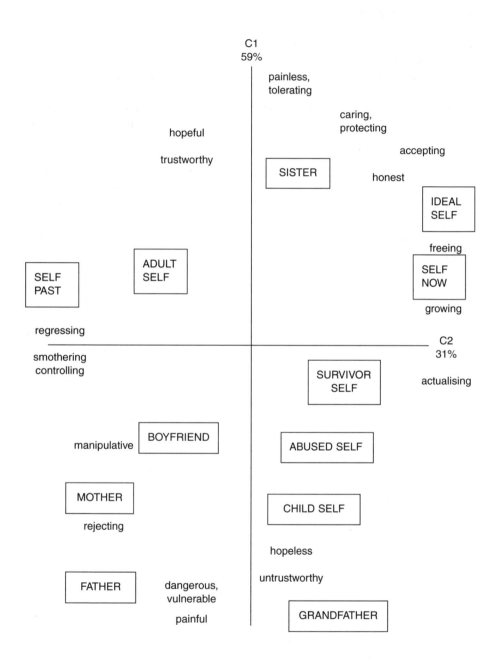

Figure 2.4   A survivor's repertory grid

Recognition of target problems

The Psychotherapy File, Reformulation Letter and the SDR or SSSD form the immediate tools for the client to learn to recognise instances within and outside therapy that TPPs occur. Each TPP is explicitly described to the client and the list of TPPs is linked to the diagram and referred to repeatedly or refined accordingly. Many survivors with severe identity disturbances (see Chapter 3) experience discontinuity, variability and sharp changes within their moods, thinking and states of mind for unknown reasons. They are likely to report problems tracking these changes at first but progressively become more attuned to their own states of mind. Symptomatic procedures (e.g., binge eating, alcohol abuse) can be pinpointed within the SSSD and methods to break these patterns discussed and devised as necessary. The client's involvement and creativity are encouraged when doing so and it is important that the therapist does not become too prescriptive at this juncture.

Between session work, self-monitoring and target problems

Therapeutic work during early individual sessions is exploratory and reflective, and the survivor's pacing of the therapy is paramount. The therapist can use the therapist–client interaction as a form of naturalistic observation to glean information about his/her relational repertoire based on transference and CT patterns. The survivor's descriptions of narrative episodes within relationships in his/her personal history and daily life can revise or confirm the therapist's hypotheses. Learning to recognise the way in which TPPs manifest themselves in daily life is the first step, revision of the problem following logically from recognition. Self-monitoring diaries of triggers, mood states and identified self-states can enhance recognition of patterns (termed procedural loops) of how one state leads to another and where dilemmas, traps, snags and distressing symptoms occur.

Later work can become much more focused and specific to the TPs and underlying TPPs which form the survivor's difficulties. These are written onto a Rating Sheet and reviewed at each session to gauge whether changes have been achieved or difficulties are being encountered (see Figure 2.5).

Structured work between sessions to break the harmful patterns identified, similar to 'homework assignments', is a vital feature of the therapeutic process. Any tasks should be fully understood by the survivor and the aims, objectives and likely outcomes discussed and made explicit. In many cases, the survivor will experience a degree of frustration when obstacles to change are encountered or he/she repeats the same harmful pattern without change occurring (e.g., 'watching myself going around the same old circuit, doing the

Patient's name :
Therapist's name :
Date :

TP
Target Problem :
TPP
Target Problem
Procedure

		S4	S5	S6	S7	S8	S9	S10	S11	S12	S13	S14	S15	S16	f-up
A RECOGNITION Rate how skilled and quick you are at seeing the pattern	more — same — less														
B STOPPING AND REVISING Rate how far you are able to stop the pattern and/or replace it with a better way	more — same — less														

AIM
Alternatives or exits

Figure 2.5   Target Problems Rating Sheet

same thing again'). Despite feelings of discouragement, repeating an unhelpful pattern allows the survivor to improve self-observation and practise the task of breaking the pattern with more valuable knowledge via 'trial and error' to some extent. Encouragement from the therapist that the survivor persists with vigour is important. The techniques applied to break patterns and revise problems must be appropriate and creative, relying upon the therapist's and survivor's invention and likely to secure achievable and lasting change. The gains of change can also be anxiety provoking and many survivors will state that the old patterns might be dysfunctional but 'make sense' or 'feel comfortable—what I know'. If the client reports experiencing difficulties understanding the TPPs and progress in changing them is repeatedly not achieved, it is important that the therapist does not attribute this to the client's lack of motivation or conclude that it is a form of sabotage. Refinement of TPs and TPPs may be required with the feedback of the client and new or more accurate TPs incorporated into the reformulation.

Revision of target problems

The actual methods used to break unhelpful patterns, be they modifying narrow, restricted RRPs, dilemmas, traps and snags or symptomatic and avoidant procedural loops, is relatively flexible within the CAT framework. For example, addressing the *victim* state of mind may require experiential methods (IRR, EMDR), alteration of the client's self-perception from *victim* to *survivor*, empowerment using power mapping (Hagan & Smail, 1997a, 1997b) and repeated tracking of current relationship patterns and learning new ways of thinking, feeling and behaving.

Supervision of clinical practice

Even the most seasoned therapist with a great deal of experience working with adult survivors of childhood abuse can become entangled in the complex transactions between therapist and client which tend to occur. The value of a knowledgeable colleague's objective perspective is essential to enhance the therapy itself for the survivor and also to avoid alliance collusions and ruptures, impasses and stagnation occurring which hinder the therapeutic process. Transference and CT patterns are powerful elements of work with adult survivors and each therapist should seek supervision and advice at differing points throughout the therapy in tandem with thoughtful introspection about interactional patterns which emerge. The level of experience and competence of the therapist will dictate the extent to which supervision is required and it is vital that a therapist's inexperience is matched with adequate supervision for the survivor's welfare in the first instance.

The value of CAT reformulation

The accuracy of CAT reformulation methods (e.g., the SSSD) was explored by Bennett and Parry (1998) comparing the flow diagram created between therapist and patient from the same single case with data derived from two alternative formulation methods, namely the Case Conflictual Relationship Theme (Luborsky & Crits-Christoph, 1990) and Structural Analysis of Social Behaviour–Cyclic Maladaptive Pattern models (Benjamin, 1974). This study examined the validity of CAT reformulation reinforcing previous investigations of its therapeutic value (Bennett, 1994; Evans and Parry, 1996). The findings of Bennett and Parry support the contention that accurate reformulation of a patient's difficulties can be achieved using CAT without a reliance upon complex, laborious methodologies. As a clinically sound process of reformulation, CAT analysis can provide a comprehensive means of conceptualising the recurring damaging patterns of procedures and relating associated with a patient's difficulties.

Roth and Fonagy (1996) comment on CAT that the 'prime value of this technique is that it offers a structure for intervention by requiring the therapist to offer a parsimonious formulation of the patient's difficulties within an interpersonally focused schema-oriented framework' (p. 11). The diagrams generated during the reformulation process act as important tools for the work to be done in therapy and exemplify this technique. It is important that the diagrams are not over-complicated or serve to confuse the survivor. Creating the diagram in CAT requires a flexible and patient approach from the therapist and each diagram is typically as fundamentally unique as the patient and his/her experiences and ways of coping with life's difficulties and relationships.

Engaging the survivor: basic considerations and interviewing

Exclusion criteria for CAT are similar to other psychotherapies, which require active engagement, attention, concentration and collaboration from a client. An acutely mentally ill or substance-intoxicated client should be managed as necessary. Drug treatments and alcohol/drug rehabilitation may be needed as prerequisites to entering a CAT treatment. Clients with traumatic brain injuries in the past often lack the basic cognitive abilities to benefit also. CAT has been applied for clients with learning disabilities in a modified format with notable success. In general, if the client's difficulties can be conceptualised within the CAT framework, then its application is warranted.

Pacing therapy within a time-limited framework demands patience and sensitivity without losing sight of target problems and the work to be done. As discussed, clients may enter therapy with full recollection of the abuse and adversity they suffered; others may recall generic or scripted memories of incidents (Neisser, 1982), only remembering outline details of events which have become fused together. In some cases, 'forgetting' may have occurred due to dissociative processes, defensive failure to recollect, or simple degradation of memories. State-dependent recall can be observed due to the effects of mood disorder such as depression, which colours recall. Demand characteristics of the therapist–client interaction may further influence disclosure due to fear, shame or confusion.

Prior to the working phase of CAT, issues of confidentiality, expectations about what can be achieved and formal practical arrangements are best negotiated immediately. Security of clinical notes and correspondence to referrer or other professionals is important to assure the client of the boundaries within which information will be contained. Anxieties should be discussed and addressed. Installation of hope is also vital, but must be tempered with realism. Informing the client that therapeutic work will at times be difficult, challenging and emotional, but tolerant and responsive with mutual respect and control, sets the scene for the work ahead. Promises of success should not be made, but encouragement and hope communicated to the client. A verbal contract and agreement about the scheduling of sessions are necessary within the initial session to provide structure for the client at an early stage. Adult survivors' sense of vulnerability within relationships and sensitivities regarding safety can be acknowledged by stating explicitly that the client will be in control of the pacing of therapy, joint collaboration reinforced as a guiding principle is vital and that every intervention is explained, discussed and agreed. Encouraging the client to voice any anxieties, discomfort or resistance and explaining that these opinions will be respected and welcomed can allay the client's uncertainties. In many cases, only the therapist's actual behaviour can reassure the client as time progresses. Words are not enough.

A caveat of importance is that reformulating the client's difficulties in CAT terms does not discount or negate the therapist's personal discretion to employ other techniques (cognitive techniques, Imagery Rescripting and Reprocessing, Eye Movement Desensitisation and Reprocessing etc.; see Chapter 4). CAT analysis can accommodate these methods without losing the global conceptualisation of the client's difficulties, the agreed targets for change and how recurring patterns or symptoms are addressed. Ill-conceived eclecticism can become chaotic, undisciplined, directionless and unsafe clinical practice, which should be avoided. Predicting the likely outcome of changing target problems should be forecast realistically with a clear vision of the intended outcome desired by therapist and client alike.

When interviewing the survivor of childhood abuse, certain areas of his/her personal history are worth exploration. The family atmosphere, the nature of relationships with parents and the influence of extended family members require discussion, particularly if the abuse is intra-family or incestuous. Parental psychiatric or physical illnesses, substance abuse and the presence of marital difficulties are very common in dysfunctional families in which abuse occurs. Blatant neglect, cruelty and exploitation are observed amidst a backdrop of dysfunction within the parental system and relationships between parents and the children are greatly distorted and skewed. For example, in incestuous families the female child may have been groomed to assume the role of the 'wife' in several ways, including a pseudo-maternal role involving sexual relations with the father. This may be the case when the mother is physically disabled or psychologically distant or absent (e.g., due to depression or marital disharmony). Secrecy maintains the status quo for some incestuous families, while a mother's denial or threats of violence towards the mother by the father perpetuate the abuse in others.

For survivors of multiply abusive parents, it is difficult to grasp or describe an abusing parent's patterns of behaviour because of characteristic unpredictability, inconsistency and impulsivity. An abusing parent may sadistically injure and verbally berate a young child then comfort, cuddle and tend to his/her wounds expressing love and devotion. Confusing images of the parents are conveyed and the survivor may defend or explain away the parent's violence (because of psychiatric illness, misuse of drugs etc.) only to recount another episode of mistreatment. Teasing out the threads amongst the contradictory parental images and stories reported by the survivor requires patience from the therapist to build a realistic and accurate picture of the nature of the relationship between child and parent.

An appreciation of the feelings generated by the abuse and how the survivor copes can be gleaned throughout the account of his/her personal history. Even very dysfunctional coping strategies such as self-injury, bingeing on food or hazardous substance misuse can represent the only solutions the survivor could employ to achieve short-term relief, and symptoms are understood in the context of the childhood environment and the survivor's developing personality. Adult and peer relationships subsequent to the abuse provide important information regarding the survivor's management of emotional closeness, his/her sense of safety and trust and tolerance of intimacy. Marital and sexual difficulties should be explored if relevant and an assessment of the survivor's access to social supports and friendships estimated.

Assessing memories for childhood abuse

Human memory suffers from errors such as simple fallibility, suggestibility and the tendency to mistake imagined for genuine memories. At present, we do not have a 'Pinocchio test' which can verify whether or not a survivor's memories for childhood abuse are true or falsified for whatever reason. A number of points are worthy of mention initially. Firstly, 'infantile amnesia' for childhood events is common for incidents before the age of three or events somewhat later (Loftus, 1993) and an inability to recall such details is not to be considered an indication of repression of abuse. Secondly, it has been shown that memories for repeated, similar instances for certain classes of events (e.g., Type II traumas; sexual abuse, physical beatings by a parent) appear 'to be retained in spots rather than complete wholes' (Terr, 1991; p. 14) as opposed to single-event Type I traumas. Deficits in access to specific details are a reflection of normal forgetting when Type II memories are reported.

Thirdly, the base rate for dissociative amnesia of childhood abuse is debatable. Herman and Schatzow (1987) reported that 63% of 53 group therapy patients showed some degree of dissociative amnesia for abuse. Briere and Conte (1993) further stated that 59% of 450 mixed-gender patients reported traumatic amnesia, suggesting that dissociative amnesia is relatively common. In contrast, Femina, Yeager and Lewis (1990) propose that, for a group of women assessed when aged 15 and then 24, total forgetting was uncommon. These authors state that survivors fail to report because of factors which inhibit disclosure such as embarrassment, a wish to protect others, feelings that they deserved punishment, a conscious wish to forget and a lack of rapport with the interviewer. Loftus, Polonsky and Fullilove (1994) propose that adult survivors do not disclose for a variety of reasons. Pope (1997) claimed that repression and dissociative amnesia do not occur as frequently as certain research findings suggest, and methodological problems in studies have biased the interpretation of the findings. In one of the most interesting studies, Williams (1994) showed that 38% of survivors interviewed 17 years later reported total forgetting for documented abuse in childhood. Therefore, experimental and clinical evidence highlights the complexity of evaluating memories of childhood abuse and it is advisable to anticipate forgetting of specific details due to the natural fallibility of memory and to avoid any suggestible questioning of a survivor.

Survivors' accounts of their recall for childhood abuse can vary considerably. It is common for survivors to claim that they recall nothing or only partial remnants about the abuse. 'Forgetting' in these cases may reflect dissociative amnesia ('traumatic forgetting'), repression of painful memories, and their emotions and meaning or natural unreliability of human memories for childhood events. In other cases, the survivor may claim that he/she cannot honestly be certain that abuse occurred and may believe that he/she has mistaken vivid dreams and emotionally laden images for factual events. Prior disclosure may have been treated with dismissal, denigration and invalidation and the survivor may have learnt not to trust his/her own perceptions of events. Denial that the abuse occurred can occur even when verifying historical evidence is available (e.g., child or adolescent records, results of medical investigations). Motivations for not disclosing include guilt and shame, embarrassment, fear of reprisal or rejection and a sense that the abuse was deserved. Helping the suggestible survivor is problematic in that a survivor who claims he/she is unsure whether abuse actually occurred requires sensitive, patient management to deliberate his/her experiences without any influence from the therapist (see below).

Memory of abuse, disclosure and the therapeutic relationship

When the adult survivor of childhood abuse enters the therapeutic relationship, a number of clinical issues become essential to facilitate the survivor's engagement in the process of therapy and to sensitively manage the obstacles to actively addressing the psychological difficulties likely to be present. Firstly, memories of the abusive event(s) may be retained as fragmentary, elusive and indescribable sensations and images which the child has resisted internalising the meaning of—with no desire to capture the abusive experiences through the organising functions of language. Integrating these fragmentary ideas, images and memories may result in the production of an overwhelming, complete picture. The survivor may need to defend against contemplating the reality and meaning of the abuse which is perceived as a more horrific solution, struggling with varying degrees of success, keeping the same reality at bay in the external world through dissociative strategies. Heineman (1998) eloquently portrays the survivor's dilemma whereby he/she 'lives in a dark, eerily kaleidoscopic inner world in which organised images and thoughts can be punctured without warning by fragmented pictures, flashes, sounds and feelings' (p. 144).

The survivor is encouraged by professionals and others alike to address the trauma under the advice that the capacity to symbolise and verbalise memories of abuse potentially allows the adult to integrate these experiences and achieve recovery. Therapy techniques that include a 'reliving' or direct imaginal exposure approaches to the trauma help by elaborating and integrating the event(s) and meanings into prior and subsequent autobiographical memory. PTSD symptoms such as flashbacks, nightmares and intrusive recollections which are experienced in a 'here and now' manner occur because the survivor cannot establish a self-referential perspective about the context of the trauma in one's own life history. Reliving the event(s) can promote a 'reclaiming' of a self-referential, autobiographical viewpoint. The presence of dissociation and emotional numbing can interfere with the facilitation of organised, integrated memories, which are 'in the past' and not 'here and now' experiences.

For some survivors, the need to avoid the horrors of facing the totality of the abusive experiences hinders engaging in any form of 'reliving'. This must be contrasted with the opinion that 'for better or worse, once we can name a thing, we own it, and it has a place in our internal world' (Heineman, 1998, p. 144). The therapist's task is to unravel this thread of fragmented experience, and to facilitate the survivor's integration of these horrific memories and images with sensitivity and active encouragement. The survivor's fear of contemplating the unspeakable reality he/she has been burdened with and the therapist's wish to place some form of narrative structure onto this reality can represent a tense problem in pacing engagement in the helping process. Imposing a false structure upon experiences which are partial and illusory can strip the survivor of the real emotional qualities of the memories and appear to be assigning sense to a senseless experience. Naming the unnameable too quickly is often a temptation, which can undermine or destroy the process of engagement for the survivor. The use of other assessment modalities which encourage the survivor to describe the whole experience and its meaning using art, psychodrama or poetry can best convey the unpalatable reality of the abuse. Timing the disclosures of the abuse during assessment and the vehicle for doing so require serious thought from the therapist.

Disclosures of the abuse can be hindered and facilitated by different approaches (Brewin, Andrews & Gotlib, 1993). The survivor's initial experience of informing others and their responses to the disclosures at that time are extremely influential (Summit, 1983) and his/her expectations regarding the therapist's validation or otherwise can affect whether the disclosure is perceived by the survivor as empathically received and contained. Retractions of disclosures are commonplace due to a parent or guardian's undermining or negating attitude. The survivor may, consequently, question memories of the events and deny their occurrence, until intrusive experiences occur such as nightmares or flashbacks. Punishment and rejection from a non-abusing or unsupportive parent further inhibit sharing the horror of the abuse itself. The survivor as a child cannot contain the craziness of the abuse, yet is not permitted to make sense of it either. As time progresses, the survivor is condemned to inhabit an illusory world where he/she perceives him/herself as irretrievably dispelled to a shadowy sense of the world and as damaged, invalidated and disbelieved. The therapist must be aware of the risk of repeating the responses of others when disclosure was first attempted and avoid colluding with this scenario.

The shame, self-disgust and abhorrence associated with the abusive acts are also prone to influence describing the events. The survivor may expect the therapist to be overwhelmed by the deviant nature of the acts that the perpetrator did, anticipating the therapist to be able to recognise the almost transparent shamefulness of the survivor's physical body and identity. For some survivors, the abuse has invaded the body and defaced the inside of his/her body, leaving a putrefying stain on the internal sense of self. The body is perceived to be a tainted object, which is disgusting and is rejected or attacked through starvation, neglect or self-harm. The psychological self is symbolically rejected also and mistreated through sabotage, similar to the concept of the 'internal saboteur'.

Somewhat differently, abuse can leave the survivor with a sense that he/she has been depleted or stripped of vital psychological capacities. Spontaneity, creativity and the mental space to think about and reflect upon events and one's own behaviour are compromised (e.g., the child's capacity to play is impaired or imbued with scenes of trauma). The perpetrator steals from the survivor, leaving a depleted body and self. Giving information to an inquisitive therapist can seem, for the survivor, a repetition of things being taken from him/her or intrusive prying. Alertness and vigilance to a repeat of such invasion or theft result in a guarded attitude to the therapist, who may be perceived as an external danger.

False memories: simple advice

The issue of the veracity of memories of abuse in childhood, whether disclosed before or during therapy, is a matter of contentious and continuing debate (Bremner & Marmar, 1998). In terms of clinical practice when dealing with disclosures or revelations of memories, the guidelines of Mollon (1998) encompassing the experimental and clinical findings regarding distinguishing false from genuine memories should be advisedly followed. The professional's behaviour towards the potential veracity or otherwise of the memories can greatly affect how the survivor addresses whichever version of the past is most appropriate. Overzealous validation, suggestions, rewarding increased details, journaling and secondary gains can influence the survivor's ability to clearly and accurately decipher the probable veracity of the memories. Mollon advises a tolerance of uncertainty without invalidation. This applies to phenomena such as nightmares and flashbacks which can be, on one hand, conceptualised to be undistorted and accurate sensory representation of externally generated experiences (Ornstein & Myers, 1996). Alternatively, they can be viewed as a general form of memory prone to social construction and normal distortion through encoding and retrieval (Tessler & Nelson, 1996). Similarly, the sensations and affects associated with abuse can be etched upon the neuronal circuitry of the survivor (Krystal, 1968), not accessible to language and difficult to verify objectively. False and genuine memories can be equally detailed and vivid in their recollection, with few differences in specific features. Memory is partly a process of recall and reconstruction subject to distortion, error and interpretation which affect their production, unlike a videotape of a sequential event, and a 'flawed process' (Brewin *et al.*, 1993).

The stance of the therapist is crucial. Two unfortunate extremes are apparent, consisting, at one end, of the belief that children's memories are unreliable and suggestible (Goodman, Quas, Batterman-Faunce & Riddlesberger, 1994; Rogers, 1995) or that children are capable of resisting incorporating false information into their recall of memories (Tobey & Goodman, 1992). Disclosure or 'remembering' childhood memories (often triggered by themes in the media, current affairs) can occur when addressing memories of other forms of abuse, misinterpreting the nature of these abusive experiences. Premature validation must be tempered with cautious tolerance of uncertainty without negating the survivor's sense of what may be real or imagined. Encouraging the survivor to come to his/her own conclusions is important and professionals must be cautious within the therapeutic alliance. Chasing or searching for memories of childhood trauma should not be undertaken.

In other instances, repression or 'forgetting' of abusive events can lead to a survivor experiencing a recollection of previously dormant or inaccessible memories (Gelinas, 1983). With the potential stress and consequences of prosecution and the raw emotional states experienced, survivors who recall abuse in a delayed form can be confused and disoriented by their vivid and intrusive qualities. The repercussions of recall and the responses of the therapist can facilitate or inhibit the survivor's involvement in further treatment efforts in these cases.

The management of traumatic memories during CAT

The practice of CAT should take into consideration the nature of traumatic memories and the complications, which surround them for the survivor. Some survivors will report vivid, emotionally laden memories; others will report only fragmented, disparate recollections. 'Chasing' traumatic memories should not be undertaken. Each therapist is required to base practice concerning disclosures of traumatic recollections on a firm knowledge of the nature of these memories and the aims of therapy in relation to them. CAT explicitly attempts to create a self-referential perspective on how the traumas may have impinged upon or changed the survivor's autobiographical knowledge. The use of specific techniques such as the Reformulation and Goodbye Letters, the SSSD and conceptualising the survivor's personality development using the Multiple Self-States Model of identity disturbance are helpful in this regard (see Chapter 3). A narrative model of the trauma's impact on the survivor's coping (whether reflexive or intentional) over time is incorporated into the CAT process.

Whether direct 'memory work' should be a necessary component of CAT depends on a case-by-case appreciation of the nature of the survivor's recollections and the survivor's capacity to engage in direct exposure to contemplating the trauma itself and meanings associated. CAT promotes organisation and integration of the trauma and elaborates the meaning and context of the trauma in the survivor's life. Coping strategies, however dysfunctional or self-defeating, are understood as part of general functioning.

Assessing other aspects of abuse: structured interviews and self-report questionnaires

Several assessment measures are useful which specifically tap the survivor's personal experiences of childhood abuse and adversity (see Meichenbaum, 1994, for a review of different methodologies and measures). The timing and explanation for asking questions about childhood abuse or traumas must occur in the context of sufficient client engagement, trust and safety. Resnick and Newton (1992) propose that a simple probe should routinely question clients that specifically asks about the possibility that abuse occurred in any form in formative years. Most clients interviewed within a variety of settings and situations will indicate whether or not any untoward events occurred and whether he/she is willing to discuss them further, never or at another time. The style of questioning should be non-threatening and respectful, accentuating that the client is in control of the entire process and its pace. Screening questions are legitimate and advisable in the initial stages of assessment and can be explored more thoroughly with the client's agreement and motivation.

Two measures that are particularly helpful to clarify the survivor's experience are the Childhood Trauma Interview (CTI; Fink et al., 1995) and the Childhood Trauma Questionnaire (CTQ: Bernstein & Fink, 1998). Both interview schedule and self-report questionnaires have demonstrated satisfactory reliability and validity for clinical use.

The CTI is a semi-structured interview approach which assesses six areas of interpersonal trauma, including separations and losses, physical neglect, emotional abuse or assault, physical abuse or assault, witnessing violence and sexual abuse or assault. Questions ascertain behavioural aspects of these events. For example, the physical neglect section inquires about a lack of supervision, deprivation of food, clothing and medical care. The emotional abuse section asks about experiences of being screamed at, criticised, humiliated, threatened with abandonment or injury. Physical abuse is described as experiences of being hit, kicked, thrown against walls, locked in, burned or choked. Sexual abuse experiences include perpetrators making sexual threats, being forced to watch others engage in sexual intercourse and contact ranging from inappropriate touching to rape. All perpetrators are inquired about and the severity and frequency of the traumatic events are rated from 0 to 6; duration is noted from age of onset to cessation of the experiences. Therefore, details of abuse with each category are obtained with ratings for the number of perpetrators, severity, frequency and duration of the trauma. Terminology such as 'perpetrator', 'abuse' or 'neglect' is avoided and multiple initial questions and follow-up probes are used.

The CTQ is a 28-item self-report scale which accompanies the CTI. Four scales are included—physical and emotional abuse, emotional neglect, sexual abuse and physical neglect—rated on a five-point Likert scale according to the frequency with which the experiences occurred (0 = 'never' to 5 = 'very frequently'; 'the punishments I received seemed cruel' (physical and emotional abuse), 'someone tried to touch me in a sexual way or tried to make me touch them' (sexual abuse). Again pejorative terminology is avoided. These assessment tools are recommended to accurately investigate a survivor's retrospective accounts of childhood adversity, allowing the therapist to obtain sensitive information in a structured manner. The CTQ's inclusion of a minimisation/denial scale can be helpful in detecting the survivor's attitude to disclosure when a documented history of abuse is known to be available.

Evaluating adult psychopathology

Co-morbidity is almost expected when survivors attend for therapy and, as discussed, the diversity of psychological difficulties associated with childhood abuse is far reaching. Inquiries about sexual dysfunctions are better delayed despite research evidence that this domain is very often affected (Mullen *et al.*, 1993).

Personality testing can show the extent to which the survivor displays relational patterns towards oneself and in interaction with others which form the substrate for any self-defeating, dysfunctional behaviours. The Millon Clinical Multiaxial Inventory (3rd edition; Millon, Millon & Davis, 1994) is a 178-item true–false answer self-report questionnaire which assesses combinations of personality dimensions related to DSM-IV personality disorders (Axis II) and symptoms (Axis I). Alternatively structured interviews for personality disorders (Structured Clinical Interview for DSM-IV; SCID-IV; First, Gibbon *et al.*, 1997) can be used for more formal categorical diagnosis. Screening scales for PTSD and childhood emotional disturbance embedded within the MCMI-3 permit evaluation of the presence or absence of flashbacks or intrusive symptoms, which can be followed further.

For symptom presentation, self-report measures such as the Symptom Checklist-90—Revised (SCL-R-90; Derogatis, 1983) provide a standardised assessment of current symptomatology, general severity of these problems and indication of caseness (whether professional treatment is warranted). Otherwise, the Present State Examination (PSE: Wing, Cooper & Sartorious,

1974) and the Structured Clinical Interview for DSM-IV (SCID-I; First *et al.*, 1997) are useful methods of assessing general psychopathology.

Assessing PTSD symptoms can be pursued if detected from interview screening questions or client accounts. A plethora of measures are available. The Clinician Administered PTSD Rating Scale (CAPS-1; Blake *et al.*, 1990) is a 30-item structured interview assessing the 17 core PTSD symptoms in terms of both severity and frequency. A social and vocational impairment scale is also included. Associated features of guilt, hopelessness and disillusionment are assessed, giving a comprehensive evaluation of the nature and content of PTSD symptoms experienced by the survivor. The Trauma Symptom Checklist (Briere, Evans, Harris & Cotman, 1995) is a relatively user-friendly and valuable self-report questionnaire that yields helpful information about current distressing trauma sequelae.

Dissociative experiences and symptoms can be assessed using the self-report and interview schedules referred to as the Structured Clinical Interview for DSM-IV Dissociative Disorders (SCD-D; Steinberg, 1993), Loewenstein's Office-based Schedule of Dissociation and Multiple Personality Disorder (Loewenstein, 1994) and Vanderlinden *et al.*'s (1993) Dissociative Questionnaire (DIS-Q; reproduced in Appendix 1). The prominence of dissociation within the CAT model of trauma attests to the importance of measuring these phenomena for adult survivors.

The challenge of the suicidal client

Briere and Zaidi (1989) report that up to two-thirds of sexually abused women have attempted suicide at some time. Assessing the risk for survivors of abuse is therefore crucial but is difficult to do with definite accuracy. A single predictor does not exist and a constellation of factors must be weighted to provide the foundation for sound clinical judgement about a survivor's potential risk to him/herself. Making such an estimation is a complex process with no guarantees and a variety of theories and methodologies are available. Each person's risk is the product of a unique set of variables and caution is paramount given the relative inaccuracy of our knowledge and the low base rate for completed suicide (Bongar *et al.*, 1998). At its simplest it can be suggested that direct questioning of the client about intent is the most valuable method of enquiry with 80% of those who complete suicide communicating intent. Taking note of the client's prior history of attempted suicide, current ideation, plans and preparation and methods is relevant. Current indicators such as feelings of hopelessness, depressed mood, social isolation and substance misuse provide the context for any suicide attempt.

Guidelines within inventories can be very useful. For example, the Suicide Intention Scale (Beck, Schuyler & Herman, 1974) examines the client's current circumstances and attitude towards suicide. Inquiries about the degree of planning, communication of intention, timing to avoid intervention, precautions against discovery and making final arrangements to die (e.g., giving possessions away) can be noted. The client's ideas about the choice and lethality of method used, seriousness of the attempt, ambivalence towards living and expectations about the likely fatality of the attempt provide a comprehensive picture of the client's overall intentions. Estimating his/her coping ability, problem-solving capabilities and sense of control is also relevant. The therapist must attempt to understand the client's motivations for contemplating suicide (e.g., to actually end psychological pain and suffering, to communicate or manipulate) and acknowledge his/her view that no other feasible option is available. Precautions or plans to negotiate assuring the client's safety at the material time must be made. Frequently, the survivor of abuse may consider suicide as a method of terminating the influence of the perpetrator's actions that entrap and control him/her to the present day.

Helping the client to understand that this notion can be reframed to be that killing oneself is the ultimate concession of power and control to a worthless, vile and deviant perpetrator can alter the client's thinking. Killing oneself is admitting complete defeat to the perpetrator. Self-injury is commonly a representation of enactment of the abuser–victim scenario towards oneself because the survivor feels deserving, defiled and worthy of punishment and attack due to guilt, blame and shame. Paradoxically, clients are often surprised to acknowledge that they are in control over the enactment of abuse towards oneself in this manner, although the impulse of self-harm can be intense and difficult to resist. Inventories such as Firestone and Firestone's self-report measure (1996; Firestone Assessment of Self-destructive Thoughts, FAST) assess a continuum of self-destructive thinking ranging from thoughts which lead to lowered self-esteem to self-annihilatory thinking, suicidal ideation and intent.

Self-harm is a commonly encountered behaviour shown by survivors of abuse that can engender feelings of helplessness, frustration and even anger for the therapist. Injuring oneself does not intuitively rest with the role of 'surviving', the latter role perceived, perhaps, as necessitating shoring up all of one's resources towards the goal of preserving health rather than attacking oneself. Those who deliberately harm themselves do so for many reasons. The motivations include tension relief to rid oneself of negative emotions (reinforced by the escape from distress), or as an expression of self-hatred and punishment because the survivor feels deserving of harm or inherently bad or evil. In these instances, it is often only the observable physical signs of injury, such as blood or a sufficient amount of pain, which satiate the intensity of the urges. Other motivations are sexual masochism in a fetishistic way (e.g., cutting or insertion of sharp objects into the sexual parts of the body) and to secure social attention, maintain dependency and coerce care or to manipulate the environment and relationships (Pollock, 1997). When these acts are compulsive, survivors report the urges to harm as intolerable and intense as if he/she is 'on a roller-coaster that you can't stop'. The therapist can experience a corresponding countertransference reaction of powerlessness, anxiety and frustration, as if the survivor is untouchable and unreachable. Every effort must be made to help the survivor divert attention from the urges and to understand the reasons and functions for the act.

Sometimes, the act of self-harm represents a direct enactment of an abuse-generated RRP (e.g., *abusing/hating* to *deserving* victim), although it is best not to assume this unless the complete reformulation of the survivor's repertoire supports this mechanism. One of the inherent difficulties of inferring to a survivor of abuse that he/she may be engaging in self-harm because of the internalisation of abuse-generated RRPs is that it suggests that the perpetrator, in some form, has left a legacy of victimisation that is continuing and the survivor is perpetuating the abuse against him/herself almost on behalf of the still omnipotent perpetrator.

This is a risky therapeutic message to present to a survivor of childhood abuse, but in some cases it may accurately convey the intrapsychological process underlying his/her deliberate self-harm. A strength within this suggestion is that it promotes the survivor to make the shift towards the surviving rather than the abusing role during self-management procedures. It can be argued that the actual episode of victimisation has finished and one of the most important tasks for the adult survivor is to address the tendency to cause continuing pain inwardly. Encouraging the survivor to recognise and revise this pattern can become a specific TPP during CAT (e.g., learning to alter the victim self-state to that of survivor). One of the potential benefits of pointing out the internalisation of the perpetrator–victim relational unit is that it does infer that changing its influence requires the survivor to battle against this urge by resuming control over one's own self-management by aggressively defying the internalised perpetrator and not engaging in self-injury. This requires a great deal of sensitive therapeutic work to encourage the survivor to take this course of action and failure to do so can feel as if the perpetrator is still 'winning' or 'in control'.

These motivations and functions are not necessarily mutually exclusive and, like most human behaviour, self-injury can be multi-determined and serve a variety of purposes. Careful attention to possible reasons for self-harm is necessary when assessing the motivations for self-destructiveness generally within a survivor's presentation.

CAT research on adult survivors of abuse

Several clinical studies have described the application of CAT for patients who have histories of severe sexual, physical and emotional abuse. A patient series study of the outcome of CAT for survivors is described in Chapter 11.

Clarke and Llewelyn (1994) reported the CAT treatment of seven adult female survivors, this study illustrating the changes in repertory grid date following therapy. Llewelyn (1997) has also reported a case study of the CAT for a sexually abused adult describing the process of treatment. Pollock & Kear-Colwell (1994) and Pollock (1996) report the reformulation and CAT of seven female survivors of extensive abuse, each of the patients having violently assaulted her intimate partner. Pollock (1997, 1998a) further described the therapy of a male perpetrator of sexual abuse who was severely abused in childhood. Golynkina and Ryle (1999) report a group of borderline personality disorder (BPD) cases with predominant histories of neglect and abuse and the relevance of dissociated self-states in the reformulation of these patients' pathology. Ryle and Golynkina (2000) describe the developmental features of 27 BPD patients with sexual and physical abuse and deprivation being evident for the majority of this sample. Outcome data from the study of Pollock (1996) established that scores on the Dissociation Questionnaire (Vanderlinden *et al.*, 1993) measuring identity fragmentation, amnesia and loss of behavioural control showed clinically significant improvement following CAT with structured changes occurring as assessed using repertory grids.

CHAPTER 3

CAT and the Multiple Self-States Model of trauma

In Chapter 2, the basic model of CAT reformulation, assessment and treatment process was described and illustrated with direct reference to the three areas of psychological dysfunction (i.e., disturbances in self, affect and interpersonal relationships/social behaviour) central to understanding how childhood abuse can affect adult functioning.

The CAT model presented here is based on a number of assumptions. Firstly, it is proposed that a continuum of severity exists in terms of the extent to which each survivor's personality development is compromised. At the lesser end of this continuum, the survivor may report acute and short-term reactions to the abuse during childhood with little direct detriment to his/her general functioning and transient psychological symptoms. The survivor's identity formation has not been affected negatively to a significant degree. At the more extreme end, the survivor shows varied and incapacitating reactions to the abuse, including severe identity disturbance, emotional distress and psychological symptoms and problems within self–self and self–other relationships. The assessment and treatment of a survivor's *identity disturbance* is assigned prominence within this model and the case illustrations described later in Chapters 5–8 report the treatment of progressively more extreme presentations along this continuum of severity in personality dysfunction.

The second assumption is that the internalisation of the perpetrator-to-victim relational unit represents a mechanism for the persistence of many of the survivor's psychological problems in terms of self–self and self–other behaviours. The model attempts to provide a means of reformulating this reciprocal role procedure and addressing it as a part of the survivor's reaction to the abusive experiences. Thirdly, it must be borne in mind that each survivor's responses to trauma are idiosyncratic and unique, influenced by a multitude of additional developmental and environmental factors.

The Multiple Self-States Model of identity disturbance

The Multiple Self-States Model of CAT (MSSM; Ryle, 1997, 1998) represents a trauma-based explanation for identity disturbances and difficulties arising from childhood abuse tracing the ways in which development of an integrated, stable, adaptive self can be compromised along this severity continuum. Within this model, trauma is proposed to cause disruption to identity development and particularly causing fragmentation into discrete, multiple, fractured self-states which are permeated by dissociation and dissociative symptoms. It is, therefore, a *trauma-induced dissociation* model of pathology.

An integrated identity is characterised by a sense of continuity in perception of oneself and others, and stable moods and behaviour patterns over time with adequate control of appropriate emotional states. The person's values, habits, likes, dislikes etc. are consistent and relatively unchanging. The person evaluates him/herself to be a mixture of positive and negative attributes and goals. Needs are acknowledged and pursued in a socially mature manner (Kernberg, 1984; McWilliams, 1994). Guidano and Liotti (1985, p. 103) describe early facilitative parenting to promote 'a full sense of self-identity and an inherent feeling of uniqueness and historical continuity'. Adversity in childhood affects the integration of identity, Fine (1988) claiming that the greatest damage occurs to self, self–other, and other–other interactions. Similarly, Ryle's model of personality integration views deficits and dysfunction in identity to originate from exposure to harsh, abusive, neglectful caregiving environments which fail to encourage acquisition of an adaptive, flexible and responsive repertoire of experiences (and RRPs) which permits stable, coherent identity formation.

As stated in Chapter 2, the core construct in CAT is the *reciprocal role procedure* (RRP), which is defined as intentional, aim-directed sequences of perception, feelings and actions in relationships, enactment of a given role and prediction of the responses of others (Ryle, 1990). An RRP describes a relational unit and includes two polarised roles which influence self–other and self–self interactions. These may include a parent- and child-derived role such as *caring* in relation to *blissfully cared for*, *abusing–victimised*, *controlling–crushed* or *contemptuous–belittled*. Individuals develop a more or less elaborated repertoire of RRPs emerging from early care-giving experiences into later adulthood. Optimal personality functioning necessitates the development of an adaptive repertoire of RRPs, which is flexible, fluidly organised and appropriately and responsively deployed in the context of relationships.

How does abuse actually traumatise?

Traumatic experiences can be defined in differing ways. The *Diagnostic and Statistical Manual of Mental Disorders* (DSM-IV; APA, 1994) states that an event is traumatic if the person has (1) experienced, witnessed, or was confronted with an event which involved actual or threatened death or serious injury, or a threat to the physical integrity of self or other, and (2) the person's response involved fear, helplessness or horror. A differing distinction is added by Terr (1991), who proposes that two types of traumatic event can occur, namely Type I and Type II traumas.

Type I traumas consist of short-term, unexpected events of limited duration which are sudden and devastating. Type II traumas are manifest as sustained, repeated events which are anticipated and cause long-standing impacts. The former is related to a better recovery pattern and is recalled as complete, vivid memories associated with symptoms of PTSD. Type II traumas, in contrast, cause greater corruption of the person's identity and more drastic strategies are evident in coping with the prolonged and repetitive nature of the traumas. Memories for events are less complete and are retained in a fragmented form. The survivor's adjustment is, to a large extent, dependent on the 'dose' of trauma experienced or witnessed and the degree of consequential pathology is also related to the duration, frequency and severity of the trauma. In some cases, the influence of the trauma can remain dormant and fail to affect the survivor until a later time, when the detrimental effects become apparent. Sexual abuse in childhood can be of both types, ranging from a single incident to chronic and repetitive assaults. The age and developmental status of the survivor is a critical factor, which affects outcome. It must be kept in mind that the additive influence of other forms of abuse and the contribution of the family environment as either a positive or negative factor must be taken into account.

Childhood traumatic experiences compromise the survivor both physically and psychologically (van der Kolk, 1994). The reason why a trauma is traumatic is conceived by Kluft (1984) as occurring when (1) the child fears for his/her own life, (2) the child fears that an important attachment figure will die, (3) physical intactness and/or clarity of consciousness is breached or impaired, (4) the child is isolated with these fears and (5) the child is systematically misinformed or 'brainwashed' about his/her situation (cited in Goodwin, 1985, p. 160). The essence of trauma is that the event(s) occur outside the normal range of human experience, cannot be assimilated and accommodated into the survivor's existing schema and violate our most rudimentary assumptions that one is invulnerable, worthy and deserving of good fortune, and that the world is meaningful, orderly and just (Janoff-Bulman, 1992). Therefore, trauma affects the survivor physically and psychologically, violating cognitive, interpersonal, emotional and social spheres of existence.

According to the MSSM, when pathology is observed because of childhood adversity or abuse, the survivor's personality is likely to show deficits in three main areas (see Figure 3.1). At the first level of the MSSM, harsh or adverse care-giving environments result in the internalisation of a restricted,

Integrated identity — Integrated identity — Identitity disturbance/ — Severe identity disturbance/
minimal symptoms   symptoms present   fragmentation into multiple   fragmentation into separated
                                          self-states, dissociation present   self-states (alters), severe
                                                                                dissociation, several forms of
                                                                                severe symptoms present

                                          Borderline Personality   Dissociative Identity
                                          Disorder (BPD)   Disorder (DID)

Figure 3.1 The continuum of severity within the Multiple Self-States Model of identity disturbance in CAT

narrow range of limited or extreme interpersonal procedures (e.g., *neglecting–deprived*) which colour future adult interactions and self-management (e.g., *punishing–injured* via harming oneself).

At the second level, a more complex disruption in an individual's sense of self-experience is described. Negative or traumatic events during development fail to encourage the operation of hierarchical procedures (called *metaprocedures*) which mobilise, connect and organise the deployment of RRPs. Features of identity disturbance are exhibited, referred to as evidence of a *dissociated personality* (Ryle, 1997). Traumatic or harsh care-giving disrupts the fluidity and connectedness of experience and dissociative symptoms are observed, including memory lacunae, loss of behavioural control, derealisation and depersonalisation. Dissociation reflects a lack of fluidity, connectedness and 'glue' within the system of self-states. Smooth changes in mood, behaviour and perception of self and others are absent, causing confusing and contradictory senses of self and discontinuity in identity across time. Failure to develop metaprocedures leads to dissociation and the production of two or more discrete self-states. A self-state includes a dominant RRP, each procedural role representing a state of mind with a distinct mood, perception of self and others, access and control of emotion. Switches between different self-states are disturbing experiences, for example from *powerless victim* to *angry abuser* (a switch within the RRP of a single self-state) or *powerless victim* to *ideally fused* (a shift from one self-state to a different state).

At the third level, the MSSM describes a deficit in self-reflection affecting consciousness and self-observation, disrupted also by dissociative processes. Disruption at level two, because of trauma or poor development of coordinated procedures, can affect level three. The capacity to recognise repetitive patterns of relating to oneself and others is defective, causing difficulties monitoring one's own responses, experiences and behaviours.

The spectrum of identity disturbance in the MSSM

The MSSM assumes a central role of *trauma-induced dissociation* in the failure to achieve an integrated identity, and the number of states, the degree to which they are dissociated from each other and amnesia between them vary along a spectrum. Reminders or perceptions that the survivor is experiencing a re-enactment of an abusing-to-victimised RRP perpetuate the fragmentation of these self-states and dissociation itself.

BPD (see Chapter 6 by Clarke and Llewelyn) is located on this spectrum (Golynkina & Ryle, 1999) where two or more subpersonalities or self-states are experienced as distinctly separate, with partial amnesia between them. The degree of dissociation is rarely absolute for BPD patients (Ryle, 1997), unlike that of dissociative identity disorder (DID). Fragmentation into numerous self-states also occurs to differing degrees. Criteria for BPD (DSM-IV, APA, 1994) include identity disturbance in the form of markedly and persistently unstable self-image or sense of self (excluding adolescent identity problems) characterised by frequent shifts in aspirations, plans and attitudes to others and oneself with an unclear, shallow and contradictory self-perception exhibited.

Further criteria are a pattern of instability and intense interpersonal relationships, impulsivity, affective instability and reactivity of mood, recurrent suicidal behaviour and gestures, threats or self-mutilation, chronic feelings of emotional emptiness, inappropriate or intense anger or difficulty controlling it, frantic efforts to avoid abandonment and transient, stress-related paranoid ideation or dissociative symptoms. Shearer (1994) has provided empirical evidence to support the link between BPD and dissociation. Furthermore, studies have indicated that up to 81% of patients diagnosed with BPD suffer from developmental effects of adversity and trauma during early personality development (Bernard & Hirsch, 1985). Childhood abuse is associated with the development of identity disturbances and dissociation along a continuum of severity ranging from BPD to DID.

The most severe end of the continuum extends to explain DID which is thought to show marked fragmentation into distinct identities, with amnesia being very prominent. Therefore, a *gradation* is implied by the MSSM from normal state-dependent memories and personality integrity through to distinctly dissociated identities in DID. This view is based on the theory that disorders which demonstrate severe dissociative processes or symptoms, such as DID, are complex forms of PTSD (van der Kolk, Roth, Pelcovitz & Mandel, 1993) resulting from chronic and damaging traumatic experiences, usually during childhood. Dysfunction within identity can be traced to each of the levels.

Level one: what the survivor internalises

At the first level, inadequate or uncaring parental environments colour the nature and content of the repertoire of RRPs internalised by the child. RRPs tend to be restricted and narrow and result in limited ways of relating to others and oneself. For example, a child who is subject to frequent physical beatings, harangued as stupid, evil and deserving of punishment is likely to internalise RRPs such as *contemptuous–contemptible*, *punishing–punished*, *terrorising–injured*. Expressing these experiences through words which describe the relational unit of adult-to-child depends upon whether the semantic meaning assigned to the totality of experiences fits the adult survivor's recollection of them.

Neisser (1982) demonstrated that multiple episodes of frequent abuse experiences become remembered as *generic* scripts which are broad distillations of the interactions between perpetrator and survivor. Specific incidents will be recalled (especially when single-incident Type I traumas have occurred) but more generally the summary script of the types of interactions during the abuse events are captured in memory through procedural rather than episodic learning. Family environments from which abuse emerges typically inhibit the child's acquisition through stimulation, play and positive involvement of more flexible and adaptive RRPs, which contribute to a sense of security, consistency and care. The child learning little more than internalised RRPs from the abuse, although interaction with significant others can compensate (e.g., extended family members, school peers, friendships, caring professionals), is unable to elaborate memories of the abuse, or acquire alternative RRPs or/and autobiographical memories remain unintegrated. Healthy management of the self is hindered and the young adult feels uncomfortable nurturing him/herself.

RRPs generated by childhood abuse can colour the survivor's self-perception and self–self and self–other behaviour for several years as he/she develops into adolescence and adulthood, patterns being maintained and reinforced often in a self-perpetuating way with restriction to the range of roles enacted by the survivor. These RRPs cannot be removed or extracted. They must be understood, reorganised, tracked, transformed and managed through therapeutic discourse and techniques. Conceptualising these RRPs and understanding their effects is a major task for any form of psychotherapy. Worthwhile therapy should address not only what the survivor has been robbed of enjoying but also it should release the survivor from the continuing influence of harmful RRPs and patterns emerging from them. The survivor carries the legacy of abuse in the form of these abuse-related RRPs and patterns and he/she must be helped to transform them to more adaptive ways of perceiving, feeling and acting.

In some instances, the survivor will claim that the experience of being victimised has created 'something new', which they definitely would not have been burdened with if the abuse had not occurred. A new object relation or, in CAT terms, RRP is internalised. Enduring traumatic abuse or pseudo-affectionate, non-aggressive sexual assaults creates a new relational unit, which is internalised and becomes part of the survivor's repertoire of RRPs. If the events occur in childhood, as opposed to adulthood, the survivor's developing relational repertoire incorporates the abusive RRP into his/her self and interpersonal behaviour, influencing other-to-self and self-to-self transactions. Survivors are aware of the need to mourn the loss of a spoilt childhood which abuse deprives them of. Many describe that the experience of abuse has given them a burden of feeling soiled, defiled, tainted, controlled and captured, with feelings of sadness, anxiety, powerlessness and pessimism. It is easy to conclude that these feelings and self-perceptions are indicative of a depressive episode. The subjective experience is described as more complex.

In other respects, the abuse causes a 'loss' for the survivor, which is directly related to the abuse. In some respects, abuse strips and depletes the survivor of basic capacities (e.g., to enjoy oneself, appreciate care and nurturance, creative thinking). Support for this notion is that sexually abused females are assessed by attachment interview schedules to report unresolved loss in their past histories of relationships (Stalker & Davies, 1995). An example is that of a 43-year-old married man who described his experiences of sexual abuse to have 'shown me the evil, dark reality of human nature. I went to a place that was starkly real and disappointing. It left me despondent, sad, hopeless'. This survivor also recalled 'I couldn't plan or set goals. I had no direction. Everything that was worthwhile was spoilt. I gave up fantasies of family life, intimacy. It all seemed wistful. Fantasies were fragile, like a shiny ball that was perfect but would inevitably be smashed. It was pointless investing in anything. Nothing that was dear mattered anymore. It felt unfixable'. He experienced unpredictable episodes of intense fear and sadness which overwhelmed him.

Abuse generates RRPs that persist in the internal life of the survivor. If the abuse is chronic and intrusive, the abuse-related RRPs are distillations of repeated variations of the perpetrator–victim relational scenario and the perpetrator's behaviour towards the child defines part of the survivor's personality as an adult. The survivor's resilience and how the environment compensates for the abuse-related RRPs influence whether the perpetrator directly moulds and shapes the survivor's personality. With increased chronicity of abuse, the more probable that the child's personality and repertoire of RRPs will be enveloped by the perpetrator's inducement of the child into certain roles with the entire relational unit internalised. Abuse-generated RRPs which have coloured the survivor's behaviour can dictate unhelpful interpersonal patterns. These ways of thinking, feeling and acting become maintained and reinforced often in a self-perpetuating way and restrict the range of roles others are expected to enact and the survivor can demonstrate. These RRPs cannot be removed or extracted. They must be understood, reorganised, tracked, transformed and managed through therapeutic discourse and techniques. Conceptualising these RRPs and understanding their effects is a major task for any form of psychotherapy. Psychotherapy should address not only what the survivor has been robbed of enjoying but also it should release the survivor from the continuing influence of harmful RRPs and patterns emerging from them. The survivor carries the legacy of abuse in the form of these abuse-related RRPs and patterns and he/she must be helped to transform them to more adaptive ways of perceiving, feeling and acting.

Emotional states that are associated with each reciprocal role and state of mind can vary, are typically idiosyncratic and affect the survivor's daily functioning. For example, a perpetrator's degradation during victimisation through physical torture and verbal denigration can induce the abused person into a *defeated*, *injured* and *despised* role with accompanying feelings of shame, guilt and self-disgust. A survivor often struggles with an inability to perceive him/herself as deserving of anything other than contempt and, in some cases, may feel fundamentally damaged. Self-blame, shame and self-loathing are common emblems of this condemnation of oneself expressed through sabotaging any successes or rewards, physical attacks on the body, a fatalistic pessimism about the future or even suicide attempts. The survivor may experience the 'voice' of the perpetrator intruding or clashing with his/her own thoughts, haunting the survivor's internal reality as if separation as an autonomous, active agent in the world has been substituted by a pervasive dependency on a tyrannical captor. A feeling of surrender, passivity and powerlessness is experienced with futility to escape this imprisonment.

Simply thinking about the perpetrator can annihilate the survivor's fragile resourcefulness and ruptures any notion of stability and cohesion in the survivor's functioning. Moods, perceptions of oneself and others, recollections of past events and continuity in one's behaviour vacillate into confusion—a state from which the survivor must break free to gain a semblance of tangible reality. Memory lapses may occur and persecutory ideas about the motivations of close relations creep in. Uncertainty about whether subjective experiences are dreamt or actual can occur and urges to cause physical harm to oneself and experience pain are outgrowths of these disturbances in identity. The external world can become a petrifying bombardment of potential attackers, causing dread, anxiety and panic with retreat to one's inner world the only option, yet this route risks vulnerability because it activates distressing memories of the perpetrator and his behaviour. The survivor has no place to stay and no place to go psychologically. An intolerable dilemma dictates the survivor's feelings.

The survivor's sense of identity is fragmented, fragile and tainted by the experience of abuse. One patient provided an impression of this by describing how her internal body cavity was like a 'filthy room where animals were starved, mistreated and imprisoned, faeces have been thrown onto the walls and floor, the smell is retching and my inner organs are decaying' (Laura; Chapter 8). Another patient described how becoming a 'social chameleon' had led him to feel as if he was watching himself from outside his body continuously trying to analyse which 'character' he was automatically assuming to fit the situation. Outwardly, this man was socially competent and personable and he maintained numerous façades with many different social groupings and members of local society. His personal life was characterised by addictive misuse of drugs, which, he claimed, provided him with a feeling of wholeness, and he felt dependently fused with his addiction as a vital activity. The utility of becoming 'many' promoted further fragmentation. A sense of unity within the self was only achievable in an altered state of consciousness when intoxicated. To all of those who encountered this patient he was balanced and invariable, yet this survival strategy added, in a self-defeating manner, to his fractionated sense of himself. The structural faults in identity lie at the root of psychopathology originating from abusive experiences. Symptoms and dysfunctional behaviours become understandable from the survivor's frame of reference if the defects in the fabric of identity are mapped and linked.

At level one of the MSSM, undesirable emotional states, self–self and self–other transactions can be understood as products of the internalisation of the perpetrator–victim relation and the subjective experiences of the perpetrator's actions which have induced or forced the survivor to experience certain roles, states of mind and emotions. Living in an abusive, rejecting or neglectful family environment, therefore, colours the range, flexibility and scope of the repertoire of RRPs acquired by the survivor (level one of MSSM). Dilemmas, traps and snags confirm and reinforce these RRPs and procedural loops entail failure to revise this procedural learning. Avoidant and symptomatic procedures are expressive of these harmful patterns of relating, thinking and feeling.

Level two: the structure of the survivor's identity

At the second level of dysfunction, the impact of trauma on the structural features of identity is given prominence. The severity of the traumatic experiences, the extent of fragmentation of the survivor's sense of self and the degree of dissociation are considered. Fragmentation refers to the survivor's sense of experiencing oneself as 'in bits', fluctuations in mood are common and he/she acts in an unpredictable and dramatic way, especially during interactions with others. The survivor's sense that he/she is continuous, consistent and stable appears corrupted. Young (1992) has referred to a 'post-traumatic personal identity' shown by survivors of chronic sexual abuse. The importance of dissociation in understanding traumatic responses has been articulated by many theorists and researchers and as a process dissociation has been described as the '*sine qua non*' of severe abuse (Gershunny & Thayer, 1999).

Dissociation is described in DSM-IV (APA, 1994) as a 'disturbance or alteration in the normally integrative functions of identity, memory or consciousness' and a number of diagnostic conditions are assignable, including disturbances in memory (amnesia, fugue states), consciousness and one's sense of reality (depersonalisation, derealisation) and identity (dissociative identity disorder, DID). Braun (1988) proposes that disruption occurs in normal integrative and perceptual processes of behaviour, affect, sensation and knowledge (the 'BASK' model). Dissociation is a feature of several mental disorders, including eating disorders, substance abuse, schizophrenia and personality disorders, specifically borderline personality and DID, the latter the most extreme example of a dissociative disorder (see Chapter 7).

Dissociation can refer to two distinct psychological processes: (1) states, such as feeling unreal, emotionally 'cut off' or in a trance-like 'emotional shutdown' of negative feelings or states of mind. For example, dissociation may be described as 'being like an automaton, on autopilot' or a 'zombie'. In certain cases of interpersonal violence, the act of violence is not accompanied by any feelings of anger or hate and the behavioural act appears split off from the congruent emotional state. Anaesthesia during incidents of self-harm may occur as urges to injure oneself build. In other cases, a state of intense absorption during actions (e.g., eating, cutting oneself) is reported or a narrowing of attention towards an object or image, (2) a reflection of a diffused, incoherent, fragmented identity which features discontinuities in self-experience because of amnesic episodes (called 'absences' or 'memory loss' by some clients), unpredictable or alarming actions and impulsivity, fugue episodes and deficits in autobiographical memories for childhood and other events, often for traumatic incidents specifically. The most extreme example of dissociation is observed when a client demonstrates self-states for which he/she is completely amnesic formed into a system of separate, segregated 'alter personalities' with a typical age, name, demeanour, predominant mood and behavioural tendencies. These alternate identities often appear to serve a particular function, being protective and parental, abusing or punishing etc. Dissociative symptoms are proposed to be characteristic of certain states of mind or emerge during shifts between states.

The therapeutic aim of CAT is to reduce the frequency of these states, defining their internal and environmental triggers and using a variety of techniques to control them. These dissociative states are often activated by interpersonal transactions and result from attempts to cope with the accompanying unpleasant emotions. Promoting integration within a client's identity can be achieved by encouraging self-comprehension and observation, blending of contradictory self-states and producing 'co-consciousness' where alter personalities are introduced into an internal dialogue, identifying the reciprocal roles associated with the self-states and modifying them into more healthy versions.

Other symptoms considered dissociative include trances, auditory hallucinations, vivid imaginary companions, somatisation and the existence of separate personalities and other diagnosable personality disorders (Shearer, 1994). Dissociation is proposed to occur as a dramatic and creative survival strategy employed during trauma or abuse which entails a range of coping methods (for example leaving one's body, being amnesic for pain/going numb, emotionally blank, a zombie-like state) and selective amnesia for periods of time during the episodes of abuse. Initially, dissociation is involuntary as a form of cognitive-emotional escape or self-hypnosis but later becomes an adaptive, habitual form of tolerating extreme physiological arousal (e.g., stressful states, heightened emotional states such as rage, anxiety, terror) and evading an incapacitating sense of entrapment and powerlessness. Lipshitz et al., (1998) have proposed that the more chronic the abuse, the greater the reliance upon dissociation. In its state-dependent, situational form, dissociation is commonly reported by rape victims (van der Kolk, 1996) and in circumstances where the survivor's life was threatened. If abuse is prolonged, frequent and intrusive the survivor may come to rely upon dissociation to cope and employ it voluntarily, becoming a functional aspect of the survivor's personal identity (Tillman, Nash & Lerner, 1994).

Dissociation is viewed as occurring along a continuum of severity ranging from habitual self-hypnosis and daydreaming to a more pathological state characterised by total amnesia between 'selves' or other personalities (Ross, 1998). Waller, Putnam and Carlson (1996) have shown that pathological features or symptoms of dissociation are indicative of extreme psychopathology and a taxon in itself (a discrete cluster of severe symptoms). In relation to the MSSM of CAT, dissociation is a prominent facet in the survivor's response to traumatic event(s).

Prolonged, intrusive and forceful abuse with a lack of validation or supporting alliances causes trauma-induced disruption to *metaprocedures* which results in deficits in the mobilisation and organisation of appropriate RRPs at level one. Discrete, separate self-states dominate the survivor's capacity to relate to oneself and others, affecting identity integrity and interpersonal domains of behaviour. Discontinuity and incoherence in the sense of self is evident and severe symptoms and reliance on dissociation are observed. Restricted self-reflection and disturbance of consciousness affect awareness of one's own mental states and behavioural patterns. Switches within and between more or less dissociated self-states further disrupt the survivor's ability to observe him/herself and to experience reality without distortions or errors of attribution for the abuse (e.g., self-blame). The case of Shelley in Chapter 8 provides an illustration of dramatic changes between and within self-states.

Within each self-state, each pole of the dominant RRP represents a 'state of mind' (or 'state of being') as termed by Horowitz (1979) with a dominant mood, perception of self and access to emotion and control of these emotions. To display and experience a state of mind as an 'abuser' drastically differs in essence from 'victim'. How being 'abusing' is expressed will differ qualitatively amongst perpetrators and the survivor's experience of this interpersonal act. They are polarised, contrasting, yet intimately related forms of action and existence also. Only one state of mind is accessible at one time. The affective states which we associate with each reciprocal role can vary, for example, being victimised can be accompanied by rage or guilt, attempts to tolerate and manage these emotions setting in motion sequences (*procedural loops*) which entail avoidant or symptomatic patterns.

A more severe structural fracture is noted also whereby the smooth connectedness between organised hierarchical layers of RRPs does not occur. Instead traumatic experiences disrupt the child's development of higher-order organising procedures (the *metaprocedures*) which promote the fluid deployment of RRPs during interaction with others. Deficits in this facet of the survivor's identity cause segregation of RRPs into a number of distinct, separated, self-states which predominate self–other and self–self transaction. Very often a degree of amnesia is evident between these self-states and switches between them are experienced as contradictory, sharp, abrupt and confusing. Golynkina and Ryle (1999) have shown that the degree of dissociation or amnesia between typically two or three main self-states can vary, most often reflecting self-states of *abusing–victimised*, *ideally caring–cared for*, highlighting how contrasting the nature of these states can be.

Level three: deficits in self-reflection and reality testing

At the third level of the MSSM, the capacity to reflect on oneself and self-observe (an RRP in itself) is impaired and fluctuations in mood, subjective experience and perception of oneself and other people are confusing and difficult to understand. Switches between self-states and shifts in responses to a reciprocal role can evoke feelings of confusion and a sense of incoherence in experience which impairs the survivor's capacity to reflect on the possible internal and external triggers to mood changes etc. Dissociation maintains this fragmentation.

Ryle's MSSM is conceptually akin to Lerner's model of the nature of disruption and disturbance in identity stability, consciousness and memory caused by trauma-induced dissociation (described by Tillman *et al.*, 1994). Lerner states that the content of identity is affected (MSSM level one), the structure is also fragmented (level two) and continuity of consciousness and memory compromised at a functional level (levels two and three). The continuum of dissociation extends along a spectrum of fragmentation where amnesia between separate self-states, discontinuity in experience, confusion and mood instability are more apparent as greater trauma is observed (Coons, Bowman & Milstein, 1988).

Practical implications of the MSSM

The direct implications of the MSSM are that the internalisation of the abusive experience is evident at level one of the MSSM, the *abusing–victimised* relational unit being an integral part of the survivor's personality continuing to affect him/her as it is sustained through triggers of the original events (e.g., men with certain physical appearances, sexual activity, specific smells or other stimuli) and enacted in self–other and self–self relationships. Very similarly to object relation models of psychopathology (Mollon, 1998), the internalisation of a malevolent representation of an abuser results in affective disturbances and defensive manoeuvres to manage or distort these representations. Unlike object relations, RRPs imply an active enactment of a total relational unit rather than static images of representations. In CAT terminology, the abusing pole of an RRP implies a goal-directed interpersonal action and the reciprocal role corresponds to the state of mind of 'being a victim' that the survivor was induced or forced into assuming.

Formulating a survivor's personality using this model permits an appreciation of the extent to which his/her personality integrity is compromised and affected. The generally asymptomatic survivor is unlikely to have encountered prolonged, frequent, invasive abuse accompanied by a dysfunctional family environment. The resulting repertoire is less restrictive with more flexibly deployed RRPs, less fragmentation into disparate self-states and a more insightful capacity to self-observe fluctuations in experience, moods and behaviours.

The degree of fragmentation into multiple self-states differs with greater numbers of states related to more severe trauma. A continuum of dissociation is also observed with severity of abuse, the most extreme example of the combination of multiplicity and dissociation (amnesia) being DID (DSM-IV, American Psychiatric Association, 1994). In most cases, little or partial amnesia is observed between two or more distinctly identifiable self-states with a degree of confusion, incoherence and dysfunction apparent when switches between states occur. BPD is proposed to be located along this spectrum of multiplicity and dissociation, of less severity than DID. Recent research by Pollock et al. (see Chapter 12) has supported the basis of the MSSM in terms of its thesis that BPD and DID exist along continua of multiplicity and dissociative processes. Estimating how severely compromised each survivor's identity appears on each level of the MSSM provides an indication of the impact of the abuse and how these problems reverberate throughout the survivor's adult life.

The MSSM further focuses target areas for clinical intervention. Addressing the internalisation of abuse-related RRPs is a prominent part of freeing the survivor from continuing reminiscences of the abuse itself and the sense that the abuser persists in invading his/her daily life and functioning. Helping the survivor to comprehend the nature of the abuse-related RRPs and verbalise the relationship created and 'defined' by the abuser can encapsulate a profoundly distressing legacy of experiences. Often the survivor will succinctly attribute a single descriptor to the perpetrator's behaviour such as 'hurting', 'perverting', 'hating' or 'destroying'. How these RRPs dictate the survivor's transactions with others and self-management can be examined. For example, a survivor who has been subjected to a sadistically punishing perpetrator will internalise the RRP *sadistically hating-in-relation-to-punished martyr* and may enact this procedure through spoiling a new, positive heterosexual relationship or causing grossly sexually masochistic injuries by self-cutting. The detection of the influence of these RRPs in general relationships and the therapeutic alliance is imperative for adequate containment and handling of the survivor (Dunn & Parry, 1997).

The joint construction of the SSSD helps the therapist and survivor to appreciate the fragmentation between separate self-states and track the movement and fluctuations between them. Environmental and interpersonal events which trigger switches can be detected and the location of symptomatic or avoidant procedures identified. Ameliorating fragmentation and dissociative processes and symptoms is an important goal at level two of the MSSM. The links along the sequences between self-state to procedural loop (with symptoms) to a differing self-state are traced and realistic exits and strategies for control instigated on the basis of the diagram. The fluidity between self-states can be promoted and amnesia or other dissociative symptoms addressed. The repetitive reference to and use of the SSSD can aid self-reflection and observation of how he/she pursues the same 'circuit' when moving from one state to another (level three). The MSSM contains aspects of structure and content of identity, both of which must be targeted during therapy for the survivor.

Clinical assessment of the MSSM

Two assessment tools are useful in applying the tenets of the MSSM to each case. The PSQ (Pollock *et al.*, 2001, Chapter 12), is a self-report measure containing eight items describing, at the pathological (right) end, experiences of instability, fragmentation, multiplicity, mood changeability and loss of behavioural control. The PSQ has been shown to be a psychometrically reliable measure which correlates positively with greater general psychopathology, dissociative symptoms, social problems, multiplicity and mood lability, and negatively with self-concept clarity and sense of coherence. Use of the PSQ can provide an idea as to what extent the survivor's personality is integrated or fragmented as described within the terms of the MSSM.

The States Grid (Ryle, 1997; Golynkina & Ryle, 1999; Appendix 1) is a form of repertory grid analysis which uses labelled self-states identified from therapy sessions as grid elements with a number of supplied constructs scored to provide a graphical analysis of the survivor's self-states and their psychological features. Changes in construct correlations and element distances can be used to estimate progress in therapy (Pollock, 1996). Golynkina and Ryle (1999) have identified six main recurring self-states in 20 BPD patients who reported histories of childhood abuse, including *abuser rage, victim rage, victim guilt, coping mode, zombie state* and *idealised*. These self-states occur in decreasing frequency as described in sequence. Identification of the survivor's self-states and their nature helps construct the SSSD, which is used as a clear account of the individual's difficulties. In combination with the Psychotherapy

File, the PSQ and States Grid can be employed to clarify the degree to which the MSSM applies to the survivor within the three levels.

Dissociation can be assessed using structured interviews and self-report measures. Steinberg (1993) produced the Structured Clinical Interview for DSM-IV Dissociative Disorders (SCID-D), which assesses the presence and extent of amnesia, depersonalisation, derealisation, identity confusion, alteration and other symptoms. The Dissociation Questionnaire (DIS-Q; Vanderlinden *et al.*, 1993) is a self-report measure that is useful for detecting the extent to which a survivor experiences identity fragmentation/confusion, amnesic episodes and other dissociative symptoms. The DIS-Q is reproduced in Appendix 1. A study by Pollock (1996) provided evidence from seven cases of adult females abused as children that CAT had a clinically significant effect on reducing dissociative experiences, including identity fragmentation and amnesia.

The CAT process and the basics of the MSSM are best illustrated by describing its application for an adult survivor of abuse who completed therapy. Each phase of CAT and its procedures, objective, methods and techniques are discussed throughout the case study.

Case illustration: Ann

Ann is a 21-year-old Caucasian woman with a long history of involvement with psychiatric services, referred to Clinical Psychology by her community psychiatric nurse. She had been admitted to hospital when 15 for multiple suicide attempts and self-harm and also to a rehabilitation clinic for alcohol dependency when 19. When initially assessed, Ann was compliant and honest in her disclosure, appearing depressed in mood. She was physically markedly thin and stated that her self-care had deteriorated over the past three months. Ann had not misused alcohol for a period of time, remaining abstinent for 10 months, an achievement she felt proud about and determined to maintain. She acknowledged experiencing intense urges to harm herself on occasions, 'gripping thoughts of suicide' and a fear that she would 'slip back to the bad old days when I didn't know who I was or what I was doing'. Her current relationship with her partner (an older businessman) was typically strained and antagonistic, yet Ann claimed to be supported greatly by long-standing friends in her community. She attended university, punctuated by episodes of absence due to 'depression and stress, not coping'. Ann presented as motivated, insightful and willing to commit herself to individual psychotherapy.

Her personal history included witnessing physical violence between her alcoholic parents, exposure to pornographic videos and her parents' friends having intercourse, and transient spells placed in statutory care. Ann's mother was described by her as verbally critical, humiliating and undermining and she claimed that she could hear her mother's voice berating her when experiencing stress. She felt that her confidence suffered and she expected failure as a result of her mother's influence. Her father was unpredictable, impulsive and physically abusive on a frequent basis. Ann stated that she would try to psychologically 'switch off my awareness' during the beatings as a means of coping. Her relationship with her sister was competitive and hostile. Both children were removed and returned to their parents' care on three separate occasions. At the age of 13, Ann was sexually abused by her paternal grandfather several times (indecent touching, oral sex). She began to misuse different substances (sniffing solvents, misusing alcohol in particular) after these events, and while intoxicated and sleeping at a friend's party Ann awoke to find that she was being raped by a male stranger. Her first suicide attempt and admission to psychiatric hospital followed. She was diagnosed as personality disordered with major depressive disorder and alcohol dependence. Her lifestyle was unsettled for subsequent years with chronic alcohol misuse and self-harm, with no positive response to professional help. Alcohol rehabilitation had been a catalyst for Ann to become motivated to helping herself when she was referred for psychotherapy.

Ann was open, while distressed about talking about the childhood adversity she had experienced. Structured interview using the CTI highlighted that she had experienced separations, witnessing untoward events, neglect and direct abuse. Self-report on the CTQ corroborated that Ann rated these experiences to have been extremely frequent and severe, lasting the majority of her formative and adolescent years, with later revictimisation (the rape). Personality testing (Millon Clinical Multiaxial Inventory—3) showed Ann to have a very negative self-perception, with features of depressive, self-defeating, passive–aggressive and paranoid dimensions. On a symptom level, Ann reported panic attacks, mood swings, vague physical complaints and post-traumatic stress symptoms (flashbacks to the abuse by her grandfather during sexual intercourse, derealisation and depersonalisation).

Ann completed the Psychotherapy File, which, when discussed with her, showed that she endorsed a dilemma regarding entering intimate relationships with others, a trap relating to alcohol abuse and a snag whereby positive events and success were forbidden due her feelings of inherent 'badness and being spoiled by the touch of others'. Ann reported frequent unstable states of mind. Her PSQ score was 33, indicating a high degree of identity disturbance, mood variability and a sense that she could experience herself as differing significantly on different occasions. Her scores on the DIS-Q indicated severe identity fragmentation/confusion and experiences of derealisation. On the Structured Clinical Interview for DSM-IV (SCID-I), Ann reported anorexic symptoms of self-starvation with significant weight loss, depressive episodes and substance dependence.

Ann was able to distinguish that she perceived herself, others, control of emotion and typical mood differently, yet a pattern tracing their variability could be described. She would often feel emotionally overwhelmed, depressed, inferior, needy and 'transparent, non-existent and alien' with others (her 'core state') who were construed as controlling, tyrannical, belittling and powerful. Ann recognised her mother's 'voice', which frequently commented on her behaviour and undermined her at these times. Her temptation to drink alcohol to 'block out the feelings' was strongest when her mother's 'voice' caused guilt that overwhelmed her. Ann considered these feelings to be unmanageable and debilitating. At times, Ann would recognise that she would act in a superior manner towards others, after which she experienced self-disgust and guilt. Ann's survival strategy had typically been to withdraw into a fantasy world where she imagined being surrounded by protective glass and untouchable, with no access to her painful feelings. Ann yearned for a blissful, loving relationship and her misuse of alcohol on a regular basis was a crude attempt to achieve this state, yet she was revictimised when intoxicated and her illusory fantasy was destroyed. Lastly, Ann identified that she felt 'like a child in a woman's body', needing social attention, and acting dramatically to coerce others to recognise her. When in this state, she felt seductive, but conflicted and uncomfortable about her sexuality and its meaning. Ann was convinced that this child-like part of herself should be blamed for the sexual abuse by her grandfather, claiming 'When I'm like that, I have the words "abuse me" written on my forehead. I get attention and sex mixed up'.

Ann therefore identified her states of mind in her own words to be 'Miss Disintegration' (depressed, needy, inferior, worthless), 'Miss Superior' (controlling, rejecting, powerful, critical/demanding), the 'Self-destroyer' (punishing, suicidal, self-harm), the 'Bubble' (blissful love, when imagining an illusory haven or relationship) and the 'Child actress' (seductive, provocative, responsible for the abuse). Ann perceived others to be 'Soul vampires', a personal reference to the perpetrator's mistreatment and cruelty towards her. The reciprocal role to the 'Soul vampire' was termed 'Miss Used' by Ann, which represents the internalised perpetrator–victim RRP. The 'Self-destroyer' represents Ann's identification with the 'Soul vampire' state, during which she felt a compulsive urge to harm herself as a form of punishment. 'Miss Disintegration' is the reciprocal state to 'Miss Superior' (derived from her parents' care of her) with severe personal dysfunction and negative feelings associated with it. Ann's idealised state (the 'Bubble') could not be sustained following the rape and she coped by misusing alcohol excessively and harming herself to control her feelings (the 'Self-destroyer'). Ann found acknowledgement of having been violated and abused difficult to accept because of the 'Child actress' whom she believed to be to blame for provoking the sexual abuse.

Countertransference responses to Ann's presentation consisted of a sense of impotence when she declared her 'compulsion' to harm herself (the 'Self-destroyer'). Her dramatic attention-seeking and blatant sexualisation of the therapeutic relationship was disarming (the 'Child actress'), her belligerence and rejection evoking feelings of devaluation and failure ('Miss Superior' in relation to 'Miss Disintegration'). Ann most typically expressed her anxieties that the therapist would be critical or contemptuous towards her (SS1). Alternatively, she anticipated the therapist would be unreliable and uncaring towards her ('Soul vampire' in relation to 'Miss Used'). Enactment of these states and their respective reciprocal roles formed the backbone of Ann's relational pathology. A dilemma was apparent in that her attempts to enter intimate relationships risked exploitation, betrayal and harm, yet avoiding relationships afforded a degree of safety but her emotional needs were unmet and she remained disillusioned and dissatisfied.

Ann completed two types of repertory grids: a standard role grid and States Grid (see Figure 3.2). The diagrammatic reformulation generated from the assessment is shown in Figure 3.3. This diagram became the platform for discussing the identification of target problems (TPs) and underlying target problem procedures (TPPs). TPPs were listed and prioritised by Ann and the therapist together. She was encouraged to maintain a self-monitoring diary of her thoughts, feelings and ways of relating to promote recognition of agreed TPPs. Ann rated the extent to which recognition improved as therapy progressed on the Target Problems Ratings Sheet.

Ann's SSSD identifies central self-states which form the structure of her personality and the dominant reciprocal role repertoire which underlies the states of mind she experiences. Her personality is affected at all three levels of the MSSM of trauma, with her sense of herself and others coloured by traumatic events during her development, instability in identity and recurrent moods, and deficits in self-observation and self-reflection. The relational unit between 'Soul vampire' and 'Miss Used' reflects the internalisation of a generic, scripted imprint of the perpetrator–victim reciprocal role. Her strategies for survival and coping, with their accompanying symptoms and dysfunction, are evident and can be clarified and tracked by both therapist and client, avoiding collusion and promoting corrective experiences and collaborative change.

Ann's Reformulation Letter was well received by her and she discussed it thoughtfully, adding further representative incidents and events that supported the patterns suggested.

Dear Ann,

The choice you made to enter therapy was, in your words, your 'last possible hope'. I recognise that you have invested faithfully in the work we have undertaken to date and that you have been determined not to give up on achieving a better life for yourself, despite your feelings that professionals have failed you many times in many ways. I have listened to your memories of your parents' 'crazy acts' and your feelings of

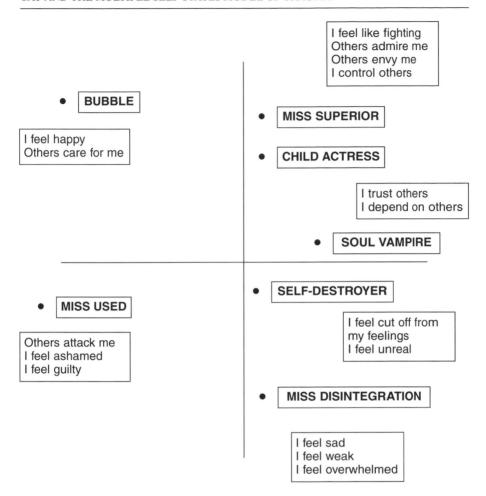

Figure 3.2   Ann's States Grid

guilt, bewilderment and longing that they would be different. You question whether they cared for you at all and whether their claims that you deserve the harm you experienced were true. Your grandfather's assault and the unfortunate incident when intoxicated have reinforced your belief that you have 'abuse me' written on your forehead. Your partner is inconsiderate, verbally abusing, 'plays mind-games' and his derogatory sexual comments upset you on a daily basis. Yet, you wonder whether any other type of relationship exists and recognise yourself to be too emotionally needy and reliant upon his presence, if not just for a sense of security.

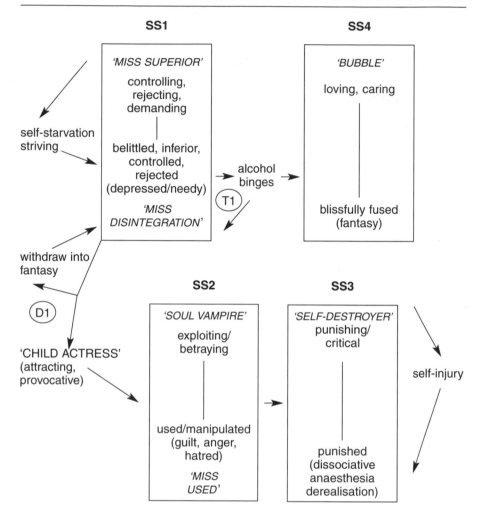

Figure 3.3   Ann's Self-States Sequential Diagram

The history you reported within and outside your family was coloured with adversity, cruelty, neglect and abuse, causing you to feel exploited, belittled, rejected and criticised. Feelings of sadness, anxiety, inferiority and confusion were common for you. You learnt to cope in differing ways, sometimes drinking alcohol 'to oblivion' or to achieve a sense of comfort and emotional warmth. At other times, you have pushed yourself to exhaustion to achieve in school and college. Starving yourself of food has maintained an illusory sense of control over events in the world and managed the confusion you have felt.

You stated that relationships have always felt 'one-sided' and you blame the 'Child actress' when others exploit or betray you. Guilt and anger lead to self-hatred (your mother's 'voice' calling you names) and a wish to punish yourself by cutting your body within which you feel trapped. Although this works in the short term and 'makes sense', you realise that this cannot continue. Being with others sometimes feels worthwhile, but this is a transient and fleeting moment which disappears quickly. Acting in a morally righteous manner, acting belittling and contemptuous towards others has destroyed several friendships and you also wish to change this pattern.

Problems that we could work towards addressing are as follows:

Target problem 1: drinking alcohol
Feeling inferior, depressed and overwhelmed, you binge on alcohol to 'block out the thoughts', which only works temporarily. Differently, you drink to achieve an illusory sense of 'bliss' that also does not last. Aim: to deal with the source of the emotions that produce alcohol misuse and to learn to cope differently.

Target problem 2: feeling uncomfortable with others
When emotionally close to others, you feel they become critical, rejecting, controlling and demanding, causing you to respond by striving to exhaustion (e.g., college work, thinness) or you control your intake of food excessively and reject your body for being 'female'. Aim: to gain control over your own life and behaviour, to achieve a balanced, self-nurturing food intake.

Target problem 3: attracting abuse
Either you feel that your need for affection and attention leads to exploitation and betrayal, causing anger, guilt and self-rebuke, or you avoid contact with others, which ensures safety but causes greater emotional neediness. Aim: re-evaluate your contribution to the instigation of the abuse.

Target problem 4: self-injury
Self-disgust and feelings of entrapment in your body result in a compulsion to punish yourself. Aim: to improve your sense of self-worth and learn to care for yourself rationally.

Target problem 5: failing to make progress
Feeling that you do not deserve to improve your life, you sabotage and devalue any achievements, ensuring further episodes of hopelessness and depression. Aim: to address the internal tendency to sabotage success that is forbidden.

Target problem 6: alone in a fantasy world or risking abuse
Either you become socially isolated and live in a fantasy world where

you are safe but emotionally needy, or you risk exploitation by entering a relationship with someone. Aim: to learn to choose a caring partner and stay involved, without subjugating yourself or withdrawing.

Target problem 7: feeling exploited and misused by men
Your expectation that men will inevitably manipulate, exploit and abuse you leads to self-blame, guilt and rage towards yourself, placing responsibility onto the 'child actress' for attracting unsavoury men. Aim: to address the continuing influence of the perpetrators upon your life.

Recognition and revision of TPs

The first sessions of active treatment for Ann included her completion of a self-monitoring diary of her thoughts, moods and interactions with others and identification of situations in which problems were experienced. The Target Problem Rating scales showed that her ability to comprehend her changeable states of mind and moods was initially poor. She was encouraged to continue to trace these patterns throughout therapy. Ann's completion of Imagery Rescripting and Reprocessing (IRR; Smucker & Dancu, 1999) addressed the RRP and associated state of mind described in SS2 ('Miss Used'). During this procedure, the emotions of guilt, shame and anger were expressed and Ann was able to review her belief that the 'Child actress' had acted seductively by attracting attention. She was able to re-evaluate the behaviour of the perpetrators and the extent of her own responsibility. Ann reported a surge of rage when she realised that she had been victimised repeatedly and her self-hatred reduced significantly along with her desire to punish herself. The enactment of the RRP within SS3 (the 'Self-destroyer') was less compulsive and incidents of self-injury decreased.

Ann's dilemma regarding contact with others (D1) was addressed by encouraging her to consider her behaviour within her current heterosexual relationship and to change the images she held of herself as deserving of abuse, subjugation and perceiving others as typically manipulative. Her partner's attitude to her changed for the worse, becoming more controlling and critical of her. Ann felt able to remain resolute in the face of her partner's behaviour without withdrawing into a fantasy world of seclusion. Her subjective feelings of inferiority and depression ameliorated and she reported feeling more capable of attaining her emotional needs by self-nurturance and friendships. The identified trap (T1) was more difficult to change but Ann could recognise the situations during which she experienced feelings of being controlled, rejected and belittled. Ann stopped her alcohol binges and remained abstinent, terming her new state as a 'dry drunk'.

Ann made a concerted effort to alter her tendency to starve herself that was an enactment of the controlling aspect of the RRP of SS1. At times when Ann could 'hear' her mother's voice berating her she persisted to struggle against the urge to engage in frenetic activity (e.g., exercise, studying) and she felt more able to appreciate that she should strive in her own interests and not succumb to the demands of her mother. The rejecting aspect of the same RRP of SS1 was manifest in Ann's disgust about her body and its female shape ('a child trapped in a woman's body'). This issue was targeted with Ann and she came to accept these parts of herself. Her tendency to procrastinate at times and to depreciate any treatment gains (a 'therapeutic snag') was referred to on a frequent basis to avoid sabotage of success, and improvement was observed on this problem.

Ann's Goodbye Letter

Towards the last three sessions of therapy, Ann was presented with the Good-bye Letter. It was particularly important to acknowledge the work completed already and to help her to concentrate on the issue of termination.

Dear Ann,
We are approaching the end of the sessions we agreed and it is impor-
tant to think about the progress made to date and what still needs to be
kept in mind and continued. You undertook some difficult work in the
early stages of therapy, concentrating on your upsetting memories of
the neglect and abuse caused by your parents and later the assaults by
your grandfather and a stranger. These incidents made you perceive
yourself as belittled, inferior and misused and you felt spoilt, guilty,
shameful and depressed because of these events. You felt urges to pun-
ish yourself by cutting your body and you coped in a haze of alcohol.
Being in a relationship was problematic and you felt 'between a rock
and a hard place' in that you risked abuse when with a partner or you
withdrew into a fantasy world, feeling emotionally needy. You har-
boured a desire to be blissfully involved in a partnership in which you
would be cared for and loved. This fantasy was easily destroyed and felt
unattainable. The problems we agreed to target have improved in terms
of your ability to recognise when and why they occur and you have
broken the unhelpful patterns, which caused you distress. In particular,
you have stopped drinking alcohol, describing yourself as a 'dry drunk'
now. Temptation to drink still occurs but you cope now by working
towards your career examinations without causing yourself to become
exhausted and appreciating that you are pursuing a goal for yourself,
an achievement you feel you deserve and is not forced by your mother's
demands and criticisms. You are appropriately angry that you have
been 'taught' to punish yourself because you blamed the 'Child actress'

for provoking the abuse. We discussed this issue extensively and you were able to express the rage you felt towards the perpetrators without placing responsibility wrongly upon the 'Child actress'. You have directed and channelled your feelings of rage into becoming determined to 'survive and thrive'.

You argued yourself that self-harm did not make sense if you want to assume the role of a survivor, despite the fleeting urges to self-harm which still persist, but you manage well. You have ended the unfortunate relationship with your partner based on your realisation that being within a partnership does not have to feature distrust, manipulation or degradation. This is an important step for you.

I have acknowledged with you that ending therapy has made you feel anxious and you worry about coping 'alone'. It is important that we address these fears and discuss any 'holes in the road' which may be ahead and prepare for them.

Follow-up

Ann was seen at three two-month intervals and at one year post therapy for review of her progress. She continued to progress well, with only two incidents of self-injury which followed the death of her grandfather (one of the perpetrators of abuse against her) and an argument with her mother. Ann was able to incorporate these lapses into her understanding of her difficulties and, at one year post therapy, she considered herself to be symptom free and generally problem free. Her scores on the PSQ and DIS-Q were below the clinical range and she sustained a stable, mutually satisfying relationship with her partner and had recently discovered that she was pregnant, Ann stating her delight at the prospect of motherhood.

Conclusion

Ann's case illustrates the presentation of a survivor of childhood abuse that can be located along the MSSM continuum of severity (see Figure 3.1) where partial dissociation, fragmented identity and significant psychological symptoms are observable. Disturbance is evident at level one in that Ann's repertoire of RRPs is coloured by negative roles and states of mind with internalisation of the abuse-generated RRP also (SS2). Discrete self-states are identifiable within her history and recurring patterns of relating to herself and others and she experienced changeable, unstable moods and self-perceptions (level two). Dissociative processes were associated with episodes of self-injury in the form of derealisation and anaesthesia. Ann found it difficult to track the shifts in her moods, behavioural responses and sense of herself across time and within relationships to others (level three). Formal psychological testing showed that Ann reported elevated PSQ and DIS-Q scores, anorexic and depressive symptoms and alcohol dependence. She was diagnosed as a mixed personality disorder with significant borderline features. CAT achieved an improved integration for Ann's identity functioning and enhanced her capacity to recognise and revise the target problems agreed with her. Ann's reliance upon self-injury and associated dissociation decreased and she began to address her dependency on alcohol through an understanding of the relationship between her states of mind, emotional disturbances and habitual coping strategies. Ann's relationship with her partner was ended by her, Ann stating 'I always knew it was harmful and unhealthy, but I felt blinkered and wanted to believe it was different than it really was'. Ann claimed she could think more clearly and effectively about her own thinking, feeling, relating and choices. She felt that she was entitled to happiness and good fortune without guilt and anxiety.

CHAPTER 4

Psychological models and therapies for traumatic experiences

CAT is a relatively new therapeutic model and what follows is a comparison of CAT to other psychological models generally and to those conceptualising and treating traumatic experiences in childhood specifically. A plethora of theoretical and practical models have been described to conceptualise traumatic experiences ranging from various cognitive-behavioural models (social-cognitive, information-processing and more traditional Beckian models) to neurobiological approaches, Ericksonian Solution-Focused hypnosis (Bell-Gadsby, 1996) and Eye Movement Desensitisation and Reprocessing (EMDR; Shapiro, 1989; Parnell, 1999). Each of these theoretical models has a unique way of understanding what exactly trauma does to a survivor, the typical impact observed and how to practically address the sequelae of childhood trauma. They all have merits and beneficial outcomes are reported for their clinical application. They also demonstrate strengths and weaknesses and CAT is similar in this respect. The present chapter aims to briefly report a selection of models and to consider the commonalities to and differences from the CAT model described in Chapter 3.

McFarlane (1988, 1996) insightfully proposed that adult survivors of trauma are victimised by having memories of the event, not by the event itself. Implicitly or explicitly, a survivor's memories are the representations, which form the substrate for psychological therapies. Addressing the direct or indirect impact of the traumatic memories, their effect upon the survivor's sense of self and the world and the meaning attributed to them is a vital aspect of enabling positive change. Most models conceptualise how the traumatic events or information continue to cause dysfunction through some form of memory substrate and theories tend to differ in the concepts used to describe how the event, long since past, still persists in the survivor's mental, emotional, biological and behavioural domains of life.

The level of inference targeted in each therapeutic modality differs uniquely and the choice of theoretical model to explain and conceptualise the traumatic aspects of the survivor's experience varies greatly. Van der Kolk (1988) stated that a spectrum of responses to trauma exists for humans ranging from distinct neurobiological changes, emotional dysfunction and disruption to attachment and interpersonal behaviour. For example, van der Kolk suggests 'the body keeps the score', emphasising the psychobiological alterations caused by trauma and also that 'emotional memory may be forever', highlighting the affective sequelae.

A diversity of models conceptualising the impact of childhood abuse and trauma has been forwarded and a selection of models is reviewed in this chapter considering their relative strengths and deficits. The value of these explanatory models is difficult to judge rationally and often the individual survivor's profile at presentation will affect which model a clinician considers most applicable. They do not have to be viewed as mutually exclusive either: the same symptoms, for example intrusive, distressing images or flashbacks, can be treated using medication, imagery-based cognitive techniques (e.g., Imagery Rescripting and Reprocessing), power therapy approaches (e.g., EMDR) or behavioural methods (e.g., Direct Exposure Therapy). It is vital that a coherent framework or model of the survivor's childhood experiences—how problems are manifested and persist and which mechanisms require addressing—is derived, no matter which technique is applied. The therapist's experience, competence and discretion will also influence the choice of treatment approach delivered.

The breadth and variety of treatments to address differing types of trauma are significant. Clinical interest in PTSD has grown extensively in the field of trauma studies and treatment. Several models focus on this diagnosis exclusively, in deference to other facets of the survivor's response and his/her attempts to more or less successfully tolerate and manage resulting difficulties (i.e., revictimisation, social behaviour and identity disturbances). The comparative similarities and differences of CAT for adult survivors of childhood trauma will be considered following a review of the model.

Post-traumatic stress disorder and childhood abuse

PTSD is defined within the DSM-IV classification system as a pattern of symptoms which often follows the human experience of trauma when (1) the person has experienced, witnessed or was confronted with an event(s) that involved actual or threatened death or serious injury, or a threat to the physical integrity of self or others; (2) the person's response involved intense fear, helplessness or horror. Symptoms which are observed include persistent re-experiencing of the event(s) in the form of distressing recollections (images, thoughts), dreaming, and acting as if the event(s) is actually recurring (flashbacks) and intense physiological responses and reactivity to cues which symbolise or resemble the traumatic events(s). Persistent avoidance of stimuli associated with the traumatic event(s) occurs and persistent symptoms of arousal also (i.e., difficulty falling or staying asleep, hypervigilance, exaggerated startle response). It has been debated whether PTSD is entirely relevant to conceptualising the long-term effects of childhood abuse.

Finkelhor (1987) has disputed whether the behaviour of the majority of perpetrators induce this type of experience, being more subtle, prolonged and 'may be less an event than a relationship or a situation' (p. 353). Betrayal, entrapment and violation are more fundamental in the context of childhood abuse than overwhelming danger, which is more akin to stranger rape or natural disasters. He argues that the PTSD model does not adequately account for the presentation of most survivors, with Kilpatrick *et al.* (1986) demonstrating that of 126 sexually abused adult females only 10% were currently found to report PTSD symptoms, with 35% claiming these symptoms were ever present. Finkelhor disagrees with the proposal that survivors of sexual abuse specifically are destined to experience PTSD as suggested by Frederick (1986) and Goodwin (1985).

Despite Finkelhor's (1990) view that the PTSD model does not account for *all* of the symptomatology and personality disturbances observed in the presentations of abuse survivors, recent research findings do point to a high prevalence of PTSD symptoms, particularly for survivors of childhood sexual abuse, which parallels the findings for those who have experienced sexual assault. Albach and Everaerd (1992) reported that 63% of 97 incest survivors were diagnosed to meet criteria for PTSD with increased symptomatology being related to reactions of freezing, dissociation and anxiety. Rowan, Foy, Rodriguez and Ryan (1994) showed that 69% of 47 survivors of childhood sexual abuse met criteria for PTSD, with symptomatology related to greater overall exposure to abuse, duration and frequency of these experiences, age of onset and the use of physical force. Similarly, Wolfe, Sas and Wekerle (1994) noted that the difference between a PTSD-positive (44 survivors) and PTSD-negative (46 survivors) diagnosis was accounted for by the nature and severity of the sexual abuse, and guilt for children (average age of 12 years). Wolfe *et al.* conclude that 'as noted by Finkelhor (1990), a PTSD conceptualisation of sexual abuse does not easily accommodate other known effects (e.g., sexualisation), and may be more suited to explaining the effects of acts of violence than to child sexual victimisation ... clearly, the notion of PTSD does not apply to all forms of sexual abuse or all abusive experiences' (p. 47).

It would be negligent not to inquire about PTSD symptoms when an adult survivor is assessed given the findings regarding the presence of PTSD symptoms evident from empirical research. A child's initial responses to abusive experiences, which are uncontrollable, unpredictable and conditioned to triggering stimuli (e.g., persons, places, smells, sounds), may present as acute trauma symptoms such as agitation, anxiety and sexualised behaviours. If the abuse becomes chronic, inescapable and intensive, PTSD symptoms may continue and intensify unabated, including flashbacks, nightmares, intrusive memories and avoidance behaviours (McLeer *et al.*, 1988).

Considering that survivors do report distressing re-experiencing, intruding and avoidance symptoms, psychotherapeutic techniques founded within good theoretical foundations that ameliorate these difficulties are worthy of consideration. Several of the models referred to below conceptualise trauma within the PTSD framework and their applicability to childhood abuse requires further debate.

Neurobiological models and pharmacological therapy

Numerous experimental studies have shown that the human response to trauma is complex and qualitatively different at a neurobiological level from the normal stress reaction (van der Kolk, 1988). Psychophysiological effects of trauma include extreme autonomic responses to reminders of the trauma and hyperarousal, neurohormonal effects (affecting noradrenaline, glucocorticoids, serotonin and endogenous opioids levels), neuroanatomical affects (hippocampal, amygdala, sensory areas, Broca's area, right hemispheric lateralisation, locus coeruleus functioning) and immunological changes (Friedman, 1991; Meichenbaum, 1994; van der Kolk, 1994). These changes indicate that the trauma sufferer is in a state of fight or flight, chronically aroused continuously in response to sights, sounds and thoughts related to the trauma, with a perpetual expectation that the trauma will recur. Internal homeostasis is imbalanced and symptomatic distress results from the survivor's reliance upon high levels of unmanageable arousal, conditioned alarm responses to reminders of the trauma, and disturbances to memory regulation, perception and information processing. The survivor's body is psychologically and physiologically geared to be 'enduringly vigilant for and hyper-reactive to environmental threat' and in 'survival mode' (van der Kolk, 1994, p. 217).

Different medications appear to affect specific clusters of PTSD symptoms, with antidepressant medication the first intervention of choice suggested by Davidson *et al.* (1993). Davidson and van der Kolk (1994) propose that psychopharmacological treatment for PTSD aims to reduce the frequency and severity of intrusive symptoms, the tendency to interpret incoming stimuli as recurrences of trauma, decreasing conditioned hyperarousal, avoidance behaviour, improving depressed mood and emotional numbing and reduction of dissociation and impulsive aggression. Monoamine oxidase (MAO) inhibitors (phenelzine, brofaramine), tricyclic antidepressants (imipramine), selective serotonin reuptake inhibitors (fluoxetine), anticonvulsants (carbemazepine), beta-adrenergic blockers (propronolol) and anxiolytic drugs (benzodiazepines) have been used in studies showing that psychopharmacological treatments for PTSD symptoms are 'at best palliative' (Solomon & Shalev, 1994) and unlikely to be of value as a long-term treatment option. Davidson and Baum (1994) proposed that prescribing medications includes more non-specific factors such as the size, dosage and even colour of the medication, with importance ascribed to the meaning of the medication, and the quality of the professional–patient relationship being critical to judgements about the effectiveness of the medication. Meichenbaum (1994) further advises that psychopharmacological interventions for trauma symptoms are promising, but only one weapon against PTSD given the lack of depth in evaluative research studies to date.

Cognitive models of trauma and PTSD

Advances have been notable in theoretical formulations of PTSD and trauma generally within cognitive psychology frameworks over a number of years. Follette, Ruzek and Abueg (1999) concluded that a large amount of empirical support exists for positive outcomes when cognitive-behavioural treatment packages are used for different types of trauma, including cases of childhood sexual abuse. Cognitive models can be defined within two main camps: (1) the *social-cognitive theories*, which focus upon the corruption of schematic belief systems by the trauma; and (2) *information-processing theories*, which propose that accommodation of the traumatic information itself is vital for successful adaptation to occur. These models conceptualise PTSD symptoms in the main and there exist a number of cognitive-behavioural models of sexual abuse specifically. Descriptions and critiques of these models follow here. The validity of these psychological paradigms is significant.

Social-cognitive models include those of Horowitz (1986) and Janoff-Bulman's cognitive appraisal theory (1989, 1992). Foa's theory (Foa *et al.*, 1992), Brewin's dual representation theory (1988), Brewin, Dalgleish and Joseph (1996), Hartmann and Burgess (1993) and Power and Dalgleish's (1997) SPAARs model represent information-processing models of PTSD. Implications for treatment are clearly made within each of these theories to address PTSD symptoms. It may be argued that the strength of these models is their ability to explain experimental and clinical data on PTSD and particularly single episode Type I trauma (Terr, 1991).

Generally, cognitive models of PTSD propose that the traumatic event(s) involve a violation of basic assumptions connected to survival, including beliefs about personal invulnerability, status within the social group, the ability to meet internal moral standards and relationship between action and outcome. Events which can be considered traumatic tend to be characterised as unpredictable, uncontrollable and those for which the individual is culpable or to blame (Meichenbaum, 1994). The individual's pre-existing schematic beliefs about self, others and events in the world are corrupted by the meaning of the event and are incompatible with this prior set of assumptions. The symptoms of PTSD are conceptualised to represent attempts to integrate the meaning of the event and its impact on the individual's belief system. Successful integration of the meaning of the event occurs when changes are made within the belief system (becoming 'sadder and wiser'). Incomplete or unsuccessful resolution is evident when this process of incorporation is not achieved. Brewin *et al.* (1996) describe *emotional processing* of trauma, borrowed partially from Rachman (1980), to depict three endpoints of processing including completion/integration (no symptoms, attentional or memory biases), chronic emotional processing (depression, phobic or generalised anxiety, continuing memory and attentional biases) and premature inhibition of processing (attention biases, impaired memory, avoidance schema, dissociative and phobic states).

Horowitz (1986) described certain reactions and phases of processing whereby traumatic information is propelled by the psychological need for new information to be integrated within existing cognitive schemata or models of self, other and the world, referred to as a 'completion tendency'. Initially, the individual may be stunned, experiencing an overload of thoughts, memories and images of the trauma that cannot be assimilated. Certain defence mechanisms are employed to ward off these forms of information and the individual becomes numb and denies the reality of the event. Oscillation is observed between the completion tendency and propulsion of the traumatic information into consciousness. Defensive manoeuvres attempt to exclude this information, resulting in phases of *intrusion* (e.g., flashbacks, nightmares) and *denial-numbing*, with integration within existing or modified cognitive schemata. Chronicity of PTSD indicates inadequate processing. Horowitz's model has been criticised because of its inability to explain why some individuals do not develop PTSD symptoms, the nature of the existing schemata, how processing fails and why delayed onset of PTSD occurs (see Power & Dalgleish, 1996, for a comprehensive critique). Although Horowitz's model has face validity and apparent explanatory power, these limitations are notable.

Janoff-Bulman's (1989, 1992) cognitive appraisal theory focuses on the importance of pre-morbid assumptions an individual holds about the world, in particular beliefs that one is personally invulnerable from trauma or harm, the world is a meaningful and comprehensible place and oneself is positive and deserving of good fortune. This set of assumptions provides meaning, structure and sense of the person's experiences and events, becoming 'shattered' by trauma due to their violent disruption. Symptoms of PTSD follow the impact of the trauma. Janoff-Bulman's model does not (similarly to Horowitz's model) detail the nature of the cognitive structures involved or why patients with psychiatric conditions pre-morbidly are more likely to develop PTSD than those who have not. Accommodation of traumatic information, adaptation of one's sense of the world being meaningful and oneself as deserving of positive life experiences, requires alteration to autobiographical memory (e.g., resolving the knowledge that one's father who should be caring, nurturing and protecting has been abusive and betraying) represents an important task for the survivor. Social-cognitive models provide ways of thinking about this aspect of trauma resolution.

An information-processing model by Foa (Foa & Kozak, 1986; Foa & Riggs, 1993) has proposed a fear network theory of trauma based on Lang's (1985) concept of fear structures. This model suggests that traumatic information is held in a memory network that comprises stimulus information about the events, reactions to the trauma and interoceptive information (e.g., bodily sensations) which links stimulus and response elements. Reminders of trauma activate this fear network, information enters the awareness of the survivor and intrusive symptoms are experienced. Avoidance symptoms of PTSD are perceived to be a reflection of the survivor's attempts to suppress or exclude traumatic information. Resolution of the trauma can only be achieved by activating the network (through Direct Exposure Therapy), allowing its modification and the assimilation of incompatible and corrective information into the memory network. Severity of the trauma may lead to a fragmented or disjointed fear network and greater difficulty integrating new information. The unpredictability and uncontrollability of the traumatising event also affect the course of integration. Foa et al.'s model has been criticised because of its reliance on a single level of representation which cannot sufficiently explain how traumatic information is structured and why poor networks develop for some and not others. Rothbaum and Foa (1996) describe the application of prolonged exposure and systematic desensitisation for rape survivors with beneficial results.

The dual representation theory (Brewin et al., 1996) is an attempt to counter the problems with single-level representation models such as Foa's. Brewin describes two levels in memory where traumatic information is represented. The first level, referred to as verbally accessible memories (VAMs), are memories that are amenable to conscious retrieval and can be progressively edited by the survivor. VAMs include sensory responses and meanings assigned to the trauma. The second level, situationally accessible memories (SAMs), are only accessible when the original traumatic cues are present. Both forms of representation are avoided in parallel during the trauma and can account well for PTSD symptoms. SAMs result in flashbacks, dreams and situational arousal, whereas VAMs account for intrusive memories, emotional responses and selective recall of the event. For successful adaptation, the survivor is required to integrate information in VAMs into pre-existing belief systems, adjusting expectations of the self and the world, and the emotional reactions associated with this incompatibility. Direct Exposure Therapy techniques activate SAMs and the experience of fresh, non-threatening information facilitates integration by creating newly formed SAMs. Both routes are important for emotional processing to be achieved. When this is not always possible chronic processing or premature inhibition of processing can occur. Brewin *et al.*'s model provides a comprehensive dualistic model of information processing but Power and Dalgleish (1997) have expressed concerns that certain limitations still exist (e.g., what the role of VAMs and SAMs in memory are generally, how information is actually accommodated into pre-existing VAM representations).

Power and Dalgleish formulated a model of emotion termed the Schematic, Propositional, Associative and Analogical Representation Systems model (SPAARS), which assumes that several different representational systems are involved in the generation of emotional disorders. Traumatic information is processed by *analogical* systems (visual, auditory, olfactory etc.) and the output from this system is fed to one or all of three secondary systems, termed *associative*, *propositional* and *schematic*. Emotional responses can be generated automatically and swiftly from analogical to associative systems (e.g., spontaneous sadness), which can then be inhibited consciously. An appraisal route also exists when information is transferred from analogical to schematic model systems and this route is generated more slowly and is prone to conscious and, to an extent, unconscious interpretation. When trauma is experienced, the schematic system appraises the event as having threat-related meaning and it is encoded at all other systems of the SPAARS. At an analogical level, sights, smells and sounds are processed. The propositional system encodes trauma facts and interpretations of the event and the schematic system detects trauma-related information that is incompatible with higher cognitive goals such as personal survival and maintaining the existing configuration of schematic beliefs. The traumatic event is, therefore, stored at all levels and unintegrated with pre-existing schematic models. Intrusive symptoms occur due to the continual appraisal of the incompatibility of the traumatic-information through activation and reactivation of the 'fear module' into consciousness. Avoidance and hyperarousal emerge from activation of this fear module also. Intervention to promote emotional processing must account for slow and fast change (automatic and controlled processing, reminiscent of 'emotional' and 'intellectual' change; Power & Dalgleish, 1997) achieved via both exposure-based and cognitive restructuring interventions.

The model of Hartmann and Burgess (1993) describes an information-processing approach that occurs in four phases: *pre-trauma, trauma encapsulation, disclosure* and *post-trauma* outcome phases. The second phase, trauma encapsulation, suggests that the event causes an alarm response (arousal, fight/flight, dissociation) followed by the storing of traumatic information ('trauma learning') at sensory, perceptual, cognitive and interpersonal levels, with re-enactment, repetition and displacement ('trauma replay') occurring and affecting the survivor's constructions of his/her survival, mastery and control over oneself and the world. Differing outcomes are described for the post-trauma outcome phase termed integrated, anxious-avoidant, disorganised and aggressive-delinquent behavioural outcomes. The authors state that interventions should aim to provide safety, strengthen the survivor's resources, resurface and process the trauma through unlinking sensory, perceptual and cognitive information, transferring the traumatic memory to the past and accommodating it into autobiographical memory. This model directly considers sexual abuse in childhood from an information-processing perspective and accounts for the relevance of the other factors such as social support when disclosure occurs.

A recent cognitive-behavioural model by Ehlers and Clark (2000) is worthy of mention because it addresses why PTSD symptoms persist. The survivor's appraisal of current threat is a focal aspect of the model arising due to negative appraisals of the trauma and its sequelae and disturbances to autobiographical memory. Therapeutic change is achieved by altering the nature of the memories of the trauma (increasing elaboration, contextualisation into autobiographical memory, weakening stimulus–stimulus and stimulus–response associations and perceptual priming) and by addressing appraisals (e.g., the fact of the trauma means 'the world is a dangerous place', re-experiencing symptoms are appraised as indicating loss of control, and 'madness', difficulty concentrating attributed to brain damage). Coping strategies (i.e., safety behaviours, thought suppression) and cognitive processing styles (i.e., selective attention to threat, pretending the trauma did not occur at all) are deemed to directly produce PTSD symptoms, preventing positive changes to negative appraisals of the trauma and the nature of the memories. This model is simple, explains the persistence of PTSD problems, and argues for specific therapy targets (elaboration of memory by reliving with cognitive restructuring) to alter appraisals and coping that exacerbate a sense of current threat.

Cognitive therapies specific to abuse-related trauma encompass elements of both information-processing and social-cognitive schema-based approaches. Cognitive Processing Therapy (CPT; Resick & Schmicke, 1992) differs from traditional Beckian Cognitive Therapy (Beck, 1967) and has been applied for women reporting PTSD symptoms who had experienced a single incident of rape (without competing pathology or incestuous histories). CPT is a variant of Direct Exposure Therapy based on information-processing models which goes beyond simple prolonged exposure techniques by helping the survivor to examine beliefs and meanings (safety, trust, power, esteem and intimacy) attributed to the event. Written assignments are undertaken to identify and modify 'stuck' points. CPT claims that PTSD symptoms emerge from conflicts or 'stuck points' between prior schemata and the traumatic information (the sexual assault itself). Identifying and modifying these conflicts is a specific target for cognitive restructuring. An exposure element of CPT aims to encourage the expression of affect through writing about and reading the scenario of the assault, training the survivor to identify and change thoughts and feelings related to the abuse, focusing on the five areas of safety, trust, power, esteem and intimacy (and a sixth termed 'frame of reference' referring to loss of causality, locus of control etc.). For example, conflict may be observed when the survivor cannot accommodate beliefs about danger and safety, trust and betrayal. These five areas are borrowed from the work of McCann, Sakheim and Abrahamson (1988), who proposed that each of these areas had two *loci*; schemata relating to the self and to others (resulting in 10 areas of functioning). Symptoms occur if prior positive schemata are disrupted or if negative schemata are reinforced by victimisation. McCann *et al.*'s model has not been empirically investigated but evaluative data from Resick and Schmicke's study indicated that 'many of the women reported substantial improvements in the quality of their lives' (p. 753) and treatment gains were persistent. Promising outcome data has been reported for a similar model for rape survivors (Foa, Steketee & Rothbaum, 1992) which consists of imaginal, *in vivo* exposure, covert modelling, role-play exercises, cognitive restructuring and thought-stopping techniques.

Imagery and experiential methods in CBT

Arntz and Weertman (1999) reviewed the forms of experiential methods used in CBT and the components that they consisted of. Two methods are most prominent: *imagery techniques with rescripting* and *historical role-play*. The former use guided imagery in three phases, where the original parent–child scene of abuse or trauma is experienced as if it is actually occurring (an exposure element); the second phase includes a rescription during which the scene is viewed by the patient as an adult who confronts the perpetrator and experiences the scene from a different perspective; and, in the final phase, a further rescription consists of the patient imagining the whole situation again from the child's point of view. During the second phase, the adult self is encouraged to comfort, secure safety for and soothe the abused child self. In phase three, the child, once rescued and safe, is asked by the therapist how it feels to be nurtured and cared for. Empowerment is facilitated and fundamental schema change is achieved.

Historical role-plays comprise the generation of a memory of an interaction between parent/perpetrator and child, a replay of the interaction as a role-play exercise (the patient enacts the child role), the therapist playing the reciprocal part. Reversal of roles is also undertaken and the patient is encouraged to try new behaviours in the interaction. The patient's cognitive and especially emotional responses are explored, defined and debated to provide a fresh way of thinking and feeling about the original scene.

Imagery techniques must be used with caution. It is unreasonable to ask a survivor if, for example, chronic physical abuse by a parent has occurred, to contemplate that parent being protecting, nurturing and loving. The rescripting element of certain imagery procedures does not always go as planned and can appear to take on a life of its own when a patient is sincerely involved in the task. For example, some patients with severe psychopathology may find it uncomfortable or impossible to comfort and soothe the child self after rescue from the perpetrator during rescription. 'Getting in touch with the inner child' (Parkes, 1990) can become a confusing endeavour for a survivor of abuse, especially those who blame themselves entirely for the abuse. In clinical practice, imagery rescription can become difficult when the child self attacks and berates the adult self for not protecting him/her, refusing to be physically touched or soothed and also on occasions when the adult self has physically beaten or verbally harangued the child self, calling the child derogatory names and generally rejecting the child. When these instances occur, this represents clinically important data about the survivor's psychopathology and identity disturbance and how the survivor relates to other parts of the self. Dissociation from the traumatic imagery or simply resistance to imagining the scenes of abuse greatly hinders these procedures and a decision must be made about actively encouraging the survivor to persist in imagining the abuse scenes or attempting to address these difficulties using different methods.

Imagery Rescripting and Reprocessing (IRR; Smucker, Dancu, Foa & Niederee, 1996; Smucker & Dancu, 1999) aims to actively alter the narrative within the abuse memories and the cognitive-emotional schemata underlying its continued recall. In part, IRR focuses upon 'inner child' work (Parkes, 1990). IRR is founded on the premise that traumatic memories for both children and adults are lacking in verbal narrative, are state dependent, encoded in sensory rather than linguistic form, are stored differently and difficult to control consciously and fixed and unaltered through time. If memories of childhood abuse are encoded as visual imagery, then imagery techniques should be beneficial to alter them and integrate the meaning of the trauma. Smucker *et al.* refer to the value of information-processing approaches such as direct exposure and guided imagery in changing traumatic images and memories. Furthermore, Smucker and Dancu (1995) describe pathogenic abuse-related schemata of powerlessness, mistrust, abandonment, worthlessness, self-blame, inherent badness and unlovability as characteristic of survivors of sexual abuse in childhood. Traumagenic beliefs and schema disturbances must also be addressed to alter cognitive processes concerning self and others. Therefore, IRR aims to decrease arousal, eliminate intrusive PTSD symptoms (nightmares, flashbacks), replace the role of victimisation with a sense of safety and empowerment, change abuse-related cognitive schemata and develop soothing and nurturing behaviour. The therapy consists of imaginal exposure of the abuse scene (visually recalling and experiencing the images, thoughts, emotions), followed by imaginal rescripting (replacing the traumatic imagery with mastery imagery) and self-nurturing imagery. The traumatic scene is first visualised from the child's perspective and mastery achieved by the adult self, the latter reprocessing the images. Connection at an emotional level is encouraged by 'adult-nurturing-child' imagery of soothing, comfort and nurturance after the adult self enters the abuse scenario, confronting and dealing with the perpetrator, removing the child self to safety and providing continuing safety and care. Outcome studies have been favourable (Smucker & Dancu, 1999), with significant changes to a number of schemata related to trauma and similar treatment gains maintained after six months follow-up.

Cognitive therapies for childhood abuse

Jehu, Gazan and Klasson (1988) described a cognitive-behavioural multi-modal therapy programme which targets self-denigratory beliefs and distortions that are directly associated with personality functioning and symptoms. Types of dysfunctional beliefs are identified, distortions recognised and alternatives jointly developed to challenge these beliefs. Distortions include *dichotomous thinking* (a minor personal flaw indicates complete badness), *overgeneralisation* (a general conclusion that all men will exploit) or *personalisation* (because a survivor did not prevent the abuse, he/she must have been responsible). Self-blaming beliefs consist of ideas that compliance means consent or that adhering to the perpetrator's treat of secrecy means that he/she must have wished the abuse to continue. Self-denigratory beliefs include distorted thoughts regarding being stigmatised, inferior or inadequate because of the fact that the abuse actually occurred to him/her.

Jehu's Belief Inventory includes statements of beliefs related to the abuse such as 'I must have been seductive and provocative when I was young' (self-blame) and 'anyone who knows what happened to me sexually will not want anything to do with me' (self-denigration). Alternative beliefs are generated using logical analysis, reinterpretation, and provision of information or activities to challenge and disconfirm the dysfunctional ideas. Other treatment procedures are communication training, anger control, and problem solving and relationship enhancement. Therapy focuses on target complaints and is structured to address certain problem areas. Jehu's approach is a practical method applying cognitive, behavioural and experiential techniques designed to target abuse-specific beliefs about oneself, the abuse itself and events in the world generally. Evaluation of treatment outcome has been positive and encouraging.

Salter (1994) proposes a 'trauma-based world view' which describes how the perpetrator of sexual abuse impacts on the thinking of the victim, referring to how abuse causes survivors to experience 'sex offenders in the head' (p. 201). This model suggests that the perpetrator's view of the world and behaviour are intrinsically linked to the survivor's beliefs system. For example, sexual trauma entails a loss of meaningful, order between events and their predictability. The view that the world is typically benevolent is corrupted, and a sense of randomness and malevolence is engendered. The trauma, further-more, undermines the survivor's beliefs about self-efficacy, control and mastery over the avoidance of negative events.

A series of cognitive distortions of processing information and its content also occurs. *Process* errors would consist of diametrically opposite beliefs to those of the perpetrator. For example, the perpetrator's grandiosity, narcissism and sense of entitlement through selfish behaviour cause the survivor to expe-rience self-effacement and denigration of him/herself. *Content* errors relate to beliefs imposed by the perpetrator upon the survivor's reality at the time of the abuse that the survivor internalises and shares as mutually understood facts—for example, the belief that the perpetrator was mentally ill and could not control his behaviour or that the child's physical response during sexual contact is interpreted as consent and participation. Content errors are distorted, define the survivor's continuing sense of reality and are shared by perpetrator and survivor.

A somewhat similar cognitive theory is the internalisation model of Wieland (1998). External actions during the abuse, including the perpetrator's behaviour, affect the survivor by a process of internalising the meaning of the event, expectations of future events and his/her perceptions of the self, rela-tionships and the world generally. Internalisation leads to propositional beliefs ('I am disgusting, worthless') which influence the survivor's behaviour (e.g., self-injury). Wieland's model adds little to aforementioned theories, but does specify a process by which the abuse itself is absorbed into the personality of the survivor. Interestingly, empirical research by Waller and Smith (1994) examining both the role of overt (self-denigratory beliefs using Jehu's Beliefs Inventory) and covert cognitive correlates (information-processing biases using a modified Stroop technique) indicated that these latter biases reflected a specific schema which involves beliefs about being contaminated by sexually abusive experiences. These findings support an internalisation of the trau-matic experience on a cognitive, information-processing level.

Turner *et al.* (1996) described a 'multimodal' cognitive approach based on the inference that incest survivors experience a form of complex PTSD. Psy-chological difficulties of this condition include deficits in affect regulation (anger, self-destructiveness), alterations in consciousness (amnesia, dissocia-tion), alterations in self-perception (guilt, shame), alteration in the perception of the perpetrator (idealisation, preoccupation with revenge), alteration in relating to others, somatisation and alteration to systems of meaning (despair, hopelessness). Therapy targets memories of the trauma and tolerance of the emotional intensity attached to the original trauma in a reflective construction of the impact of these events. Issues of identity and relatedness, 'narrative themes' such as helplessness, guilt, loss and maladaptive cognitive schemata about self-blame, alienation and trustworthiness are a central focus for change. The survivor's subjective meanings about the trauma are considered and reinterpretation of distorted reasoning and assumptions altered. This method therefore incorporates information-processing and schematic-level interventions. The treatment format consists of individual and group therapy with medication (fluoxetine). Preliminary outcome data for six survivors attests to a decrease in PTSD symptomatology and traumatic themes. These cognitive approaches are easily grasped by survivors and provide a structured, effective, targeted method of intervention for a wide range of psychological problems after abuse.

Attachment theory

Bowlby (1969, 1973) proposed that the child develops internal working models which are mental constructions forming the basis of personality. Sroufe and Rutler (1984) stated that these working models are so relationship bound that the child internalises both sides (or roles) of the attachment figure-to-attached-person experience and learns care-giving while receiving care. These models form the template for emotionally significant relationships in adulthood demonstrating stability, consistency and elaboration as time progresses. Crittenden (1985) proposed that early acquired working models are resistant to change and often difficult to revise due to self-confirming experiences and maintenance. Alexander (1992) and Alexander *et al.* (1998) have applied attachment theory to abusive and incestuous families, reporting that *insecure* attachments (particularly fearful attachment styles) are exhibited by survivors. These patterns emerge from general family dysfunction and the interdependence of negative attachment patterns amongst family members affecting perceptions and relational balances within the family. In effect, parents' insecure attachment patterns are precursors to the development of similar patterns for the child through a failure to attune to the child's emotional states, compromising the child's capacity to reflect upon his/her own thoughts, feelings and perceptions, with relational imbalances being directly evident between parent and child (Gelinas, 1983; Ryan, 1989).

A *dismissing* pattern exhibited by an abuser can lead to the child idealising the perpetrator, blocking memories of the abuse, and difficulties showing intimacy typical of a neglectful and disinterested parent (Feeney & Noller, 1996). An abuser who demonstrates a *preoccupied* pattern, focusing excessively on negative and traumatic memories, will exhibit anxious, dependent and jealous adult relationships resulting in role reversal and parentification of the child (Gelinas, 1983). A *fearful avoidant* pattern shown by an abuser is often associated with reliance upon denial, dissociation, poor impulse control and substance abuse and preventing a non-offending parent from protecting the child (Anderson & Alexander, 1996). Abuse, as stated, can constitute several forms ranging from active rejection and abuse, distancing and neglect, punishment, role reversal, unpredictable and unsatisfactory care and vacillation between acceptance and rejection (Main & Goldwyn, 1994). The reasons for the perpetrator exhibiting these behaviours and their effects upon the child are a reflection of intergenerational transmission and the contextual nature of abusing environments. Alexander *et al.* (1998) report that insecure attachment patterns were evident in 92 cases of incest, with 60% judged as fearful/avoidant and 21% as preoccupied. The attachment pattern predicted distress and depression above the effects of abuse severity with personality disorders being predominant (avoidant, self-defeating and borderline features).

The authors conclude that symptomatic presentations, such as PTSD symptoms, dissipate as time progresses and interpersonal problems do not, as originally suggested by Finkelhor (1990), and symptoms show intransigence whereas relational imbalances and internalised patterns of attachment produced by the abusive environment itself persist and pervade the survivor's current adult relationships (e.g., partner, child). Insecure attachments are most prevalent in the histories of physically abused and neglected children (Carlson, Cicchetti, Barnett & Braunwald, 1989) and later adult intimate relationships may show 'traumatic bonding' (Dutton & Painter, 1981), the survivor entering partnerships in which revictimisation occurs in a self-defeating process. The therapeutic alliance itself is an attachment pattern where recurrent, internalised patterns of relating are expressed. Promising forms of psychotherapy for dysfunctional attachment patterns within a self-psychology perspective have been reported (Shane & Shane, 1997) targeting 'relational configurations' maintaining pathological relationships and symptoms.

Psychoanalytic approaches to abuse

Psychoanalytic ideas have contributed greatly to our appreciation of the relevance of traumatic childhood events to adult psychopathology. Differing models of psychoanalytic thinking exist to account for trauma, for example, Jungian approaches (Kalsched, 1996) and more traditional psychodynamic therapies (Heineman, 1998; Gartner, 1999). Freud's original ideas (see *Further Remarks on the Psychoneuroses*, 1896; *Three Essays on Sexuality*, 1905; *My Views on the Part Played by Sexuality in the Aetiology of the Neurosis*, 1906; *Introductory Lectures*, 1917; *Beyond the Pleasure Principle*, 1920; *Inhibitions, Symptoms and Anxiety*, 1926; *An Outline of Psychoanalysis*, 1940) about the relevance of trauma in childhood remain influential in psychoanalytic practice today. He proposed an 'economic model' of trauma, claiming that childhood sexual abuse lay dormant until the memories were activated through the advent of puberty, causing the meaning and affect associated with the memories to overwhelm the ego, producing symptoms. The survivor's mind is overwhelmed and overstimulated by the abuse, the quantity of 'accretion of excitation in the nervous system' cannot be tolerated and symptoms are formed due to helplessness. The internal source of trauma, the memory itself, retraumatised the survivor and feelings of helplessness and traumatic anxiety were experienced. Freud later revised his theory somewhat and his model implied that dynamic tension emerged between internal fantasy and the external event. The traumatic events overwhelmed the pleasure principle, being expressed in dreams, symptoms and transference themes and a damaged self. *Repression* became a central mechanism to account for the notion that memories and affects were pressed back down out of consciousness.

Janet's theory of trauma and dissociation (1889) furthered psychoanalytic understanding of abuse, citing dissociation to be central to pathology. *Dissociation* differs from repression in that the former describes a changing state of consciousness splitting the mind, and primarily at the time of the trauma. The objective of dissociation is to provide a means of psychological escape from the situation with a fracturing of identity evident when relied upon habitually. Both can occur and are not mutually exclusive. These processes remain significant concepts to understanding responses to trauma in present psychoanalytic thinking.

Object relations thinking on the nature and impact of childhood abuse has been prominent and helpful in conceptualising the internalisation of the abuse experience and accounting for symptoms of survivors (Westen *et al.*, 1990). 'Object relations' describes the process whereby specific representations of self and other become internalised and organised in meaningful ways into cognitive, affective and motivational patterns which guide interpersonal behaviour (Westen, 1991). These include the complexity of representations of significant others, affect in relationships, the capacity for emotional investment in relationships and moral standards and understanding of social causality (Freedenfeld, Ornduff & Kelsey, 1995). Intrapsychic representations of self and others form the structural and dynamic substrate of personality, and sexual and physical abuse impairs the survivor's functioning in these domains (Marcus, 1989). Pistole and Ornduff (1994), Ornduff, Freedenfeld, Kelsey & Critelli (1994) and Freedenfeld *et al.* (1995) describe the use of projective testing (the Thematic Apperception Test), with sexually abused and physically abused children indicating impairments in these areas of personality. Specifically, their object world is malevolent, with an expectation that interactions will be hostile and unprotective, the world an unsafe and dangerous place. Representations of others are less complex and undifferentiated and show less integration (greater concrete, transitory, unorganised and contradictory representations). The typical affective tones ascribed to relationships are negative and a lack of capacity to emotionally invest in relationships is evident.

Understanding of logical attributions and causality in human relationships is impaired. Abused children expect contact with others to be conflictual and painful, with fantasies of aggression attributed to others permeated with per-petrator–victim expectations. Sexual preoccupation and guilt dominate the thoughts of sexually abused children (Pistole & Ornduff, 1994) in addition. It is argued by Gediman (1991; cited in Pistole & Ornduff, 1994) that 'one can-not have survived abuse without internalising the interaction of abuser and victim' (p. 392); the object relational world of the survivor is impaired and affected in a structured internal fashion. Object relations psychotherapy aims to integrate these deficits using the therapeutic relationship as the vehicle for changes (Stewart, 1996).

Mollon (1993, 1996) describes a distinctive and insightful model of distur-bances of the self conceptualised in psychoanalytic terms. Trauma impinges on seven aspects of self-functioning, accounting for the impact on the survivor both in terms of the structure and experience of the self. First, the perpetra-tor's actions and explanations for them impose a false reality onto the sur-vivor, denying him/her the capacity to develop a separate subjectivity and sense of reality. Second, helplessness and passivity engendered by the abuse compromise the survivor's sense of personal agency, control and autonomy. This causes some survivors to assert a semblance of control or power by mim-icking the perpetrator role, termed identification with the aggressor. Third, the survivor's objective sense of self is affected by creating an image of him/her-self as damaged, guilty and shameful because of the degradation within the abuse, and the perpetrator's tendency to implicate the survivor as responsible for the abuse. Being used as an object of self-gratification engenders feelings of worthlessness and inferiority. Fourth, on a structural level, the survivor experiences a 'shattering' of the self with little stability or integration. Fifth, the delicate balance between objective and subjective self becomes skewed in either an inward or outward direction, the survivor becoming self-absorbed and preoccupied, with an incapacity to engage with others, or excessively focused on others. Sixth, illusions of self-sufficiency may become prominent whereby the survivor distrusts everyone and fails to attach to others, avoiding intimacy. Lastly, abuse within the family violates the survivor's sense of lineage and sense of origins, affecting identity, with childhood recalled in a disjointed and confused manner.

The use of transference relationships, especially self-object dimensions, is vital in tandem with emotional insight for positive change. Self objects refer to the survivor's tendencies to engage with the therapist in an unconscious way of relating to restore or develop the self within an empathic therapeutic alliance. Mollon (1996) describes Meloy's (1993) use of the concept *stranger self object* whereby the survivor internalises a fantasy that a predator (the per-petrator) exists in the internal world and the child will become preyed upon. Pollock (1997, 1998b) further illustrated this link between abusive experiences and internalisation of the predator–prey dimension. The therapist's manage-ment of the therapist–survivor object relation is critical to avoid further damaging or empathically failing the survivor when his/her internal world is vastly corrupted and negatively coloured.

Eye Movement Desensitisation and Reprocessing

Eye Movement Desensitisation and Reprocessing (EMDR; Shapiro, 1989, 1995) has been a controversial treatment procedure categorised under the rubric of 'power therapies' (Figley, 1997). EMDR was originally designed to address trauma (both Types I and II) with claims of significant clinical effectiveness, client acceptability and satisfaction (Poole, de Jongh & Spector, 1999) and rapid improvement in a single session (McCann, 1992). EMDR has been applied to different disorders additionally including phobic states, panic disorder, depression and personality disorders with claimed success. Training in EMDR has flourished since its inception and it has been marketed with enthusiasm as a 'miracle . . . extraordinary and profound . . . the most revolutionary, important method to emerge in psychotherapy in decades' (Shapiro & Forrest, 1997).

As a procedure EMDR consists of a number of phases, including client history-taking, preparation and assessment, desensitisation, installation, body scanning and closure. The client generates a composite image representative of the traumatic event consisting of a negative cognition, physical sensations, emotional responses, sounds, smells etc. The client focuses upon this composite image and the therapist employs a series of saccadic hand movements across the client's field of vision, which the client follows with his/her eyes (knee taps, bilateral audiosounds etc. have been used). The desensitisation phase consists of a number of series of saccadic eye movements while focusing upon this image, repeated until the client's anxiety or distress diminishes. The installation phase comprises the client attending to the image and installing a positive cognition through further saccadic eye movements. The validity of this positive belief is increased throughout the procedure.

Changes are noted for all distressing components of the traumatic image. EMDR is based on Shapiro's (1989) Accelerated Information Processing Model, which proposes that traumatic information causes a neurological imbalance in physiological systems without achieving adaptive resolution. The system is unable to function and the traumatic information is retained and stored neurologically in a disturbed state and is continually triggered internally or externally in a distressing, state-dependent form as intrusive and re-experiencing symptoms of PTSD. Eye movements are hypothesised to trigger the physiological mechanism that activates the information-processing system, achieving integration and successful resolution. EMDR has been described for survivors of rape and childhood sexual abuse (Shapiro, 1989; Shapiro & Forrest, 1997) with success although controlled studies with independent evaluation have not been conducted.

EMDR has its followers and its critics. Conclusive empirical evidence is absent for EMDR although 13 published controlled studies attest to positive outcomes in PTSD symptoms, which is the greatest number for any form of treatment method to date (see Poole, de Jongh & Spector, 1990, for a review). The rate of change is more rapid compared to other therapies (e.g., Direct Exposure Therapy) with less intervention time required.

Critics of EMDR range from being scientifically sceptical to virulently denouncing of its theoretical basis and capabilities. Rosen, Lohr, McNally and Herbert (1999) state that Shapiro's theory amounts to 'neurobabble' and 'what is effective in EMDR is not new, and what is new is not effective' (p. 10) and also that EMDR makes claims that are unfounded. Richards (1999) provides a measured analysis of the debate surrounding EMDR, pointing to the evidence that the 'active ingredient' of this procedure has not been identified and includes components of imaginal exposure, cognitive restructuring and self-control techniques. It is pertinent to add that EMDR is best applied as part of an overall treatment process rather than a single 'miraculous cure' (Rosen *et al.,* 1999).

EMDR appears to be most successful for single trauma and Shapiro (1995) asserts that 'no prolonged molestation victim . . . can be fully treated in this manner' (p. 154). Despite the controversy that surrounds EMDR generally, its use with survivors of abuse in childhood, adulthood or both cannot be ascertained but, as is the case with any current treatment procedure, its clinical utility will be determined as time progresses. On a personal level, having found EMDR to be effective within clinical practice in many cases for a diversity of disorders (Pollock, 2000), the application of EMDR appears promising for survivors of abuse. EMDR does not consider the developmental and relational impact of abuse even though reduction of distressing PTSD symptoms can be achieved. It corresponds, therefore, to another form of information-processing treatment for traumatic memories and symptoms. In cases of abuse in which PTSD symptoms are evidently present, EMDR is appropriate. Parnell (1999) reports a series of case studies using EMDR for adult survivors of childhood abuse with notable success, although empirical data is absent to allow scrutiny of the outcomes achieved. In conclusion, EMDR is a powerful and creative technique that can be beneficial when incorporated into other formulations of childhood abuse.

Finkelhor's Four Traumagenic Dynamics Model

David Finkelhor's (1987) model of different 'dynamics' that account for many of the diverse symptoms and psychological problems associated with sexual abuse has been a powerful explanatory theory. A *traumagenic dynamic* is an 'experience that alters the child's cognitive or emotional mentation to the world and causes trauma by distorting the child's self concept, worldview or affective capacities' (p. 354). Trauma distorts assumptions and the coping responses a child displays may have been adaptive during the abuse, but dysfunctional at a later date. The four dynamics operate before, during and after the abuse and explain the impact of the trauma in many domains of the child's and later adult's life. The dynamics are as follows:

- *Traumatic sexualisation.* During the abuse, the child's sexuality is moulded in developmentally inappropriate ways by rewards by the perpetrator, learning that sexualised behaviour can be used as a form of manipulation and an excessive focus on the physical body, and unpleasant feelings become associated with sexual themes. The consequences of this dynamic are that the child becomes confused about sexual identity and norms, intimacy and sex are fused, sexual aversion occurs and sexual preoccupation is observed. Behaviourally, excessive masturbation or play may be seen, sexual aggression, promiscuity or flirtatious behaviours and sexual dysfunction in adulthood.
- *Stigmatisation.* The child may develop self-perceptions as worthless, shameful and guilty, often conveyed directly by the perpetrator. When he/she realises that the abuse was socially and morally corrupt, the child is likely to form attributions about how and why these events happened, blaming him/herself because 'I must have done something'. Negative reactions to the child's disclosures (e.g., dismissiveness, invalidation) exacerbate this self-perception. Consequences of stigmatisation include feelings of guilt, shame, alienation and poor self-worth, leading to substance abuse, self-injury and criminality.
- *Betrayal.* The betrayal of trust, whether by a parent or a manipulative perpetrator outside the family, causes dramatic damage to the child's capacity to invest in relationships and accept care from others. One adult survivor described to me how her perpetrator of six years of sexual abuse towards her was a charming, well-respected man within the extended family who told her she was his 'protégé', sending her for expensive music lessons and paying for her to attend operas and musicals. She described how she pictures him as a 'Trojan horse' character who, once he gained her confidence and trust, violated her under the guise of her being 'special'. Her sense of betrayal was enormous. Children who feel betrayed often demonstrate mistrust, anger and hostility, depression and guilt, exhibited behaviourally as discomfort within intimate relationships, marital difficulties, aggression and delinquency and risk of future revictimisation or exploitation.
- *Powerlessness.* The disregarding of the child's wishes and consent, and fear of injury and harm, cause a sense of disempowerment as his/her body is used as an object for someone else's gratification. The inclusion of threat, physical violence or cruelty within the traumatic experiences results in a

sense of being trapped or coerced for the child who cannot take any effective action to prevent or stop the continuation of the abuse. PTSD symptoms appear most associated with the dynamic of powerlessness due to the inducement of fear and apprehension. Nightmares, flashbacks, anxiety and a desire to exhibit or retrieve some semblance of control (e.g., by restricting one's food intake) may occur, with the possibility of the child learning to become controlling and abusive towards others through aggression or other criminal activities.

The value of group approaches

Group formats for adult survivors of childhood abuse are commonplace and come in a variety of different packages. A review by Meichenbaum (1994) suggested that empirical data is lacking as to whether group versus individual therapy (or a combination of both), short or longer term, structured or unstructured, with male, female or mixed co-therapists, improves the delivery and outcomes of the therapy provided. Some group programmes focus on the 'there and then', others more so on the 'here and now' in the survivor's life and the place of the memories of abuse and their effects. These groups differ substantially in their structure, driving theoretical approaches, contents and delivery. It is important to state that clinicians' creativity and resourcefulness are most prominent compared to reliance on empirical findings.

Finkelhor's model forms the basis of Zaidi's (1994) time-limited group programme which is partly educational, cognitive-behavioural and uses exposure techniques also. The targets of the programme are to increase understanding of abuse to reduce stigmatisation and self-blame, confronting memories of abuse, teaching the abused child to decrease guilt and isolation, expressing anger and hostility by rejecting the internalised messages employed by the perpetrator, reducing obstacles to intimacy and addressing traumatic sexualisation and empowering the survivor to plan for the future.

Brandt (1989) described a short-term group for female survivors which involves the retelling of the abuse, writing letters to the perpetrator which are kept and not mailed and discussion groups which cover topics of trust and intimacy, relationships, phobias and sexual problems. Kearney-Cooke and Stiegel-Moore (1994) report a feminist psychodynamic group approach which addresses the loss of childhood experienced by the survivor, writing a narrative which redefines her life and body and the installation of constructive hope and positive reframing of the abuse experience in the context of her personal history. Survivors are taught techniques to deal with emotional distress, guided imagery is used to address traumatic memories, a re-enactment of the abuse itself is undertaken using experiential techniques and exercises deal with feelings of shame and self-loathing. Breaking the cycle of revictimisation in the survivor's relationships is given prominent attention. Longer-term groups for survivors of incest include Gold-Steinberg and Buttenheim's (1993) format, which centres upon helping the survivor to retell the narrative story of the abuse. An innovative approach by Alexander *et al.* (1989) involves survivors discussing a given theme or topic common to incestuous experiences (e.g., negative self-perceptions, alienation, and trust) in dyadic discussion groups that rotate to a new partner sequentially. Kirschner, Kirschner and Rappaport (1993) describe a group approach that attempts to 'depathologise' the survivor's experiences, uncover the history of the abuse, reduce the impact of symptoms and, in addition, confront the perpetrator if necessary.

Westbury and Turry (1999) report a comparison study which assessed the effectiveness of group treatment for sexual abuse survivors over individual therapy alone showing that, with a 10–12-week group, anxiety and depression were ameliorated most significantly by the group approach. The content of the group was based on the body-focused feminist model which, again, required survivors to 'tell their story' in a safe, empathic environment. Integrative Body Psychotherapy was used as a holistic method of addressing cognitive, emotional, physical and spiritual aspects of the trauma, including body-focused relaxation, personal boundaries exercises, coping with dissociative and re-experiencing symptoms and guided visualisations of safety, inner wisdom and containment. Certain feminist therapy techniques were also included in the group sessions. Cognitive-behavioural therapy within a group setting for adult survivors of abuse has been reported (Young & Blake, 1999) and more self-help oriented groups also, with promising outcomes (Ainscough & Toon, 1993). The application of CAT groups for survivors is reported in Chapters 9 (Teresa Hagan and Kath Gregory) and 10 (Mark Stowell-Smith, Michael Göpfert and Susan Mitzman).

CAT in relation to other psychotherapies

As an integrative psychotherapy, it is pertinent to consider what may be unique about CAT and how it is similar or even equivalent to other theories of psychotherapy, particularly cognitive and psychoanalytic psychotherapies. Ryle (1978) began the debate about generalities in psychotherapies with discussions about the perceived common language for the psychotherapies and how analytic ideas could be redefined in cognitive terms (Ryle, 1982). As CAT has developed, refinement of the relation of CAT to both forms of psychotherapy from which it derives its name has continued (Ryle, 1990; Leighton & Ryle, 1995; Marzillier & Butler, 1995). A trend has been observable as psychotherapy practice and research have become more reflective with advances in theory and its implementation more fine tuned and evidence based. Cognitive therapies have gradually introduced methods for conceptualising the interpersonal aspects of a patient's problems as suggested by Young

(1994a, 1994b), Young and Lindemann (1992) and Alford and Beck (1997). For example, Bucci (1997) describes 'emotion schemata' and Safran and Segal (1996) describe 'dysfunctional cognitive interpersonal cycles' that emphasise the repetitive, self-confirming nature of a patient's behaviour in relationships that lead to distress.

Young (1994a) proposed that 'early maladaptive schemata' (EMSs) are acquired during development, representing cognitive structures which influence and distort information processing, are typically affect laden and affect the patient's behaviours, which are designed to avoid or compensate for the schema. In the practice of Schema-Focused Cognitive Therapy (SFCT), the EMSs are often presented to the patient as internal, stable, resistant structures using analogies that they are 'buttons', 'viruses' or 'devils' (Young, 1995) which must be managed and starved of ways of behaving, thinking and feeling which maintain them. Young does describe in detail how each of the 14 EMSs affect the therapy relationship; for example, the *abandonment/instability* EMS can result in the therapist being perceived by the patient to be a transitional source of safety and stability, and a vehicle to disconfirm that abandonment will predictably occur.

The *mistrust/abuse* EMS can be best managed within therapy by complete honesty, attention and discussion paid to the patient's anxieties about trust and intimacy and the expectation that the therapist will be abusive. SFCT is, therefore, focusing on how the patient's EMSs directly affect relationships generally and the therapeutic alliance also. The emphasis upon an EMS as a semi-autonomous, agentic entity existing within the patient and forming the resistant structure of his/her personality centres the source of problems inside the patient, which can be alarming to some (Pollock, 1999).

Experiential techniques are favoured in SFCT, including dialogues in imagery with parents, 'inner-child' work, description of different facets of the self (such as the abused, angry, protective parts of the self), especially with patients diagnosed with personality disorders. For borderline personalities, Young suggests the patient may experience schema modes such as the abandoned child, angry/injured child, abusing parent, detached protector and healthy coper. 'Flipping' between schemata and modes requires tracking and conflict between them addressed. Furthermore, SFCT aims to tailor the style of therapy as an 'antidote' to the patient's schemata as they present themselves, and acknowledgement that the therapist's own schemata may 'erupt' towards the patient within the context of limited reparenting (Young, 1995).

The critique by Marzillier and Butler (1995) provides an interesting comparison between CAT and cognitive therapy that acknowledges that CAT has similarities in terms of its structured, time-limited, focused approach with specific goal-setting tasks and emphasis on active collaboration. Similarities exist in the patterns targeted (e.g., traps and snags as 'vicious cycles' and negative thinking), identification and modification of underlying, internalised schemata, acceptance that unconscious motivations influence behaviour and the importance of implicational meaning as defined within the Interacting Cognitive Subsystems model (ICS; Teasdale & Barnard, 1993). The authors conclude that cognitive therapy and CAT 'have several points of convergence both in theory and practice; CAT is, as its name clearly indicates, a "*cognitive therapy*" ' (p. 137). The emphasis on theoretical analysis of both these therapies is noted, and that the temptation to translate techniques from one language to another may whitewash their unique differences.

An in-depth account of dialogue between Leighton and Ryle (1995) considers 'How analytic is CAT?', with a number of points raised by Leighton regarding the right of CAT to describe itself as analytic in any sense. (I would refer the reader to Chapter 8 in Ryle (1995a). Ryle's defence of CAT is that the innate warfare of Kleinian object relations thinking and Freudian structural dynamics negates the active and constructionist capacities of human existence and the influence of development contexts and culture.

Attachment theory (Bowlby, 1969, 1973) shows a close resemblance to CAT concepts and explanation for the intergenerational transmission of abusing relations. Ryle (1995a) suggests that Bowlby's ideas regarding 'internal working models of relationships' is very similar to CAT RRPs derived from early care-taking experiences and proximity-seeking through biologically driven attachment processes, RRPs also equivalent to Stern's (1985) Representations of Interactions that have been Generalised (RIGs) whereby, through parental attunement to the child's affective state and facilitation of his/her capacity to reflect upon experience, the child internalises discrete procedural knowledge about interactions. Bowlby proposed that the child develops internal working models which are mental constructions forming the basis of personality. Sroufe and Fleeson (1986) stated that these working models are so relationship bound that the child internalises both sides (or roles) of the attachment figure-to-attached-person experiences and learns care-giving while receiving care. Shane and Shane (1997) conceptualised 'relational configurations' to underlie self–other transactions within an attachment and self-psychology framework similar to CAT RRPs.

These models form the template for emotionally significant relationships in adulthood demonstrating stability, consistent expectations and elaboration as time progresses. Crittenden (1985) claimed that early acquired working models (early RRPs) are resistant to change and often difficult to revise due to self-confirming experiences and maintenance. CAT conceptualises a lack of revision to harmful patterns of relating to oneself and others to reflect problems within the procedures of the survivor and the effects of self-confirming dilemmas, traps and snags. The difference between CAT and attachment theories is that RRPs are considered to involve knowledge, affect and action, which the latter theories address separately, although the similarities to explain personality development are very apparent.

Commonalities and differences, strengths and weaknesses

A number of areas are relevant when comparing CAT to other forms of theoretical formulation of trauma and therapy. I refer here to the conceptualisation described in Chapter 1 and the three domains of *disturbance of self*, *affect dysregulation* and *interpersonal/social problems* when discussing the theoretical and clinical utility of CAT. It could be questioned whether CAT provides a useful means of conceptualising the effects of traumatic experiences on the development of the self. CAT does infer a psychological construct (the RRP) to explain how generic, Type II traumatic experiences in childhood are represented in implicit memory, similar to Young's early maladaptive schema, Bowlby's internal working models and Bucci's emotion schemata. CAT can be differentiated from psychoanalytic, attachment and cognitive models by its central emphasis on RRPs and the premise that sign-mediated language is important in the process of internalisation of self–self and self–other components. Reasons for non-revision of these stable internalised representations and disturbances in identity development and functioning are also accounted for. The nature and severity of disturbances in self are conceptualised specifically within the MSSM's three levels and targets for therapeutic work identified. A central role is assigned to the concept of dissociation, which is compatible with modern theories and empirical research regarding traumatic experiences and psychopathology.

The relative influence of the internalisation of the perpetrator–victim dimension is well accounted for in the CAT model of identity disturbance and given specific prominence when conceptualising the nature of the psychopathology observed. This does not preclude the possibility that the traumatic experiences have not been internalised to a detrimental extent and that the survivor's developmental trajectory has compensated for early adversity. The MSSM attempts to acknowledge also that the severity of impact of any combinations of childhood abuse differs from survivor to survivor in terms of the type and pattern of symptoms experienced, the extent of identity disturbance and the severity of personality dysfunction generally. Dissociation and identity disturbance have been shown by empirical research to be related to severity of childhood abuse and trauma and the MSSM accounts for these facets of survivors' responses in childhood and later adulthood.

Affect dysregulation is understood to be intrinsically related to the states of mind induced by the internalised, abuse-generated RRPs and their continuing effects on the survivor's identity. Symptomatic problems are proposed to indicate dysfunctional, self-perpetuating patterns of self–self and self–other relationships. In many senses, the interpersonal parameters of childhood abuse suggest that emotional disorders and symptoms are a reflection of problems in the survivor's capacity to relate to oneself and others. The MSSM of CAT accounts for the areas of dysfunction suggested by McCann and Pearlman

(1990; safety, trust, power, esteem and intimacy) whence RRPs such as *vulnerable–dangerous* (safety), *betrayal–exploiting* (trust), *abusing–victimised* (power), *contemptuous–belittled* (esteem) and *corrupting/using–violated/used* (intimacy). Finkelhor's traumagenic dynamics of traumatic sexualisation, betrayal, powerlessness and stigmatisation are similar in this respect.

The *interpersonal/social problems* exhibited by some survivors are understood as false solutions generated to cope with the meaning and longer-term effects of the abuse and its compromise of the survivor's developing identity. Each survivor's creativity and resourcefulness in the manner in which he/she copes is acknowledged and connected to the overall reformulation of the survivor's patterns of thinking, feeling and acting. In addition, the survivor's capacity to defeat him/herself, destroy progress and inhibit healthier parts of identity is also recognised and addressed.

It must be stated that CAT has little to say about the development and treatment of PTSD symptoms, unlike many other models. It can be suggested that several techniques and intervention models are available within the therapist's 'tool-box' to treat PTSD and these can be easily incorporated within a CAT framework without losing sight of the survivor's personality functioning as defined by the MSSM, as long as therapeutic integrity overall is not jeopardised.

Conclusions

Childhood abuse is an interpersonal event or episode which has a multitude of potential effects at several levels of analysis, whether it is cognitive, affective, psychosocial or neurophysiological. It is important to derive a well-informed appreciation of the predominant difficulties for each case and to offer the form of intervention which will be of most benefit. It is unlikely that any psychotherapy or technique can be advocated as appropriate for every survivor because of the heterogeneity of developmental outcomes and uniqueness of survivors' creativity in dealing with adversity.

Whether it is always wise to address memories of abuse directly is a contentious issue (see Chapter 2) and CAT does allow the survivor to achieve a coherent personal narrative of the generic experiences of abuse during the reformulation process. CAT can be undertaken adequately without the survivor retelling every detail of the abuse scenarios and the search for historical truth can be managed sensitively and treatment progress achieved without any direct 'memory work'. The use of techniques such as Imagery Rescripting can enhance the reformulation process in CAT and other methods (e.g., EMDR, imagery work) can be interwoven into a CAT reformulation with reasonable ease, avoiding the loss of an overarching conceptualisation of the survivor's procedures and troublesome patterns. This is particularly relevant when nightmares, flashbacks or other PTSD symptoms are associated with the reciprocal roles and states of mind induced by the victimisation itself (i.e., powerless, guilty victim).

The following chapters (5–8) describe further case illustrations of the application of CAT and the MSSM of childhood trauma. The chapters progress in tandem with the increasing severity of psychological disturbance proposed by the MSSM and further demonstrate the processes of reformulation and practice of CAT.

Part II

CAT practice and illustrations of the model

CHAPTER 5

SUE LLEWELYN AND SUE CLARKE

Adult psychological problems and abuse

All therapists, who are trying to respond constructively to clients who have disclosed childhood sexual abuse, will make use of some theoretical understanding of what the effects of abuse are, and how they may be mitigated. It is our experience that CAT is well placed to offer both an understanding of the effects and how to help. Having worked extensively with survivors we have found CAT helpful, and we hope in this and the next chapter to explain how and why.

We need to start with some of the significant questions about childhood sexual abuse and its consequences. First, why does it appear to be so devastating for the survivor's psychological adjustment in some areas of life and not others? And next, why do many survivors appear to be so vulnerable to relationship difficulties and further victimisation? Related to this, there are two further key questions which arise when trying to help resolve difficulties: how can therapy help without causing yet more pain through questioning existing coping styles, and how might the therapeutic relationship itself both reveal and help to heal some of the pain? Any therapeutic approach, such as CAT, needs to be able to offer some answers to these questions. In this chapter we will look at how CAT approaches a client with a less severe presentation of distress, while in Chapter 6 we will examine the insight that CAT can provide for therapists working with clients with BPD, and how CAT may seek to stabilise and manage more severely distressed clients.

The sequelae of childhood sexual abuse

First we need to consider the effects of abuse. Numerous studies have attested to the evidence that survivors of sexual abuse are likely to experience a range of distressing symptoms which disrupt their sense of self, their ability to regulate emotion and their personal relationships (see also Chapter 1). These symptoms include depression, poor self-esteem, anxiety, relationship and sexual difficulties, substance misuse and revictimisation (Cahill, Llewelyn & Pearson, 1990; Kuyken, 1995). We do not wish to claim that childhood sexual abuse by itself causes all these symptoms, as many children who experience sexual abuse may also experience physical and emotional abuse, as well as disrupted parenting and economic difficulties, and these will play their part in developing psychological difficulties. Also of course people may develop these difficulties without having been abused, and significant numbers of abuse survivors do not appear to develop any psychological sequelae whatever. Nevertheless, it does appear that childhood sexual abuse is linked directly to a variety of forms of personal distress (Mullen *et al.*, 1995; Neumann, Houskamp, Pollock & Briere, 1996), and that the existence of some link is now established beyond question.

Why should this be so? Several theories have been suggested to account for this and have suggested appropriate treatment approaches, including the post-traumatic stress model (Foa, Zinbarg & Rothbaum, 1992; Horowitz, 1986); the traumagenic dynamics model (Finkelhor, 1987); the developmental model (Alexander, 1992; Cole & Putnam, 1992); the transactional coping model (Sparracelli, 1994) and, lastly, CAT. All models have sought to explain the variability of effects and their duration, and to offer therapeutic interventions. It is the contention of this volume that CAT represents a particularly helpful approach, primarily through the concept of reciprocal roles, which is explored collaboratively via the reformulation and SDR.

The contribution of CAT

CAT is an active treatment in which client and therapist together explore the history and meaning of the client's experience, and seek collaboratively to develop other more helpful ways of relating to the self, others and the world. Before demonstrating this through a case example, some of the key concepts of CAT will be explored as they are used with abuse survivors.

Procedures

As outlined in Chapter 2, all of us develop patterns of thoughts, feelings, actions and behaviour in our dealings with ourselves and the world, which CAT labels procedures. Most of these are carried out without conscious awareness, and do not cause difficulties. Many survivors of childhood sexual abuse do, however, develop some characteristic procedures which cause them distress. Typically these procedures are patterns of behaving which at one time helped the child to survive. For example, in order to escape the attentions of her stepfather, Julie put on a considerable amount of weight as she had heard him comment on her attractive figure. As an adult, Julie wanted to develop sexual relationships with men but was anxious about sex given her prior abusive experiences. Her persistent overeating acted as a snag, which helped her to sabotage her desire for relationships and to maintain a distance from men. Other clients may develop a pattern of interacting with others in which their own needs are subjugated. For example, the placation trap occurs frequently amongst survivors although of course it also occurs with many other clients. Here the survivor, told by the abuser that she is to blame for the abuse, may have developed a strategy of pleasing others to cope with her own sense of worthlessness. This leads to neglect of her own needs, leading to an outburst of apparently selfish resentment, which only goes to prove, in the survivor's view, how worthless she really is and how much she needs to try to please people.

Recognition of procedures is one of the early tasks in a CAT therapy. Together with the abuse survivor, the therapist tracks repeated patterns of interaction (neurotic procedures) which seem to cause the client distress. For example, Shirley reported that she had acted in a placatory way with her husband for years, but deeply resented his paternalistic assumption of responsibility for her. This was demonstrated clearly in a series of everyday interactions, including his refusal to let her drive herself to appointments, and her unwillingness to cause him pain by refusing his offer of help. These interactions often resulted in either sullen withdrawal by both partners, or explosive rows which caused distress all round. After finding evidence for such patterns, therapy proceeds by helping clients first to monitor and then to develop alternative procedures, for example, by encouraging Shirley to refuse her husband's offer while accepting his concern for her, and to drive herself to therapy sessions.

Reciprocal roles

As in any other relationship, an abusive relationship establishes two roles, or poles: the perpetrator and the victim. To be in this relationship (which the child cannot normally avoid) he/she has to learn how the other person behaves, and to anticipate their behaviour. Even if the child does not want to be there, the child comes to understand what is being asked and how to respond. The greater power of the abuser (usually an adult with whom the child has some relationship which usually requires obedience and respect, or at least deference) means that the child normally has little choice about this learning. Furthermore, the child is invited or coerced into responding to the adult in ways that reciprocate the adult's behaviour. The adult perpetrator by his/her actions creates the space for the victim's response. Being abused by an adult or older child facilitates the development of a spectrum of roles: 'appeaser', 'collaborator', 'passive victim' and so on. But most crucially for CAT, the child inevitably also learns the other side of the relationship: the 'aggressor', the 'blamer' and the 'perpetrator'. This capacity to predict and understand is not a matter of choice. The child is forced into it simply as a result of the adult's actions. The child learns whether or not he/she wants to do so. What this means is that the child knows not only how to be abused and suffer but also how it is possible to abuse and cause suffering.

As we know, adult survivors of abuse normally come to therapy because of their distressing symptoms, which often include difficulties in relationships and self-abuse. Most therapists when meeting a survivor of abuse react with empathy and distress on learning the story detailing the plight of the abused child. These therapists may then be surprised and confused by some of the anger and abuse which the client may turn on themselves or others. For example, Anne, a woman raped repeatedly by a neighbour when she was a child, expressed only fear of the man but no anger. She felt instead that she was and is basically bad, and that she deserved the abuse. She feared that as a 10-year-old she was too sexy for her own good and was therefore responsible for what took place. When reminded of her abuse, for example by a television programme, Anne abused herself either by cutting or by bingeing. Her belief in her own badness was expressed verbally with bitterness and hatred. When asked if she would feel this way about another little girl who might have been abused, she replied no, it was uniquely herself who was so bad.

Other clients may not only reciprocate abuse towards themselves but will also abuse other people, although the form of this abuse is not always direct. For example, Jenny developed emotionally passionate and sexualised relationships with girl friends but abandoned them angrily as soon as they expressed any physical desire for her. Her triumphant but also anguished accounts of her behaviour with them sounded emotionally abusive. Sometimes the abuse may be physical: for example, Heather was abusive towards her own children, which distressed her a great deal. Having been abused both sexually and physically as a child, Heather had little experience of good-enough mothering on which to draw when she herself was faced with crying children and was receiving little support from her partner. When her small daughter would not stop crying, she hit the child's legs and arms repeatedly, until both she and the child were exhausted. The image of the screaming child still haunts Heather, who cannot forgive herself for what she did, especially as she was herself a victim of similar attacks by her own father, which had accompanied the sexual abuse. We will discuss the issue of abuse towards others further in Chapter 6.

The concept of reciprocal roles can help the therapist to make sense of what is happening for the client, and to share this with the client. For example, it was possible to discuss with Heather how she, as a child, learned that there were two possible ways to be in the world: either powerful abusive parent who demanded obedience and conformity, or weak passive child who was terrified and powerless. When her own children cried endlessly, she had no model of what to do, other than to do as her parents had done, which was to hit the children. But there was more to it than just an absence of an appropriate role model. Faced with the relentless crying in a cramped flat with angry neighbours, Heather again felt terrified and powerless, at the mercy of the powerfully crying children and the potentially critical neighbours. This echo of her childhood plight was so painful that she attempted to escape by flight into the other role: that of the powerful abuser. Sharing this perception with Heather allowed her to understand her abusive behaviour, start to accept it, and hence to change.

Analysis of reciprocal roles helps the therapist as well as the client. Sitting with an angry, withdrawn client who exudes contempt for the therapist as well as desperate neediness can be confusing. Understanding that the abused client may be oscillating between herself as a frightened victim and herself as an angry survivor may help the therapist to avoid being drawn into unhelpful reciprocation with the client. For example, Jenny's therapist felt irritated and rejected by Jenny and was tempted to respond by withdrawing from therapy. By discussing the reciprocal roles in supervision, Jenny's therapist felt more confident in helping Jenny to a clearer understanding of the impact she was having on others and herself when she felt threatened by intimacy.

Reformulation

As described in Chapter 2, a key technique is the development and delivery of the reformulation. Almost inevitably in the case of the childhood sexual abuse survivor, this involves a retelling of the abuse (assuming it has been disclosed by the time the reformulation is presented) and its consequences. It is not obvious how helpful it is to explore the abuse in great detail. For some clients this may be experienced as a repeat of the original trauma, and the therapist's desire to know what happened may appear to the client as gratuitous and intrusive. A study by Ehlers et al. (1998) reports results which suggest that the helpfulness of retelling the story in detail, and going over it, depends on the individual client. They found that adult women who had coped with appalling rape trauma by withdrawing psychologically (in order to save their lives, possibly paralleling the strategy of dissociation which is used by many child victims of abuse) found re-experiencing the trauma in treatment as much more traumatic than did those women who had coped by resisting and fighting. For the latter group, re-experiencing the abuse, albeit in the safety of therapy, reinforced their sense of survival; for the former, it unhelpfully underlined their helplessness.

What this means is that the therapist has to tread carefully if the client is not merely to be reminded unhelpfully of earlier traumatic experiences. Trying to unearth more trauma is also probably not helpful. The point of reformulation is to try to understand how the client came to the present set of difficulties, and to understand how coping strategies, devised by the child in distress, may now ironically be causing additional problems to the adult survivor.

In the reformulation, then, the main emphasis is usually on trying to understand the meaning of the abuse, which normally entails spelling out its role in engendering the reciprocal role of abused, worthless, invaded and powerless, to a powerful abusive invasive other. The procedures developed by the survivor to cope with this powerless position are spelled out. For example, when faced with a sense of powerlessness that painfully echoes the past, a survivor may seek to grasp the powerful abusive role and attack herself, or she may dissociate and withdraw, or she may seek refuge and comfort in substance use. The reformulation suggests to the client how these procedures may have developed in response to endured childhood pain. The role of the therapist is to hear and record the pain, and to explore how it has led to procedures that are now unhelpful. Central to this is a recognition of the survivor's existing coping strategies. CAT does not consider that clients choose to live in pain: rather that they only have repertoires available to them that may have been developed under adverse circumstances. For example, Mike was the child of alcoholic parents who often left him in the care of his older brothers. Mike's reformulation included an account of how, following repeated episodes of sexual and physical abuse from his two older brothers, he had attempted to escape by excelling at school and gaining the attention of teachers. Mike nevertheless felt that, being dirty, he did not deserve success and unaccountably sabotaged himself by not turning up for a series of crucial school examinations, fearing that the craved attention would actually result in himself being exposed as the bad and worthless wretch that he felt he was. These feelings were particularly strong when he was with powerful others. Throughout his post-school career, Mike prevented success from ever happening by sabotage or withdrawal, always choosing obscurity. Mike construed himself as worthless despite evidence to the contrary, and when he felt he might get attention this activated a reciprocal role of the bad and attention-seeking wretch to a powerful and punitive other. Originally developed as a strategy to cope with his absent parents and abusive brothers, Mike's alternating craving for attention and withdrawal caused him considerable confusion and pain.

It is important to value the survivor's existing coping repertoire, and not to undermine it from a superior, expert position. Examination and questioning should only take place when the client is prepared for this. The goal of the reformulation is not to expose the client as mistaken or inept. Interpretations of unconscious material should be avoided as they can be experienced as invasive and not helpful. The collaborative therapeutic relationship (see below) is crucial here.

A sympathetically written reformulation can also help abuse survivors to a closer understanding, and hence acceptance, of their own contribution to maintaining their own pattern of distress. Through an exploration of recipro-cal roles in the reformulation and subsequent therapy, survivors may be able to own parts of themselves, which had previously been denied and which were thereby having an influence that could not be addressed or modified. The reformulation aims to contain the client's experiences and hence to make them manageable. For example, Heather could only start to move beyond an inchoate feeling of shame and self-loathing, to explore the fact that she had physically abused her children when she came to understand what led her to behave in ways which she, of all people, could have seen was damaging. CAT is not about blaming the victim, or heaping even more guilt onto the survivor: rather it is trying to help survivors to see how the parts of themselves that they often fear and loathe have come about. Leiman (1992) introduces the concept of the tool, whereby the work of therapy, or transformation of emotion, can take place. The reformulation is the tool whereby client and therapist can start the work of transforming the pain into something more manageable.

A collaborative relationship

Central to the experience of childhood abuse is powerlessness. Studies of the therapist–client relationship where the client is a sexual abuse survivor (e.g., Draucker, 1999) suggest that above all, therapists should seek to provide sup-port and empowerment for survivors. One of CAT's basic tenets is the impor-tance of maintaining a collaborative relationship between therapist and client, in which therapist and client are positioned side by side to examine the client's issues and attempt to devise resolutions. Empowerment of the client is a cen-tral aim of CAT; this does not mean gaining power in abstract terms, but empowerment in real, day-to-day control over the self, so that the survivor becomes the driver, not the passenger in his or own life. What this means is being able to know about and make choices when faced with dilemmas and dif-ficulties. By relating collaboratively with the client, the CAT therapist is con-veying a belief in the client's own potential to make choices and take control.

Homework tasks

Being a survivor of childhood sexual abuse is not a diagnosis, and no one set of symptoms results from it. It is unlikely therefore that any one set of treatment techniques will help all survivors (Llewelyn, 1997). Not being wedded to an exclusive theoretical base for intervention, the CAT therapist may choose to use a variety of interventions following reformulation. These include behavioural, cognitive, psychodynamic and family-oriented interventions and techniques, which are applicable because they are related closely to the understanding developed in the reformulation. In other words, the techniques are not delivered randomly, without regard for their theoretical underpinnings, but are anchored in the theoretical understanding offered by the reformulation. One technique that may be used is role-play to encourage appropriate assertiveness: the client may have little experience of being able to express opinions and may need active practice. Another technique is letter writing. For example, Sharon was very angry with her mother both for apparently failing to protect her from sexual abuse, and for appearing to prefer Sharon's older sister. Sharon was deeply afraid of her mother, and did not realistically feel able to confront her even as an adult. Instead she wrote, but did not post, a long letter to her mother in which she spelled out her new understanding of their relationship, which she had acquired in therapy. From a completely different perspective, most CAT therapists will also make use of an analysis of transference, given the powerful reciprocal roles which almost always surface in therapy with childhood sexual abuse survivors. Here the therapist will normally use an SDR to trace the re-enactments of significant reciprocal roles within the therapy itself.

The use of rating scales (see Chapter 2) encourages the therapists to ensure that tasks are completed, and that the time between sessions is used to full effect. Homework with childhood sexual abuse survivors can be particularly helpful when clients are feeling insecure and vulnerable (see Chapter 6), or where the client is trying to develop awareness of repeated patterns such as the placation trap.

Time limit and focus

CAT therapists normally agree with their clients a clear framework and duration for therapy following reformulation. The effect of this is to encourage a clear focus on the work to be achieved by therapy, and to encourage swift progress, in any way consistent with the reformulation. The systemic underpinning of CAT suggests that positive changes made in one area may well lead to changes in another in a virtuous cycle. Further, the Reformulation and Goodbye Letters represent tools which the client takes away from therapy, and which permit change to be not only consolidated but also initiated after termination. Evidence from psychotherapy research (Howard, Kopta, Krause & Orlinsky, 1986) suggests that effective therapy often occurs fastest in the early stages of therapy, in a negatively accelerating fashion. While this has not been investigated specifically with CAT, it seems likely that CAT's willingness to develop a focus carefully but relatively quickly will contribute to its effectiveness. As implied earlier, it may well be that the experience of abuse per se is not the focus of therapy, but rather the disturbed interpersonal relationships and self-management which have developed subsequent to the abuse. One last important issue about the time limit is the constant attention paid by CAT therapists to termination issues: these may be particularly salient for abuse survivors who have experienced a sense of loss in their childhood, either of significant others or of trust.

CAT in practice

Some of the key features of therapy have been outlined, so now a case is presented of a fairly straightforward example of CAT in practice. All names and identifying details have been altered in order to preserve confidentiality.

Case illustration: Caroline

Caroline was referred by her GP following several consultations in which she described bouts of weepiness, difficulty in concentration and suicidal thoughts. Psychotropic medication had been used with little effect. Caroline was a 26-year-old nursery nurse who lived with her boyfriend; the latter was known to the services as a casual drug user. Caroline did not use drugs, and had apparently always managed not to participate in unsafe sex with Dave. On her most recent consultation with the GP she revealed that she had been sexually abused when a child, and nervously accepted a referral to a psychologist to discuss this further.

When Caroline first attended, she appeared quiet and compliant. Her therapist asked her about her own history and requested her to complete the Psychotherapy File. It was noticeable that Caroline almost always wore black clothes to sessions except when she came after work wearing her nursing uniform. She completed the Psychotherapy File promptly, highlighting particularly the placation and social isolation traps. Her therapy lasted 16 weeks, including the four weeks prior to reformulation. Her initial depression scores using the Beck Depression Inventory were within the moderate to severe range.

After a few weeks of meetings, the therapist felt that she and Caroline had established a reasonable relationship, and the beginnings of an understanding of the snags and dilemmas which Caroline experienced. She was initially unwilling to talk much about the abuse by a neighbour, or about memories of her father who had since died, and an early separation from her mother. It was often hard to engage Caroline in therapy, and the therapist felt as if she were sometimes having to pull Caroline out of a withdrawn watchfulness. After four sessions, the following Reformulation Letter was given to Caroline, which she agreed was reasonably accurate.

Dear Caroline,

Over the past few weeks you have told me about yourself and how you feel that some of the events that happened when you were a child seem to have affected you to the present day. Your father died when you were seven years old in an accident at work, and you and your brother went to stay with an aunt who lived nearby while your mother tried to rebuild her life and career by moving away in order to cope with the loss. Despite knowing that the accident was not your responsibility, you always felt that your normal childish naughtiness must have somehow contributed to his accident and that your mother blamed you for the loss. Feeling guilty you tried to please the adults around you, and this included the aunt's elderly neighbour who then sexually assaulted you. It seemed to you that this was again your own responsibility, and that you could not tell your mother, who appeared to you to be vulnerable, and more in need of your protection than you were in need of hers. Not wishing to inflict your distress on her or your aunt, you continued to submit to the neighbour's abuse, which you felt to be deserved punishment, until he moved away following his own divorce.

You eventually moved back to live with your mother again, who was pleased that you were so easy to deal with, especially as your brother had difficulties at school. You learned that if you were a 'good girl' your mother was happy. It seemed that you must at all costs hide your 'bad' side. When you eventually left home, your boyfriend Dave started to demand that you accept his desire to have relationships with other women, which you accepted in your desire to please him. Nevertheless you felt distressed and angry, and on several occasions you contemplated suicide. You wanted to be funny and witty like his other friends, but often felt as if you were either worthless or bad. Despite all of this you were able to complete your training as a nursery nurse, and to make good relationships with the children you cared for, even if sometimes you found it difficult to feel comfortable with the other staff in the nursery.

It now seems as if you find your life a tremendous effort, and you feel trapped in a variety of ways:

(1) Hoping to please other people you try to do as you think they want, which eventually leaves you feeling abused and taken for granted. This happens particularly with Dave. This sometimes results in

> *your angry outbursts, which make you feel guilty and more con-vinced of your badness, and need to please other people.*
>
> *(2) Feeling low in confidence, you often choose to avoid people, and withdraw from social situations, as for example when you go out with Dave's friends. People then apparently assume you are not interested in them, and do not seek to include you in conversations. This proves to you that you are boring, which further reduces your confidence.*
>
> *(3) While you enjoy some things about your relationship with Dave, part of you feels uncomfortable with him. You also fear that he might reject you, as you feel you are not as easy-going as he wants. On the other hand, you are not sure you want to be like this any-way, but to assert your own view feels unacceptable, so you tend to submit to his views or risk being rejected and abandoned.*

> *In our sessions together I hope that we will be able to become aware when these patterns occur. They may also happen in therapy: for instance, you may find yourself wanting me to tell you how to think or do things, for fear I may think badly of you if you express your own views. Becoming aware of this will be the first step in trying to find other ways of improving yourself and your relationships with others. I look forward to working with you.*

Following this reformulation, Caroline and her therapist spent several sessions exploring the traps and dilemmas which they had both noted. Caroline observed how she tried to please people in many inappropriate ways, such as volunteering to stay behind at work and tidy the nursery after hours, which no one else did. As homework, Caroline monitored this. Together Caroline and her therapist then discussed ways in which she could set more appropriate lim-its. After six sessions they drew up a Sequential Diagrammatic Reformulation which described the reciprocal roles that appeared to represent Caroline's relationship patterns. This can be seen in Figure 5.1. There were two major reciprocal roles, the most dominant RRP being a powerful and dangerous other to a weak and abused self.

Caroline felt herself most often to be located in the weak state, and was afraid of asserting herself lest she behave in abusive dangerous ways. In addi-tion there was an abandoning, withdrawing other to an abandoned, sad and hurt self. Although her relationship with Dave was not very rewarding, at least she did not feel entirely abandoned by him, since she coped with the hurt she felt as a result of his affairs with other women, by withdrawing emo-tionally herself. She felt that this was less awful than the pain of his aban-doning her completely. There was also some hint of an idealised state in which a loving and ideal self reciprocated a loved and held self, but this was rarely accessed.

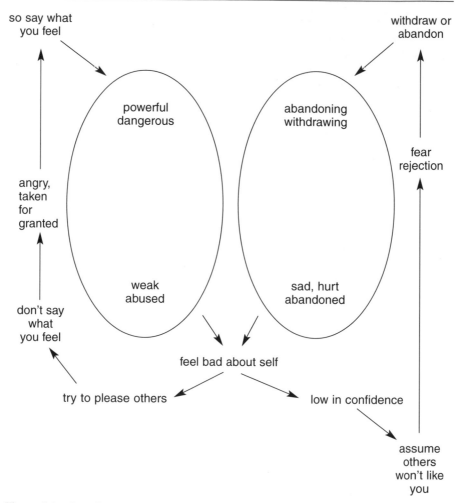

Figure 5.1   Caroline's Sequential Diagrammatic Reformulation

Procedures which linked these states were drawn out, and Caroline was encouraged to see how her attempt to avoid the pain of being responsible for harm led her to behave in weak and passive ways, which was easily taken advantage of by others. Her attempt to placate others was described as a procedure for avoiding responsibility for causing harm because of her assumed inner badness. This 'badness' was linked to her fear of being abandoned again which led her to accept Dave's behaviour, and either to blame herself for being so demanding, or withdraw in pain from any emotional contact. Caroline experienced a great deal of relief at seeing so clearly the patterns that underlay the feelings which had so long troubled and confused her.

For the following two or three sessions, Caroline and her therapist worked on devising more appropriate exits than her existing procedures of placation and avoidance. She tried to discuss with Dave how hurt she was by his behaviour, and how her response of emotional withdrawal meant that their subsequent relationship was even less rewarding for them both. The therapist also talked of how Caroline's passivity and withdrawal in the session had an impact on the therapy itself, and how Caroline's gradual exploration of her inner emotional world could allow her to take more risks in, but gain more from, relationships.

It then emerged in session nine that Caroline was still troubled by memories of the abuse which had occurred when living with her aunt. This happened most often when she was having sexual intercourse with Dave, an event which she disliked and avoided if possible. It further emerged that Dave was dependent on Caroline for money from her small income for his street drugs, which she did not use and disliked, but which seemed to guarantee his dependence on her. Despite the fact that she did not appear to obtain much happiness from her relationship with Dave, she felt both that she deserved little better, and that at least he would not leave her like both her mother and father had done. Therapy then turned to an examination of Caroline's fears of abandonment and her grief which she felt after her father died, and when her mother left her in the care of her aunt. Caroline wept openly about this, apparently for the first time, and started to express feelings of anger for both parents. By session 11, however, she said that she had visited her father's grave for the first time, and had spoken by telephone to her mother about her father's death. Her mother had told Caroline details of her father's accident that she had not known before, which made it even clearer that Caroline's sense of responsibility was inappropriate. The therapist drew attention to the SDR and how Caroline had managed not to follow her usual procedures of avoidance and self-blame, which delighted Caroline. She then drew a parallel with her experience of abuse, and how she now accepted that she had not been to blame for the abuse, and that if this was the case she could not have such a firm conviction in her own inner badness any more.

Between sessions 12 and 13, the therapist was off sick for two weeks, which Caroline found difficult. Her initial assumption was that somehow this was her own fault, which represented an enactment of her reciprocal role of dangerous and powerful (causing hurt) to a weak other (the sick therapist). The distress of this feeling then caused her to move into another role enactment, that of being the abandoned and hurt client reciprocating an abandoning and powerful therapist. She was able to tell the therapist how she felt both guilty and angry, and how this changed quickly into hurt and withdrawal. The therapist then used this re-enactment to explore Caroline's habitual responses to hurt, and how this had been replayed in therapy. They also discussed more appropriate and reality-based ways of dealing with incidents such as the therapist's illness, and how Caroline might recognise and prevent such triggers from plunging her into her hurt state in the future. This was explicitly linked by the therapist to the forthcoming termination of therapy.

The final three sessions concerned ways of maintaining Caroline's increased sense of self-esteem, and her self-knowledge. Throughout therapy she had completed weekly rating sheets concerning her unhelpful procedures, as detailed in the reformulation, and she was delighted to see how much she had improved. At session 15, the therapist gave her the Goodbye Letter, as follows:

Dear Caroline,

We are now approaching the end of therapy and I wanted to write down how I think we have progressed during therapy. We looked at how you have felt trapped in a pattern of trying to please people, especially Dave and your mother, and how this led you to feel taken advantage of, and hopeless about the future. We saw how as a child you had taken on responsibility for things that were not your responsibility, and having done this, how difficult it was to accept the care that your mother and aunt did try to offer. You felt either responsible, dangerous, blameworthy and powerful, or else weak and abused. Feeling responsible seemed so terrible that it seemed better to be weak and abused, but this too hurt. Seeking to avoid this pain you have tried to establish relationships, but you have felt afraid of being abandoned as happened when you were little. It appeared to us that as an adult, as well as when you were a child, the only way you could find a way out was to withdraw, avoid people, and to suppress your own needs and feelings. We saw how today that can lead you to avoiding saying what you really think for fear you might harm someone, choosing instead to stay quiet, although feeling angry inside. With me too you were initially rather withdrawn, as if waiting for me to tell you the right answers.

We also saw how sad you had been when your father died, and how you had never felt able to grieve for him for fear of upsetting (hurting) your mother. At the same time you hated feeling so vulnerable and hurt, and we wondered if your withdrawal from relationships sometimes resulted from a choice to be the one who puts up with things and withdraws, rather than be the one who is abandoned and hurt. We wondered how that might be replayed in your relationship with Dave, and how it also happened sometimes between us in therapy.

During therapy we also looked at how memories of the sexual abuse you told me you experienced as a child have continued to bother you, and we spent quite a few sessions looking at your feeling of badness and your sense of self-blame. Gradually you have been able to accept that the responsibility was not yours, and you have been able to accept that your way of coping was the best you as a child could devise at the time. You have also developed more confidence in your own value, and your qualities.

In addition, during therapy you began to question your relationship with Dave and the extent to which he had appealed to you maybe because he acted in a powerful and confident way, and relieved you of being responsible for anything. We also wondered if maybe your acceptance of whatever he does comes from fear of being left. You have questioned whether staying with him and accepting his way of life would ever succeed in making you happy: you are still thinking about this. My sense is that it will be important for you to continue to challenge the trap of trying to please, which we have been looking at, as well as the dilemma of feeling either responsible and to blame, or weak and powerless. Related to this is your fear of being abandoned that we thought might have led you to choose a partner who, although unreliable, does seem to need you. Maybe the choice is not as clear cut as this, and you do have a chance to take care of yourself without harming other people, or being hurt. We have noticed how with me you have become more confident in being able to express your feelings, and how nothing bad seems to result when you do this.

Therapy ended as planned after session 16. Although Caroline had been asked if she wished to write her own Goodbye Letter, she decided not to do so as things had been busy at work and at home, as she was planning a forthcoming fiftieth birthday party for her mother. The therapist accepted this both as a healthy sign of Caroline's decreasing need to please, and also as a form of rejection given the imminent termination of therapy by the therapist.

Follow-up

Three months after termination, Caroline attended for follow-up. She was wearing brightly coloured clothes for the first time and appeared much more relaxed than ever before. She reported having finally decided to leave Dave and to move in to share a flat with a girl friend. She still had feelings of self-doubt, and found it hard to accompany her girl friend on evenings out, but she was able to start to enjoy some interests of her own. Her relationships at work had improved as she no longer felt obliged to stay behind to help beyond her regular hours, and had agreed some limits with the nursery manager. She still felt apprehensive about the future, but memories of her sexual abuse rarely troubled her. Psychometric assessment using the Beck Depression Inventory (Beck *et al.*, 1961) revealed a score within the slightly elevated range, which was a significant improvement.

Overview

Caroline's therapy experience was reasonably typical of how a CAT therapist might address the difficulties of a childhood sexual abuse survivor, whose difficulties are not overwhelming. Most of the psychopathology observed is evident within level one of the MSSM (see Chapter 3), with little identity disturbance. Although issues of abuse and memories of abuse are addressed, they rarely form the most important focus of therapy. Rather, the reciprocal roles that are developed as the child grows up and which are enacted in the present form the focus of treatment. The sexual abuse is incorporated into the client's world through the relationships developed. Each client will therefore have evolved a unique set of meanings surrounding the abuse experience. Caroline's story showed how she became vulnerable to depression, impoverished emotional and sexual relationships, and a repeat in adulthood of an emotionally abusive relationship with Dave. In a brief, focused therapy not all these issues were addressed in detail, but the aim of CAT is to help clients to move on, or to 'unstick' them. The therapist has to be adaptable since no two clients are alike. Nevertheless some themes do tend to recur with abuse survivors: poor self-esteem, damaged ability to relate to others with appropriate assertion, and poor self-management skills. These have to be addressed while respecting both existing coping strategies and the survivor's ability to function well in many other areas of life.

Conclusion

At the start of this chapter we asked, why does childhood sexual abuse appear to be so devastating for the survivor's psychological adjustment in some areas and not others, and why do some survivors appear to be so vulnerable to relationship difficulties and further victimisation? We have suggested that the reciprocal roles first established in childhood and later elaborated via patterns of procedures may, for some survivors, result in vulnerabilities which can lead to self-harm and psychopathology, although this does not happen in survivors where coping responses are healthier. We also asked how therapy can help without causing yet more pain through questioning existing coping styles, and how the therapeutic relationship itself both reveals and helps to heal some of the pain. CAT therapists work collaboratively with clients, aiming to understand and support the client in developing awareness of procedures and replacing dysfunctional procedures with healthier ones, including those which occur in relationships such as the therapeutic relationship. In this way CAT addresses significant aspects of the abuse experience as it is revealed in therapy.

CHAPTER 6

SUE CLARKE AND SUE LLEWELYN

A case of borderline personality disorder

In this chapter we focus on childhood sexual abuse (CSA) survivors who, in addition to the problems outlined in the previous chapter, also experience profound difficulties in maintaining a stable and consistent sense of themselves, or their relationships with others. They may have entrenched interpersonal difficulties and a deep fear of abandonment. They may engage in impulsive or self-destructive behaviours and experience frequent fluctuations in their mood. Such clients are likely to fulfil the criteria for borderline personality disorder (BPD) (DSM-IV; American Psychiatric Association, 1994). Compared to survivors without borderline disturbance, their problems are more complex, severe and difficult to treat.

Having summarised the research findings that link CSA and BPD, we will describe the Multiple Self-States Model (MSSM; Ryle, 1997) of BPD and the general ways in which CAT practice needs to be adapted for this client group. This is followed by a discussion of a particularly damaging feature of BPD— revictimisation—and the way in which this may affect the therapeutic process. Throughout the chapter, clinical vignettes are used to illustrate the problems and processes. In the final section, we present an example of CAT in practice with a BPD male survivor. Some details and all names have been changed to preserve confidentiality.

Relation between BPD and CSA

Although both biological and environmental influences are considered to play a role in the origin of borderline disturbance (Linehan, 1993; van Reekum, Links & Boiago, 1993), research efforts have focused mostly on early experiences. Physical and sexual abuse repeatedly features in the histories of borderline clients (Ogata *et al.*, 1990) and is reported more frequently than it is by other clinical groups. Eighty-six per cent of borderline clients reported CSA, compared to 21% of other psychiatric inpatients (Bryer, Nelson, Miller & Kroll, 1987). CSA is reported by 67–87% of borderline outpatients (Herman, Perry & van der Kolk, 1989; Shearer, Peters, Quaytman & Ogden, 1990; van der Kolk, Hostetler, Herman & Fisher, 1994). This is in contrast to 26% among non-borderline outpatients (Herman *et al.* 1989). Although the link between CSA and BPD is now beyond question, it should never be assumed when it has not been reported. Even if therapists have good grounds to suspect a history of CSA, they should be respectful of conscious or non-conscious motivations that may prevent their clients disclosing.

BPD and the theoretical contribution of CAT

Most theoretical models of BPD acknowledge the importance of childhood trauma in the aetiology of the disturbance. They differ, however, in terms of the emphasis placed on traumatic experience versus biological vulnerability (cf. Ryle, 1997; Linehan, 1993). Models also differ in terms of the core component status assigned to different features of BPD.

According to the MSSM, BPD originates in a failure to integrate experience as a result of early trauma or neglect (Ryle, 1997). It is best understood as reflecting the changing dominance of a restricted range of partially dissociated, and sometimes extreme, self-states or reciprocal role procedures (RRPs). These RRPs determine the individual's management of the self and relationships with others. When RRPs are partially dissociated, the individual's sense of both themselves and others is unstable, discontinuous and fragmented. He or she has little or no sense of a stable identity, and emotional and social experience is constantly shifting. Dissociation originates in childhood trauma or neglect and inhibits two aspects of psychological development: (1) the metaprocedures that normally connect, coordinate and mobilise the RRPs are disrupted by exposure to unmanageable distress and/or incoherent and contradictory experiences; (2) the capacity to self-reflect is diminished.

The roles of dissociation

Dissociative processes are, therefore, at the core of the MSSM of BPD. The relationship between dissociation, CSA and BPD is now well established (Herman *et al.*, 1989, Ogata *et al.*, 1990). Dissociation refers to a splitting of experience: elements of the experience are not integrated into a unitary whole or a unitary sense of self (van der Kolk, van der Hart & Marmar, 1996). Dissociation occurs both during the traumatic event and post-traumatically (Chu & Dill, 1990). The continued use of dissociation also prevents the development of more adaptive ways of coping.

Dissociative processes enable abused children to cope with the immediate trauma. For example, Emma escaped from the reality of her abuse experience by psychologically leaving her body to be abused, while she retreated to a safe corner of the room. In another case, Jenny, having been told by her abusing father that sexual intimacy was reflective of their unique and secret relationship, denied the abusive reality of her experience by only permitting herself to acknowledge the special nature of their relationship. In both cases, the abused self and abusing other is denied as a defence against profound emotional distress and/or disillusionment.

The consequences of such protective strategies are that BPD survivors are unable to link their experience into a coherent whole, or provide an integrated account. This, in turn, has a profound effect on their emotional and social development and underlies the most damaging features of BPD. Dissociative tendencies are likely to diminish survivors' capacity to learn from experience or attribute responsibility correctly. The high rates of revictimisation (Clarke & Llewelyn, 1994; Clarke & Pearson, in press a), self-blame (Jehu et al., 1988) and self-harm (van der Kolk, Perry & Herman, 1991) found amongst CSA survivors may, in part, be explained in this way (see below).

Why do such tendencies persist into adult life? Once abused children have learned to dissociate in response to trauma, they tend to continue to do so in the face of subsequent stress. In adulthood, dissociation is reactivated and maintained by traumatic associations or further trauma (Ryle, 1997). Because BPD survivors have such a fragile identity, dissociative state switching may also occur as a result of non-reciprocation from another person. BPD survivors are likely to be unaware of the triggers to their dissociative symptoms or state switches. For example, Emma was unable to explain her sense of terror on entering an olive green-painted corridor until she recalled that the bedroom in which she had been abused was also olive green, a conditioned anxiety response. In another case, Trevor became scornfully dismissive whenever he failed to recruit an admiring response from someone he admired, a learned response that escaped scornful exposure.

CAT practice with BPD

The therapeutic goals outlined in Chapter 2, such as establishing a collaborative relationship, reattribution of blame and reformulation of symptoms, also apply to survivors with BPD. However, the primary aim of CAT with this client group is to enhance their ability to integrate their experience (Ryle,

1997). This should occur at three levels: (1) the integration of past experience into a coherent personal narrative; (2) the integration of behaviour, cognition and affect; and (3) the integration of the BPD survivors' sense of identity (Kennedy & Waller, unpublished). Although this process is likely to be a life-long task in traumatised individuals, CAT can make an important beginning, particularly with respect to enhancing survivors' self-cohesion.

Given the challenge of the task and difficulties establishing an alliance, BPD clients should be offered longer therapy contracts (24–30 sessions) than with less complex groups. The optimum number of sessions is often difficult to judge. For this reason, we sometimes contract for 12 sessions initially and then decide on the number of remaining sessions to offer. The primary focus of CAT with BPD clients is to develop their recognition of dissociated self-states and thereby enhance self-cohesion. With the exception of high-risk, self-harm-ing procedures (see below) or snags that may impede the therapeutic process, relatively less attention is given to the description or revision of target prob-lem procedures (TPPs) than with less complex cases. CAT has unique features specifically designed to facilitate integration such as the Reformulation Letter and the SSSD.

Reformulation

A central aim of this document is to construct a coherent narrative of sur-vivors' history in order to help them integrate past experiences and associ-ated memories and emotions. Present difficulties are understood in the light of their early experience. The tone of the letter should be tentative and, if possible, trial hypotheses should be offered during the session before being put in writing. Reformulation should always be a collaborative process and therapists should be willing to revise them in the light of new material. If therapists suspect that emotional or cognitive elements of their clients' expe-rience have been split off, this is best addressed by describing concrete exam-ples, rather than by interpretations of non-conscious motivation. In our experience, the latter may lead to BPD clients feeling misunderstood, blamed or even persecuted, whereas the former reassures them of their ther-apists' ability to acknowledge and accept the denied features of their experi-ence. The Reformulation Letter should end with a description of the ways in which survivors' difficulties may impede the therapeutic process, including snags, paying particular attention to potential threats to the therapeutic alliance (reciprocal role enactments). A well-constructed Reformulation Letter plays a crucial role in developing the therapeutic alliance. It models a process of reflective understanding of clients' difficulties, provides a thera-peutic focus and places the relationship with the therapist on the therapeu-tic agenda.

Clients may be overwhelmed by the most carefully written Reformulation Letter. Moreover, a list of TPs and TPPs can seem disjointed and fragmented. For this reason, we follow the main letter with a summary statement illustrating the interrelationships between the TPs and TPPs (see case example). The summary statement can also be revised and extended, in the light of new understandings.

Self-States Sequential Diagram

The second important CAT tool for this client group that serves to facilitate integration is the SSSD. This aims to develop clients' capacity for self-reflection and self-cohesion yet further. The cognitive component of this task is best achieved by an elegant description of the main self-states that govern the most problematic or high-risk procedures (see below). In most BPD cases, this will include abusing, idealised, cut-off and abandoning self-states. The development of the SSSD may begin in the first session with a very simple diagram. Colour coding RRPs and related procedures can help clarify the links and interconnections.

Self-cohesion is also enhanced interpersonally, by offering clients a corrective therapeutic relationship. As noted in Chapter 5, given the strong emotions attached to child abuse, non-CAT therapists may relate to just one end of the RRP and over-identify with either the victim role or abuser role. Understanding the reciprocal nature of the self-states helps therapists avoid this. Although some unhelpful reciprocation is inevitable, frequent reference to an accurate diagram reduces the possibility of therapists continuing to reinforce clients' existing reciprocal role repertoires. Inadequate diagrams that fail to describe clients' experiences should be reconsidered and revised as therapy progresses.

Work with this client group should always be supported by ongoing supervision. Given that therapists cannot report what they have not recognised, the use of audiotapes and transcripts is a valuable way of assessing the accuracy of diagrams. These can also provide detailed information on therapists' ability to identify RRP enactments optimally. Successful therapies with BPD clients are highly dependent on therapists identifying threats to the therapeutic alliance. Bennett (1999) has shown that therapists with good outcomes identified 83% of RRP enactments, compared to 34% identified in poor outcomes. The Therapist Intervention Coding (TIC) scales can be used to assess CAT competence. This empirically developed measure can be used to determine therapists' ability to identify content (history, current events, stories etc.) or process (transference, countertransference manifestations) links and relate these to, or revise, clients' diagrams (Bennett, 1999). Although the final version of this scale has not been published to date, an early version is available in Ryle (1997).

Termination

Abrupt and potentially traumatic terminations should be avoided by offering phased follow-ups. In our experience, about 50% of BPD survivors may require a second intervention. Group work can be an efficient and effective way of extending the insights developed and providing more time for revision. These may incorporate CAT formulations which focus on the survivors' abuse experience, or on particular difficulties associated with abuse (psychosexual or eating issues).

In the following section, we discuss the understanding and treatment of a very damaging feature of BPD: revictimisation (van der Kolk *et al.*, 1991).

Revictimisation

In Chapter 5 we outlined the process whereby abused children may internalise abusing to abused reciprocal roles and the implications of this for survivors' relationship with themselves (their intrapersonal, self-management procedures) and their relationships with others (their interpersonal procedures). We have found a reciprocal role framework to be invaluable in helping survivors understand the distressing phenomena of revictimisation, that is, the tendency to experience further abuse in adult life or to become abusive, either towards themselves or others. Although this tendency is well established amongst CSA survivors with borderline disturbance (Russell, 1986), recent research suggests that the form and function of revictimisation may be gender specific.

Gender-specific effects

Sexual abuse among the male population is now becoming more widely acknowledged, as men seek help to deal with abuse-related problems. Although it is generally accepted that prevalence rates for CSA are an underestimate for both sexes, males are believed to under-report to a greater degree than females (Dalkin, 1997). The reasons for this are thought to be cultural in that male socialisation discourages any show of vulnerability (Dimock, 1988). Male survivors may be reluctant to view themselves as victims, as this may be seen to undermine their masculinity (Dalkin, 1997).

Given the reluctance of male survivors to disclose their abuse, less is known about the long-term effects of CSA for men. Studies have described a number of sequelae that are common to women, such as self-blame, disturbances of self-esteem, PTSD, relationship difficulties and sexual compulsiveness (Dimock, 1988; Myers, 1989). However, they also include difficulties that are less frequently reported in women such as confusion about gender roles and sexual preferences, homophobia (Dimock, 1988; Myers, 1989) and excessive and uncontrolled aggression (Rogers & Terry, 1984).

In addition, it is commonly believed that male survivors are more likely to become abusers than female survivors are. Between 70% and 80% of adult male sexual offenders report being sexually abused as children (Longo, 1982; Gonsiorek, Bera & Le Tourneau, 1994). This finding should be treated with caution, however, given the lack of evidence concerning the proportion of male offenders that have not been abused. Nevertheless, female survivors are more likely to be victimised than to abuse, either by allowing themselves to be exposed to the abuse of others or by engaging in self-abusive behaviour (Russell, 1986; Fromuth, 1986; Clarke & Llewelyn, 1994; Waller, 1991). Such gender-specific effects suggest that men and women cope with their abuse experiences differently. Using repertory grids (Francella & Bannister, 1977), we conducted two small-scale patient series studies to assess the personal constructs of male and female survivors.

Our first study (Clarke & Llewelyn, 1994) was conducted with seven female survivors, all of whom showed borderline presentations and had revictimised either by self-harming or experiencing abusive relationships. With one exception, the women significantly identified with their child self or victim self and saw men in general as abusers before therapy. Thus their sense of themselves was predominantly as child-like victims. In addition, they had an expectation of abuse in relationships with men. Following CAT, this victim identification disappeared and the women showed a more positive identification with their ideal self. However, therapy had no impact on their construal of men. We argued that therapist gender might account for this lack of change, as the first author (SC) had again conducted the therapies. It may be difficult for a female therapist to have an impact on clients' construal of men.

The second study (Clarke & Pearson, in press b) was conducted with four male survivors, all of whom had revictimised by being physically or sexually abusive to women or children and two of whom were suicidal. All four men showed a borderline presentation; two also showed features of a narcissistic disturbance. In contrast to the female survivors, two of the men significantly identified with their abusers, rather than their child self or victim self. Moreover, those men who had histories of being abusive identified negatively with their victims, suggesting little acknowledgement of the damage they had done or identification with their own victim-hood. The men also showed a failure to identify with men in general.

CAT produced no change in the male survivors' identification with other men. Again, therapist gender may account for this lack of change, as the first author (SC) had conducted the therapies. However, the abuser identification disappeared after therapy. In addition, all of the men showed an increased identification with their victims following CAT. This change appeared to be confirmed by behavioural effects: two of the men reported dramatic reductions in their abusive treatment of women.

It is interesting to note that homosexual orientation appeared to be predictive of a paradoxical psychological effect in both studies. In our female survivor study, the only participant to identify with the abuser role was a bisexual woman who reported using her promiscuous relationships with men to taunt her female lover. Similarly, the only participant to identify himself as a victim in our male survivor study was homosexual; he had apparently rejected the stereotyped masculine abuser role. This interpretation should, however, be treated with caution given the small number of participants involved in these studies.

What are the theoretical and clinical implications of these two studies? Firstly, as we have noted in Chapter 5, survivors of childhood sexual abuse are not a homogeneous population. Cultural influences are likely to play an important role in determining how children cope and what they learn from sexually abusive experiences. Female survivors may be more likely to internalise a powerless victim role; male survivors may be more likely to internalise a powerful abuser role. We should, however, be mindful of the exceptions to these patterns. According to object relations theory (Ogden, 1983), each of these identification patterns necessitates a disavowal of the reciprocal role. Victim identification requires that the powerfully destructive aspects of the experience are disavowed or projected; abuser identification requires that the more helplessly vulnerable aspects of the experience be likewise denied. Given that a core component of borderline disturbance is personality fragmentation, an important role of therapy is to facilitate the integration of disowned facets of the survivor's personality. In other words, therapists should avoid an over-identification with either the victim self or abusing self. As we have noted before, this is best achieved by describing observable events, rather than interpreting hypothesised defences.

Secondly, therapist gender may influence the extent to which male or female survivors can change their perceptions of gender roles. Despite a growing awareness of female perpetration, it remains the case that the majority of abusers are men (Gonsiorek *et al.*, 1994). Although it may be easier for most survivors to engage with female therapists, changes in their construal of men may be more likely with a male therapist. Some preliminary data collected in our clinic (Clarke & Pearson, in press a) suggests that a resolution to this dilemma may be individual CATs, followed by survivor groups, co-facilitated by both a male and female therapist.

Suicidal ideation and self-harm

Suicidal or self-harming urges are another feature of revictimisation. The association between childhood sexual abuse, borderline disturbance and deliberate self-harm is well established (van der Kolk *et al.*, 1991). Given the 8–9.5% prevalence suicide rate for BPD (Stone, 1990; Paris, 1993)—comparable to that reported for psychosis—self-destructive tendencies should always be taken seriously and a risk assessment conducted as a matter of priority. This should include questions concerning the frequency of suicidal thoughts, the possibility of suicidal plans and factors that may prevent these from being enacted (see Maris, Berman, Maltsberger & Yuflt (1992) for a more thorough discussion of risk assessment). Having completed an assessment of risk, CAT therapists should then determine the intra- and interpersonal contexts in which self-harming urges or acts occur. These should be described fully as TPPs in both the Reformulation Letter and the SSSD.

In our experience, CAT therapists sometimes fail adequately to describe or understand self-harming procedures. This may be because such acts are so alien to therapists' personal experience that they challenge their ability to sustain a therapeutic stance, or because the description of self-harm evokes negative emotions (Dunn & Parry, 1997). Such avoidance by therapists has serious consequences, however. It communicates to clients that self-harm cannot be considered or discussed, which may reinforce their sense of shame and hopelessness (Favazza & Conterio, 1989). In addition, CAT therapists are less likely to be therapeutically disempowered by the associated risks of self-harm, when this has been described and understood.

Although there is a relative paucity of empirical work in this area, a general consensus exists that self-harm occurs for a variety of reasons. Differing theoretical accounts emphasise different functions. As each of these can inform our CAT understanding of self-harm, we shall provide a brief theoretical overview with clinical illustrations in the following section.

Psychodynamic explanations focus on attempts to deny, or ward off prohibited anger by turning it towards the self (Menninger, 1935). According to this model, self-harm serves the dual function of self-punishment and reparation. For example, Gemma felt powerless to resist the sexual demands of James, whom she described as being physically repulsive to her. At the same time, she recognised her dependence on him, both to provide a reassuring presence and to taxi her around. Gemma appeared to cope with this dilemma by becoming emotionally numb while having sex. Although this provided some short-term relief, sex was followed by flashbacks and olfactory hallucinations related to her CSA experience. At such times, Gemma felt guilty and shameful. This triggered an intense urge to burn her genitals. Once this was achieved, Gemma's self-disgust was purged.

Behavioural explanations (Linehan, 1993) stress the importance of the functional consequences of self-harm in terms of (1) attention or care and (2) escape from demands (interpersonal), or (3) tension relief (intrapersonal). Not understanding this can cause difficulties in therapy. For example, Julie was encouraged to attend therapy to help her cope with her CSA experiences.

From the onset of therapy, however, her flashbacks and nightmares had increased in frequency and Julie felt increasingly overwhelmed. She was unable to communicate her struggles to her well-meaning therapist, who continually stressed the benefits of disclosure. In desperation, Julie took a small overdose. Fearful that she might have harmed herself, she then told her therapist about her overdose by phone. Having organised medical care, her therapist expressed her concern and offered Julie additional sessions to cope with her elevated symptoms, hence rewarding the suicidal behaviour.

To date, the tension reduction account of self-harm is the only model that has been tested empirically. Haines, Williams, Brain and Wilson (1995) have shown that amongst self-harming male prisoners tension relief (measured by marked reductions in psychophysiological responding) accompanies the imaginal presentation of self-harming incidents. Dissociative processes—which may be identifiable at a physiological level as production of an endogenous analgesic, endorphin—play a key role in the tension relief hypothesis. Prospectively, dissociation is a predictor of both self-harm and of suicide attempts (van der Kolk *et al.*, 1991). Clinical observations suggest that self-harm may served the dual function of inducing, and obtaining relief from, dissociative states.

For example, Harriet's frustration increased steadily throughout the day. First, she had an unresolved misunderstanding with her sister. Then a delayed train made her late for her therapy session, which was shortened as a consequence. As her tension increased, self-harming urges and images increasingly preoccupied her. Cutting was a well-established routine that had reliably relieved distress for a number of years. On entering her flat, she went straight to her source of razors. Harriet felt no physical pain whilst cutting and her distress eased on seeing her blood. She spent the remainder of the evening in a numb state, until she retired to bed emotionally and physically depleted.

In another case, John, who had experienced agoraphobia for years, experienced a panic attack while waiting to see his psychiatrist. On his return home, John became preoccupied by the possibility that the psychiatrist had ridiculed him. He felt insignificant, vulnerable and exposed, emotions that were reminiscent of those he experienced while being subjected to his father's scornful abuse. As his distress increased, John felt increasingly unreal, disoriented and cut off from his surroundings, which faded visually. He described this experience as if he were trapped in a vast tunnel, the only way out being the established exit of self-harm. By this time, he was fixated by his urge to self-harm. He experienced no physical pain while cutting, but began to feel more real and connected with his surroundings as he watched his blood flow.

This overview illustrates that self-harm occurs for a variety of reasons. In our opinion, to describe self-harm merely as an enactment of an abusive self-state oversimplifies the potential range of functions it can serve and has little prescriptive value.

We shall now present an example of CAT in practice with a male survivor with borderline personality disorder in order to illustrate some of the treatment issues described above.

Case illustration: Mark

Mark, an attractive 35-year-old man, had been admitted to a psychiatric hospital for depression and suicidal ideation six months before his referral for CAT. Since this time, he had been prescribed antidepressants and was living in sheltered accommodation. The referral letter mentioned a CSA disclosure that Mark had made during his hospital admission.

Mark failed to attend his CAT first session, but responded to a follow-up appointment. He said that he had been feeling desperate since the break-up of his marriage two years previously, when his wife disclosed that she was having an affair and he had attempted to harm her lover. Following a short prison sentence, he moved to another part of the country. He felt unable to make contact with his daughters while he continued to have vengeful fantasies about his wife's lover. He described having mood swings (from depressed and hopeless to rage) and self-harm by cutting at least once a week.

Although Mark had considered suicide prior to his hospital admission, the hope that he might resume his relationship with his daughters prevented him from doing so. He had recently overdosed on his medication, in an attempt to get some prolonged sleep. On occasions, Mark also drank alcohol to excess and abused drugs. This had caused some problems at the hostel, where he was expected to remain abstinent and participate in residential activities. Mark thought it unreasonable that he should not be allowed to stay in his room and listen to his music. Mark's behaviour had caused a number of verbal disputes with other residents and staff and he had been told that his continued placement was dependent him being more compliant.

Mark's mood appeared flat and the therapist noted that there was a strong smell of alcohol on his breath. She suggested that his missed appointment and apparent need to drink might reflect his difficulty attending the session. Mark replied that he attended his appointment only because he had been told to do so. The therapist wondered if feeling resentful in response to the demands of others appeared to be a familiar pattern for Mark. She suggested that it might be easier for him to make an informed decision about his commitment to therapy, if he had some understanding of what it involved. She outlined the framework of CAT, explaining that it required him to be actively involved in developing understandings. This would require that his thoughts and feelings were not dulled by alcohol, and that both she and he did not repeat his 'defiant to demanding' patterns in their sessions together. To her surprise, Mark reassured her he wanted to continue with therapy and would remain sober.

Although he failed to attend the next session, he then requested another appointment.

Mark began his second session with a muffled apology, saying that he spent the week feeling conflicted about therapy. The therapist applauded his efforts to attend and invited him to discuss his concerns. Mark said that he had spent the week drinking. Although he recognised his need for help, he had vowed to himself that he would never let anyone get close. When the therapist suggested that this concern was understandable given his early experiences, Mark became noticeably withdrawn. She explained that in order to help him, she would need to know something about his history, adding that her aim was to understand how his past related to his present difficulties, rather than to ask him to describe traumatic events before he was able to cope with this. Mark seemed reassured by this.

With respect to his early childhood, Mark was a reluctant historian. He briefly told the therapist that he had experienced both emotional and physical abuse from both of his parents. These experiences were described without any associated emotion. When the therapist noted that no mention was made of Mark's sexual abuse experience, he said firmly that he was not prepared to discuss this. The therapist suggested that cutting off from his distress enabled him to cope with these experiences as they occurred. She noted the absence of emotion in his account and suggested that he continued to blank out feelings associated with the memories. Mark nodded.

He had less difficulty describing his early adult life and appeared eager to impress or amuse the therapist with his anecdotes of risqué adolescent gang life and criminal activities. His accounts of behaving aggressively were coupled with reassurances that these were not his 'true self'. The therapist noted his difficulty accepting his abusive tendencies but suggested that—just as he had learned to cut off from his own distress—he had also learned to detach himself from the distress of others. She began to illustrate these diagrammatically in terms of abusive to abused and cut-off states. As the therapist suspected that Mark might withdraw from therapy, the following Reformulation Letter was presented in the third session. At this time, the summary sheet only described the difficulties numbered 1–4. The remaining descriptions (5–6) were added at a later stage in therapy.

Dear Mark,

You came to see me feeling at the depths of despair. You were overwhelmed by painful emotions attached to the breakdown of your seven-year marriage and the loss of your wife and two young daughters. You described your sense of shock, betrayal and rage at Linda's affair, your threats to kill her lover, Ben, and the resultant prison sentence. As this vengeful rage continued to preoccupy you following your release from prison, you decided to move to another part of the country in an attempt to put some safe distance between yourself and your past. Although this strategy has prevented you from acting out your rage towards Ben, your sense of utter despair, hopelessness and failure continues to haunt you.

Helplessness in the face of injustice and abuse is a familiar theme in your life. You grew up in a family of four children. As the eldest son, you were expected to take responsibility for the younger children. When things went wrong, you took the blame. This took the form of violent verbal and physical attacks, from both of your parents. You have also briefly disclosed the fact that your father sexually abused you. This undoubtedly served to confirm your sense of yourself as helplessly vulnerable in a brutal world. For this reason, you learned to cut off from your vulnerability and terror and empowered yourself with anger. You would vent your rage on objects or other people. This led to further beatings from your father which in turn hardened your defiant defence.

Your teenage years were spent re-enacting your family script. You led a gang, which vented its anger on more vulnerable young men. Your male friends respected you for your tough brutality. By the time you were 18 the tables had turned on your father—you both knew he would never get the better of you again. You resented any form of demand from others. So you walked in and, defiantly, out of a series of jobs. Any source of frustration was an opportunity to pick a fight. You described living off anger—it was a source of energy and power. At the time, you had no sense of compassion for your victims. Only later would you feel guilt or remorse for the damage you had inflicted.

A road traffic accident brought this lifestyle to an abrupt end. Linda nursed you while you were recovering in hospital and, for the first time, you discovered that you could be cared for. Within six months you had married. Although you worked exceptionally hard to be good enough for her, you could never convince yourself of your worthiness. In addition, your resentment and sense of defiance grew as you sacrificed your drinking and fishing trips to meet Linda's demands to invest in the home. Your relationship became more hostile and verbally abusive. When you discovered her affair, you resorted to your old ways of coping. Feeling abused and betrayed you threatened abuse. This was followed by the loss of your marriage and your imprisonment.

Perhaps this is why you now withdraw from the world to cope. In an attempt to dull the pain and block out the memories, you have taken to drink and drugs. The relief is only brief, however, and is followed by a compulsion to harm yourself by cutting or overdosing. The seriousness of your self-harming behaviour resulted in a referral to me.

Initially you attended therapy because you were told to do so. During the past two weeks, I have been impressed by your efforts. Your sexual abuse remains so profoundly distressing that you have only been able to allude briefly to this. We will need to be mindful of your need to pace yourself and avoid repeating some of your old patterns of relating in our relationship. For example, you may try to please me but then feel resentful of my demands, become defiant or leave therapy prematurely. I suspect that your missed sessions with me following my requests for sobriety may have reflected this pattern. You have expressed a long-standing belief that relationships inevitably lead to disappointment or abuse. I sense that you are beginning to trust me, but I also suspect that your desire to attend our sessions is coupled with anxiety about being vulnerable with me.

During the next few weeks, we can work together to develop shared understandings of your difficulties and begin to identify some ways you might begin to relieve your distress. I shall look forward to this opportunity.

Summary

Because my childhood was characterised by violence and abuse, I learned to cut off from my helpless vulnerability and terror and use anger to empower myself. It seems as if I am:

1. Either a powerful and violent brute, or a helpless victim.

In the past, I empowered myself with rage for protection. More recently, I keep my distance from others to avoid conflict or disappointment. But my life has no meaning and seems empty. The attempts of others to encourage me to reinvest in life feel like unmanageable demands. I cope by becoming defiant.

2. If I must, then I won't.

Sometimes others withdraw in response to my defiance. My mind is filled with memories of the past and I feel overwhelmed by hopeless despair and loneliness.

3. I attempt to fill the void with drugs and drink.

Although this brings temporary relief, feelings of loss, anger and vengeful fantasies break through. Reminded of my past aggressive acts, I feel shameful and guilty.

4. In an attempt to punish myself for my destructive thoughts and acts, I vent my anger on myself by self-harming. This provides some relief by making me numb and occasionally recruits professional care.

However, the effects of self-harm are short lived and my distress breaks through again. It seems as if my life is doomed to fail, as if

5. I am inherently unworthy of success or attachments.

I constantly anticipate disappointments and failure. Sometimes this snag becomes self-fulfilling. At other times,

6. I feel I have to put 100% effort into everything I do—I must perform perfectly.

I cannot sustain this, however, and become depleted and resentful that my efforts are not acknowledged or reciprocated.

Mark described the letter as being accurate and said that he felt both unnerved and saddened by it. Its presentation marked a somewhat idealised phase of therapy. Mark's self-harming urges diminished. He read the letter every night and showed it to all the members of staff at his hostel. He began voluntary work for the homeless, working 12-hour shifts and organised fishing trips for the hostel residents. The therapist noted the marked shifts in Mark's presentation from untrusting and withholding to disclosing personal information about himself; from passively withdrawn to frenetically active and social. She reminded him of the similarity to his description of his efforts to please his wife and suggested the possibility of let-down, disappointment and exhaustion were he to sustain these expectations of himself. A description of his idealising procedure was added to this Reformulation Letter (6) and perfectly caring, performing roles were added to his diagram, noting that these also applied to his current expectations of therapy.

This idealised phase ended around the sixth session, when Mark's fishing partner took a serious overdose and was admitted to hospital. Mark felt angry and disappointed with him. The therapist suggested that he may have been reminded of his own vulnerability, but Mark denied this. Another resident at the shelter had received a visit from his daughter. Mark felt envious and this triggered vengeful thoughts about his wife's lover. Mark noted the accuracy of the abusing role on his diagram, although he felt uncomfortable with this description. During the weeks that followed, he reported dreaming about his family, spending more time alone and a re-emergence of his self-harming urges. His diary showed that these followed hopeless despair about the loss of

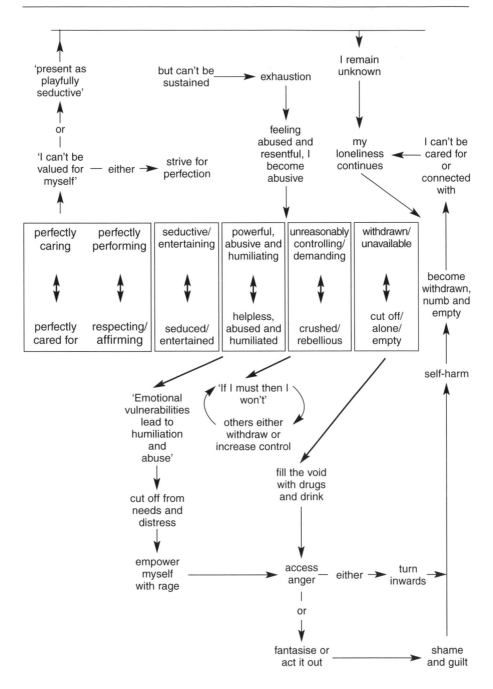

Figure 6.1 Mark's Self-States Sequential Diagram

his family. Despair led to drinking, which disinhibited vengeful fantasies. These led to self-blaming and self-shaming thoughts about his violent tendencies, which in turn led to self-harming urges. In the past, self-harm was followed by emotional relief and a sense of having purged himself from guilt. On some occasions, it also led to professional care. A detailed description of his self-harming procedure (4) was added to the summary sheet of Mark's Reformulation Letter.

Although reports of vengeful and violent fantasies towards others also featured in his therapy sessions, Mark was reluctant to bring accounts of his despair to therapy. Whenever the therapist attempted to focus on distressing issues, Mark became playfully defiant. For example, he would change the subject with a wry smile, fantasise about running away or winning the lottery. The therapist repetitively identified such incidences as attempts to divert them both from his distress. She included an entertaining-to-entertained role on his diagram, noting that the cost of this was that he failed to learn that he could be accepted for himself or recruit care for his distress. Mark's entertaining presentation continued intermittently, nevertheless.

During the ninth session, Mark revealed that he had been unable to discuss his childhood experiences with Linda, or allow himself to be known by her. Further discussion indicated that his inability to disclose his CSA experiences stemmed from the threats these posed to his manliness. The therapist suggested a parallel in his relationship with her, noting the possibility of a missed opportunity for a different experience in therapy.

Accounts of angry outbursts with others characterised the sessions that followed. When the therapist inquired whether Mark might be angry at her, he denied this, adding that he never felt angry with women. He acknowledged, however, that his defiant role might account for his reluctance to complete his homework. He also reminded the therapist that he had not self-harmed throughout his therapy. In an attempt to simplify the task of monitoring his RRPs and procedures, these were colour-coded during the session. While they were doing this, Mark acknowledged a conflict between his need for care and expectations of abuse. When the therapist linked this to the therapy processes, Mark discussed his concerns about the termination. On leaving the 13th session, he gave the therapist a hug.

Mark completed his diaries the following week and these showed an improvement in his recognition of his colour-coded state shifts and procedures. He was difficult to engage in the session, however. He whistled throughout the therapist's suggestion that his concerns about termination or the meaning of his hug should be discussed. The therapist identified the defiant role on his map, noting his continued ambivalence about the demands of therapy. She also noted, to herself, her sense of being rendered therapeutically helpless throughout the session. As Mark left the room, he briefly reached out to stroke the back of the therapist's neck.

Mark began the next session by disclosing self-harm following a drinking binge. He was unable to recall the precipitating events, however. The therapist referred to his parting gesture the previous session and suggested that, given his history, it would be understandable if he misconstrued her efforts as an invitation for physical intimacy. Pointing to the *abuser-to-abused* RRP, she suggested that his sense of vulnerability, in relation to herself, may be intolerable and that his attempts to engage her sexually may represent his need to redress the balance of power. She reminded him of his comment that he could not be angry with women. Although Mark initially laughed at this suggestion, he later disclosed that his self-harming act had followed sexual thoughts about the therapist and guilty feelings. A *seducer-to-seduced* RRP was placed on his diagram.

This session appeared to mark a more productive phase of therapy. During the weeks that followed, Mark used his colour-coded diagram daily to recognise his state shifts and procedures, occasionally managing to pre-empt them. Although Mark's CSA was not described during the entire therapy, he was able to discuss the long-term legacy of this experience. He disclosed traumatic nightmares and his attempts to diminish these with drugs and alcohol. He also discussed his long-standing concerns about his sexuality. He began to recognise that he publicly inflated his masculine power in an attempt to conceal his private doubts. Although this insight helped Mark acknowledge the damage he had caused others without punishing himself by self-harm, he noted that he could never forgive himself for some events. For this reason, some time was spent discussing the possibility of Mark completing a long-distance pilgrimage as a penance, in an attempt to reconcile himself with his past destructive acts. Mark said that he would plan this following therapy. He also expressed some ambivalence about the possibility of change, as if claiming a new life implied a betrayal of the love he felt for his daughters.

Understandably, Mark's anger concerning the injustice of his early life continued, as did his concern that he might act this out. He recognised both his progress and his continued vulnerability. Although the description of his experience in terms of RRPs had enabled him to think more clearly about himself than before therapy, on some occasions the dominant states continued to be his only sense of reality. Mark described mixed feelings about the ending of therapy. On the one hand he felt relieved, but on the other hand he now had a painful awareness of his potential to relapse without support. For this reason, phased follow-up appointments were offered and the Goodbye Letter focused on his 'snags'. During the final session, the therapist noted a quiet sense of intimacy in the room. The Goodbye Letter was as follows:

Dear Mark,

We have now come to the end of our session together and it is time to say our mutual goodbyes. Although our time together has been brief, I think you have begun to make some significant changes during the last few months.

When I first saw you, you were overwhelmed by powerful feelings concerning the break-up of your marriage. Sometimes you were consumed by rage and intent on revenge: to you, your wife was a bitch and her lover a bastard whom you wanted to kill. At other times, you blamed yourself for being unworthy of her. As you swung from rage to inadequacy your anger was either directed outwards or inwards. We began to recognise that beneath this anger was an unbearable sense of vulnerability and sadness about your life. With the aid of your diagram, you began to recognise the self-defeating nature of your struggle to avoid your human vulnerability and need, by hiding behind your rage.

We also began to recognise that you had other ways of keeping yourself and others distant from your emotional distress. When we got close to this, you would try to divert our focus by attempts to entertain or flirt with me. You recognised this as your 'one of the lads' role. Although this enabled you to keep others distant while relating on a superficial level, you never felt appreciated for yourself or cared for. As I declined your invitation to relate in this way, you risked being known by me and became aware of the possibility that you could be accepted for yourself. This has enabled you to acknowledge your need for friendships and you now take small risks in relationships outside of therapy. You have pursued your fishing interests and begun to find some enjoyment in life. We both recognise, however, how difficult it is for you to do this. Three important factors restrict your progress.

The first of these is your tendency to rubbish anything that isn't perfect. Sometimes, you avoid any challenge or demand because, if you can't do it perfectly, it's not worth doing. The second factor is the sense of betrayal you experience when you recognise any satisfaction in your current life, as if loving your daughters and claiming any current happiness is incompatible. The third factor is your deep sense of badness and desire to punish yourself for your past behaviour.

You have begun to make small steps in overcoming these snags. You're trying to acknowledge the value of being 'good enough' rather than perfect. You are just beginning to accept your right to claim some satisfaction in your current life. You now recognise that the possibility of a future relationship with your daughters is dependent on your beginning to move forward. You also acknowledge the very damaging effect that your self-harming behaviours and suicidal tendencies could have on your daughters. We have recently discussed the possibility of your obtaining some peace or self-forgiveness for your past acts by completing a pilgrimage, or some other form of reparation ritual.

> *Saying 'goodbye' to each other will undoubtedly stir feelings of loss. You have expressed a sense of feeling unprepared for the ending of therapy and vulnerable. We both recognise that our sessions represent the beginning of an incomplete process. During our brief time together, however, you have begun to change. Your self-harming urges have diminished considerably. You are beginning to be more understanding and accepting of yourself and make some small claims on a happier life with a few friendships. We both recognise that it will be difficult for you to maintain your progress on your own. When you feel you are struggling, it might be helpful to remind yourself of our time together, read my letters and reflect on your map. You will also need to be mindful that your three snags do not undermine your efforts.*
>
> *Although I shall miss our sessions, I recognise that it is timely for you to try and consolidate your progress on your own. I shall look forward to our follow-up meetings during the next few months.*

Mark attended four follow-up sessions, at one, three, six and nine months. He had maintained his progress; he was beginning to form some trusting relationships with other men and was planning to live independently. At his final follow-up, he requested a referral to a group of male survivors of sexual abuse.

Mark's progress was confirmed by a series of self-report questionnaires completed before and after therapy, and at nine-month follow-up. These included the Millon Clinical Multiaxial Inventory III (MCMI-III; Millon *et al.*, 1994), a 175-item measure that assesses Axis II disorders (using DSM-IV criteria; American Psychiatric Association, 1994); the Dissociation Questionnaire (DIS-Q; Vanderlinden *et al.*, 1993), a 63-item measure of dissociation; the Personality Structure Questionnaire (PSQ; Pollock *et al.*, 2001; see also Chapter 12), an eight-item measure that assesses personality integration, and the Symptom Check List (SCL-90-R; Derogatis, 1983), a well-known assessment that provides a general measure of symptomatic disturbance (Global Severity Index; GSI). Higher scores reflect higher levels of disturbance for all these measures. Mark's BPD score on the Millon decreased after therapy (94, 61). Although it increased slightly at follow-up (65), it remained below the threshold for BPD (85). Without exception, Mark's scores on the remaining assessments showed a consistent decline during the three assessments: DIS-Q, 3.03, 2.32, 1.41; PSQ, 39, 37, 22; GSI, 2.93, 1.82 and 1.39.

Overview of therapy

This therapy demonstrated that BPD survivors like Mark can achieve some integration of past experiences, affect and sense of identity, without CSA experiences being described in detail. It is possible that Mark would have been unable to cope with more focused attention to his CSA experiences, and that this may have precipitated him leaving therapy prematurely, or acting impulsively. As it was, CAT led to measurable improvements in Mark's BPD disturbance, personality integration, and dissociative and general symptomatology. This laid some important foundations for Mark to then embark on some trauma work, if he so chose. Throughout this and the previous chapter, we have argued that, although CSA survivors share common features, they are not a homogeneous group. For this reason, individualised formulations are required that can identify the disavowed features of survivors' experience and personality, as first steps towards facilitating integration. The Object Relations framework and unique formulatory tools of CAT are well suited to this task. Throughout the therapy, reformulations and diagrams should be regarded as a provisional hypothesis, to be tested and refined on a session-by-session and moment-by-moment basis. For BPD survivors, the healing process cannot be hurried and may require a series of therapeutic experiences. The theoretical coherence, structure and relationship focus of CAT provide an invaluable contribution to this end.

CHAPTER 7

A case of dissociative identity disorder

Dissociative identity disorder (DID; DSM-IV, American Psychiatric Association, 1994), formerly multiple personality disorder (MPD; DSM-III-R, 1987), is the most extraordinary psychopathological condition, to the extent that professional scepticism that it exists at all has been continuous over many years (Dell, 1988; Hilgard, 1994; Ross, 1998) and where Seltzer (1994) claimed the condition to be a 'psychiatric misadventure'. The diagnosis constitutes the presence of two or more distinct identities or personality states, at least two of which recurrently take control of the person's behaviour, accompanied by an inability to recall important personal information that is too intensive to be explained by ordinary forgetfulness (DSM-IV, 1994). Substance misuse or organic conditions do not account for these features for the diagnosis to be made. Secondary signs and symptoms include 'voices' talking or coming from inside the person, a sense that another persona is taking control, amnesia for childhood events, blank spells, flashbacks to childhood incidents of trauma, being told by others of unremembered events, feelings of unreality and other dissociative symptoms such as depersonalisation (feeling like one is in a dream or detached from one's own body), derealisation, trance and possession states (Loewenstein, 1991).

Persons with DID are also documented to experience affective symptoms, sexual dysfunctions, auditory hallucinations, substance abuse and to be the most self-destructive diagnostic group (Coons et al., 1988; Armstrong & Loewenstein, 1990; Ross, 1998). Therefore psychiatric co-morbidity is very common and neurological conditions are also observable for a subgroup of DID patients (Brown, 1994). As a true diagnosis, its prevalence is debated, yet clinical investigations of series of patients diagnosed as DID have been undertaken across cultures (Boon & Draijer, 1993; Sar, Yargic & Turkin, 1996; Putnam et al., 1986; Coons et al., 1988; Ross, Norton & Wozney, 1989). The accusation that misdiagnosis is common (Kluft, 1991) and the controversy surrounding whether DID exists at all have complicated our understanding of this extreme condition of personality dysfunction, partly due to the complexity of the clinical picture associated with DID and difficulties building theoretical models to inform treatment (Putnam, 1989).

When treatment is provided, DID patients appear to fare well and improve significantly depending on the clinical status of the case (Ellason and Ross, 1997). Horevitz and Loewenstein (1994) suggest that three groups of DID patients exist. The first are high-functioning patients who show little personality disorder co-morbidity, can master affect, control dysphoria and engage well within the therapeutic relationship. Secondly, DID patients with complicated co-morbidity, especially BPD, and complex PTSD symptoms are less amenable to treatment, and the third group are termed enmeshed patients who currently live in continuously abusive relationships and destructive lifestyles. A gradation in response to psychotherapy can be expected based on the complications within these cases of DID.

Patients with DID provide accounts of severe identity disturbances, discontinuity and confusion in their sense of self, and curious experiences due to disruptions of consciousness, memory and emotion (e.g., finding oneself in a location without any memory for travelling, being unable to recognise family members, being informed of behaviour not remembered due to amnesia, *déjà vu* experiences and a sense of unreality). Cohen, Giller and Lynn (1997) have published an interesting and insightful volume of poems, writings and other forms of self-expression made by DID patients describing the subjective reality of the condition, one patient referring to her sense of her identity as a 'frightened puzzle', another claiming that she felt that she resembled 'fragments shattered like broken glass, some edges sharp, poised to cut and wound, to strike out, others dull, no glint, unpolished, flat, lifeless'. The inner experience of the DID patient appears to be a confusing experience, perceiving oneself as populated by distinct, separate identities of which one has little knowledge or control over, accompanied by bizarre and distressing physical and psychological symptoms.

Separate identities, referred to as 'alter personalities', with unique personality characteristics including names, ages, behaviour patterns, moods, habits and talents (Coons *et al.*, 1988) are reported. These characteristics can include typical intense affective states such as anger, depression, and suicidal and self-abusive urges. 'Functional' alters have been reported, for example, a 'protector' or 'rescuer', 'persecutor' or 'destroyer', 'helper' or 'comforting dead relative' alters. The presence of each alter is indicated by distinctive changes in accent, voice, dress and demeanour, with associated features including differing handwriting or signatures and bilingualism (Lewis *et al.*, 1997). Ross *et al.* (1989) report child alter personalities to be most common (86% of 236 cases), with 'protector' (84%) and 'persecutor' (84%) alters also evident, the median number of alters present being two personalities at the time of diagnosis. Putnam, Post and Guroff (1986) also describe child alters to be prevalent in 100 DID patients, with the number of alters ranging from one (termed a 'dual' personality) to 60 (median of 9, mode of 3). Switches between personalities are usually spontaneous, with a wide range of ages recorded for the first appearance of the alter (range 1–32 years, median of 4). Psychopathological states (depression, mood swings, suicidal ideation) and physical symptoms (headaches, unexplained pain, gastrointestinal disturbances) are specific to different alter personalities. Awareness of alter personalities tends to be varied, with continuous awareness of alters in some cases and total amnesia occurring in other cases. Conflict between alters has been expressed as an 'internal homicide', reported by approximately half of the cases in the Putnam *et al.* study.

Conceptualising DID has been dominated by two main theories. It has been argued that traumatic childhood experiences are efficient external causes for severe identity fragmentation, dissociative processes and symptoms to occur after the abusive episode or event has ended, but becoming a habitually employed defensive response by the victim to deal with psychological pain and distress (Elliott, 1997; Gershuny & Thayer, 1999). DID can be considered to be an extreme response to trauma during development whereby the victimised individual creatively survives by escaping the psychological or physical pain by altering consciousness (e.g., memory, attention) with short- and long-term effects on identity integration.

Objective evidence supports the relationship between different forms of childhood abuse, dissociation and the diagnosis of DID (Wilbur, 1984). Putnam *et al.* (1986) report that 68% of 100 cases of DID experienced physical and sexual abuse (incest in 68% of cases, repeated physical assaults in 75%). Ross *et al.* (1989) document 88% of 236 DID patients to have reported either physical or sexual abuse. Convincingly, Lewis *et al.* (1997) discovered objective records of severe abuse in 11 of 12 cases of DID patients charged with murder, concluding that the study 'established, once and for all, the lineage between early severe abuse and dissociative identity disorder' (p. 1703). Ross (1998) critically reviews the trauma model of DID, with clear recommendations for scientific scrutiny of this model, acknowledging that the trauma and socio-cognitive models (the alternative theoretical stance to understanding DID) suffer from three main deficits, including ideological and anecdotal rather than scientific evidence, both models being viewed as mutually exclusive and a lack of scientific experimentation conducted to support either perspective. It is likely that each case of DID is a mixture of different influences and aetiologies which vary substantially.

The Multiple Self-States Model and DID

The MSSM of CAT defines the condition of DID to be at the most extreme end of the spectrum of dissociation and identity disturbance, with BPD an intermediate condition which features a lesser degree of dissociative pathology (Shearer, 1994; Pollock *et al.*, 2001), specifically amnesia between separate, distinct self-states. Alter personalities with amnesic barriers represent, theoretically, the most severe end of trauma-induced personality fragmentation (Ryle, 1997). Pollock *et al.* suggested that DID patients do demonstrate greater evidence of dissociation than BPD patients and normal personalities, yet the contention that fragmentation into multiple selves is greater for BPD than DID patients was not entirely supported (see Chapter 12). Therefore, DID appears to be a more severe dissociative condition than BPD but the presence of amnesic barriers and the configuration of alters may indicate an extreme means of achieving less identity fragmentation. It is concluded that different influences are relevant for BPD and DID when applying the MSSM, in that the BPD patient suffers from multiple, partially dissociated self-states whereas the DID patient suffers from extreme pathological and disabling dissociation and lesser fragmentation itself. Of course, it could be argued that if a DID is amnesic for other alters then confusing multiplicity is not subjectively experienced. The BPD patient may be the most unstable form of disorder for differing reasons to the DID patient. CAT should aim, therefore, to diminish reliance and influence upon dissociative processes and symptoms in DID patients to promote integration.

Within the MSSM as applied to DID, disruption is most notable at levels two and three. At level two, dissociation is extreme and segregation into discrete self-states has become so pervasive that self-states have become perfused with amnesia and transformed to separate alter personalities. An *idealised protecting* in relation to *rescued, nurtured* RRP within a self-state may become the 'protector' alter, a self-state consisting of *persecuting, tyrant* in relation to *abused, angry* representing a 'persecutor' alter. Amnesia occurs between self-states and within the two reciprocal roles (states of mind) of the dominant RRP. Compartmentalisation and splitting are complete and encompassing at level two. Awareness of switches or shifts is absent or dramatically impaired in DID because of amnesia. At level three of the MSSM, self-reflection is also severely compromised between self-states due to dissociation and pronounced switching between self-states.

Ross (1998) has proposed that successful integration of DID patients during psychotherapy should not attempt necessarily to decrease the number of personalities of identities (or self-states in CAT) but to limit the conflict and switching between them, promoting 'co-consciousness' between identities through 'blending' of self-states, decreasing symptomatic distress and interpersonal dysfunction. Horevitz and Loewenstein (1994) describe the *rational* treatment of DID patients to be based on three phases: (1) stabilising the patient; (2) addressing trauma and resolution of the patient's reliance upon dissociative defenses; and (3) integration of other personalities with post-integration interventions. The process of CAT and its main objectives show a number of similarities with these three phases, particularly stabilising the patient's experiences, feelings and behaviour and integration of dissociated aspects of identity. Coons (1984) described six criteria indicating complete integration in DID characterised by continuity in memory, an absence of dissociation, a subjective sense of unity, an absence of alternate personalities, a modification of transference consistent with fusion and the presence of previously segregated feelings. The development of more stable personalities or co-consciousness and cooperation between alters accommodating conflicting or contradictory impulses and feelings and working through traumatic events are specific targets for psychotherapy. The identification, naming and recognition of distinct self-states in CAT is in accordance with these aims. Increased awareness and self-reflection reduce triggering of switches or shifts accompanied by amnesia. Integration of disparate self-states and identities is a focal aspect of CAT, with changes to symptomatic procedures related to harmful recurrent RRPs.

Case illustration: Laura

Laura was a 35-year-old Caucasian woman who was unemployed and lived with her sister, both her parents being recently deceased. Psychiatric input and support had been provided by several professionals over a number of years because of Laura's multiple physical and psychological complaints. Her presentation had caused diagnostic confusion, Laura's difficulties being labelled as personality disorder in general terms, with features of factitious disorder. She did have a series of vague physical complaints with successive medical interventions. Laura's history of involvement with professionals had typically become conflicted and antagonistic, resulting in the discharge of her case because of her hostile behaviour.

Laura's behaviour included frequent incidents of self-harm by cutting her arms, breaking her arm with a hammer and overdosing. She showed evidence of major depressive disorder and BPD (fear of abandonment, impulsivity, suicidal gestures, feelings of emptiness). Most significantly, Laura was reported to frequently show a dissociative state for which she was completely amnesic; during this state she would assume the personality, demeanour, attitude and behaviour of a seven-year-old child. Switching to this alternate personality was triggered when Laura was woken from sleep by loud noises (e.g. fire engines, doors slamming) or as a response to prolonged stress. At first, the veracity of Laura's child alter personality was understandably disputed, reinforced by a deterioration in professionals' attitudes towards her when she became demanding.

Laura's personal history was relatively unremarkable until the age of eight when she experienced a four-year episode of repeated sadistic gang rape which included being bound, and physically, verbally and sexually assaulted. Laura did not disclose her experiences to anyone because she was threatened to remain silent, risking violence otherwise and blackmail with photographs taken of her by her perpetrators. Two male perpetrators committed the majority of the offences. To Laura's surprise, the abuse stopped with no explanation. Her weight increased significantly and she became reclusive, looking after her elderly parents. She did not experience any heterosexual relationships and denies any post-traumatic stress reactions following the assaults. She recalls her self-esteem to have been very poor during her adolescent years and she described herself as 'ugly, withdrawn, dirty and pathetic'.

At the age of 17, Laura was subjected to a serious rape by a co-worker. This revictimisation resulted in stress-related constipation, which required surgery and installation of a stoma. While being catheterised by three nurses Laura experienced her first flashback to the sexual assaults in childhood. Laura disclosed the abuse to one of the nurses and a social worker was assigned to her case. She, coincidentally, received threatening letters from one of the perpetrators at that time which she gave to the social worker, who was unfortunately removed from the case without explanation. Laura's response was to attempt suicide because of this loss (attempting to jump from the hospital windows). Psychiatric review was not provided. She was discharged to the care of her sister.

Laura's dissociative symptoms were evident during the initial episode of assaults, when she would become detached from the experience via depersonalisation, psychologically 'removing' herself from the room, with little recall for specific details of the incidents. She recalled further that she had coped with being raped by focusing intensely on a ticking clock and the sound of a nearby fridge-freezer. Laura's sister stated that Laura had first demonstrated the 'child-like state' at the age of eleven, although the family simply tolerated her behaviour without undue concern.

When in the dissociated state, Laura would talk in childish language, say that she did not recognise her sister, claim that her parents were alive and that she would attempt to leave her present home to travel to her 'real' home. She would search for toys that had been mislaid and become confused and upset by the presence of her stoma. She was entirely amnesic for her experience of this state and voiced her suspicion that others, particularly her sister, were lying to her. On one occasion, Laura had been discovered by police walking in busy city traffic with no concern for her safety. On another occasion, she contacted the police stating that she had been kidnapped by her sister.

Prior to the initial assessment by the therapist, Laura's episodes of dissociation were increasing in frequency and she reported feeling severely depressed, hopeless and suicidal. Nightmares and flashbacks to several incidents of abuse were occurring frequently, triggered by certain smells, sounds or situations (attending a dentist, gynaecological examinations). She had recently disclosed that she had secreted a syringe of insulin and sleeping tablets to secure an opportunity to kill herself. Laura had recently been hospitalised because of her dissociated episodes, but discharged herself after an argument with her responsible consultant. She was not afforded psychiatric support.

At initial interview, Laura presented as an overweight, timid woman who minimised any concerns or complaints. She appeared forlorn, fatigued and depressed. She expressed her sense of defeat and hopelessness about her circumstances and the deterioration in her coping and moods. She sighed frequently and complained lethargically about 'things just go from bad to worse'. Laura was open and honest and appeared to have maintained a sense of humour about situations that had been stressful. Her sister was very supportive and willing to continue helping her. Otherwise, Laura engaged well, her reality testing was satisfactory and there was no evidence of acute mental illness.

The assessment of Laura's case took account of Coons' (1984) advice that 'only taken together can all of the personality states [in dissociative disorders and MPD] be considered a whole personality' (p. 53) and that the functions of alters are analysed to understand the personality structure of the DID patient. Armstrong and Loewenstein (1990) further comment that considering 'alternate personalities "separately" sets up a test situation that is incomparable with the clinical reality of MPD' (p. 449). Laura was diagnosed based on DSM-IV criteria for DID and clinical indicators evaluated using Loewenstein's (1991) semi-structured Office Mental Status Examination for Complex Dissociative Symptoms and Multiple Personality Disorder (OMSE-CDS-MPD), which probes for symptom clusters including process symptoms (e.g., state and identity changes, switching), amnesia, affective, PTSD, somatoform and autohypnotic symptoms. Laura was considered to demonstrate a dual form of DID with one identifiable child alter for which she was completely amnesic, this dissociated state demonstrating distinct linguistic usage, demeanour, perceptions and behaviour. She also reported time loss (referred to by her as 'the memory loss'), disremembered behaviour (acting like a child, looking for toys etc.) and fugue states during which she attempted to travel to the home where she lived when aged seven. Laura showed no signs of autohypnotic symptoms. She also demonstrated flashbacks, nightmares, anxiety reactions triggered by numerous stimuli, emotional detachment and avoidance behaviour. Her mood was predominantly depressive, very changeable, characterised by self-blame and hopelessness, with transient suicidal ideation caused by minor stress on a daily basis. Laura's medical history indicated several surgical operations mostly for gastrointestinal complaints suggestive of somatoform symptoms.

Psychological testing using the Millon Clinical Multiaxial Inventory—3rd edition (Millon et al., 1994) showed elevations on scales assessing borderline, negativistic, schizotypal, paranoid and avoidant personality attributes. Symptomatically, Laura showed evidence of major depressive disorder, PTSD and somatoform symptoms. Severe personality pathology and symptom distress were clearly observable. Laura's Full Scale IQ was average, with no evidence of neuropsychological dysfunction. Findings from neurological examinations were unremarkable.

A decision was made to administer the Rorschach Comprehensive System (Exner, 1991) when Laura presented in her age-concordant state and when experiencing the dissociated child alter state. This was based on the hypothesis that the transition to the alter personality represented a dramatic defensive strategy providing a means of escape from the constraints of reality and a 'survival tool'. On testing, Laura showed traumatic responses to the projective stimuli (e.g., perceiving scenes of rape and torture in several Rorschach plates, aggressive and trauma responses, dissociation and depressive themes). When readministered the same test while in the child alter state, Laura's responses were appropriate to those of a child, with no evidence of trauma, aggression, dissociation or depressive content.

Laura's scores on the Dissociative Questionnaire indicated elevated scores on scales measuring identity confusion/fragmentation, amnesia and loss of behavioural control. Her PSQ score was 28, suggesting that her sense of identity, moods and behaviour were changeable. The Psychotherapy File revealed endorsement of a number of dilemmas and traps and marked instability in relation to her sense of herself, moods and experiences.

CAT for Laura

Laura's case was complex in that she presented with difficulties which would typically result in exclusion from psychological treatment (her history of suicidal behaviour, current presentation of self-injury and DID; see Calhoun & Resick, 1993). She agreed to 24 sessions of CAT on an individual basis. She expressed a mixture of optimism, anxiety and desperation in her attitude to entering therapy. Laura was provided with the Reformulation Letter, compiled from several sources, paying particular attention to the self-report of her traumatic experiences and how she managed her difficulties after these events. The letter was as follows:

Dear Laura,

At the time that I agreed to meet with you, your daily life appeared to be moving from crisis to crisis. You said when we discussed transferring to my care that you were sad that you had been abandoned because you felt you were too much trouble for your previous psychologist and you asked if I could guarantee you that I would not let you down and would rid your life of all its problems. You told me about how you felt doctors and other professionals had stopped helping you because you believe you were demanding. We must keep these thoughts in mind.

You spoke openly of your feelings that your parents had left you prematurely when they died and you felt vulnerable, lonely and depressed. They did not know about the traumas you had endured over the years, you decided not to disclose what had happened because they were ill and elderly. You cared for them with dedication and their deaths were very hard to accept.

The traumas you have experienced at the hands of others have had a major effect on your thoughts about yourself and the world since. The abuse was painful on a physical and mental level, causing you to feel trapped, guilty, to blame for not confronting the perpetrators and a 'dirty object'. You cannot understand why you did what they told you to do when you were abused and you said that this made you feel like a 'prostitute', 'a fly in a web' and a 'fish caught on a hook'. You feel that the perpetrators were 'thieves' and 'burglars' who violated your body. You mentioned how you coped at the time, by taking yourself outside your body, 'shutting down' so that you would not remember the event or absorbing your attention on the surroundings (ticking of the clock). You coped by gaining weight, becoming reclusive and hurting yourself because you felt that you deserved the pain you suffered. You have felt trapped by the memories of the abuse, recurring flashbacks and nightmares and the fact that the perpetrators kept photographs of the abuse and threatened to send them to your parents. At times you have felt depressed and suicidal, but failing to kill yourself when you attempted to do so has reinforced your sense of worthlessness.

You stated that you dream of being saved by a 'fairy godmother' and being 'Cinderella' for a while. Unfortunately, you felt sad that this would never happen and you stated that you were frightened of change and progress, often making up or exaggerating problems to keep professionals interested and maintain the level of dependency you needed. The difficulty in doing this has been that professionals have rejected you (the last thing you wanted!) because they have felt deceived.

Recently, any build-up of distress has led to you coping in a dramatic way, becoming a young child in 'the memory loss'. When you feel suicidal, frightened of being abandoned or let down or distressed by nightmares or flashbacks of the abuse, it appears that you resort to escaping in a drastic manner. The problems we need to target are:

Target problem: feeling trapped by the abuse

You continue to feel under the spell and threat of the perpetrators of abuse and re-experience these appalling events daily. You enact this abuse towards yourself by attacking your body, which you consider to be dirty and not your own. The stoma represents the perpetrators and when you feel it attack you, you hate it and attack it.

Target problem: feeling distrusting of others/professionals

You seek care and human contact with others, particularly professionals, whom you hope will be a saviour and ideal carer, taking away your pain and distress. You feel that, inevitably, professionals will become weary of your neediness, disappoint you and reject you, leaving you feeling 'high and dry', unwanted and abandoned.

Target problem: uncertainty about relationships

Either you seek a relationship and risk being abused and hurt or you avoid a relationship, becoming more emotionally needy, reclusive and dissatisfied because you are undeserving.

Target problem: depression, suicidal thinking and overeating

Feeling abandoned you feel depressed and worthless, thinking of suicide. If you attempt suicide and it does not work, this confirms your sense of worthlessness and failure. Otherwise, you cope with the depression by overeating, which causes you to feel disgusted at yourself and unhappy.

These are the problems we need to work on to help you recognise and break these harmful patterns and states of mind.

Laura's response to the letter was positive and she voiced her thoughts that her parents had betrayed her by dying and that she had previously felt angry at professionals providing care for her but felt 'I couldn't say anything in case I annoyed them . . . if I got better, they'd pay less attention to me'. In addition, Laura completed the States Grid (Figure 7.1), which helped to identify the self-states she experienced. This information was also used to construct the SSSD with her (Figure 7.2).

Laura was able to add names for each state of mind within the self-states. Laura's response to the diagram was to state 'It's a bit scary. Seeing it in black and white is very different to talking about things. It makes it more real'. It was agreed with Laura that the distress she experienced when in self-state three should be addressed first to attempt to eliminate her flashbacks, nightmares and panic symptoms, her sense of blame for the abuse and to diminish her feelings of being snared and trapped by the perpetrators. This would also have the aim of decreasing Laura's urge to self-harm by enacting the dominant RRP of *attacking/abusing* in relation to *used, trapped* by a self-management procedure.

Laura's individual CAT was preceded by IRR (Smucker *et al.*, 1996; Smucker & Dancu, 1999) to address her experiences of flashbacks,

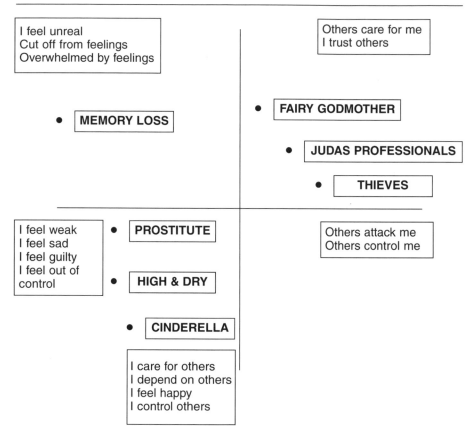

Figure 7.1   Laura's States Grid

nightmares and other traumatic symptoms. It was anticipated that she would have difficulty engaging in this form of treatment because of her habitual tendency to dissociate, yet within a trusting and safe therapeutic relationship Laura was able to undertake the procedure. IRR targeted a number of vivid, distressing memories of the abuse. These events included gang rape, bondage, physical assault and demeaning sexual acts, Laura being threatened to secrecy and told that she deserved the abuse because she was a 'whore and a dirty prostitute'. The frequency and intensity of PTSD symptoms decreased and Laura was able to reattribute the responsibility for the abuse with the perpetrators based on her realisation that she had been blackmailed, had tried to resist the perpetrators, and had been tied up and beaten when she had become obstructive. IRR allowed both therapist and client to define the RRPs between perpetrator(s) and Laura during the series of abusive events as 'thieves, burglars' in relation to 'prostitute'. Laura recognised that the self-perception as a prostitute was inaccurate and she described feeling, initially,

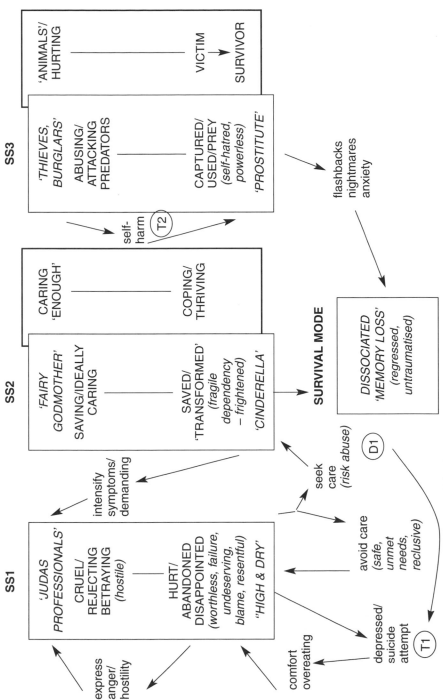

Figure 7.2 Laura's Self-States Sequential Diagram

angry about her sense of having been victimised and then her feelings of determination to survive and to 'make sure they (the perpetrators) don't spoil one more minute of my life'. Laura reported that she had decided to end her self-harm because she believed these acts were a reflection of the entrapment she still experienced by the perpetrators. Laura's recognition and revision of this target problem occurred rapidly and was maintained throughout and after therapy.

Between the second and third session Laura telephoned the department, requesting that the therapist contact her immediately, her appointment being scheduled for the following day. When the telephone call was not returned on the same day, Laura contacted the department to state that she did not wish for the therapy to continue, and she was admitted to the local hospital's Accident and Emergency department because she had broken her forearm with a hammer. She did attend a subsequent appointment and stated that she had injured herself because she believed the therapist had 'let me down, abandoned me when I needed help'. Her refusal to attend the arranged appointment was explained by Laura as 'if I reject you first, then you can't reject me'. This incident provided further evidence of the self-states 'Judas professional' in relation to 'High and dry' and the pattern was discussed with Laura openly in a non-confrontational manner. Laura recognised that her behaviour was an example of the expression of this self-state.

On another occasion (session seven) Laura had made a telephone call to the department in a distressed state, claiming to be suicidal, requesting the therapist to contact her immediately. On the following day, Laura again contacted the department, stating that she wanted to end therapy, that she had cut her arms with a knife and that the therapist's failure to contact her had again been the cause of her reactions. Laura did attend her next appointment, demanding an explanation for the therapist's lack of interest. The sequence of events and Laura's responses were discussed, demonstrating that the therapist had been perceived as *saving, caring* and, subsequently, *cruel, betraying* and *rejecting*. Laura's fragile dependency (SS2) had become intensified and she felt 'high and dry' (SS1), suicidal and had injured herself in frustration. She had also experienced a spell of three days during which she entered the state of 'memory loss' and regression to the child alter personality. It was discussed with Laura that perfect, ideal care was impossible to provide, that she was unrealistic in her perceptions of professionals and that the 'fairy godmother' did not and could not exist for her. Laura voiced her belief that if she could not be guaranteed perfect care she would always experience difficulties trusting professionals. The therapist was fully aware of and vigilant towards Laura's sensitivities to rejection, abandonment and betrayal.

Laura's compliance with the caring regime for her stoma had periodically become erratic, whereby she would refuse to change the stoma, cutting it on a number of occasions and describing it as a 'living thing, it moves and attacks me'. Laura equated her stoma with her perpetrators and felt it was a constant reminder of the abuse and continued assaulting her. The stoma was irreversible and the task for Laura and the therapist was to facilitate her tolerance of the presence of the stoma. Laura disclosed further that she had elected to have surgery to produce a stoma as a means of self-harm. The stoma symbolically represented her 'dirty insides being outside' which she could assault, an enactment of the RRP in SS3 towards herself and the stoma, which represented a perpetrator. Encouraging Laura to learn to manage the stoma with minimal contact and involvement with as little interference in her daily life as possible was an important achievement for her, further releasing her from a sense of being attacked and trapped.

Laura's dilemma (D1) regarding entering adult relationships, including those with professionals, was affected by restricted options. She could avoid relationships, feeling dissatisfied and emotionally needy or enter a relationship with the expectation of being abused or hurt. Safety and trust were difficult to secure for Laura and, although she recognised the influence of this target problem procedure, she found it difficult to revise actively. She fantasised about her 'first proper kiss', being dated and learning to express her femininity without being fearful of sexual attack. She was encouraged to attend night classes about aromatherapy and beauty therapy, which she enjoyed. Laura made a list of activities, which she felt she had been deprived of doing due to her reclusive adolescence and adulthood and, despite being reticent about deserving to enjoy herself, she pursued these activities positively.

During later sessions (session 12), Laura announced that her parents had returned as 'ghosts', were physically present in the consulting room and had decided to 'take my pain away'. Laura's presentation was somewhat similar to that observed when she was in the dissociated child alter state in that she was childish, untroubled, calm and fixed in her beliefs. Her reality testing was impaired yet not as severely compromised when compared to the child alter state. Laura insisted on talking to her 'dead' parents, preparing meals for them and suggesting that others should be able to see her parents. The therapist conceived this change to indicate a stress-induced psychotic state, similar to the child alter state and reflecting Laura's flight into an escape. Unfortunately, Laura stated that she could not be sure whether her parents would remain with her and she spoke openly of killing herself to 'go with them'. It was introduced to Laura that her reactions were indicative of her fragile dependency in SS2 and fears about being left 'high and dry' and abandoned, her parents the source of blissful, idealised care. Laura's invention of her parents' 'ghosts' is reminiscent of another form of regression fantasy similar to the appearance of the child alter personality.

Laura was encouraged to consider methods of mourning her 'lost childhood', which she equated as a direct consequence of SS3, feeling that the 'thieves' had stolen her enjoyment and innocence of adolescence. She decided to do so in two ways. Firstly, she made an audiotape of her abusive experiences, ending with statements about her desire to retrieve the happiness she believed had been stolen from her. She then cut the audiotape up into small fragments, placed them in a tin box and buried it in a ritualistic manner in a local park accompanied by a friend. Laura recalled this to have been an extremely powerful, fatiguing event, stating also that it provided closure for her to the legacy of the abuse. Secondly, Laura obtained two balloons, representing her parents, and released them by the sea. She tied a letter onto both balloons (kept anonymous) disclosing the abuse to her parents and saying 'goodbye'—something she felt she had been denied when they died.

Laura would consistently report a worsening of flashbacks, nightmares, anxiety and depressed mood when the therapist took holidays or raised the issue of termination of therapy in the future. She stated that she feared that the therapist 'did not exist anymore' and would not return, although she reported coping with these absences and stress by making internal dialogues and conversations with a miniature image of the therapist (a sustaining introject of the therapist and new RRP).

Laura was encouraged to discuss the RRPs of SS3 and her self perception as a 'prostitute' who was captured and used by her perpetrators. She describes feeling that her perpetrators called her a 'whore', a 'prostitute' who deserved the abuse. She was blackmailed into continuing the abuse with threats by the perpetrators that they would show people photographs taken of her during sexual acts. On one occasion, when she did not attend when they 'summonsed' her, she was raped, beaten and threatened as 'punishment'. A concentrated effort was made to analyse Laura's conception of herself as a 'prostitute', the way in which the perpetrators had imposed a version of reality upon her interpretations of the abuse and how she believed herself to be a 'fish caught on a hook', 'a fly in a web' and captured. Laura found it difficult to entertain the idea that she was, in truth, victimised by the perpetrators and she existed within a false version of reality imposed by the perpetrators which maintained her sense of being controlled and preyed upon, fearful of 'being summonsed' again.

Movement towards perceiving herself in the role of a 'victim' represented a stepping stone from 'prostitute' to 'survivor', which encouraged Laura to reject and redress her sense of being captured. She also felt that self-harm towards the 'bad, guilty, deserving prostitute' made more sense to her than an attack towards a 'victim' (who has suffered enough) and a 'survivor'. Laura initially resisted contemplating thinking of herself as a victim because it had connotations of powerlessness, self-pity and vulnerability. This was discussed as a transitional step to shed the pretence that the perpetrators created for her and she accepted that becoming a survivor was the end-state goal to be achieved. Gradually, Laura was able to transform her self-perception towards being a victim, then to a survivor.

Laura did not demonstrate any incidents of self-harm following the initial incidents and an attempt to remove two of her toenails after an unpredictable encounter with one of the perpetrators in her local district prior to entering therapy. Her adherence to a regimen for managing her stoma improved, although her dislike for the stoma remained. Scores on the Dissociation Questionnaire and PSQ decreased to just above normal levels, with a significant reduction in PTSD symptoms, anxiety, depression and the frequency of episodes of 'memory loss' (the dissociated state). Changes to the first two target problems were reported, together with a decrease in the extent to which she suffered depressed moods, urges to self-harm and less need to comfort eat in isolation.

Power mapping and CAT

Power mapping is a technique devised by Hagan and Smail (1997a, 1997b) which can be incorporated into CAT reformulation and therapy. A brief synopsis of the theoretical foundations of power mapping and its application is described for Laura's case as illustration. A lack of access to material power has long been equated to the development of mental health difficulties (Smail, 1993). In childhood, the power differential is most influential whereby the adult world causes a proximal effect on the child, who is dependent and reliant, unable to comprehend the wrongfulness of a perpetrator's abusive acts or to challenge the predicament which he/she faces in an abusive environment, particularly a dysfunctional family. The inequalities and lack of access to material power can continue throughout childhood into adulthood and remain a significant aspect of a survivor's difficulties.

Hagan and Smail (1997b) propose that helping the survivor of childhood abuse to identify, objectify and redress the lack of power available is an important task in promoting more effective lifestyles and changes to personal resources. The misuse of power in the past and the present lies at the heart of many psychological problems exhibited by survivors, and increasing access and means to achieve power can be guided by the technique of power mapping. Power mapping can be helpful in providing a conceptual tool to guide conceptualising, measuring and monitoring a survivor's perceived access to power, to facilitate achieving resources by targeting plans of action to practically change circumstances and increasing opportunities. The technique can be combined with the reformulation phase of CAT, which aims to foster a meaningful, historical description of the survivor's problems, including questions such as 'Why am I the way I am?' and 'Why do I stay this way?' (Hagan, 1999). Understanding leads to recognition, promoting the potential for revision and a subsequent reduction in distress and continued suffering.

Power (and its absence) within a survivor's life is relevant given the conceptualisation of the impact of childhood abuse by Finkelhor (e.g., powerlessness, stigmatisation), McCann *et al.* (lack of power, a distorted frame of reference where causality and locus of control are evident) and in theories of learned helplessness and social rank theories of domination–submission (Gilbert, 1992). The perpetrator's misuse of power and control, the effects of systematic terrorism on a physical and psychological level and sexual exploitation promote the radical imbalance of power for the child.

The 'terrain of power' and the practice of power mapping

Hagan and Smail (1997a) report how the domains of material power can be defined, termed the 'terrain of power'. The four main sources of power include material resources (employment, money, education etc.), home and family life (relationships, children, parents), social life (friendships, leisure activities) and personal resources (understanding of the past, intelligence, confidence). A circular drawing of power domains is devised, with the survivor defining the segments where power resources are relevant at an individual level. The level and control of resources within each segment are rated prior to intervention, as shown in Figures 7.3 and 7.4. As can be seen, differences can be observed in differing domains. This provides a diagrammatic means to clarify the availability and control over power in a survivor's life.

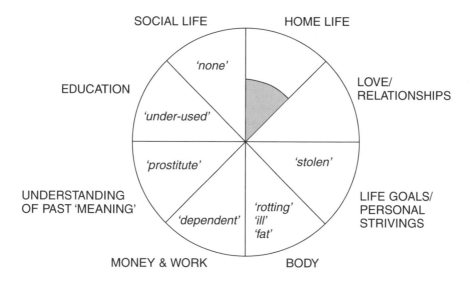

Figure 7.3   Laura's power map (pre-intervention)

Power mapping for Laura

Power mapping was introduced to Laura at a stage in CAT therapy when she was asked to contemplate the shift from 'victim' to 'survivor' within SS3. The decision was made to introduce power mapping at this time because self-blame, guilt and powerlessness complicated Laura's state of mind associated with the victim role. Laura considered the diagram to be easy to understand and she was able to describe the lack of access to and unavailability of resources in her life (see Figure 7.3).

For Laura, few segments showed any significant perceived level or control of resources. Interestingly, Laura was of the opinion that her lack of material

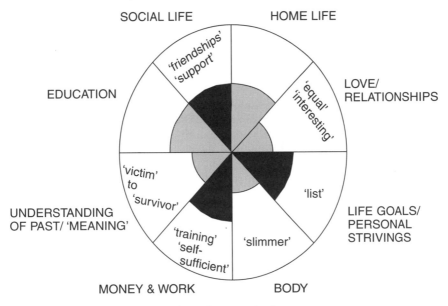

Figure 7.4   Laura's power map (post-intervention)

Level of resources	Control over resources	
NONE	None at all	☐
LOW	Severely restricted	▨
MODERATE	Limited/shared with others	▨
HIGH	Fully available	■

Figure 7.4 (continued)   Key to measuring levels and control of resources in power maps. NB: Levels of resources increase from the inner part of the power map to the outer part. Maximum access and control over resources are achieved when each segment (e.g., regarding relationships, money etc.) is considered high and fully available (all three parts of the segments are blackened from inside to outside)

power and inability to fulfil her ambitions were partly related to her sense that the perpetrators of the original abuse remained in control of her, would 'turn up at any moment and it would start all over again'. She believed her capacity to influence her lifestyle and pursue personal strivings and goals was curtailed by a psychological paralysis stemming from her feeling that she could be victimised at will by the perpetrators. In other ways, Laura reported her sadness and grief because the power map conveyed the lost opportunities throughout her childhood as a result of the effects of the abuse. At times she felt sad about these losses; on other occasions she reported anger towards the perpetrators, indignation that she had suffered during the victimisation and fantasies of murderous revenge. Laura determined that she was entitled to feel such mixed emotions and a practical and progressive step for her was to concentrate her efforts on acquiring resources to obtain greater purchase in the domains of the constructed power map.

The map shows that Laura defined herself and her personal history in terms of being a 'prostitute'; she felt that her life goals had been 'stolen'. Her relationships with others were hindered by her feelings of low self-worth and shame. Her body was perceived to be 'rotting', 'ill' and overweight. She was dependent upon state welfare money and lived a restricted lifestyle, predominantly staying at home. The career for which she had trained was 'put on hold' because of the rape and development of physical illnesses. Laura yearned for friendships and a romantic relationship. The impact of the abusive experiences on Laura's access to power and control in her life is clear from the map prior to intervention to change the evident imbalances.

Laura's power map towards the end of therapy is shown in Figure 7.4. As a crude outcome measure, the map illustrates that she has achieved notable changes in several areas. In particular, Laura did not perceive herself to be as curtailed by the psychological control she believed was exerted indirectly upon her by the perpetrators. She was able to clarify the issue surrounding who was to blame for the abuse and the misuse of power, recognising that she had been 'blackmailed and terrorised' throughout the episode of the abuse. Extending her social contacts (other than contact with professionals) helped Laura to feel less reliant upon presenting to professional services with vague somatic complaints. She acknowledged that previously her dependency upon medical services had been driven by a wish for care and social attention.

She developed a 'wish list' of goals and personal strivings that she pursued with vigour (e.g., attending the opera, holidays), she consulted a dietitian and began to lose weight and undertook exercise, retrained at college for a new career and enrolled in a drama group, acquiring several friendships. She reported her self-esteem to have improved substantially and she could 'imagine something else for me other than being sick and stuck in the past'.

Power mapping represents a simplistic and comprehensible tool for identifying and transforming the deficits in adult survivors' access to material means for influencing their environment and current predicament. Powerlessness is a common aspect of the histories and lifestyles of survivors who often do not develop any purchase on improving their situation during and after childhood. The legacy of the childhood abuse continues relatively unchanged. Power mapping can be applied in any case in which problems are detected in the current predicament of an adult survivor.

Commentary

Laura's presentation was extreme and rare in clinical settings. The choice of providing CAT for her difficulties was based on the relevance of the MSSM to conceptualise her problems and experiences and because the tools of CAT were of relevance (i.e., the empathic narrative of the Reformulation Letter, SSSD, enhancing her capacity to track her own patterns of experiences and self-observation, explicitly defining dilemmas and traps, management of the therapeutic relationship). The centrality of the childhood abuse in understanding her difficulties and its impact was explicitly stated within the SSSD and the residues of trauma were linked to Laura's creative manner of coping and experiences of severe dissociative states and symptoms. Her case is representative of significant dysfunction at all three levels of the MSSM. As a case illustration of an extreme presentation conceptualised using the MSSM, Laura's problems represented a challenge to any form of psychotherapy and differing methods (IRR, power mapping) were interwoven within the scaffolding framework of a CAT analysis to good effect without losing sight of the integral clinical picture.

CHAPTER 8

Forensic romances and violence in the therapy room: the challenge of the abuse-to-abuser dimension

Twinkle, twinkle, little star
Oh how blond and dead you are
In pain you give much more deserved
Forever more my hate preserved.
(Poem sent to therapist by patient Shelley)

A specific outcome of the intergenerational transmission of childhood abuse occurs when a survivor repeats the apparent cycle of abuse or violence in adulthood. The inclination to harm others is but one of the potential consequences of abuse and, once again, it is implausible and simply wrong to assume that it is inevitable that every victimised child or adolescent will become an abusing adult (Falshaw, Browne & Hollin, 1996).

There is empirical evidence that abuse may increase the probability of a progression to violent or sexual offending and that it is the fact of abuse itself and not the type of victimisation which may result in any category of criminal behaviour (Epps, Swaffer & Hollin, 1996). Burgess, Hartmann, McCormack and Grant (1988) refer to a process of 'trauma learning' whereby the survivor attempts to modify the sensory, perceptual and cognitive alterations that occur with the abuse, with concomitant behavioural dysfunction as a reflection of ongoing abuse or repetition of the abuse itself, the survivor alternating between the behaviour of victim and perpetrator. This theory has an immediate resonance with CAT theory and reformulation.

Similarly, Heide (1992) proposed that violent re-enactments are symbolic revenge against the original perpetrator or an extreme need to achieve a sense of control and dominance within relationships (Browne & Finkelhor, 1985). The same authors refer to criminal activities indicative of the four traumagenic dynamics mentioned in Chapter 4. *Traumatic sexualisation* relates to survivors engaging in prostitution in a defensive manoeuvre to achieve mastery or control within a sexually deviant relationship; *stigmatisation* leads to substance abuse and general criminality; *betrayal* is associated with a vulnerability to enter abusive relationships, with underlying hostility and aggression experienced by the survivor resulting in reactive, defensive violence by the survivor (Briere, 1984; Pollock, 1996); and *powerlessness* may promote an extreme need to achieve control, power and a sense of efficacy through victimising others. For example, the behaviour of males who demonstrate violence during dating relationships is best predicted by having directly experienced severe abuse by their father (Alexander, Moore & Alexander, 1991).

Despite the contention that physical abuse encourages physical violence (Dutton & Hart, 1992) and that sexual abuse is directly implicated in the generation of sexual violence (Bagley, Wood & Young, 1994), the implied linear relationship and pathway are obscured by protective factors, further vulnerability due to the 'victimogenic' lifestyle of survivors and the fact that divergent outcomes are typical of childhood abuse (Egeland & Sroufe, 1981). The influence of the survivor's gender has been suggested to influence reactions and adaptation to the abuse, with males externalising their emotional distress and females internalising the same (Dembo et al., 1992).

CAT postulates that the survivor has been induced or actively forced to assume a victimised, subordinate role, internalising both facets of the dominant RRP inherent within the perpetrator–victim relationship. To state that the perpetrator 'defines' the victim by his/her behaviour may oversimplify this process as discussed in Chapter 1 although, in some cases, the strength and impact of prolonged, chronic subordination and childhood abuse can permeate the internal world of the survivor. CAT emphasises the internalisation of both reciprocal roles created by the *perpetrator–victim relational unit* and, if no further elaboration of RRPs occurs, adaptive procedures are not acquired by the survivor in subsequent relationships, this abuse-generated RRP dominating future interactions of self–self and self–other patterns. The case illustration described here highlights the ways in which a prior history of extensive victimisation in childhood can imbue the survivor's adult behaviour and dictate the nature of interpersonal relationships.

CAT and forensic practice

CAT has been reported for offenders with an emphasis on the offender-to-victim projective identification system inherent within the index offence itself and the origins of these patterns from the offender's history and personality functioning (Pollock & Kear-Colwell, 1994; Pollock, 1996, 1997, 1998b). Crimes which lend themselves to CAT analysis tend to be interpersonally based, such as sexual offences and violence within relationships, but acquisitive offences such as arson, theft, criminal damage and substance abuse (Leighton, 1997) can be interpreted within this personality–offence framework.

The perpetrator of an interpersonal offence can be construed to induce the victim into a certain role (e.g., through grooming, deceit, imbalance of power, sadistic aggression) or to crudely force him/her into a subordinated role. For example, the *predator–prey* relation (Meloy, 1993) suggests that the victim role is defined by a crude projection by the perpetrator who ensnares, captures and misuses the victim (Pollock, 1997). On other occasions, a perpetrator may employ violence in response to a partner's behaviour. For example, a woman may resort to extreme violence to prevent a husband leaving the relationship within the context of a hostile dependency and conflicted relationship (Pollock, 1998b). Conceptualising interpersonal offences using CAT analysis can explain the curious switches in an offender's behaviour as demonstrated within the imposed construction or script. The emotions associated with states of mind induced by the act of being abused such as powerlessness, self-hatred, shame, guilt, rage, corruption of one's sexuality or masculinity can reverberate and affect the survivor's later behaviour. The concepts of 'identifying with the aggressor' and 'victim rage' are relevant to conceptualising certain survivors' destructive behaviour towards others. Formulating the survivor's reactions in these terms can be of benefit within some cases.

An offender's fantasies of crimes such as rape or murder are cognitive scripts of the relational unit between offender and victim enacted during the actual offence and practised, rehearsed and reinforced mentally prior to the crime (Ressler, Burgess & Douglas, 1988). Pollock (1997) reported two cases of offenders who showed noticeable shifts in their self-states during crimes. One offender initially bound, gagged, beat and sexually assaulted a young boy, berating him for being unclean and worthless, only to force the victim to injure the offender by cutting his stomach prior to releasing him. Within the same RRP (*punishing–punished*) of a given self-state, a reversal is apparent during the offence. In the second case, a rapist's offending was understood as a switch between two distinct self-states (*idealised–worshipped* to *punishing–defiled*), the victim being idolised then, following rejection of the offender's advances, defiled and punished for this rejection. Splitting is often evident between such contrasting and contradictory self-states and is typical of the personality-disordered offender. Often an entire projective identification system operates at the core of the offender's personality, and therapy and rehabilitation must focus upon altering this internal relational structure to achieve sustainable change. Skills acquisition (e.g., anger control) and reducing dynamic, changeable factors related to the offending (e.g., substance misuse, sexual arousal patterns) are important yet often insufficient on their own to prevent reoffending in certain cases. A determination and analysis of the link between the offender's personality functioning and the idiosyncratic enactment of the crime, including the offender–victim relational unit, must be made in order to understand the motivations for the offence and sequential pattern which emerges (Pollock, 1998b).

'Forensic romances' and violence in the consulting room

The very nature of the benevolent, attentive and unconditional relationship with another human being cultivated within the therapeutic situation can encourage an unrequited affection between patient and therapist. Discrepancies in perceptions of the shared intimacy can, of course, occur in either direction or in a dysfunctional reciprocal fashion. Therapist and patient are comparatively vulnerable to each other and a complex variety of interactions is often exhibited. Thoughtful clinical analysis and conceptualisation of the nature of the emerging emotional attachment are necessary to avoid stagnation, rupture or even dissolution of the relationship entirely.

Violence from a patient towards a therapist is not uncommon, especially in forensic practice (Buckley & Resnick, 1994). The notion that helping professionals are at risk of harm from a patient is an obvious reality, yet counterintuitive because we may entertain fantasies that the process of assisting will facilitate healing and gratitude for both parties involved. When a patient declares or exhibits intense, intimate love towards the therapist, this indicates a juncture where the management of transference and countertransference issues is critical based on a coherent and exact formulation of the patient's psychopathology and therapy goals. The nature of the involvement can range from appropriate dependency to benign infatuation to morbid or obsessional emotional engagement. It is the latter extreme version that can be accompanied by threatening behaviours such as unwanted pursuit, repeated contacts of differing types and, in certain instances, violence or even murder. A case illustration is described here of an adult female who attempted to kill her therapist following a crescendo of threatening behaviours within the therapeutic relationship. The vicissitudes of endeavouring to help this patient are reported and the clinical formulation of the therapist–patient relationship is described applying CAT theory and principles.

The nature of obsessional love

The term 'erotomania' or 'delusional love' has been evident in psychiatric nosologies since its first description by Esquirol (1965), later expanded upon by de Clérambault (1942), Ferdiere (1937), Kretschmer (1918) and Seeman (1978). Its status was reviewed by Segal (1989) and later the diagnosis was incorporated within modern psychiatric diagnostic systems (as Delusional Disorder, Erotomanic Type (DDET) in the *Diagnostic and Statistical Manual of Mental Disorders—3rd edition*; DSM-III-R, 1987). It refers to 'an erotic delusion . . . that one is loved by another' (DSM-III-R, 1987; p. 199) that persists for at least a month, other psychotic symptoms and bizarre or conspicuous behaviour absent, with the object sought being unattainable because of higher social or financial status. The object sought is perceived to be the first to fall in love and to have made amorous advances. Explanations for these beliefs include the perceptions that the patient is being victimised, the object can communicate through mind control or extrasensory perception, or that the object made the initial contact and is demonstrating unrequited love (Harmon, Rosner & Owens, 1995).

The classic type of erotomania consists of the delusional form observable secondary to a major disorder (schizophrenia, or depressive, bipolar disorder) and Ellis and Mellsop (1985) proposed that the primary form, as a monosymptomatic delusion, is extremely rare. Lehman (1980) stated the view that 'it would be advisable not to perpetuate the existence of this questionable syndrome in the literature'. Later research by Gillett, Eminson and Hassanyeh (1990) supported this opinion, identifying only three cases of primary DDET in 11 patients. Kienlen *et al.* (1997) reported that approximately one third of stalking criminals identified were psychotic and very few have a diagnosis of DDET. Despite ambiguity and imprecision amongst definitions of erotomania, there is clinical evidence that it occurs most often as a secondary symptom of a major mental disorder, particularly schizophrenia (Rudden, Gilmore & Frances, 1980) or symptomatic of organic disorders including brain damage (John & Ovsiew, 1996), and sexual (Kaplan, 1996) or chromosomal disorders (Silva, Ferrari & Leong, 1998). Delusional erotomania has been recorded in male forensic patients (Menzies, Federoff, Green & Isaacson, 1995; Taylor, Mahendra & Gunn, 1983), across differing cultures (Phillips, West & Wang, 1996) and in homosexual cases (Boast & Coid, 1994). It has a chronic course with variable responses to psychopharmacological interventions (Gillett *et al.*, 1990).

Typically, the behaviour of these patients can be classified as 'stalking' or 'obsessional following' which 'seriously alarms, annoys, harasses, or terrorises the person and serves no legitimate purpose . . . and causes substantial emotional distress to the person' (California Penal Code, 646.9). The frequency of violence generally in these criminal cases ranges from 2.7% for 74 DDET types of obsessional followers (Zona, Sharma & Lane, 1993) to 36% for 14 cases reported by Mullen and Pathé (1994). Meloy (1996) cited figures, across 10 studies incorporating 180 cases, suggesting that 75% of assailants who threaten violence are not and that 2% of cases culminate in a murder. Pursuit of the object tends to occur in multiple forms (letter writing, physical approach, telephone contact; Meloy, 1997) and continues for many months to several years. Dietz (1988) examined letters sent to celebrities and politicians ($N = 65$), concluding that the most probable recipient of violence is a third party standing between the person and the sought object, and that fewer than 5% of sufferers are violent.

Distress and self-defeating behaviour are prevalent features of the sufferer's plight, often resulting in imprisonment because of harassment of the victim (through letters, telephone calls, repeated approaches or actual attack). The notion that the risk of violence towards the object can occur is well documented in cases of DDET, research by Menzies *et al.* (1995) suggesting that multiple delusional objects and a history of prior antisocial behaviour were useful predictors of dangerousness in males. Mullen and Pathé (1994b) state that erotomania in any form can result in the patient placing the target of the morbid infatuation in a situation of 'at best harassment and at worst violence' (p. 614). Distinguishing whether a given case is a secondary or primary erotomania is crucial for the management of the condition and it is clear that the latter type is conceptualised to represent a symptom of personality pathology.

Mullen and Pathé (1994b), clarifying types of *pathological love*, stated that a 'pure' erotomania (without the presence of a mental disorder) did exist, emerging as an expression of a vulnerable personality and forming the totality of the clinical picture. A distinction is here made between DDET as a primary diagnosis or as a secondary symptom of a more prominent psychiatric disorder and 'pure' erotomania which exists as the dominant and singular feature of the patient's complaints and presentation. Personality characteristics of the patient are given substantive weight by the authors, who claim that 'the emergence of the disorder is usually to some extent understandably related to the patient's personal and social situation as well as underlying character structure' (p. 619). The pre-morbid personalities of the 'pure' cases of erotomania are described as demonstrating specific characteristics such as social ineptitude, isolation, poor self-worth, suspiciousness or assumed superiority, a fear of intimacy and rejection and sensitivity to narcissistic injury or criticism. In most cases, a precipitant can also be identified (e.g., loss of a companion, failure of a valued relationship) which preceded the onset of the erotomanic presentation.

Attachment disturbances, personality pathology and erotomania

Insecure attachment patterns have been implicated as substrates for a number of psychopathological states (Rosenstein & Horowitz, 1996). Obsessive love and pursuit of the unrequited object have also been linked to specific types of attachment pathology and personality disorders. Bartholomew and Horowitz's (1991) theoretical typology of *secure, fearful, preoccupied* and *dismissing* attachment patterns can be used to describe the obsessional follower's behaviour (Meloy, 1998). This model is founded on a matrix of combinations of positive and negative models of self and others. For example, the fearful, preoccupied and dismissing patterns account for stalking behaviours. The *fearful* pattern concerns development of a negative self-worth, chronic anxiety about rejection and abandonment, affective instability and intimacy anger (Dutton, Saunders, Starzomski & Bartholomew, 1994). The individual is caught between pervasive distrust of others and a desire for intimacy coupled with an extreme sensitivity to rejection and chronic frustration of attachment needs. The fearfully attached individual vacillates between care-seeking and self-reliance without resolution to this dilemma. The *preoccupied* attachment pattern refers to an individual with a negative self-image who seeks approval and validation from idealised others. This pattern is also associated with high intimacy anger and features of borderline personality organisation, including unstable affects, denial, idealisation/ devaluation, projective identification and obsessional thinking (Dutton & Golant, 1995; Meloy, 1996). The *dismissing* pattern is perceived to relate to remoteness and emotional distancing in relationships aimed at preserving a positive self-image and antisocial and narcissistic personality pathology. Meloy speculated that these personality problems resulted in more vengeful and retaliatory pursuit of the object, rejection perceived as a narcissistic wounding causing intense anger.

An attachment style is understood in CAT terms as a reflection of a dominant RRP within a self-state. For example, the fearful attachment pattern of Bartholomew could be conceptualised as a *betraying-to-exploited* RRP resulting in a confusing *dilemma* whereby seeking care (side one of the dilemma) risks being disappointed, hurt, rejected or abandoned and avoiding involvement with another frustrates attachment needs (the other side of the dilemma causing loneliness, depression). Symptomatic management of both unsatisfactory aspects of this dilemma may occur through sabotaging a relationship by inducing the other party to reject or abandon (confirming the first side of the dilemma) or coping with emotional emptiness via drug misuse or binge eating for comfort. The preoccupied pattern may be described as a subjugation of oneself (e.g., RRP of *subjugating martyr-to-idealised lover*) to gain validation and approval through placation and self-sacrifice. Anger emerges when the need for affection and endorsement is frustrated.

Meloy's (1998) psychodynamic hypotheses suggested that an acute or chronic rejection of the patient challenges narcissistic fantasies of a special, idealised and destined emotional bond. This generates feelings of shame and humiliation, which are defended against through rage that fuels pursuit in the form of a desire to damage or destroy, control or harm the originally admired object. A disturbance of narcissistic equilibrium and vulnerability is inferred to set the stage for malignant aggression. A preoccupied attachment pattern and borderline personality organisation allied to social incompetence, loneliness and isolation are further markers for the development of eroto-manic behaviour. Evans, Jeckel and Slott (1982) proposed that erotomania could be conceived as a variant of abnormal or pathological mourning for the lost object and Goldberg (1994) conceptualised erotomania as an expression of 'lovesickness'. The sufferer yearns for and fails to mourn for the lost object, denial impinging upon reality testing, often displaying 'paradoxical conduct' (Segal, 1989) by interpreting disavowal of any emotional bond by the object (no matter how strongly conveyed) to be secret affirmation of love designed to 'test' the patient's perseverance.

Meloy (1996) reported that DSM-IV Cluster B personality disorders (bor-derline, narcissistic, histrionic and antisocial) were prevalent amongst criminal stalkers, with the commonality that they display identity disturbances which affect the capacity to establish relationships with others. Dependent and avoidant features may also be evident, depicting the contrasting approach and withdrawal associated with patterns of confused interpersonal relating. Meloy (1998) proposed that a form of pure erotomania could be identified which he referred to as *borderline erotomania*. An object relations framework was used to formulate this condition as 'an extreme disorder of attachment . . . apparent in the pursuit of, and the potential for violence toward, the unrequited love object' (p. 477). The attachment or emotional bonding is grossly disturbed (tumultuous, intense and discrepant to the attachment of the loved object), non-delusional in form, with no loss of reality testing, and occurs in the con-text of borderline and narcissistic personality pathology.

It has been demonstrated that preoccupied or insecure attachment patterns (Bartholomew & Horowitz, 1991) underlie the personality pathology of ero-tomanic patients with personality disorders common. Borderline personality and preoccupied adult attachment patterns have been identified as related to the potential for violence (Pollock, 1997; Pollock & Percy, 1999) and a predis-posing factor for obsessional harassment (Meloy, 1998). The importance of this attachment pattern is that it implies that patients with borderline erotomania experience identity disturbances which, in the face of perceived rejection or frustrated bonding (usually a factual relationship has occurred), evolves into a wish to injure or kill the previously loved, now hated object of affection. The motivation is to destroy the once admired and pursued object because of intol-erable frustration, rejection, abandonment (accompanied by rage, loss and anx-iety) and a desire to claim ownership of the other person. Obsessional thinking and anxious preoccupation fuel the need to possess the person, unrequited love triggering narcissistic injury and trauma. Ideas expressed by borderline ero-tomanic patients include a sense of entitlement to own the pursued object ('if I can't have you, no one will'), a romantic image of fusion through death (a macabre variation of 'till death do us join') and a 'felt quality of perfection' (Rothstein, 1984, p. 17) exhibited in masochistic subjugation and pride in per-sistence despite repetitive rebuff. In a similar vein, Zona, Sharma and Lane

(1993) proposed that erotomania can be categorised as pure erotomania, love obsessional (no prior contact between the patient and sought object) and simple obsessional, in which a prior relationship has 'gone sour'.

Kienlen et al. (1997) conducted the only investigation of attachment pathology in criminal stalking cases, showing that the majority (63%, 24 cases) experienced a change or loss of primary care-giver during childhood, and that parental separation or divorce, death, abandonment or imprisonment was common, as was traumatic abuse (55%, 20 cases). Obsessional harassment was precipitated by loss of an intimate relationship (marriage, child custody). The authors proposed that preoccupied attachment patterns were demonstrated by criminal stalkers and their obsessional following and harassment were predisposed by early attachment disruption and precipitated by loss, resulting in the display of pursuit behaviour to vent anger or grief and to compensate for recent loss.

Harmon et al. (1995) suggested that the attachments in obsessional harassment cases could be differentiated via their nature (amorous/affectionate or persecutory/angry) and whether a prior relationship had occurred (personal, professional, employment, media, acquaintance or none). The authors reported that nine of 48 cases of menacing or harassment exhibited personality disorder, consisting of borderline, narcissistic, schizotypal and mixed types, the harassing behaviours being very similar to DDET cases.

Conceptualising stalking/obsessional following and violent attachments (intimate abuse of a partner) from an object relations perspective, Meloy (1998) and Dutton and Golant (1995) disagreed regarding the subphase of object relations models of development (Mahler, Pine & Bergman's separation–individuation phases, 1975) in which obsessional followers were disturbed. Meloy proposed that the differentiation and practising subphases were critical, Dutton and Golant considering developmental disturbances during the rapprochement phase as important. These problems are inferred from the failure to attain complete psychological separateness, manage separation anxiety, develop a perception of oneself as a distinct entity and tolerance of an optimal distance from the parent. It is clear that theoretical notions regarding the underlying pathology of obsessional love, following and harassment are derived from the hypothesis that the achievement of psychological separateness has not occurred satisfactorily and loss cannot be tolerated or grieved for without resort to motivated pursuit or emotional expression. The implications for the development of a working alliance in psychotherapy for these patients are obvious.

Erotomania and the therapeutic relationship

Involvement between professional and patient is construed in this model as professional contact, and can be amorous/affectionate or persecutory/angry. A change is often observed within the relationship from positive engagement to angry, hostile and victimised. This pattern is commonly encountered with borderline personality disorder, the sudden shifting in perceptions of the therapist representing the defensive process of splitting and a reflection of idealisation and devaluation of the same object. Miller (1985) reported that 55% of 480 forensic psychiatrists had been physically threatened, and 14% attacked. Similarly, Buckley and Resnick (1994) surveyed 90 clinicians, showing that 26 had experienced stalking, a further 24 claiming that patients had waited for them outside their workplace or home, with 13 incidents of damage to the clinician's property. Multiple occasions of stalking or harassment were reported. In a recent review of psychologists' safety concerns in the USA, Corder and Whiteside (1996) reported that cases involving legal issues were more likely to feature threats, stalking and physical attacks by clients with little security provided by legal sanctions for DDET patients, but more rational responses for those with borderline erotomania whose reality testing was less compromised (Anderson, 1993).

Lion and Herschler (1998) reported nine cases of stalking of professionals, proposing that certain patients develop a *deranged transference* which all therapists should be attuned to and capable of detecting in its early stages, be alert to boundary violations and the potential for escalation and the use of legal consultation and open confrontation of the patient regarding the consequences for the patient who persists. Our own countertransference responses to a patient's intrusive, threatening or abusive behaviour can vary greatly. Fear, anxiety, rage, hate and shame may be experienced, accompanied by a desire to avoid, flee, control, reject or punish the patient. Lion (1995) commented on clinicians' use of denial to diminish the seriousness of threats made by rationalising the patient's behaviour as improbable, a reflection of mental illness and designed to affect decisions the clinician may make. It is essential that therapists feel equipped first to understand and conceptualise what is being enacted within the therapeutic frame and space, avoid the allure of colluding unwittingly with transference patterns emerging and employ pertinent therapeutic strategies that will deflect and regulate potential ruptures of the therapist-to-patient relationship.

There have not been any systematic studies of psychotherapy for Mullen and Pathé's 'pure' erotomanic type, Meloy (1988) describing psychodynamic hypotheses but not issues in therapy itself. He provides guidelines (Meloy, 1997) for ensuring adequate risk management of stalking (e.g., a team approach, documentation and recording, protective orders, treatment, imprisonment) as measures to address the reporting of relational intrusions that disrupt the safety of treatment and often precede potentially dangerous actions by the patient.

A case illustration is presented here that describes the reformulation, treatment and management applying CAT for an adult female exhibiting borderline erotomania. Particular reference is paid to how CAT conceptu-alises the difficulties that arose within the therapeutic relationship and meth-ods used to understand and manage these problems as they emerged during therapy. CAT has been reported in a number of studies for personality-dis-ordered patients who present within the criminal justice system and forensic services with promising outcomes (Pollock, 1996, 1997, 1998b). The case presented furthers the application of this form of psychotherapy for offenders.

Case illustration: Shelley

Shelley is a 24-year-old Caucasian single woman referred for a psychological opinion prior to sentencing by the courts. Her offences were several, including criminal damage to a church, sending abusive 'poison letters' to strangers whose names she had obtained from obituary columns of newspapers and attempting to poison her mother and boyfriend of six months. The letters to bereaved strangers would, typically, begin with terms of sympathy and poetry, deteriorating to profane and vulgar statements about the deceased relative. She had a previous history of criminal damage when she broke into her mother's home, writing obscenities on walls and defecating in a bedroom. Shelley had four prior admissions to psychiatric hospital, with outpatient treatment (including medication and group psychotherapy) being deemed unsuccessful due to her poor engagement with professionals. She was diag-nosed as suffering from mixed personality disorder (borderline, narcissistic, histrionic, passive–aggressive and psychopathic features) with associated major depressive episodes and panic disorder.

At interview, Shelley was dismissive, sullen, and terse and gave an air of adolescent rebelliousness and resentment that she faced prosecution for her actions. Her explanations for the crimes were that she poisoned her mother and boyfriend 'because I hate them, I wanted them to know what it's like to suffer slowly'. The letters to the relatives of the recently deceased and crimi-nal damage to her mother's home and local church were afforded no expla-nation by Shelley, though she presented as remorseless, gleeful and triumphant about her destructiveness. The therapist felt uneasy, anxious and distrustful towards Shelley.

Shelley's personal history was difficult to obtain from her, her responses being bland, superficial and uninformative. Shelley's only complaint was that she felt misunderstood and her feelings and opinions were not respected by others, especially her recent boyfriend, whom she accused of abusing her 'mentally' and who 'played games with my affection'. She stated that her only child of four was in long-term foster care and she expressed little interest or emotion about him otherwise. She did not divulge any personal information additionally which was directly indicative of significant difficulties and she refused to complete any psychometric testing or medical evaluation. Corroborating information from professional records suggested Shelley's developmental history was tragic and adverse.

Shelley was documented to have experienced repeated, invasive and sadistic sexual and physical abuse by her parents, who belonged to a pseudo-religious 'church'. The abuse consisted of her parents' involvement in grossly indecent ritualistic sexual abuse, and facilitating the same between their daughter and other members, occurring from the ages of approximately 6 to 11. She was subsequently placed into local authority care. During this time in care, Shelley was convicted of arson at a hostel and involvement in opportunistic prostitution. Her son had been conceived unplanned during a superficial relationship and he was accommodated elsewhere after she made verbal claims that she did not 'want him because he wasn't a baby anymore' and threats to kill him and herself on several occasions. Her admissions to psychiatric hospital typically followed periods of depression, social withdrawal and panic symptoms. Shelley's self-injurious behaviour had included cutting her arms and legs, attempting to cut out her heart with a knife and asking acquaintances to physically beat her when intoxicated. Psychiatric records had diagnosed a delusional disorder (paranoid type), trance-like states and mutism and she claimed that evil spirits possessed her.

At a second assessment interview, Shelley was more forthcoming and less guarded, stating that she was frightened by her circumstances and despondent about her future. She showed herself on occasions to be overwhelmed by emotion, expressing rage at her parents and boyfriend for mistreatment of her. Again, she felt at a loss to describe or explain her subjective experiences, claiming to be 'mystified' by her feelings about herself and others.

Shelley's recall of her adverse past was fragmented and vague in details and she expressed a sense of terror and shame when she contemplated her parents' abuse of her. On occasions she felt that she could deny these events had ever happened and, at other times, the horror of the abuse intruded upon her as disturbing images and frightening nightmares (not of the abuse itself) accompanied by hypervigilance and anxiety. A decision was made to recommend a community disposal with outpatient treatment to the court. Shelley was subsequently seen on a weekly basis for 24 sessions of individual CAT.

At the first session following the end of the court case, Shelley was pleased with the outcome, expressing her thanks to the therapist who had given verbal and written evidence to the court suggesting psychotherapy should be the preferred option in her case. At times, Shelley was overly dramatic in her appreciation and requested a 'hug of thanks' at the session's end. When the therapist stated that physical contact with patients generally was not a part of therapy, she became angry, verbally threatening and upset, then immediately apologetic, stating 'I have to leave you now. This is a mess. You won't want to see me again'. The therapist was left with a sense of confusion and concern wondering whether he had been excessively rigid in denying her physical contact. At the second session, Shelley reported that she had binged on alcohol and cut her legs with a knife because of 'depression'. Her mood was morose and disinterested initially, then became very focused on the therapist, asking personal questions 'to get to know him'. Shelley expressed her admiration for the therapist because he had 'spoken up' for her at court and was the only person willing to help her. Her mood lifted noticeably and she became almost excitable and childish in her views about the 'new future' she was about to enter through therapy.

She agreed enthusiastically to complete the CAT Psychotherapy File (a description of differing self-states, dilemmas, traps and snags completed by the patient; see Appendix 1) and psychometric testing, which indicated that she reported extensive identity disturbance, and dissociative, post-traumatic and anxiety symptoms. Her attachment style was assessed using Bartholomew's Relationship Questionnaire, indicating a predominantly preoccupied and dismissing attachment profile (low on secure and moderate on fearful patterns). She completed neuropsychological testing and medical procedures with no organic problems evident. Structured interview and self-report measures indicated severe personality dysfunction (borderline, narcissistic, histrionic and antisocial features).

At a third session, Shelley reported greater stability in her feelings and behaviour and attended with comments of thanks to the therapist scribbled onto ripped pages of a Bible. She commented that the therapist had a 'golden glow around his face', his wristwatch 'sparkled' and she felt 'hypnotised' by his words. She requested an extra weekly session to reward her for 'working so hard' and, when the reason for this was questioned and discussed, Shelley became irritable and verbally abusive, dismissively stating that she 'couldn't be bothered anyway, I've got other things to do'. The therapist felt sensitive about channelling Shelley towards the tasks of therapy on occasions when she appeared belligerent and uninvolved. An alarming event occurred after this session when Shelley was discovered to have threatened four consecutive patients of the therapist during a routine outpatients clinic and attended the department demanding an emergency appointment with threats of killing herself or someone else, refusing to leave the premises. Shelley was removed by security and failed her next appointment without contact.

At a subsequent appointment, Shelley produced a knife when she entered the consulting room, accusing the therapist of 'letting me down', being neglectful of her feelings and uncaring. Shelley then became tearful, apologetic and self-pitying, surrendering the knife compliantly at the end of the session. The following day, Shelley left a series of abusive and derogatory phone messages on the department's answering machine stating that the therapist was 'toxic, a murderer of harmless souls. You need to be saved from your suffocating marriage. We must free our souls through death or marry them in sleep . . . It is my duty to save you'. Shelley also posted two letters to the therapist stating her intention to kill him and his family for his uncaring behaviour towards her. The therapist was followed from his workplace and Shelley admitted during a later session that she had been responsible for an attempted 'hit and run' by car, injuring the therapist minimally. She explained that her hostility had built up as a consequence of her perception that she had been denied unlimited contact with him and the incident had been preceded by superficial self-injury, which was unsuccessful in allaying her rage.

Patterns within Shelley's interpersonal behaviour towards the therapist in this case included rapid oscillation and instability in her perceptions of herself and others, accompanying moods and interactions. At times, she appeared disengaged or rejecting of the therapist, at other times seeking a symbiotic fusion with an idolised therapist, the threats towards him representing splitting between perceiving him as a perfectly caring saviour and a frustrating, neglectful carer. The therapeutic relationship in Shelley's case was fraught with disturbance and ruptures, compromising her capacity to form an active collaborative alliance with the therapist. Previous professionals appeared to have been 'grist for the mill' and Shelley's ability to productively use the therapy process and therapist as an object and to reflect upon her own psychological processes was questionable. Notwithstanding the severity of Shelley's personality dysfunction, it was felt that CAT would be appropriate for her.

A notable improvement in Shelley's degree of engagement with the therapist was evident after discussing the Reformulation Letter. This letter describes the patient's history, how problems have emerged throughout his/her development and a tentative list of target problems, including predictions about transference issues, which is presented to the patient and revised according to his/her feedback. Jointly, Shelley and the therapist produced a list of target problems (TPs) and related target problem procedures (TPPs). The patient was requested to rate the extent to which she was able to recognise the influence of these procedures in her general behaviour and relationships and also rate the degree of revision achieved. Her Reformulation Letter is reproduced below:

Dear Shelley,

So far, our contact has been challenging and, at times, confusing. I have become aware that your life has been dotted with difficult times and, although you may have preferred not to talk about these events with me at the beginning, it is clear that you have suffered a great deal at the hands of other people. You have said that it is easier to ignore the past and not to think about what these events have meant to you.

When we spoke at the start of our contact you clearly expressed your anxieties that you would be forced to revisit these disjointed memories.

We have agreed not to do so. Your story of care from others in your childhood and later contains feelings about having been hurt and having suffered because of other people's badness and cruelty. At times you describe being terrified, guilty and wanting to hide from everyone, but needing help from people also. On other occasions you have felt a 'blind rage' because of the suffering you experienced and wanted to hurt other people in revenge. Harming yourself makes sense because it reflects the internal suffering you have come to know well.

Disappointments in relationships have been common for you and you describe a 'constant hope' that someone will not fail you. When people do fail you, you feel neglected and feel a desire to hurt that person, as you have been hurt. Boyfriends take without giving and you feel drained and emotionally empty. Your mother in a similar way appeared to care very little for you and failed to show any interest or concern for your welfare. These experiences have coloured how you feel in relationships as an adult and it is important that we make sense of them and help you to develop methods to change them.

You say that you feel happiest when you are angry and feel powerful because you're making others understand the suffering you felt in the past and now. The emotional pain of being mistreated is too difficult to tolerate. You said that thinking about this pain is also too hard to do. There are a number of problems, which we could attempt to understand and change:

Target problem 1: coping with suffering

The world of relationships is dominated by the emotional suffering of yourself or others—you feel that no other possibilities can occur. You feel that hurting others 'gets in first' and making others suffer teaches them about the pain you have felt.

Target problem 2: wanting to destroy others or yourself

At times you hurt yourself and cause suffering on behalf of those who were cruel (self-harm) or you expose your feelings of rage through violence. Feelings of power and revenge make you feel better and you continue to act in this way.

Target problem 3: feeling depressed and bingeing on alcohol

Because you experience boyfriends and some friends as taking without giving in returning, you feel drained and fatigued. To rid yourself of these feelings of depression, you drink alcohol 'to the point of oblivion', which makes you more depressed and physically ill.

Target problem 4: feeling disappointed by people

Your expectations of a perfect partner become quickly disappointed, you feel neglected, angry and try to force the person to give you the affection and care you want. Sometimes you feel anxious about ruining the relationship and try to obtain forgiveness, acting in a clingy, dependent way. At other times, you feel angry and want to 'teach a lesson' by using violence. Your feelings fluctuate from intense love to intense anger towards the same person. These patterns continue to influence your life and cause distress for you and others. During our work we need to focus on recognising and changing these problems.

Initially, a list of the dominant RRPs (described in her own words) and self-states within Shelley's repertoire of relating to herself and others was made to clarify the nature of her interactions with others and herself. These included the following RRPs:

A1 *Idealised saving*	to	**A2** *Rescued, dependent*		Self-State 1
B1 *Neglectful, rejecting*	to	**B2** *Needy, rejected*		Self-State 2
C1 *Taking, sucking*	to	**C2** *Depleted, deflated*		Self-State 3
D1 *Sadistic, attacking*	to	**D2** *Suffering victim, victim rage*	Self-State 4

Shelley was presented with an explanation of this analysis that was linked to symptomatic procedures (her dissociative trances, alcohol misuse and self-injury), avoidance and placation traps avoiding the expression of hostility and destructive envy and her sabotage of progress via snags. Shelley's response was positive and reflective, adding and adapting the Reformulation Letter and preliminary diagram.

Shelley labelled SS1 as the 'knight in shining armour' in relation to 'special lover', SS2 as 'defective mother' to 'needy child'. Regarding SS4, she described a 'destroyer' in relation to two differing roles termed 'suffering victim' and also 'victim rage'. SS3 was named as the 'vampire' state to 'drained'.

Shelley completed a form of repertory grid, termed the States Grid (Golynkina & Ryle, 1999), which generates a two-dimensional spatial plot showing how each identified self-state (e.g., knight in shining armour, needy child) is construed by the patient, as shown in Figure 8.1. Constructs (descriptors such as 'I feel guilty') are supplied and those provided by the patient are also incorporated. This provided a means of clarifying how best to depict the relationships between each of the self-states. Shelley's jointly constructed SSSD is shown in Figure 8.2. She was encouraged to identify, name and track shifts in experiences within and between these self-states and procedures underlying symptoms and distress.

Within the SSSD sequential patterns could be identified which accounted for her changeable presentation. Firstly, the sharp oscillation between her wish for blissful fusion with a partner and her wish to destroy that person represents a *state switch* from *rescued/dependent–idealised/saving* (SS1; A1/A2) to *needy/rejected–neglecting/rejecting* (a transition state of SS2; B1/B2) to

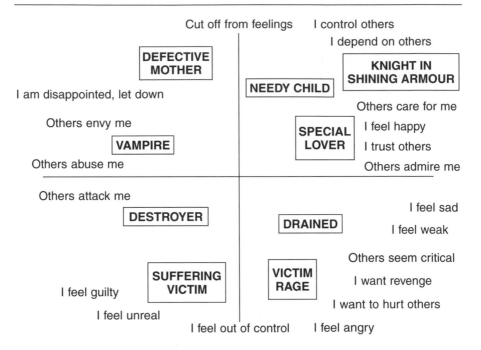

Figure 8.1   Shelley's States Grid: two-component graph

sadistic/attacking–suffering victim (SS4; D1/D2). The dramatically contradic-tory nature of self-states 1 and 4 is indicative of splitting.

A *response shift* (an alteration in the reciprocal response made to the same role of an RRP) is shown within Shelley's reactions to being victimised. On occasions she reported feeling terror and shame associated with experiencing a state described as *suffering victim.* Enactment of this RRP towards herself resulted in self-injury (trap 1). The panic, sense of psychological paralysis and immobilisation accompanying this state led to social avoidance and a strong desire for help and support from others (a move to SS1, A2). Very differently, she would also describe feeling enraged about the mistreatment she suffered (victim rage: D3). Her hatred resulted in a compulsive need to gain revenge via remorseless identification with the triumphant *sadistic/attacking* role of SS4, D1 (trap 3). To an extent, assuming the reciprocal role of D1 compen-sated for her core pain of shame, fear and hatred (D2 and D3). Shelley con-sidered this manoeuvre to be her only feasible strategy to survive the abuse and her recurring distressing states of mind.

Quite clearly, it also vastly increased the probability that she would harm someone or commit an offence. Shelley was able to insightfully comment that poisoning her mother and boyfriend (enactment of the 'destroyer' role) was designed to induce them to 'suffer, make them feel what it's like to suffer'. Her

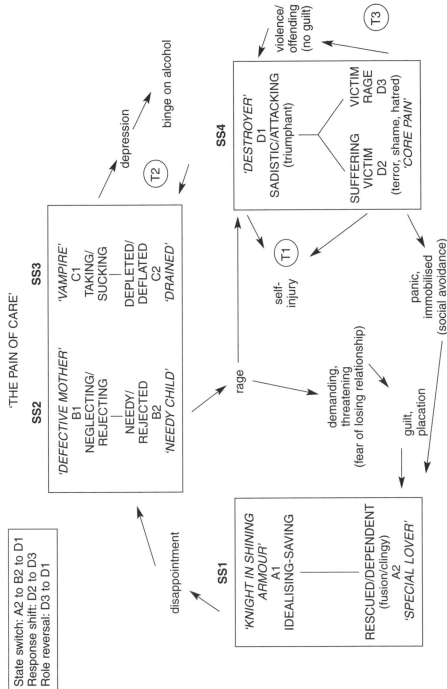

Figure 8.2 Shelley's Self-States Sequential Diagram

statements about her motivations for poisoning her mother and partner ('to make them feel what her pain felt like') can be understood as a form of communicative projective identification to dramatically induce pain and express her rage. The therapist's countertransference reactions at initial interview were also a reflection of his sense that he could be the recipient of Shelley's destructive attack.

Otherwise, Shelley could discriminate between the quality of the relationship she experienced with her mother (SS2; B1 to B2) and her boyfriend (SS3; C1 to C2). Shelley perceived her mother's care of her to be an example of passive mistreatment through disinterest, indifference and emotional neglect. Shelley's relationship with her boyfriend was described differently, characterised by deliberate, active mistreatment whereby Shelley believed her devotion and love were taken without reciprocation. She pictured her partners to be 'vampires' (C1) and she felt 'drained' (C2). When in this latter state, she would feel depressed and suicidal and binge on alcohol to change her moods (trap 2). RRPs B and C were amalgamated by Shelley into a single self-state when constructing the diagram because she believed that these RRPs denoted 'the pain of relationships'. The diagram was presented to Shelley and her reaction was, in the first instance, one of confusion, then sadness, stating 'there are parts of me that I hate'. She immediately acknowledged the vacillation in her feelings towards others from intense infatuation and love to overwhelming hatred when disappointed. Behavioural examples of this pattern (threatening patients, abusive messages to the therapist, threatening to kill him) were discussed with her. She volunteered in addition that when she felt especially stressed she could 'hear my mother's voice. It calls me names, screams at me'. This voice was experienced as an inner dialogue most of the time but also as an external auditory hallucination when Shelley was severely distressed. The RRP of SS2 B1–B2 resembled the quality of Shelley's relationship to this voice.

The SSSD was a central tool shared between therapist and patient, which was used to track her changing perceptions of herself and others and her emotional states. The transference relationship was also understood in these terms and openly discussed with Shelley. She progressed well over a number of sessions, reporting that the reformulation provided her with a sense of coherence and containment, clarifying her reactions and perceptions for her, enabling her to gain more purchase on her own experiences.

Shelley rated each of the TPs identified for recognition and revision over the sessions. TP1 (coping with suffering) stemmed from Shelley's tendency to define relationships as either attacking or victimised and she appeared to solve this restriction in relating by identifying with the sadistic/attacking RP of SS4. Others suffered rather than her and she implicitly communicated to others her own feelings of terror, shame and fear. Helping Shelley to devise different methods of coping with her own feelings of having been victimised and to recognise that this limited pattern of relating only resulted in rejection or was enacted in self-injury was a major step in therapy. She completed cognitive imagery techniques that involved communicating her emotional pain to the perpetrators and expressing her hatred and rage within the therapeutic setting. The link between being victimised, feelings of shame and rage and her need to express hatred through harming others was acknowledged and the notion that Shelley's most adaptive option was to become a 'survivor' was introduced. Shelley was initially resistant to the idea that the role of a survivor could be more powerful in the long term for her compared to the potent empowering strength she derived from the victimised role ('victim rage'; D3). Conveying to Shelley the triumph of becoming and being a survivor rather than a victim allowed her to alter her self-perception and, concurrently, she reported that her urges to self-injure decreased dramatically. Clearly, TP1 and TP2 (wanting to destroy yourself or others) affect each other when change occurs.

TP3 was addressed by encouraging Shelley to retrospectively examine her choices of men and friends in the past, how she subjugated herself to secure her position within a relationship, despite its dysfunctional nature, and to understand the importance of asserting her own wishes. She stated that 'perhaps being on your own is safer than being with a bastard, just to be with one', which demonstrated that Shelley contemplated solving this problem of relating by avoidance of intimacy altogether. The negative side of this option (i.e., unmet needs, isolation) and her confusion about obtaining intimacy and affection 'at all costs' was raised with her. Shelley learned to perceive relationships as discretionary and to bolster her definition of herself as independent and capable rather than enslaved and constrained by harmful relationships. Her depressed moods improved and cravings for excessive alcohol decreased. TP4 (feeling disappointed by people), and the fluctuating feelings that were associated with this problem, were managed through the vehicle of the transference–countertransference patterns as they emerged with the therapist and others. Shelley could quickly recognise her experience of hatred towards other people and the shift in her perceptions of them as 'letting me down'. Helping her to realise that she was projecting images of her parents onto others (as 'defective carers', sadistic, attacking 'destroyers') encouraged Shelley to be more objective about her reactions in interpersonal situations and delay her attributions that they were similar to her parents or boyfriends in the past.

Positive changes were achieved for TP1 (coping with suffering), TP2 (wanting to destroy others or yourself) and TP3 (feeling depressed and bingeing on alcohol) in that she reported being able to recognise their effects upon herself and relationships and changes to associated difficulties (depressed moods, frequency of binges on alcohol, episodes of self-injury, feelings of shame, rage and guilt) were observed. At follow-up review, after three- and six-month intervals, Shelley had entered a new relationship and reported that she still experienced significant doubts about her partner's fidelity and trustworthiness, but she was able to avoid perceiving him as described in the RRPs of the self-states addressed in therapy. She recognised her partner's faults and that 'no one is perfect'. Self-injury had stopped completely and she was abstinent from alcohol. Shelley reported that she did not send letters to the recently bereaved and voiced her embarrassment about her destructive behaviours in the past.

A CAT analysis of post-traumatic nightmares

During the fifth session, Shelley disclosed that she had been 'bothered by dreams' since childhood and particularly of late, during which she awoke in a heightened anxiety state (breathlessness, palpitations, sweating) and often 'screaming and crying'. She felt confused by these dreams, which she claimed were 'just replays of what happened'. Shelley, at times, felt also that her day and night were 'all folded into one' and she was preoccupied, socially withdrawn, emotionally labile and fatigued during the following day. Shelley requested to work on why she experienced these dreams and she wanted them 'taken away'. Her dreams were repetitive in their themes and Shelley kept a self-monitoring diary of the dreams over a three-week period. Four recurring dreams were recorded.

Dream one. 'I am watching an old lady, she's ill and can't protect herself, being physically beaten by two men in an alleyway, I don't stop them or anything, I think they sexually interfere with her too, the funny thing is that I feel glad that she's getting hurt.' Her response to this dream was confusion, feeling guilty about the fact that in the dream she did not help the woman and ashamed of her reactions to the event. She mentioned also feeling somewhat relieved and elated that she was not injured herself and 'someone else was suffering, not me this time'.

Dream two. 'I am being sexually hurt, I'm not sure if it's a man or a woman or an animal. The place smells like a fusty church. I can't breathe, then I look down and see that one of my legs is missing, it's been bitten off. I panic, I feel helpless, I shout for help and a lady passer-by walks over. I beg her for help. She just laughs and walks on.' Shelley's response to this dream was that she felt failed by others, that she deserved the attack and she was injured for life. After this dream she would report becoming convinced that she could smell the scent of the church on her clothes and hair, feeling contaminated.

Dream three. 'A faceless person, like a heavy weight on top of my body, crushing me down. I lose my breath and pass out. I then wake up in a panic and screaming.' This dream evoked a state of heightened anxiety, an acute fear for her safety and a sense that she was extremely vulnerable and in constant danger.

Dream four. 'I'm in a garden, as a little girl. I'm wearing a floral dress. It's a sunny day. I'm dancing for my mother. I can see how pleased she is, smiling, applauding. She's proud of me. I then get an uneasy feeling, like being jealous, uncomfortable. There's a man, a stranger. My mother's talking to him, very attentive. She's flirting. I think, 'Who is he?' I dance more and begin to cry. My mother continues to ignore me.' Shelley's reactions were of envy, rage and anxiety, stating that this dream generated a nauseous feeling and despondency.

The CAT model of trauma or therapy does not provide any distinct recommendations about addressing nightmares or flashbacks per se. Psychoanalytic thinking has informed our conceptualisation and treatment of dreams and nightmares within therapy to date. Hartman (1984) proposed that dreams and nightmares were stress–response imagery with a short natural history, becoming diluted within weeks or months of the trauma or blending into other dream elements. Lansky and Bley (1995) differentiate vivid, affect-laden memories which are unmodified forms of traumatic experiences with 'true' dreams in which dream work is observed (i.e. screening, secondary revision), manifest and latent content can be detected and the dreams serve a defensive function. Several therapeutic approaches do not incorporate intervention strategies to manage nightmares and it is easy to be critical of direct exposure-based techniques which appear, from a psychoanalytic perspective, to be a forced reliving of the trauma scenario and collusion with the manifest, surface content of the dream or nightmare only. Shelley's dreams could be considered indicative of an ongoing 'post-traumatic state' because of their chronicity and habitual content.

The understanding and treatment of Shelley's upsetting dreams were guided by two sources. Firstly, based on her self-monitoring, a definite pattern emerged whereby the occurrence of the dreams coincided with events during the previous day in which she reported feelings of shame, rage and psychological fragility. These included being ridiculed as malingering by a health tribunal medical consultant, being rejected by the females in her sheltered hostel for 'flirting and being too manipulative' and an incident in which a group of men made derogatory sexual comments about her style of dressing. Her dreams were most often directly about traumatic incidents with danger, interpersonal attacks, fantasies of blissful care and fusion and a responsive failure in emotional attunement from others. She reported a sense of vulnerability and enhanced neediness on the day before the dreams, following the experiences of shame and self-denigration. This description coincides with the psychoanalytic model of Lansky and Bley, who proposed that part of the post-traumatic state included true dreams which had manifest and latent content, a screening and defensive function and served to modify affects of shame and guilt from the day material into less overwhelming emotional states. The dreams were also attributed to transform the fractured, traumatised and shamed sense of identity into a more engendered self-representation (e.g., self-state).

Secondly, the themes and content of each of Shelley's dreams could be conceptualised within the self-states of the SSSD constructed with her. The dreams centred upon fantasised interactions and relations, which reflected the core RRPs and self-states as defined in the diagram, with little need for convoluted interpretation of unconscious motivations and complex dream work. Shelley was asked to explore the dreams from this perspective, explicitly framed within the assumption that the dreams may be expressions of and vehicles for transforming her sense of shame, self-denigration and anxiety and mending her fractured and disorganised sense of her identity. In dream one, it is interesting that Shelley watches someone else being attacked (projection of the 'sadistic/attacking' RRP) and she is physically and psychologically intact; yet feels guilt for not intervening and shame for reacting with a degree of pleasure and relief. In dreams two and three, Shelley reports scenarios in which she is herself injured by an assault, her sense of self damaged with associated feelings of fear and shame. The fourth dream appears to be a representation of her fantasised relationship with her 'defective mother' in which she is empathically failed, disregarded and her attention usurped by a male stranger. Shelley could also link the behaviour of the female passer-by (in the second dream) to a feeling of being abandoned when suffering abuse and requiring assistance from others.

In Shelley's case, she had experienced prolonged, chronic Type II childhood trauma (Terr, 1991) and her recollections of the abuse were indistinct and unclear in terms of specific details. Her dreams were not simply replays of the abuse as affect-laden memories. The therapeutic task for these distressing dreams was to explore the connections between Shelley's experiences of shameful events and the content of the dreams themselves, using Lansky and Bley's hypotheses about the transformation of shame to fear and reconstitution of the self within the content of the dreams. Shelley's dreams did show evidence of an increased neediness and a sense of having been repeatedly empathically failed. The dream content was also indicative of her fractured sense of identity and changes from shame to fear, although discussion about her reactions to these dreams provoked shame once again.

Shelley linked the feelings of shame to the 'suffering victim' RRP ('deserving' the assaults, projection of the victim role in dream one onto another, then guilt and shame for doing so) and her feelings of rage to this shame also ('victim rage' of SS4). It is evident that she derived some emotional relief from identifying with the '*sadistic/attacking*' RRP, but once again experienced self-admonishment for this. During the period when Shelley disclosed the dreams and their content, she demonstrated a change in her attitude to the therapist, becoming more irritable and hostile. The therapist could sense that Shelley was withdrawing from the work at this time. She reported that she was experiencing strong, almost compulsive fantasies about killing the therapist as a response to feelings of shame and rage. Her reactions were explored within the reformulation and Shelley considered these thoughts to be more manageable and understandable subsequently. She voiced her belief that the rage associated with being in the victimised role was empowering, and made her feel stronger and more psychologically 'solid'. Victim rage appeared to emanate from her experiences of shame and represented a means of integrating her sense of a fractured and incohesive identity.

Commentary

It may be questioned to what extent childhood abuse is a predisposing factor for the development of severely disturbed attachment patterns and erotomania. The reason as to why one survivor rather than another begins to repeat or re-enact abuse in adulthood is difficult to ascertain in all cases. Is it victim rage which catalyses the wish to act destructively? Is it simply a repetition compulsion (van der Kolk, 1988) to re-enact the abuse scenario as an attempt to gain a sense of mastery over the feelings which accompany abuse? Or, perhaps, the sado-masochistic dimension of the original relationship is replayed towards others as well as oneself? Research by Burgess, Hartmann and McCormack (1987) has suggested that there is insufficient evidence to propose that enacting the abuser role towards others results in a sense of mastery over the original trauma itself, despite the intuitive logic of this hypothesis.

Victim rage can positively facilitate the transition from the role of victim to survivor and many abused adults become determined that they will not suffer further on behalf of the perpetrators, stating that they reject the illusory control and terrorism the perpetrator created in the relationship. The vast majority of survivors could not contemplate causing anyone else to suffer, knowing the reality of victimisation and its effects. Their compassion is intact and strong. On the other hand, the fundamental capacity to empathise with the suffering of others may be limited for patients such as Shelley. She caused pain and suffering to exact revenge against others as a form of communication (to induce the pain she felt in others) and also to express her rage. Shelley was remorseless about her violence, believing her actions to be justified and righteous. In her case, it was clear that she identified with the aggressor (SS4; D1) or 'destroyer' as a means of coping, which is a form of *abusing–victimised* RRP. This manoeuvre was also a maladaptive way of grasping power and triumph over devalued and hated people. When a survivor demonstrates this strategy, the risks to self and others can be serious. Of course, these patterns can be inferred to dictate dysfunctional learning or deficits in impulse control (van der Kolk, 1988).

Shelley displayed an intense hatred for others and, at times, herself. As stated by Akhtar (1999), 'Hatred . . . places the individual in a state of psychic bondage' (p. 102) and, similarly, Kundera proposed that 'hate traps us by binding us too tightly to our adversary' (1990, p. 24) and can form the stable, yet preoccupied and tormented basis for masochistic attacks on oneself. This hatred appeared to fuel her experiences of rage towards anyone whom she perceived to be mistreating her, a direct legacy from the abuse she suffered during her development. Unfortunately, Shelley's hate also constrained her to the internalised RRPs derived from past victimisation and formed a central facet of her perceptions of others.

Violence has been suggested to represent a particular response to trauma whereby the expression of rage acts as a means of restoring one's sense of self (Pollock, 1995) or indicative of a 'disintegrative product' (Feldmann, 1988) stabilising the fragmentation in the self when stressed. As suggested by Dutton (1998) in *The Abusive Personality*, 'rage is the magical elixir that restores an inner sense of power' (p. 103). CAT views aggressive behaviour and affects such as rage, anger and destructiveness as extensions of the survivor's repertoire of procedures, be they symptomatic, avoidant, interpersonal or self-managing. It is likely that each case needs consideration of differing explanations to account for the relationship between the original abuse and adult offending, if a link exists at all.

What does CAT add to our conceptualisation and management of cases such as Shelley? Her dramatic changeability and unpredictable risk to herself and others were serious challenges for any competent therapist, her actions causing confusion and anxiety for anyone who tried to take responsibility for helping her. The shifts in her perceptions of herself and others, her moods and behaviour were difficult for Shelley to predict. Her capacity for self-reflection was so compromised that it could be argued that she did not represent a good candidate for psychotherapy in the first instance. Indeed, a great deal of effort and persistence was required to encourage Shelley to engage in the therapeutic process, with ruptures to this relationship tolerated and stagnation in the process anticipated. Helping Shelley to make sense of her own subjective reality and empathically communicating to her that these experiences did have a pattern and could be changed installed hope and recruited her participation.

The patient's reformulation developed as therapeutic contact continued and the view that she demonstrated borderline erotomania was inferred after differential diagnosis excluding other potential disorders. Shelley demonstrated a mixed profile of attachment patterns, particularly preoccupied and dismissing. She was considered to exhibit borderline, narcissistic and histrionic personality features with antisocial and psychopathic tendencies. Her reality testing was intact and she was not deluded. Her behaviour was more accurately understood as emanating from her attachment and personality pathology. It is interesting that Kienlan *et al.* (1997) cite two cases of stalking that had fatal outcomes where narcissistic and antisocial features were observed in tandem with a predominantly dismissing attachment style. Childhood adversity and abuse were reported also. Shelley's case mimics this combination of factors. CAT enables both therapist and patient to jointly construct an accurate understanding of dysfunctional patterns. Symptoms and other problematic patterns (dilemmas, traps and snags) are incorporated into the diagram also and targeted inside and outside therapy sessions. The challenges to the therapeutic relationship are conceptualised and managed as indications of definable transference and countertransference patterns, shared with the patient and worked on collaboratively. The link between attachment pathology, personality features, transference patterns and relational behaviour is openly analysed and addressed.

One of the benefits of a relational model of psychotherapy in these types of cases is that it explicitly guides the therapist through the confusing and continually changing sequential patterns within the patient's behaviour, facilitating the tracking of sudden, unexpected shifts in perceptions of self and others, relating and moods. The patient is encouraged to recognise these dysfunctional patterns and revise them accordingly. The therapist is provided with a concise tool to avoid collusion, prevent stagnation or rupture of the therapeutic alliance and manage the difficulties which arise within and outside sessions. Being able to accurately predict when a patient may become threatening or aggressive and understanding the reasons for this behaviour are paramount in order to facilitate appropriate responses to these instances. In one sense, accurate prediction can forestall escalation into violent behaviour (or its development and occurrence at all) through the use of a CAT reformulation. CAT provides a unique method to conceptualise the attachment pathology of patients who engage in intense, obsessive relationships and clear guidance regarding management and treatment processes in these difficult and challenging cases.

A further strength of CAT as a process of reformulation is that it focuses on the centrality of restricted, unelaborated patterns of relating which dominate the patient's interpersonal behaviour. The RRP of *abusing-to-victimised* and the distorted pursuit of idealised care can imprudently govern interpersonal relating, with little or no adaptive alternatives evident in the repertoire of certain patients. Helping the patient recognise and actively address these issues to deter repetitive, dysfunctional transactions is critical and CAT explicitly defines the effects of these patterns within and outside the therapeutic relationship.

CHAPTER 9

TERESA HAGAN AND KATH GREGORY

Group work with survivors of childhood sexual abuse

Group work with survivors is seen not just as a valuable adjunct to individual therapy but as a powerful treatment in its own right. Many clinicians also intuitively feel that a group approach is to be favoured. While there has been a sustained interest in offering group-based help for survivors utilising a diversity of techniques and approaches from a range of therapeutic models (e.g., Herman & Schatzow, 1984; Hazzard, Rogers & Angert, 1993; Blake-White & Kline, 1985), much remains to be developed here. There is little consensus on client inclusion criteria, duration of therapy, degree of disclosure of the experience of abuse, gender mixes or degree of structure, and there is a need for more empirical outcome research with particular attention to addressing high drop-out rates. Most evaluations of this type of work suggest a number of advantages that may accrue over and above what can be achieved in individual work. The provision of a forum where survivors can meet together and share experiences is thought principally to allow them to experience that they are not alone, and not different (and not worse) than others, thus addressing the stigmatisation they feel. It is also hoped that they will form new relationships and develop a sense of trust in others, and that these processes can begin to reduce the guilt and self-blame which are prevalent.

One of the problems which can be seen to beset such group work is high drop-out rates as survivors can find the work too anxiety provoking or feel they do not belong in a group mainly because of the complexity of their problems. For survivors who have a long association with mental health services, their difficulties do not make any sense to them and they often present with a confusing and complex array of problems which persist but lack any coherence. Llewellyn (1997) has drawn attention to this problem with the therapeutic literature itself. Survivors report that it is hard to gain any purchase on their experience of themselves and others and few, if any, have found diagnoses helpful (see Community Health Sheffield, 1999).

It seems that the experience of childhood sexual abuse is a particularly difficult area in this regard. There are a number of features of this history which one would expect to lead to such problems. Being 'singled out' as different and the target of abuse (as many report) leaves a lasting impression which can be difficult to revise in individual work. Childhood sexual abuse remains a taboo topic which results in there being an absence of any consensual reality within which a survivor might situate their experiences (Sullivan, 1953). Having access to and participating in a shared discourse is a main means by which we all make sense of our experiences. Indeed for many survivors this absence is exactly what was engineered by the abuser(s) to ensure their victim was rendered powerless. Such a resource can only be provided in a group context, by the lived experience of building a shared understanding with others. It is the essentially social nature of our reality and the isolating features of childhood sexual abuse which give group working an inherent logic. Such considerations have informed the approach we have been developing—that there is a fundamental sense in which group work can be particularly useful to this client group.

It has been argued elsewhere about the need in mental health care to access and provide both conceptual and material resources for clients if they are to have any realistic opportunity to change (see Hagan & Smail, 1997a, 1997b) and the lack of attention to these matters is a main criticism of individualistic approaches to helping, particularly within the dominant schools of psychotherapy. In our work we aim to provide clients with both the conceptual means to make sense of their experiences and the material context of a group in which such a tool can be used. The issues at stake can become clearer if we consider the nature of secrecy a feature which dominates survivors' accounts of their past. A secret shared with a therapist can remain a secret now held in trust by the therapist and remain an unrevised organising principle.

The provision of conceptual and material resources

CAT holds out much promise for working with survivors as reformulation forms an explicit step in the process of helping. The task of reformulation involves the development of a plausible hypothesis to account for the origins of problems. This is prepared as a sympathetic and respectful statement of how the survivors learned to cope with the conditions with which they were faced in childhood. It helps to identify their activity in this (how they made use of whatever skills and abilities they had), and how their coping strategies were the best ones they could adopt at the time and how these strategies enabled survival. Ryle (1990) has made an important conceptual advance in his notion of procedures—as the active and meaning-laden patterns of behaviour, thinking and feeling which have developed in response to childhood (and other) experiences. These procedures are not to be seen as an error or a mistake in thinking which needs correcting in later life and which appears to be the target of at least some versions of cognitive-behaviour therapy but reflect stances which were taken up in relation to the circumstances of life. These stances are often basic and formed uncritically at an early age when language may not be well developed. Furthermore, they are not necessarily articulate or verbal matters at all. These are important considerations as survivors repeatedly report that they can recognise the patterns being described but have little awareness of having made any choices in them, either then or now. As this was the only sense that they could make from the situation in which they found themselves and what was communicated to them, the feeling of unrevised childhood conceptions remains pertinent.

Some group work within CAT has suggested offering members individual reformulations, which are then shared with other group members and worked with in the group setting (Duignan & Mitzman, 1994). We have preferred to facilitate a group reformulation process because the group context itself can be important in achieving the reformulation desired. In order to facilitate the process of group reformulation, we have developed a conceptual tool entitled 'lessons learned to survive', which serves the same function in the group as the Psychotherapy File in individual work. While the latter assists both clients and clinicians to identify the patterns/procedures which are in evidence today, the diagram we have developed attempts to trace their possible genesis, showing how they could have developed and become elaborated over time. Group members have found this tool to be particularly useful and practitioners with whom we have discussed this work have expressed an interest in utilising it in their work. The tool draws principally upon group members' own accounts of their difficulties. However, we have been influenced by and incorporated aspects of other work in this area: notably Ryle (1990) in the centrality of achieving a workable reformulation to frame the therapeutic work undertaken; Finkelhor and Brown's (1985) work on tracing the effects of trauma in childhood; Mollon's (1996) work on what he terms 'core beliefs' showing 'this is the way my world works'; van der Kolk *et al.* (1996), in understanding the possible linkages between self-harm and the reduction of unacceptably high levels of arousal among trauma survivors; and Bass and Davis (1996), particularly their section on 'honoring what you did to survive'.

The linkages between past experiences and behaviour now

Finkelhor and Brown (1985) have developed a very useful organising framework, which draws out the linkages between childhood sexual abuse and subsequent problems using a model of traumagenic dynamics, all of which can be seen to relate to the misuse of power. The modelling of links in this way shows how childhood sexual abuse can lead to particular kinds of behaviour and experiences that in turn can lead to a wide range of problems and to this extent can be seen as similar to the identification of problem procedures in CAT. Following Finkelhor's lead, we have found it useful to draw up a diagram of such proposed linkages as a tool for use by survivors themselves, mainly using clients' own accounts and their words as shown in Figure 9.1. The diagram reflects *the meaning of the abuse,* and how survivors' actions and subsequent experiences can make sense, not as faulty, distorted ways of seeing and acting, or dividing experience into psychological impact and behavioural elements (as Finkelhor & Brown do) but as a means of capturing the very wide range of experiences brought by survivors. The summary statements used in the diagram are regarded as the somewhat inarticulate ground rules and consequent actions, which can be gleaned from a person's account of their difficulties. As such, clients are unlikely to have such clear statements sitting in their heads or to have consciously and deliberately made such decisions (although some did). Rather it is a shorthand way of summarising and identifying the meaning underlying their way of living—how the world is and was for them.

Modelling the effects of childhood sexual abuse as a therapeutic tool

The diagram is not a fixed one, but a therapeutic tool. Over time it has been modified and elaborated by clients and clinicians adding further patterns and cross-linkages in order to encompass the very wide range of difficulties encountered by survivors, which can include hallucinations, delusions and obsessions. The diagram shows how *for much the same reasons* one survivor may find herself self-cutting while another self-neglects. Any one survivor may do both at different times and in different situations. The diversity in experience is not a problem for psychological models of this kind, which would as noted by Finkelhor and Brown (1985) anticipate a whole array of effects. Making sense of the past can enable a person to make more sense of the present, to engage with an understanding of themselves in a new way, begin to see the meaningfulness of their experience, how in a sense it can be regarded as sensible and not just plain crazy. When the meaning of the abuse is taken as the central concern, using such a conceptualisation also shows how so-called *non-contact forms of abuse can be just as damaging as contact abuse.* Other models which are not psychological (e.g., medical models or epidemiological ones) face grave problems when trying to account for the varying effects of childhood sexual abuse as outcomes are not standard across individuals. It is hard to account for the fact that some survivors show few ill effects of their traumatic experience, while others carry long-term and corrosive difficulties which have warranted psychiatric diagnoses. The attempts made to categorise the abuse into more and less serious forms overlook these psychologically salient issues. Case material in which details have been changed and which does not relate to any one individual illustrates this matter quite clearly. The following account captures the deeply disturbing nature of some forms of non-contact abuse and can also prove traumatic to read.

Case illustration: Susan and the ritual with the mirrors

Susan was referred on discharge from the psychiatric unit where she had been admitted following a serious suicide attempt. While on the ward she had disclosed childhood sexual abuse by her father from the age of four. The staff members were not sure that this was related to her problems as he had not actually had intercourse with her, but they thought she might benefit from talking things through. Susan was the eldest of four daughters of an 'army' family, which meant that she spent her childhood travelling around from country to country living in army accommodation. She said that this was a very isolating way to live as friendships were difficult to maintain, there was little continuity in neighbours or schools and they had little if any regular contact with others outside of the family.

The story of her torture at the hands of her father was hard for her to tell. Having been forbidden to ever mention what had taken place in her childhood, Susan still felt disloyal and in terror of revealing family secrets. Her father was alcohol dependent and a bully who discouraged any member of the family from having contact with anyone outside of the home. He frequently battered his wife and took pleasure in humiliating all of them. He had always been obsessed about hygiene, insisting that each member of the family go through mindless and time-consuming cleaning of themselves and the house at all hours of the day and night. No one ever defied him or challenged his right to rule.

On coming home from school, she remembers how her father started to sit in an armchair, which provided a good view of the back entrance to the house. He would sit with a scowl on his face, watch her come in and then proceed to question her in the finest detail about who she had spoken to that day, what she may have done wrong and what the penalties would be if she put a foot wrong. He soon started to insist that on entering the house from school each day she should remove her underwear at the door and put them in the wash bag immediately (he said he had to be sure 'she was clean, in case any of the louts at school had been touching her'). Soon he elaborated this ritual and she was then required to remove her underwear at the back door where he could see that 'she did it properly' and she was required to get onto the kitchen stool to enable her to reach the kitchen sink and she had to wash 'the filthy things' and then show them to him. She then had to hang these on the clothes line in his direct line of sight. They had to be pegged out in a certain way, and she remembers him touching himself 'in a strange way' as he watched her completely obediently following his instructions. He would then sit looking at the underwear and talk about 'how dirty girls were' and she remembers how he would work himself up into a fever pitch of both anger and sexual excitement and rub his penis violently.

Day by day this ritual was elaborated upon, whereby, on seeing her come in the gate, he would take the wall mirror down and place it on the floor at his feet. She was required to stand over the mirror with her legs apart so that he could look at her genitals. If her legs shook in her fear of his wrath, he would say that she was deliberately trying to make it difficult for him to see what she had been up to. As time went on her father added more and more elements to the ritual. For example, she was required to curtsy for him, touch herself for his pleasure, and so on. Above all she had to exactly follow his instructions or suffer the consequences.

These performances went on year in and year out, all through her childhood and into her teenage years. He took great pleasure in elaborating these rituals, often to the point where she would forget one or other element and be punished for the omission. He convinced her that she did all of this for her own pleasure, that she was 'filthy' and that she smelled bad, especially around her genitals. To this day Susan suspects that on entering a room everyone can smell her and she scrubs herself with powerful cleansers until she is sore.

Susan dreaded coming home from school and started having panic attacks on the way home. She first collapsed on her way home from school at the age of five and was branded by her teachers as an attention seeker. Her father told her that if she ever told anyone about *her* filthy habits (very early on she was convinced that the rituals were her own) she would be taken away. Interestingly her mother was always absent at the time Susan came home from school and even when she begged her mum to be there, she never was, and would come home later and later as demanded by her husband.

It would be difficult to call this anything other than childhood sexual abuse and the question of him physically touching her is quite irrelevant to any understanding of Susan's difficulties, which were severe depression, self-neglect, nightmares and multiple suicide attempts. The central issue is that of power—the misuse of parental power.

As was apparent in this case, when medical models are accepted, staff routinely disregard such case histories as constituting serious childhood sexual abuse and often minimise the importance attached, as there was no physical contact reported. This is a serious error we have come across many times throughout the mental health services.

Making meaningful links: the use of the diagram in practice

In working through this model with survivors we are going further than their immediate understanding of themselves, offering them a tool with which to gain some purchase on their experiences. In our group work with survivors these are some of the most powerful sessions, where the room is filled with the noise of new understanding. Despite the fact that many of them have made use of a whole range of sources of help, often over many years, they claim that they have never been given the means to understand themselves in this way before. They begin to see how the experience of abuse in a situation of powerlessness forces the victim to make an accommodation (i.e., learn the lessons necessary to survive) and these in turn can lead to serious problems. The sessions we devote to reformulation in this way are also experienced as very painful as group members revisit their childhood experiences and realise the full extent of their misuse at the hands of others. Learning ways to manage this distress also forms a key part of the group working.

Here an outline is offered of each 'thread' in the figure showing how the multiple and complex problems with which survivors present could develop. In order to take account of the varying levels of difficulties with which survivors present, the diagram also suggests how difficulties could over time become elaborated into problems, forming patterns which could begin to fit with psychiatric diagnoses (labels from diagnoses are included in the diagram as these are part and parcel of the fragmentary understandings with which clients have presented) and how such mental health problems could then become sedimented with the passage of time, particularly if the person has spent long periods of time in a psychiatric hospital, where opportunities to take part in the normal social world are severely curtailed. Further sedimentation could then lead to further disability, the patterns taking a chronic course.

Moving reformulation from the individual to being a group task

In previous adaptations of CAT for group work, clients are offered individual reformulations of their difficulties, and these are then shared with the group as a whole. This is not the preferred method of working with our groups as it poses clients the problem of trying to make sense of essentially private experiences (which are taboo) on their own or with one other person (the therapist), who may not have sufficient legitimacy in the clients' eyes to speak with relevance to their experiences. Especially in the case of childhood sexual abuse, one of the most profound difficulties facing survivors is that they have never had the necessary social validation of their experiences. This is a key process by which all of us make sense of our world and our experience (i.e., the social world frames reality). For topics and experiences which are not

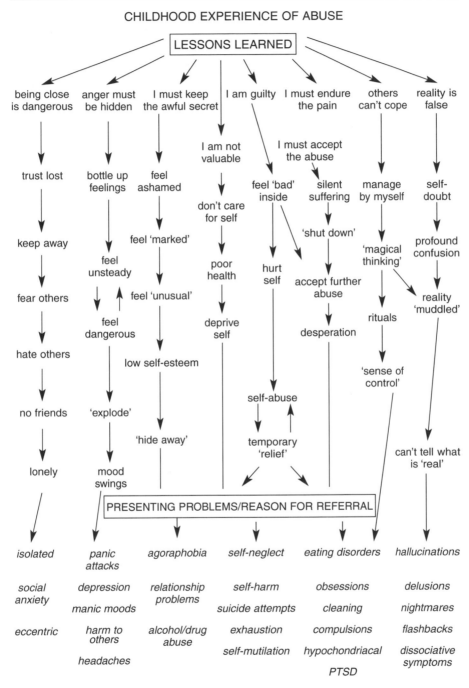

Figure 9.1   'Lessons learned' (passage of time—sedimentation)

taboo, hidden and denied, it is so easy to make sense of things that we barely think about it—there is a whole world of meaning embodied in our culture in which we are immersed which 'makes sense' of what we see, think and feel. The survivor has not had access to such and this is partly why they feel they are 'mad'. The tool could be regarded as our attempt 'to fill the vacuum in our cultural forms' (see Mollon, 1996).

In our work with survivors we have found it preferable to provide clients with the conceptual means (tools) by which they can in a group context reformulate for themselves, and discuss the particular ways in which they have been affected within a non-pathologising process of clarification. The group then can be seen as important in providing clients with a social world of shared meanings which is not available to them elsewhere.

Tracing the linkages

Although, for simplicity, the linkages are drawn out on the diagram and in the following text as if they are linear, i.e., one thing leads to another, when you start to work with the model it becomes clear that the cross-linkages between pathways are numerous and complex. There could be many arrows put in this way but this makes the model look too complex and daunting at first glance. We have also found it helpful to look at one strand at a time.

'Being close is dangerous': broken trust, loneliness and social anxiety

Learning that 'being close is dangerous' quite sensibly leads survivors to adopt the strategy of keeping away from people as they cannot be trusted. This can function in lessening the frequency of the abuse. Most survivors have had little reason to revise this stance and in fact go on to generalise it to other situations and people and are puzzled in adult life to find that (unlike others) they have no friends, have never had friends, they fear other people, have never spent much time with others to be able to be at ease in social situations and feel very lonely. Even when they find themselves in situations that look promising, where a friendship may be struck, they find themselves keeping others at bay. Many survivors describe how good they are at keeping other people at bay and have been told countless times through their lives how fierce and off-putting they can be to others. When trust in others has been profoundly shaken (unless you are without sense) you are unlikely to run the risk again. Some survivors are referred for help because they are isolated, suffer chronic social anxiety or use medication to control anxiety, while others are seen as frankly eccentric, 'odd' and hard for others to understand. In this way group members find it easy to see that the less opportunity they have had for practising being with people and knowing 'how to go on' or learning the rules which apply in social situations the more likely they are to continue to have problems.

'Never express angry feelings—angry feelings must be hidden inside': bottling up anger, panic attacks and depression

Similarly with regard to the control of feelings, most survivors report that they could never have expressed (or even acknowledged to themselves) how angry they were (and are) with the abuser(s). Being powerless in relation to the abuser, they had to learn to hide their anger inside or suffer the consequences. Many of them report that they now *automatically* bottle up their feelings, especially angry ones, and sometimes shake with the effort. A common problem reported by survivors is panic attacks, which they can remember experiencing very early in life and which in descriptive terms resemble intense anger that has had to be held down. It is usually in situations in which they feel there is no escape (resembling the circumstances of their abuse) that they still have such 'attacks'. Bottling up explosive anger over a long period of time can feel very hard to manage. One consequence of this is that many survivors actually feel quite dangerous, that they could kill, and believe that if they ever let go of their anger it would be uncontrollable, overwhelm them and destroy others. Many of them report violent and torture-based fantasies which go through their minds (and incidentally confirm what a bad person they must be to think in this way). Sitting on such powerful and explosive feelings also takes up a great deal of energy and many survivors consequently feel flat, depressed and exhausted.

Some survivors also have been a source of danger to others and report almost 'seeking out' situations in which they can let rip, goading others into anger to justify an explosion, and some have violently attacked others. Some simply avoid any situation in which they might get angry for fear of the consequences and may become agoraphobic. A further consequence of bottling up feelings is that survivors find they can have extreme mood swings. They can lose any sense of confidence in themselves when without warning they suddenly find themselves flying into a rage at what appears to be the slightest provocation, and others who have any contact with them routinely treat them with great caution. This further confirms their sense of being dangerous. Severe headaches and a history of migraine are also common. Many survivors also use alcohol and drugs to deaden their feelings.

'I have to keep secrets inside': having to keep awful secrets, and being of no value

Survivors have often been made to keep secret what was done to them and feel the burden of having to carry this, with the accompanying sense of deep shame. Keeping secrets also fuels the need to keep away from others because if anyone was to get too close they might discover the secret and reject them. To be the carrier of shame is painful and leads to an overwhelming sense of low self-esteem. Many survivors seem unable to look others directly in the face and present themselves in hunched and cowering ways which can be interpreted by others as 'sneaky' and to be avoided. Many hide away and have severe agoraphobia and profound difficulties in forming relationships with others. This feeling is further strengthened by some of the other linkages shown in the diagram (e.g., the lesson learned that 'I am not valuable'). When treated as of no worth, for others to do with as they will, survivors point out that it would be quite illogical for them to take good and respectful care of something that has no value. Thus many survivors report worrying levels of self-neglect, depriving themselves of food, sleep, comfort or any form of self-nurture which most people would take for granted. Many also report the tendency for them to give things away to others, those considered to be worthier.

'I am guilty for what took place': guilt and the acceptance of further abuse

Survivors often describe many instances of abuse throughout their lives, how subsequent and current partners have abused them, and sometimes it seems like no matter how careful they are in selecting partners, others feel at liberty to abuse them. Many report having been raped on numerous occasions, not bothering to use condoms, enduring physically and emotionally violent relationships and feeling like they are somehow branded by their childhood as a victim, calling out to others to carry on where the original abuser(s) left off. Of course, one of the lessons they took with them from childhood was the fact that they had to accept abuse. That was the way it was. They did not have the power to stand up to the abuser(s) or to find ways to stop it and no one else did this for them, leaving them to conclude that they must accept abuse as a fact of life. Having no experience of preventing abuse, they find that in the course of other relationships they simply allow others to abuse them—the pattern is the same and they feel they have no right to question what feels like the natural order of things. Many end up desperately unhappy and using refuges to save their lives when their partners become increasingly dangerous.

Survivors also report how they can dissociate and blank off from abusive experiences, cut out the physical and emotional pain which is involved and simply endure the experience. They find that they have the capacity to endure much misuse, sometimes without even flinching, such is the control they learned to exercise as children in the face of their abuse, and that the capacity to become numb was helpful.

'No one can help me here, I'm on my own': too much responsibility too young and the desperate attempts to gain control, leading to 'magical' behaviour (obsessions and rituals)

Many survivors soon found that no matter what they did they could not escape the abuse, and also that those around them to whom they might turn for assistance appeared not to be able to help either. Thus they concluded that they simply had to manage by themselves. Children have access to few resources which they can actually control, and often resort to forms of magical thinking which at the least give the sense of some control, however illusory that may be. Many survivors report the little ways in which they tried to help themselves, 'reasoning' with fate that, for example, if they saw five blue cars that day then they would be safe, or if they repeated things to themselves or counted objects incessantly then all would be okay. As with any magical and therefore practically ineffective strategy, the tendency when it does not work is to do it even harder and assume that it is simply a question of effort. Some survivors also report finding themselves 'filling up' their mental space with such mind-numbing rituals during the abuse as it was a means of not having to attend to what was taking place (e.g., counting patterns on the curtains). Many survivors come for help when this has taken over their lives (e.g., in severely controlling their eating, or other obsessive rituals).

One particularly common obsession for survivors is cleaning, as if they are constantly trying to wipe away the 'dirt' in what can become a ritualised pattern, not just to the point of having sparkling houses—although many of them do—but to the point of total exhaustion, for example being unable to leave the house before checking and rechecking certain items, saying some set piece and the wealth of other obsessions most therapists hear about in their everyday work. It seems that the illusion of control offered by magical thinking is important to their psychic survival. Of course it is also possible that sheer coincidence could also function to feed such obsessions as there may have been a moment when the abuse did not occur just when they enacted a ritual.

'It's all my fault': a false sense of 'control' in preference to a nightmare world, feeling guilty and the logic of punishment and self-abuse

One way or another, most abusers manage to convince the child that it is the child's fault that the abuse took place, and we have countless versions of this. Survivors explain that they were too pretty, seductive, naughty etc. If they were blamed for being attractive, for example, survivors may do anything to make themselves unattractive (e.g., put on significant amounts of weight, or stop eating in an attempt to lose weight and their 'dangerous' breasts, disfigure themselves, never bathe to ensure they smell bad). There is a sense in which one can feel responsible for anything that one 'does', or finds oneself doing: the feeling/experience of participation, even if forced, leaves a sense of agency and therefore culpability. Survivors report feeling 'simply bad' inside as one of the worst aspects of abuse which feeds into and is fed by the other linkages outlined. They all feel different in some fundamental way from other people— a feeling which is enhanced by the common experience that other members of the family were not (or claim they were not) abused. Survivors describe this sense of being different as like a mark they carry with them, and many of them develop agoraphobic tendencies, a terror of being seen by others, and stay indoors, not daring to expose themselves to the gaze of others.

Feeling that they are marked and 'bad', it also seems right to abuse themselves. Survivors often report painful levels of self-abuse which can include constantly insulting themselves in their everyday thoughts, shaving their heads, cutting themselves, nipping themselves, beating themselves, alcohol abuse and, of course, attempts to get rid of themselves in suicide attempts. Continuing to abuse themselves also feels fitting—this is exactly what they think they deserve, and the world would seem out of kilter if they were not routinely punished in this way.

Another aspect of their experience which can lead to repeated self-harm is the feeling of temporary relief that often accompanies, for example, self-cutting. This was the way it was in childhood, that after each painful experience of abuse they knew that there would follow a time of relative peace and relief until the next time (this is also reported by many clients who have been physically abused). The abuser(s) would often follow a pattern, the warning signs of which would be all too clear to the victim. After such episodes some survivors report that the abuser would then leave them alone for a while, and they could allow their anxiety levels to fall, experience at least some peace and rest and let down their guard. They now repeat the experience in adulthood in order to feel, even if momentarily, a sense of peace. It is almost as if survivors feel they have to 'pay' for a sense of peace and calm—they have learned a pattern of intense pain, high arousal and then shut down. For their highly disciplined bodies and minds, pain precedes a state of calm. Many survivors report that for the most part they are not able to feel any sense of bodily (and the concomitant psychological) comfort and that the alternative to repeated self-cutting, for many of them, would be to remain in an intolerable state of high arousal, highly anxious and constantly watchful, their body filled with adrenaline. The self-cutting is a means at their disposal (within their power) of securing temporary relief.

Also in childhood, some survivors 'preferred' to take responsibility themselves for what took place, as this allowed them to retain a sense of a reasonable world (i.e., 'if I am responsible then the whole world is not like this') and the survivor can also maintain the illusion of control if it is within themselves.

It can be too overwhelming for a child to accept that there is nothing they can do and that the world is a terrible and unpredictable place for them.

'My reality is false and cannot be trusted': blanking out, hallucinations and delusions, lies

Many survivors report that the way in which they endured the abuse was by blanking out, at least mentally 'leaving' the situation until it was all over, and they find themselves doing exactly the same today, whenever they feel they are in a threatening situation. Few feel they have any sense of control over this and in the group work it is common for survivors to find that the topics under discussion are so threatening that they have difficulty staying with the group in the room. They simply cannot attend to what is taking place. This can be such a frightening experience that survivors lose all faith in themselves, they no longer trust themselves or their own thinking, as frequently and automatically they find that their conscious attention to things simply takes off and they are left, sometimes in dangerous situations unable to act. Many survivors have described how, for example, they have stopped driving as they cannot trust themselves in this way. Such a profound sense of self-distrust leaves survivors prone to intense bouts of self-doubt and anxiety and lacking in any sense of confidence with which to face the world or make any decisions.

Others report that their sense of reality about what was going on was so skewed by the power of the abuser that they now have little faith in their own rational processes. Abusers convince children that what is taking place is not really happening, that it is their imagination, a common lie being that they were dreaming. The message is driven home that this is a forbidden topic which attracts severe punishment and threats whenever attempts are made to name what their body and their mind know was taking place. Children depend on adults for the naming of reality and this trick convinces many survivors that they are truly mad, that they conjure up events in their own heads.

Another way in which profound confusion accompanies abuse is that it often takes place in total silence, where the activity is not being commented upon in the normal way in which most 'social' events (i.e., those we share with another) are. It is also often accompanied by strange and unusual behaviour on the part of the abuser(s), who at some level know that there are no words for what they are doing, and survivors are often left with a very powerful sense of something peculiar going on, but not having the means to describe the experience, even to themselves. When total power is held over another, there is no social requirement to observe the 'rules' of polite interaction, for example, to communicate with the object of your attentions—you just do what you like.

It should then be no surprise to find that some survivors report feeling totally confused and unable to grasp/remember what took place. Rather they have experiences which can feel hallucinatory or delusional. Many also do have frank hallucinations and delusions wherein the content often metaphorically 'captures' what was going on. It is almost as if their psyche obeys the requirements of the social situation and the demands of self-preservation. They register the experience in the only permissible form. This is probably one of the reasons why many survivors find themselves drawn to creative writing, this being a fitting form in which to capture elements of their experiences.

Also there may be a sense in which traumatic events are not grounded in reality by normal processes (e.g., talking them through with others), taking on a life of their own as the victim repeatedly tries to make sense of a much distorted world. Over the years the faces and feelings involved in the abuse keep coming back unbidden and cloud the reality of situations today. Thus many survivors report that any trigger (a smell, a tune, a time of day, an activity) brings the experience back—flashbacks over and over again. This happens both in their sleep (when their guard is down) and in their waking life. It may also help to explain the painful finding that when survivors join our therapy groups and begin to build up trust they let their guard down, only to find that they then begin to feel much worse than they did before coming for help. We routinely warn survivors about what may happen in the group work and we have found that these phenomena tend to decrease as the survivor makes more and more sense of their experiences. To be told that they are mentally ill, as a means of apprehending their experience, simply confirms for them what the abuser(s) have said all along, that their reality has no meaning with which others will concur, and sediments their sense of themselves as worthless.

The links spelled out above are those which survivors have been able to develop in the group work, where the similarities of their experiences allow them to meaningfully confer and experience validation for their formerly entirely private and lonely experiences. The linkages are not causal in any positivistic sense of the term, but are links of meaning. They are entirely a psychological matter. The figure provides a general template within which each survivor can map their own experiences and it can be seen that the threads are not mutually exclusive and there are many possible cross-linkages that can be made. Essentially such clarification seeks to undo the mystifications of power and increases their sense of meaning.

We encourage each individual in the group to map for themselves their own linkages on the diagram, to identify concrete examples from their own lives to illustrate how the thread is experienced by them, and we work together in specifying the traps, dilemmas and snags which can easily be added to any of the threads. Group members appear to find it relatively easy to identify which 'threads' apply to them and which do not and each member aims to construct his/her own unique mapping. Some survivors have been able to identify 'threads' which were relevant in the past, but no longer have the same significance and can see how they have changed. The reciprocal role procedures are also identified and worked through, particularly the *abuser–abused* RRPs. This can be particularly painful work. This work forms the basis of plans for change and the group also provides a context in which experiments with being different can be tried out, not just in imagination but *in vivo*, with their companions in the group. Secrets really do cease to be secrets when worked with in such a group context, wherein survivors report feeling that they have been given a real opportunity to revise their past with others.

Acknowledgement

We would like to acknowledge the contributions of J. Czarnocka, J. Ward, A. Konyk, S. Martindale, L. Wilkinson, L. Clancy, A. Daykin and C. Todd, and the survivors themselves, who do not wish to be named.

CHAPTER 10

MARK STOWELL-SMITH, MICHAEL GÖPFERT AND SUSAN MITZMAN

Group CAT for people with a history of sexual victimisation

The topic that we are considering here is a complex one that combines three potentially diverse aspects in one clinical situation, namely, group therapy, CAT and the clinical issues presenting when dealing with people with a history of sexual victimisation. It will not be possible to do these three aspects justice in a reasonably comprehensive way. We are writing this chapter as part of a reflection on work in progress; this is not our complete work but belongs to the whole community of professionals and clients to whom this is relevant. For the purpose of this chapter we will focus on people where the victimisation has occurred during their childhood and we will illustrate our analysis with details of our clinical experience and work.

Brief group psychotherapy

Group therapy, CAT and the various aspects of a past history of childhood sexual abuse each have their own literature and potentially quite divergent theoretical constructions. Often people tend to muddle through all these differences because they cannot afford in their everyday work to be too purist in their approach. As has been stated in a different context, each particular modality of psychotherapy can become abusive when used exclusively and is seen as having universal validity (Göpfert, Webster, Pollard & Nelki, 1996). Furthermore, when looking at the more successful ways of working with complex problems such as a history of severe trauma, the pioneers of such therapies tended to go beyond the boundaries of their purist modality, or start combining frameworks of therapy (Göpfert & Barnes, 1994). Some authors have distilled principles of integrating ways of working (e.g., Norcross & Goldfried, 1992). Since our subject links at least two modalities and combines them with a particularly complex area of clinical work, we start with a brief outline of how this integration has been done by others.

Firstly, Agazarian and Peters, when writing about their model of group therapy, postulate that each part component of therapy requires its own theory (Agazarian & Peters, 1981). In their case this means that the group requires one set of theoretical tools, whereas the individual in the group and the understanding of the individual in the group setting require another set of tools. The requirement is for these theoretical frameworks to be compatible with each other, while being and remaining fundamentally different, so that each can provide some explanatory power in a complementary manner to help make up the whole picture. In Agazarian and Peters' model the two main approaches are (classical) psychoanalysis and systems theory as Kurt Lewin has developed it (Lewin, 1951a, 1951b). This approach to using compatible but divergent theoretical approaches contrasts with another, second way of trying to combine divergent ways of constructing psychological space. This is exemplified by Wessley Carr (1994), who has described what can happen when bringing together seemingly different frameworks such as Christianity and psychoanalysis. He argued that any integration of two such different frameworks creates a new, third framework, which may be unpredictably different from its two original constituents.

In our experience these two points of view are not as different as they might appear at first sight. A number of authors in the field have tried to put together an 'integrative' amalgam of both (e.g., MacKenzie, 1990; Marziali & Munroe-Blum, 1994). It might be important to emphasise, though, that there is value in keeping distinctions both alive and clearly visible when combining different frameworks of psychological understanding. The same would apply to intervening therapeutically and in integrating differing approaches to create a third, new approach to help address particular issues.

Ours is work in progress within this area of differing approaches, not yet with any finite outcome. Initially, we will begin by outlining some select contributions to group therapy, followed by some aspects pertinent for the treatment of sexual abuse, and a discussion of how these two perspectives can be combined with a CAT approach. This account will be interwoven with some clinical illustrations.

Being part of various groups is an essential part of the human condition, as is being in a relationship. A relationship is dyadic whereas a group is a triad or more. Just as various forms of individual therapy are specific adaptations of a 'relationship', so the various approaches to therapeutic group work represent an attempt to create the essential human quality of 'being part of a group'. Not surprisingly, one basic assumption of the more purist approaches to group work tends to be that the essence of human beings is social rather than individual, both at the conscious and unconscious level. Barnes, Ernst and Hyde (1999) have defined 'group' as a collection of people who come together with a common aim, which differentiates them from 'not-group', thus drawing a boundary. Boundaries are necessary in order to develop cohesion but they also bring with themselves the potential for internal and external tension and conflict (Barnes *et al.*, 1999). Barnes *et al.*, using concepts of Stock Whitaker, outline that all therapeutic (and other) group activity can be mapped along three dimensions: the type of group member, the purpose of the group and the type of group. Hence the starting point is: 'Who do you want to help? What can be achieved? How can the group be set up to do this?' (Barnes *et al.*, 1999).

A dimension of both the relationship and being-in-the-group is the difference between female and male. Culturally the corresponding social roles are that of mother and father, which are stereotypically differentiated into passive, nurturing and care-taking, as against active, independent and repressive of emotions. These stereotypes have been increasingly challenged over recent decades and various forms of feminist group work have sprung into existence (e.g., Butler & Wintram, 1991) aiming to focus particularly on the social aspects of gender role. Similarly there are men's groups that have addressed the psychological consequences of sex stereotyping upon men (Price, 1988). Gender-specific groups allow for particular gender-related identity issues to be the focus in a way that is akin to gender-specific organisations in other contexts. There are particular clinical situations when gender issues might be central to what has to be dealt with, such as in sexual victimisation.

There are numerous other groups reported on in the literature, usually defined by clinical diagnoses such as eating disorders or BPD. Usually these are groups with a structure that may include some training purpose such as anxiety management or social skills training. Other groups with a specific purpose could be groups to explore one's attitude to money, or sexuality. Groups for women with a history of childhood sexual abuse, for instance, may well be better seen as belonging to this category if they deal with specific issues such as sexuality or relationships. Often women with a history of sexual victimisation end up being referred for anger management if anger and frustration are an important consequence of the abuse. There is always a possibility that referring people to such groups carries a risk of pathologising and revictimisation by the professional system. This is particularly pertinent with people with histories of childhood sexual victimisation where issues of shame are central to the after-effects of the experience, and labelling can easily reinforce rather than resolve.

A further feature of brief psychotherapy groups is that they may have a large educative component. For instance, one of us (MG) had previous experience with a physiotherapy group for patients suffering from chronic fatigue syndrome. This educative group provided the means of support, mutual understanding and exploration for its members that they would have found difficult to accept from any other kind of group. Another particularly interesting model is that of Linehan (1993), where a whole series of training modules in groups is combined with individual therapy for people with complex needs. There is good evidence for the efficacy of this approach, which integrates many different ways of thinking, including a hefty dose of developmental psychology, with one-to-one and group therapy in what is a variant of cognitive-behaviour therapy called Dialectical Behaviour Therapy (DBT). It also seems to work well for women who have been sexually abused.

There is some concern in the literature about the more psychoanalytic, exploratory, interpretative group work and its ability to make people feel worse or unsupported (e.g., Piper, Rosie, Yoyce & Azim, 1996). Another, not unrelated and recurring concern in the literature is the difficulty of running closed, time-limited groups for people with more complex issues. In respect of CAT groups Maple and Simpson (1995), who provide a comprehensive account of the general interface between CAT and group analysis, have aired this concern. One conclusion that they reach is that CAT and group analysis can be integrated in a variety of formats and settings. However, CAT groups should be longer than the initially conceptualised 12 sessions for people with more complex problems. The relationship between time-limited, closed groups and people with complex psychological needs has been most succinctly formulated by Marziali and Munroe-Blum (1994), who reviewed the literature and also reported on the basis of their clients' experiences. In general, they found that outcome was worse in that people failed to get better, or continued to slowly deteriorate in terms of their capacity to function socially. More importantly, people tended to feel invalidated if interventions 'went above their heads' or did not seem to reflect an accurate enough understanding of what it was like for them to suffer from complex problems. They felt most comfortable with an empathic, validating response, a principle that is well established elsewhere in the literature (e.g., Linehan, 1993). Marziali and Munroe-Blum's model of interpersonal group psychotherapy emphasises the need for the therapist to recognise when the therapeutic alliance 'goes off track', not dissimilar to Safran's cognitive model of rupture-of-therapeutic-alliance therapy (Safran & Muran, 2000). There is some evidence that this may well be an important ingredient of good therapy generally (Hubble, Duncan & Miller, 1999).

Applied and training groups apart, the model of group therapy most commonly practised in Britain is group analysis, developed by Foulkes (Foulkes 1964, 1975) and taught by many institutions across Europe, often in collaboration with the Institute of Group Analysis, London (IGA). Group analysis is based on the assumption that human beings are social rather than individual. The individual is the basic biological unit but the group is the basic psychological unit. Foulkes described the group metaphorically as a 'hall of mirrors'

(Foulkes, 1964), linking this to early experiences of being cared for, where 'mirror reactions' are an essential lever in developing a differentiated self from the caring fused self of mother-and-child.

Barnes *et al.* (1999) define group analysis as a process which relies on the therapist (usually called group conductor) being able to utilise their own thoughts and feelings as a crucial part of the observations of the whole group process. The field of observations is defined by the type and purpose of the group (the group's task), which closely links with the role of the conductor (the therapist's task). There needs to be clarity with, and adherence to, this role so that the analytic activity of the group can take place within its clearly defined boundaries. Analysis occurs in the group and by the group including the conductor. The conductor's role predominantly is to provide the containing setting by looking after the boundaries of the group, which requires dynamic administration to ensure that the anxieties of being within a group are optimally protected by what is going on externally to the group. Setting up a group is a task that requires the setting up of a working relationship between the conductor him/herself, the group (initially in the mind) and the organisation within which the conductor is working. The aim is to set up a good-enough-group. Barnes *et al.* emphasise that there are no absolute rules for setting up and conducting groups, that there are only consequences to be worked with (Barnes *et al.* 1999). Thus group analytic principles do not have to be taken as exclusive but as potentially enhancing and enriching any other way of working in groups in a complementary way. Group analysis pure would have to be considered with the caveat of the findings and conclusions of Marziali and Munroe-Blum (1994) as running the risk of alienating people, at least those with more complex needs, unless their need for validation of their experiences is carefully attended to.

In conclusion, there are many other modalities of group therapy not mentioned. There are other ways of working with groups using concepts derived from Sullivan's work (Sullivan, 1953; MacKenzie, 1990), which are all very useful and important contributions to the field. The interested reader is referred to the literature, especially MacKenzie's book on time-limited group therapy, for further information and reference.

Cognitive analytic group therapy

Although originally developed as a model of brief individual psychotherapy CAT has continued to address a range of non-individual applications. For example, in Ryle's *Cognitive Analytic Therapy: Active Participation in Change* (1990) suggestions are made in relation to the application of CAT with couples. CAT concepts have also been applied to an understanding of psychologically damaging work environments (Walsh, 1996), while Dunn and Parry

(1997) and Kerr (1999) have applied the CAT model as a way of understanding the dynamics between community mental health teams and their more damaged, borderline clients. A number of factors unite these applications. These include emphases upon the dialogical or reciprocal nature of interactions between either the self or other, the self and particular subsystems and the application of the SDR as a descriptive device that can represent and illuminate this activity.

The first reported application of the CAT model in a group setting was described by Mitzman and Duignan (1993) and Duignan and Mitzman (1994). This first paper explores the process of CAT group therapy by focusing upon one man's experience within a group and concludes that the SDRs acted as an active therapeutic agent within the group, containing distress and encouraging participation and disclosure. In a comprehensive review of the theory and practical application of CAT within groups Maple and Simpson (1995) report the development of a number of CAT groups. These include groups which have been conducted as part of a psychotherapy outpatient service, within a day hospital and a counsellor training group in which understanding was facilitated of the counsellors' own reciprocal role procedures. Two of us (MG and MSS) have conducted groups which combine psycho-educational material about the process of CAT therapy along with the more traditional elements of CAT groups. These elements were combined as a means of considering whether the provision of educational material might serve to contain a group of self-selecting patients from a waiting list of a psychotherapy outpatient department.

In the majority of cases, the CAT groups described by Mitzman and Duignan (1993) and Maple and Simpson (1995) adhere to a structure that broadly corresponds to the one offered in individual CAT. That is to say, they are time-limited groups, conducted by one or two therapists, utilising prose and diagrammatic reformulation to delineate repetitive patterns and states of both intrapersonal and interpersonal activity. The reformulation, recognition and revision of these states and associated patterns are seen as central to the enterprise of both individual and group-based CAT. In many cases the prose and diagrammatic reformulations are generated during the course of individual sessions that precede the start of the group. One well-used format is for members to then introduce themselves within the group by way of reading out their own reformulation letter. Subsequently individual SDRs are introduced. These remain available and visible to group members for the duration of the group, either in their existing format or by being copied or transcribed on to a large sheet of paper. Group reformulation and Goodbye Letters might also be introduced as a way of addressing the group process. Maple and Simpson (1995) provide an example of how the group Reformulation Letter might retain contact with the practice of CAT by, for example, describing group dilemmas. They describe a group in which it was necessary to be:

either masked, isolated but safe, keeping true thoughts and feelings inside for fear of ridicule, aggression, rejection or disappointment

or

vulnerable, exposed and likely to be looked down on, rejecting others before they can reject and abuse me. (Maple & Simpson, 1995)

One effect of early reformulation is to accelerate and bring to the surface issues or processes that in a longer-term group might remain dormant. Once activated an advantage of the CAT group over individual CAT is that the group allows for the development of multiple reciprocal role enactments that can be immediately examined within the context of the group. Welldon (1996) argues that the potential multiple transferences within a group are particularly relevant for the sexually abused patient who may bring to therapy a well-developed feeling of uniqueness. This in turn may evoke collusion from the therapist by making him or her feel protective and responsible about them. Within the group, different forms of transference mean that this sense of suffocation can be avoided. In turn, these different forms of transference or reciprocation allow further opportunities to know and understand the patient.

A final feature that we wish to emphasise here is one that distinguishes CAT group therapy from longer-term, psychoanalytically informed therapy that purports to promote deep, psychological changes and psychological growth. Ryle (1995a) has argued that a form of time-limited therapy such as CAT does not claim to promote psychic growth; rather the limited focus of CAT is to 'unblock' obstacles to psychic change by highlighting recurrent patterns of inter- and intra-psychic functioning. In so doing a foundation is created in which psychic growth might occur. The following material illustrates these more modest aims in the treatment of a woman with a history of incest within a CAT group.

Katie was a 38-year-old divorced woman who had been recruited by her father into an incestuous relationship from the age of 7 to 16. Her relationship with her mother was cold and distant. She participated in a CAT group that combined four sessions of individual CAT leading on to 20 group sessions. She took with her into the early group sessions an SDR that posited three self-states organised around the themes of ideal care, abandonment and emotional disengagement. By group session five it seemed that Katie had attempted to configure the group so that she and another male group member were the group parents, looking after and tending to its more needy children. She referred to a programme that she had seen on TV that had described a 'fat camp'—a holistic residential treatment centre, providing a comprehensive range of physical and psychological treatments for obesity. Throughout subsequent sessions the 'fat camp' became a metaphor to which Katie frequently referred and which appeared to represent her desire to make the group into the perfectly caring environment in which she could both give and receive perfect care. Failure to attain this sense of perfect care within the group appeared to provoke in Katie a state shift into emotional disengagement. Over the course of the group Katie came to understand this type of shift as emerging in the context of her earlier history in which she had sought some form of perfect care to rescue her from her neglectful mother and predatory father. As with the group, the failure to attain perfect care led her as a child into what she termed an 'emotional deep-freeze' in which she engaged with others but always in a detached, superficial way. Within the group the SDR allowed her an insight into this state shift. In turn she resolved that she would endeavour to remain emotionally in touch both with herself and others in the group without becoming over-involved. She was able to successfully achieve this goal within the group and a parallel began to emerge outside of the group in which she began to maintain relationships with others without becoming too entangled in their lives and difficulties.

One survivor's experience of an early CAT group: a case illustration

In 1988 the first CAT group was piloted at St Thomas's Hospital, London, closely replicating the structure of an individual 16-week CAT. Susan Mitzman (SM) and Dr Imelda Duignan (ID) conducted the group, receiving weekly supervision from Dr Anthony Ryle and Ian Simpson, Group Analyst. Candidates for the group were selected from patients on the waiting list who had been assessed as suitable for individual CAT. The group was heterogeneous, time limited and semi-structured. The group comprised four males and four females between the ages of 18 and 37 years, representative of the diverse mix of social class and ethnicity of the catchment area. One female patient, June, had a history of brief reactive psychoses; the remaining patients were diagnosed with personality disorder. One group member had previously received formal individual therapy.

There were concerns regarding both the marked gender disparities, and the extent of psychiatric disturbance, within the proposed group. The women in the group were ethnically diverse: of the four women, two were Jamaican and one, Elizabeth, was Anglo-Chinese. The women in the group were of poor to average educational attainment, and generally passive in their interactions with others, with the exception of Elizabeth, a 19-year-old student whose brief and unsatisfactory interpersonal relationships were characterised by 'beating others' or 'being beaten'. Elizabeth spoke at length of fighting violence with violence. She carried a knife for self-protection and graphically described her physical assaults upon others whom she perceived as 'wronging' her.

The four men were Caucasian, two being graduates, and one a postgraduate, all of whom were highly articulate. Peter had endured a catalogue of experiences of physical attack, gross violation and humiliation at the hands of others. John, a narcissistic male, had been physically abused by his father. John spoke of constantly 'being bullied' or having his 'bubble burst'. He would diminish others by 'bursting their bubbles' as a means of defending against imminent attack. James feared being overwhelmed by dangerous feelings, expressing superiority and contempt for others. He intellectualised his difficulties and struggled to accept anything 'good' from others.

Over the course of four weekly individual sessions, each patient received a psychiatric and psychometric assessment, completed the Psychotherapy File and developed both a prose and Sequential Diagrammatic Reformulation. The individual sessions contributed an educational component to the early phase of therapy in as much that they provided firm boundaries, fostered realistic expectations and increased motivation and optimism, while also modelling patient–therapist collaboration.

Patients were informed that, following the four individual sessions, they would form as a group from week five, when they would share their prose reformulation with the large group, as a means of introduction. On week six, and at all subsequent group meetings, the eight SDRs were combined and reproduced on two A4 sheets and placed on an accessible central table. Initially, the group conductors acted as modellers, actively offering individual and group interpretations which were linked to the SDRs. Group members soon became familiar with their own and others' SDRs. The SDRs acted as tools for addressing reciprocal relationships and transference material within the group. Group members were encouraged, over time, to use the SDRs to develop 'exits' from their unwanted procedures, within the context of the group. The group met for 12 weekly 90-minute sessions, and Goodbye Letters were exchanged in the final session.

Group members were predominantly characterised by *abusing–abused, attacking–attacked* self-states, initially raising some concern about the group's robustness and potential for containment. From the outset, however, group cohesiveness and the rapid acceleration of the group process were markedly apparent. The heterogeneous nature of the group, in combination with early, individual reformulation, the sharing of prose reformulations in the first group session, and the active use of SDRs in subsequent group sessions, were considered to be crucial factors in influencing firm boundaries, group cohesiveness and engagement.

June was a pleasant, somewhat dowdy, 35-year-old Jamaican woman with a history of brief reactive psychoses and depression. The group was June's first experience of psychotherapy. She had sought therapy in order to relieve and make sense of her isolation, depression, shame, low self-esteem and powerlessness. In individual sessions with SM, June expressed a need to 'come to terms' with her unsatisfactory relationship with her mother, whom she experienced as critical and rejecting. June's husband demonstrated little affection, repeatedly exploiting June's placatory behaviour. June expressed a 'lack of entitlement' and chronic low self-esteem, striving to be a 'good wife and mother', assuming undue responsibility for others, while receiving little appreciation. She felt increasingly resentful and isolated, fearing the expression and strength of her anger and dissatisfaction. June experienced intense guilt and shame, and disclosed (for the first time) that during her early to mid-teens a sexual relationship had developed between June and two of her older brothers. June, conflictingly, described the sexual relationship as pleasurable, being the only source of intimacy and 'love' she had received as a youngster. June's presenting complaints were characteristic of, and consistent with, a history of childhood sexual abuse. Her SDR depicted her self-states, which were organised around themes of deprivation, powerlessness, lack of value and angry loss. June's experience of the group is briefly described below, illustrating the crucial role of her prose reformulation within the context of her group experience and the facilitation of therapeutic change.

During the individual sessions it had not seemed appropriate, and indeed there was insufficient time, to gain a detailed account of June's experience of abuse. June did, however, briefly describe regular penetrative sex with an older brother over a number of years, sometimes taking place in the presence of the younger brother. It was emphasised that the decision to share the experience of abuse would reside with June, and that June's Reformulation Letter would serve as her introduction to other members during the first group meeting. June felt that her Reformulation Letter should make some reference to her abuse experiences. The contents of this letter are reproduced below:

Dear June,

You were born in Jamaica and when you were 2½, your parents left you in Jamaica with your grandmother, when they emigrated to England taking your two older brothers with them. Your grandmother cared for you in the best way she could, but she was cold and undemonstrative and you never felt close to her. At the age of 7, you joined your parents in England, who by now were strangers to you. You were reunited with your older brothers, and your parents went on to have four other children. Throughout your childhood, you 'skivvied' after your brothers and sisters, while feeling estranged and a 'cuckoo in an unfamiliar nest'.

You received very little warmth or care from your parents. Because you were the main carer at home, you rarely left the home, and had no opportunity to make friends of your own. You became particularly close to your two older brothers, who supplied you with the warmth, comfort and intimacy you so desperately craved. Both your parents were punitive and strict, and they parented you by firm discipline, rather than caring for you in the way you would have wished. You were unable to communicate with your parents in any meaningful way, and it was as if 'a brick wall' separated you from them. You have given up trying to 'reach out' to your mother, and you are left feeling angry and confused.

As a result of your early experiences, you feel that you deserve no care or respect from others, and you feel ill equipped to care for your own children, and to establish equal relationships with men. You have become disillusioned with your parents, and also with men, and you have given up hoping that things will ever be any different. You are left feeling guilty and a failure. As a consequence you find yourself submitting to the needs of others because you are afraid of confrontation. At times, your hidden, angry feelings 'break through the surface' to the extent that you fear you may 'lose control'. You are unable to assert your needs, as you feel guilty and undeserving of anything better. Thus, in your close and intimate relationships, you demand nothing, and therefore get nothing back in return, except hurt and disillusionment. This makes you feel increasingly worthless and depressed. When you think of your early life the pain becomes unbearable, and instead of confronting the hurt and anger, you 'shut down' and are left feeling empty and more depressed. You are joining the group to try to make sense of your confusion and distress.

June's early separation from her mother and the ensuing themes of remoteness and isolation extended into her adolescence. This was experienced as emotional detachment (as if being separated by a 'brick wall') during the period of extensive (parental) physical, and (fraternal) sexual, victimisation. Her experience of marginalisation appeared to be maintained, and exacerbated, by 'secrecy', fearing that the risk of intimacy would inevitably expose her 'unacceptable' and 'bad' self. This dilemma was mirrored in the group. June initially appeared uncomfortable and withdrawn from the group, rarely contributing. With gentle facilitation, June was 'eased' into the group and she gradually gained sufficient confidence to movingly articulate her childhood deprivation and harsh and neglectful parenting.

In the beginning of the middle phase of the group, June sent her apologies explaining that she had suffered a brief psychotic episode. June, however, was keen to rejoin the group and she returned the following week, remaining in the group with no further missed sessions. This was of interest, given that a history of previous psychiatric hospitalisation is associated with increased likelihood of failure to complete therapy (Hazzard *et al.*, 1993). The containing structure of CAT, the cohesive nature of the group and the identification of RRP re-enactments via SDRs may have protected June from further fragmentation, and safeguarded the group from dangerous regression and destructive transferences. During June's absence the group expressed their sense of loss, fearing that they had failed to acknowledge and 'hold' June sufficiently. It was hypothesised that the men held a fantasy they had acted as aggressors projecting their victim selves into June, and were holding the responsibility for her fragmentation. The group welcomed June back with genuine warmth and relief, acknowledging that her presence had been missed.

Throughout the middle phase of the group, June spoke of frightening childhood experiences, of 'running away from home' on several occasions, and described 'deeply painful memories' which she wished to share with the group. John, who had presented as markedly narcissistic both on assessment and in the early phase of the group, expressed support and warmth for June. John likened June's need to run away to his own experience of staying away or coming late to the group, as a means of inducing loss in others, and feeling that his presence had been missed. John felt 'personally to blame' in that June had 'not been getting enough from the group'. June responded by saying that she had been 'touched' by her welcome back. She remarked that others had 'talked of many of the things' she had been unable to express for herself, and she spoke of her anger and bewilderment at her parents' rejection of her, hinting at the sexual involvement with her brothers.

In the penultimate session, June announced that she had asked her mother to read her prose reformulation in an attempt to communicate the pain of June's childhood and her mother's remoteness. Consequently June and her mother had begun to 'talk for the first time'. Having 'rehearsed' sharing her reformulation with the group and experiencing acceptance, we suspect that June was able to risk 'reaching out' to her mother. Experiences of social and familial stigmatisation (real or perceived) exacerbate the core experience of abuse and trauma, and June's partial disclosure of her abuse within the group, and to her mother, was seen as pivotal to the resolution process. Simply 'telling their story' may be insufficient for the 'victimised' patient to achieve reparation (Tyson & Goodman, 1996). In addition, prose and diagrammatic reformulation is seen to facilitate the exploration and recognition of past trauma and current unconscious re-enactments within the context of the group.

In the final group meeting June expressed 'special thanks to the men', declaring that the group had provided her with the first experience of men who did not set out to denigrate her (and whom clearly had the potential to do so), but who were 'able and willing to listen' to what she had to say. Nicholas and Forrester (1999) argue that reassurance from a heterogeneous group has more validity as empathy is received from those whom, in another setting, may be experienced as threatening and unable to understand, and who are unlike a therapist, whose role it is to be accepting and 'kind'. June believed she 'deserved to be heard', feeling as if 'she could move mountains'. It was recognised that June had, on many occasions, been able to appropriately offer, as well as derive, guidance and support within the group. At this juncture, SM commented on June's marked physical transformation during the latter phase of the group, when she had emerged from the anonymity of her dark, dowdy clothes, wearing (appropriately) younger, brighter clothes and had altered her hairstyle. June also shared with the group that she was considering pursuing higher education, or possibly applying for part-time work.

All members of this early pilot CAT group demonstrated statistically significant improvements across a range of post-treatment measures, with the exception of Elizabeth, who dropped out after attending two group sessions. At one month's post-treatment follow-up, five of the patients, including June, felt that the group had fulfilled their expectations and wished for no further help. Two patients requested further therapy and were subsequently referred to a long-term group. Specifically, June demonstrated marked shifts in her presenting symptoms of isolation, guilt and shame, consistent with Carver, Stalker, Stewart and Abraham's (1989) view that time-limited groups offer an ideal setting to address patients' experiences of stigmatisation and powerlessness. Cahill, Llewelyn and Pearson (1991) state that short-term approaches are less likely to have an impact upon dysfunctional family relations, low self-esteem, trauma symptoms and sexual dysfunction. Given June's rapid change in the group, there were concerns that June's belief that she 'could move mountains' may represent a 'flight into health', and it is possible that a longer-term group intervention may have offered greater potential to address this specific concern with more opportunity for reality testing. At three months follow-up, however, June continued to make good progress and wished for no further intervention.

Different group genres in the treatment of people with a history of sexual victimisation

A literature on the group treatment of people who have experienced child sexual abuse has evolved from the late 1970s and has continued to accumulate throughout the following decades. Within this literature a number of forms of group genre are described. These include single-category, homogeneous groups of child sexual abuse victims, victims treated within the context of a mixed category, heterogeneous groups, time-limited and open-ended groups, and structured, focused groups along with unstructured psychotherapy groups. In this section we will review some of the studies that have described these applications to the treatment of this population.

Many of the early descriptions of group-based treatment describe relatively short-term, structured programmes applied to groups of child sexual abuse victims. Examples of this include work by Tsai and Wagner (1978), Herman and Schatzow (1984), Goodman and Nowack-Scibelli (1985), Alexander *et al.* (1989), Carver *et al.* (1989) and Roberts and Lie (1989). Some of the variations within this genre include differences in the number of group sessions (between 4 and 18), whether the group is open to incest victims or anyone who has been sexually abused, styles of group leadership, and single or co-led groups comprising either an all-female or male–female team. Mennen and Meadow (1992) suggest that common to a number of these studies is the contention that the time-limited group enhances the participants' capacity to work on their problem through interaction organised around a collective understanding of a shared experience. For similar reasons such groups are said to discourage regression and difficult, destructive transferences (Sanderson, 1990).

One argument made for group therapy with homogeneous groups of sexual abuse victims is that it can provide a corrective emotional environment in which internalised family rules about secrecy and disclosure can be confronted and challenged (Goodwin & Talwar, 1989). In the short-term structured group it is commonplace for therapists to adopt a directive stance, for example, encouraging group members to tell their story, share something of their abuse experiences, reduce isolation and change their position within their families. A recent study that illustrates the position adopted in the short-term, focused approach is detailed by Longstreth, Mason, Schreiber and Tsao-Wei (1998). The authors describe a series of treatment groups comprising up to 12 females with a history of sexual victimisation meeting for 16 weekly sessions of 90 minutes duration. Specific group sessions offered a mixture of both structured and unstructured activities. The therapists addressed in a structured fashion some of the known emotional sequelae of child sexual abuse, such as self-blame, shame and body image distortions, while utilising the group process as a way of validating each woman's experience of abuse and her response to it. Group outcome was assessed through the use of the SCL-90-R (Derogatis, 1983) and a calculation of further health utilisation costs. The authors report that all of the women who completed the programme showed statistically significant reductions in all but the SCL-90-R's hostility subscale at a one-year follow-up. Despite this, however, the frequency of consultations with general practitioners did not change (Longstreth *et al.*, 1998).

In addition to these shorter-term groups a number of longer-term survivor groups have also been described. These are invariably less structured and utilise group process as a treatment factor. Mennen and Meadow (1992) suggest that in the absence of substantial empirical research decisions about the duration of group psychotherapy for the survivors of child sexual abuse are made on the basis of leaders' preferences, financial considerations and 'practice wisdom'. Cahill, Llewellyn and Pearson (1991), however, report that issues such as continuing difficulties with family of origin, relational problems, chronic post-traumatic or dissociative symptomatology, sexual dysfunction and impaired sense of self are, however, unlikely to respond to relatively short-term interventions. Hence, some indications about the length of therapy might be drawn from existing knowledge about the likely responsiveness of particular types of problem or psychopathology.

Ganzarin and Buchele (1987) described a long-term model of psychoanalytic group psychotherapy with incest survivors, the focus of which was insight into the ways in which representations of victim and perpetrator became manifest in patterns of transference and countertransference. The authors argue that the intensity of such reactions cannot be modified over a short period and, therefore, requires the framework of the longer-term group. Donaldson and Cordess-Green (1994) have described an integrated model of long-term group therapy for incest victims. This has something in common with previously reported CAT groups in as much as it combines a period of assessment, preparatory individual sessions followed by commitment to a longer-term, unstructured therapy group. Nicholas and Forrester (1999) describe long-term, psychoanalytically informed work with child sexual abuse victims in a heterogeneous psychotherapy group. They emphasise the role of projective identification as something that both perpetuates and helps us understand traumatic abuse and provides examples of how both 'abused' and 'perpetrator' parts of the self can be projected into other group members, the group as a whole or subgroups. Over the course of the long-term group the survivor is helped to reintegrate projected parts of the self so that relationships with both self and others can occur in a more integrated fashion. A particularly striking example of this type of group environment is provided by Welldon (1993, 1996), who describes a group analytic approach with groups containing both victims and perpetrators of sexual abuse. Her contention is that this combination is beneficial to both. For example, perpetrators can become aware of the extensive physical and psychological consequences of their actions when confronted with members who resemble their victims. By contrast, victims may be assisted to move from quiet compliance to the expression of anger and self-assertion in relation to group members who correspond to their erstwhile abusers (Welldon, 1996).

Nicholas and Forrester (1999) argue that one important interaction we must consider when assigning the sexually victimised to group treatment is the degree of traumatisation in relation to the transference environments provided by these different group modalities. Their contention is that short-term, homogeneous groups maintain group interaction at a relatively superficial level. Homogeneity of problems, such as difficulties with anger control, alcoholism or the psychological consequences of child sexual abuse, often leads to the development of a common focus or task. An advantage of this in the treatment of victims of child sexual abuse is that it might lead to a degree of group cohesiveness that in turn leads to early disclosure of abuse experiences and their psychological sequelae. While this might limit the opportunity for exploring transference, within the group the sense of 'us all being in this together' is something that has a containing effect upon the survivor. This containment might be less immediately attainable in a heterogeneous, unstructured group. In this respect Nicholas and Forrester suggest that the homogeneous group may be most suitable for victims who are acutely affected by PTSD-type symptoms and for whom dealing with the added stress of transference may be more than they are currently equipped to handle.

Van der Kolk (1993) dismisses the usefulness of a long-term homogeneous group for survivors on the basis that it can produce excessive dependency and idealisation of the therapist. He adds that coupled with this is a tendency for members to bond together against the outside world and in so doing actively impede the reintegration of the isolated, mistrustful survivor. These comments echo Reyes, Reyes, and Skelton's (1997) observation that the victims of trauma may compensate for an obliterated sense of self by identifying with a class of things, for example, victims of sexual abuse. Having said that, authors such as Sanderson (1990) and Courtois (1988) have reported successfully working in long-term groups with victims of both incest and sexual abuse.

There is some agreement (Tyson & Goodman, 1996; Mennen & Meadow, 1999; Nicholas & Forrester, 1999), however, that the heterogeneous, dynamic group that focuses upon here-and-now interactions offers a better alternative. We discussed earlier how the early experience of sexual abuse infuses the victim's sense of self and his or her relationships with others with the idea of abusiveness. For some, intimacy, attention and sexual abuse are coupled together so that intimacy can only be attained on the basis that abuse is either elicited or enacted. Welldon (1993) and Nicholas and Forrester (1999) have argued that the mixed, dynamic group provides an appropriate transference environment in which these dramas can be worked through. In a robust, well-contained group the survivor can begin to renegotiate a different form of internal working model for relationships with both self and others from those often engendered by early abuse. Our impression is that this is also attainable within the heterogeneous CAT group.

Westbury and Tutty (1999) summarise the findings on both short- and longer-term survivor groups and note that most studies report statistically significant changes in areas such as depression, self-esteem, and general psychiatric and trauma symptomatology. The same authors, however, suggest that caution must be exercised in considering the findings from the majority of these studies as they suffer from a weak research design in which pre- and post-test psychometric scores alone are compared. An exception to this is the Alexander *et al.* (1989) study, which employed a control group and reported statistically significant changes in participants' levels of depression and general symptomatology when compared to the control condition.

Some common issues in the group therapy of the sexually victimised and limitations of group therapy

Commonly, people with a history of childhood trauma and deprivation end up becoming helpers through a process of being 'parentified' (Göpfert *et al.*, 1996), usually either in relation to younger siblings or in relation to a needy and demanding parent. A common coping strategy may then be the sense of competence derived from helping others that can take the form of a professional career. In a group this can then generate a dynamic of people helping each other and not bringing 'themselves'.

Another common experience is the 'anti-group' (Nitsun, 1994), which represents the split-off destructive part of a group. Clinical experience as collated by Nitsun indicates that this is an inevitable part of any group process. In the case of people with a history of sexual victimisation it might be a representation of a re-enactment of the victimisation, not entirely unlike the process of revictimisation though as part of the therapeutic group experience. The following example brings the roles of 'helper' and of 'victim' powerfully together.

John was referred with a history of incest in the context of an abusive family culture involving at least three generations of his family. Childhood memories were a blur of a smell of alcohol and semen, the vision of trouser legs of grown-up people and also a strong sense of being special. He had developed a sense of competence out of a combination of being special and of looking as responsibly as he could after his mother. He had chosen a career as a psychotherapist, working with an organisation which provided for a population with a high proportion of people with a history of sexual victimisation. John was very interested in joining a CAT group to deal with some very intensely self-destructive patterns in his life. Amongst other issues his reformulation highlighted his tendency both to help people while simultaneously having an intense sense of being abused. This he enacted in the group where he rapidly became the helpful co-therapist. However, as a result, other group members felt patronised by him, and he eventually left the group, saying that he could not participate in any other way other than helping the people in the group. Since they did not want this he preferred to leave. Afterwards, other group members shared that John had told them about joining a magic circle at around the same time that he had joined the CAT group. This left the group with the need to understand. They thought that John had really decided that the 'magic circle' was where he wanted to be. The group's perception was that it was mainly a group of people with histories of sexual victimisation and the image of satanic rituals came to people's minds. Some of these perceptions were based on evidence from discussions with John. In conclusion, it appeared that John had re-enacted his abusive experiences in a powerful, unconscious and destructive way, which provided a collusive experience with others in the form of a 'magic circle', while only being able to get involved in therapeutic work in the role of therapist, even when asking and actively seeking therapy because of the overwhelming impact of some self-destructive patterns in his life.

It is important to acknowledge that as professionals many of us have a background of trauma and victimisation, as well as a propensity to become involved in the revictimisation of our patients by way of role enactment as in the above example. The way this is enacted in a group is different but group therapy does not protect us from it, as the above examples may illustrate.

It has been increasingly recognised that sexual abuse and rape are part of a much wider picture in which either unconsciously or (especially in times of war and ethnic strife) consciously the purpose is to humiliate the victim. The abuser thus may be trying to take care of his/her denied humiliation and shame because of his perceived inferiority. The power of the abuser gives his/her abusive mindset the power to determine other people's identities within the abuser's network of relationships. This is an essential part of the pattern of 'grooming', which can be crucial in understanding and therapeutically dealing with the effects of victimisation. This wider, often systemic pattern of grooming and humiliation can be the much more damaging part of sexual victimisation. As previously discussed, the psychodynamic concept of 'projective identification' is often used to provide an explanatory theory for the way in which humiliation is transmitted in the perpetration of such abuse. It is our contention that using projective identification purely as a pathological term describing how one person's split-off aspects can be successfully lodged in another person can be limiting. It may also prevent the therapist from taking into account wider, systemic aspects of what needs to be dealt with and is not always helpful, especially if it means that the pathology gets too firmly lodged in the person using mechanisms of projective identification. We would see projection and identification and any combination of these as normal mental mechanisms which underlie much of human cognitive functioning, perception and communication in particular. As such, while projective identification may be used for purposes that are incompatible with constructive relational functioning, it may also provide a foundation for mental states such as falling in love. This is an instance of a mental state that involves a degree of projective identification that would hardly be seen as 'disowning' for defensive (i.e., pathological) purposes. This is not to deny the immense usefulness of 'projective identification' as a mental mechanism but merely illustrates the need to free it from its association with pure pathology.

Another common process that occurs with the sexually victimised is one in which the sense of self is threatened with obliteration. This process is highly relevant to the dynamic that might develop within a group and can be explained through the little-known theory of Bi-Logic elaborated by the Chilean psychoanalyst Ignazio Matte-Blanco (Matte-Blanco, 1975; Rayner, 1995). Bi-Logic is based on the premise that the human mind (conscious and unconscious) has two kinds of logic operating simultaneously at any one time, namely a 'logic' which is as if all things are the same, and relationships between subject and object are symmetrical, reversible; whereas the other, more familiar Aristotelian logic would be based on differences between things, and would say that subject–object statements cannot necessarily be reversed, such as 'John is the father of Mary' does not equal 'Mary is the father of John'. Yet in the unconscious, as defined by Freud, this is exactly what happens with the associated consequences of the disappearance of space and time because of the disappearance of such difference.

Reyes *et al.* (1997), using concepts of Bi-Logic, observed that victims of trauma seem to have an obliterated sense of self due to the 'disappearance of difference'. This results in a loss of internal access to their emotional experience and a need to utilise projections onto the external to gain access to it as from outside with the help of tangible frameworks that give some sense of control and safety. For instance, they quote the case of a refugee who had lost her whole family, including her two-year-old daughter, in an act of torture and terror but had herself survived. She could talk about it when bringing a friend's two-year-old daughter whom she was minding to her therapy. The sense of self tends to be substituted by a sense of belonging to a class of things (e.g., a victim of abuse might belong to the class of 'victims of abuse' which then replaces the sense of personal identity). In this way it can become a container of otherwise unmanageable feelings. Reyes *et al.* define the effects of trauma as a loss of the internal world which instead is mainly replaced by the need to project or displace. This in turn results in an increasing sense over time of identity being bound up with belonging to a mere 'class' of people in the logical sense of the word (e.g., the class of victims of abuse). The resulting fragmentation and alienation can often lead to a 'class' struggle, an example of which will be given below (Reyes, Reyes & Skelton, 1997).

These concepts are complex and their discussion goes beyond the scope of this chapter; however, they do add to an understanding of the dynamics of sexual victimisation, and what may or may not be achieved within a group setting. If someone with such experiences is seeking help a number of generally unpredictable things can happen.

Lisa described a history of childhood sexual victimisation. As an adult her female partner went off with the female counsellor who was supposed to help them with their relationship, an event that illustrated the tendency of people with histories of victimisation to be revictimised (Chewning-Korpach, 1995). Lisa was severely traumatised by the latter experience and her life completely disintegrated, with loss of job, contraction of her social network and difficulty engaging with therapeutic help. She was eventually offered a group which she attended but again the group was constantly reinforcing her sense of victimisation, and all her experiences in that group tended to be constructed by her as confirmation of her status of being a victim, further adding to her 'revictimisation'. She eventually engaged with an individual therapist; however, the interpretations and understanding offered by the therapist initially did not make an impact upon her. There were some moments when she felt less anxious and able to reflect upon her own difficulties and was able to contrast these difficulties to her memories of her life before the break-up of her relationship. At such times she observed her female therapist's capacity to cope with the relationship difficulties with her just as she had previously done with her partner of many years standing. It was her identification with the therapist, coupled with the therapist's positive commitment to her, that allowed her to begin to reconstruct her life to some degree and then consider what further therapeutic help she might need to sort herself out. She could then use therapy again, as it was not fused experientially with abuse and revictimisation in the way that it had been in the group.

In Sharon's case the outcome was less fortuitous. She described a very serious history of traumatising incest, exacerbated by having been raped by a doctor in a casualty department when she had taken an overdose under the influence of alcohol. On a later occasion a patient on a psychiatric ward had raped her. She then went on to 'consume' therapist after therapist. She was very bright and pursued degrees in psychology and law which informed her use of professional services. Whenever professional helpers either failed to comply with her wishes or confronted her, the situation would inevitably end up with her having an experience of 'revictimisation'. Sometimes these experiences would be reinforced by some imperfection of professional practice that in turn would lead to her going to extensive lengths in complaining about the professional concerned through all available professional and legal channels. By contrast, if professionals were accommodating Sharon would eventually drop them as useless. Invariably they would have to suffer recurrent and serious infringements of professional boundaries that led them to feel abused. The only groups this woman could engage in were groups of campaigning victims and she had become a leading figure in the user movement of this area at one point. For Sharon, the conclusion must be that she had completely contracted into an identity of being a victim of abuse.

The therapist familiar with CAT will recognise that there are elements of reciprocal role concepts in the described effects of traumatisation. The crucial issue, however, is that they are a direct result of fragmentation through the experience of severe trauma. In a group, especially if there are more than one or two such members, there can be a profound effect on the group matrix, which at times can lead to great difficulties. This is apparent in the following case example where impoverished, rigid but unconscious roles were enacted and remained inaccessible for therapeutic modification.

Anne was a 32-year-old woman with a history of childhood sexual victimisation, having been sexually abused both by an uncle and neighbour. Her mother left the family home when she was four and she described a distant, uninvolved relationship with her father. As an adult she entered into recurrent abusive relationships with men. She also described a neglectful, physically and sexually abusive relationship with her own children, all of whom had been taken into care. In her individual sessions Anne announced 'If people are cruel to you, you are cruel to others'. This was represented within an SDR that posited a self-state based around an 'abuser–abused' RRP. Her goal within the group was to explore and find some exit from a pattern in which she was either a victim or perpetrator of abuse. Within the early sessions of the group she moved between quiet passivity to dramatic, premature disclosures about her own abuse and her abuse of one of her children. After one of the early group sessions she reported that another male group member, John, had approached her outside of the group and suggested that they sleep together. An emotionally charged group session then followed in which John was accused by the group of behaving in a sexually predatory manner towards Anne (John did not return for the remaining group sessions). Soon after this session Anne went on to disclose how she had made herself intentionally homeless. Accompanying the various practical explanations that Anne offered for this act was a comment that she needed to re-create a situation in which she could survive in the face of threat and danger. Her homelessness stimulated much concern and excitement within the group. Various offers of help were made that eventually led some group members covertly meeting with Anne outside of the group. This both corrupted the boundaries of the group and seemed to filter into the life of the group in an insidious and destructive fashion. At a point when the anxieties created by this situation seemed to be reaching a crescendo Anne dropped out of the group. In the final session one of Anne's would-be rescuers, Alan, commented how Anne had left a trail of destruction behind her within the group.

Technically, then, patients such as these may need an externalised object to replace what has been lost internally, as a 'scaffold' as Reyes *et al.* call it, to assist in accessing internal experiences externally. This may be possible to achieve either in an individual or group-based CAT in which a form of scaffolding is provided by reformulation. However, there is a considerable risk that a pattern may be identified as a reciprocal role but it may then not 'respond' to the more cognitive attempts to formulate and co-construct issues with the patient. What may help in such situations is difficult to predict. It could be a group of any format, be it feminist in orientation (e.g., Butler & Wintram, 1991), or heterogeneous and open-ended, or individual work if a group cannot help. Ultimately it is a question of the quality of the therapist and of the person having suffered such trauma, and what links they may be able to make, beyond the definitions of therapeutic modalities.

Concluding comments

We have reviewed some of the issues in the group treatment of the sexually victimised and considered some of the precedents for applying CAT in a group format. We believe that the optimal integration of a therapeutic group model and CAT has yet to be achieved. In particular we are aware that there is a large body of research and concepts from social psychology, including some very detailed work on roles and role behaviour, that could be fruitfully integrated with the concept of reciprocal roles with which there are overlaps.

We are currently considering how the traditional co-constructive approach of CAT reformulation could translate to a constructivist group activity. As part of a group approach, group members would construct SDRs within the group. This would contrast with the more traditional model in which diagrams are constructed with the therapist and then taken into the group. Our impression is that this creates an inevitable tension between the dependency generated through the setting of individual reformulations with a professional and the autonomy that is fostered as part of a group therapeutic approach. The resulting dependency tends to inadvertently reinforce the helplessness that is so often part of the 'victim-of-abuse' identity of our clients. It is for that reason also that we prefer to avoid the term 'survivor' as it is so strongly identified with 'victim'. While we totally support the notion that victimisation has occurred and that responsibility belongs to the perpetrator (and the cultural context if it condones the perpetration of sexual victimisation), we believe that the notion of being a 'victim' can reinforce helplessness.

Acknowledgement

The authors gratefully acknowledge the contributions of Brigitta Bende and Sarah Mackereth, who were part of a project developing time-limited groups using psycho-educational and cognitive analytic concepts. We are grateful for financial support from North Mersey Community Trust and the practical support of the Liverpool Psychotherapy and Consultation Service in completing this project, which will be reported in detail elsewhere.

Part III

Clinical issues in applying CAT

CHAPTER 11

Clinical outcomes in the application of CAT for adult survivors

Evaluating the effectiveness or efficiency of psychotherapies is not an easy task and producing an adequate evidence base for psychological therapies generally is a complex endeavour (Roth & Fonagy, 1996). Comparing clinical outcomes for differing forms of therapy suffers by failing to evaluate the complex interplay between patient, therapist and technical variables and, realistically, manual guided practice of psychotherapies cannot capture the unpredictability and vicissitudes of delivering psychotherapy and the idiosyncratic and often uncollaborative contribution of some clients. Co-morbidity of disorders further complicates interpreting outcomes and it is impractical in a busy, demanding clinical setting to exclude needy clients who are distressed or in crisis.

When a survivor of childhood abuse is referred for help, CAT is only one option for the therapist. Which psychotherapy best suits the client is the most important consideration and the therapist must be pragmatic, informed and responsive to the client's needs and wishes, a matter of 'horses for courses' rather than a decision dictated by guru-like evangelism for favourite psychotherapies. Certain clients with certain difficulties will respond best to particular ways of thinking about their problems and managing them. Good clinical practice, to my mind, requires the therapist to be flexible, responsive, attuned and honest about his/her competence to deliver the psychotherapy of choice and to facilitate access of the service elsewhere. Advice and supervision by colleagues and mentors can be helpful. It must be accepted that even those clients with a specific disorder which is claimed to be responsive to a form of therapy may not benefit from psychotherapy. An appreciation of this frailty in our knowledge base and capacity to effect change is a crucial prerequisite to good practice, despite the constraining demands of clinical settings.

What follows is a description of a patient series that received CAT for abusive experiences in childhood. At this stage in the development of CAT, innovative practice and case series evaluation studies must precede formal evaluation, with the objective of expanding the theory and practice of the therapy. Therefore, the description to follow amounts to an exploratory piece of small-scale research which hopefully will form the platform for more rigorous psychotherapy research as defined by Salkovskis (1995) and Roth, Fonagy and Parry (1996). This is not a controlled study comparing CAT to other interventions with independent measurements of outcomes. Any positive changes mentioned are limited by these deficits in the study design and reflect within-group improvements. The series consists of 37 adult survivors treated by the author using CAT. When an additional technique (IRR, EMDR, medication) was also employed, this is stated.

Patient series

Twenty-two (59.4%) clients were treated on an outpatient basis, the others as inpatients in a psychiatric hospital, medium-secure unit or prison. Thirty-one were female (83.7%), six were male. The average age at that time of referral was 24 years of age (SD = 10.4; range = 18–41 years), 28 (75.6%) were married or cohabiting, three were divorced and six were single. Only three clients were employed at the time of the study.

All of the clients, after being interviewed using the CTI, disclosed multiple forms of abusive experiences which were, on average, rated to have been moderately frequent and severe, occurring over a seven-year period (SD = 4.3; range = 1–14 years). The average number of perpetrators was greater than two (SD = 1.4; range = 1–6), who were predominantly male (in 29 cases, female in 4 cases, mixed in 3 cases). Eighteen clients (48.6%) reported sexual revictimisation in adolescence or adulthood.

Eleven clients had been admitted to psychiatric hospital on one occasion, nine had received prison sentences or detention in a secure hospital, the remainder denying any history of institutionalisation. Twenty-seven (72.9%) had received some form of individual or group psychotherapy in the past for their problems and 26 survivors (70.2%) were currently receiving psychotropic medication and had been for an average of 1 year and 11 months (range = 7 months to 8 years 3 months).

Assessment

Each client was evaluated using the Millon Clinical Multiaxial Inventory—3 (MCMI-3; Millon *et al.*, 1994), Symptom Checklist-90–Revised (SCL-R-90; Derogatis, 1983), Dissociation Questionnaire (DIS-Q; Vanderlinden *et al.*, 1993) and the Post-traumatic Stress Disorder—Interview (PTSD-I; Watson *et al.*, 1991). A repertory grid (Kelly, 1955) was administered with supplied elements including *self-now, self as victim, self as survivor, ideal self, perpetrator(s), mother, father, person who feels guilty* and *person who should feel guilty* (see Pollock & Kear-Colwell, 1994; Pollock, 1996). Ratings of the extent of recognition and revision of target problems and the number of incidents of

Pre- and post-therapy assessment scores

Table 11.1   Pre- and post-therapy scores (at completion of therapy, 3, 6 and 9 months follow-up) for 37 clients

Measures	Pre-therapy	Completion	3 months	6 months	9 months
MCMI-3					
Disclosure	64.8	61.2	59.4	54.3	60.4
Defensiveness	51.4	48.6	53.9	59.6	55.5
Debasement	72.3	68.5	63.4	68.3	66.3
Schizoid	60.1	54.9	62.9	61.3	54.9
Avoidant	84.2	53.6	54.9	60.2	60.4**
Dependent	71.4	42.4	43.9	41.1	42.2**
Depressive	79.9	60.6	54.9	53.1	50.9**
Histrionic	42.5	42.9	45.7	51.3	54.9
Narcissistic	21.6	32.6	33.9	42.6	40.1
Antisocial	32.9	24.2	20.6	33.6	32.8
Aggressive–sadistic	42.4	40.1	43.5	40.1	42.9
Compulsive	59.6	50.6	54.9	60.2	62.4
Passive–aggressive	63.3	60.2	54.6	50.2	50.9
Self-defeating	94.6	74.9	70.6	70.3	72.6**
Schizotypal	42.6	47.9	52.6	50.4	45.6
Borderline	88.4	72.3	70.2	63.4	61.6**
Paranoid	92.3	87.6	89.4	86.7	91.3
SCL-R-90					
Somatisation	42.3	26.9	22.4	21.0	19.9**
Obsessive-compulsive	70.1	43.6	39.4	27.4	20.4**
Int. sensitivity	75.3	73.4	72.4	74.3	72.6
Depression	69.4	60.4	54.4	43.3	32.9**
Anxiety	54.6	42.4	30.9	30.1	27.3**
Hostility	61.1	40.9	30.4	27.8	20.1**
Phobic anxiety	78.4	47.6	30.4	24.7	21.2**
Paranoid	79.4	77.6	78.4	72.6	78.9
Psychoticism	72.3	32.9	36.4	32.6	29.9**
Global Severity Index	70.4	60.4	54.9	50.6	42.3**
PTSD-I					
Re-exp	17.8	9.2	8.7	8.9	9.1**
Intensive	28.4	14.8	12.7	13.9	14.6**
Avoidance	32.6	21.8	17.6	15.9	16.4**
DIS-Q					
Identity/frag/con	3.2	2.4	2.1	1.4	1.5**
Amnesia	3.0	2.1	2.3	2.0	2.4**
Dep/dereal	2.7	1.4	1.0	1.1	0.8**
Absorption	0.4	0.6	0.4	0.4	0.7
TP Ratings					
Recognition	1.4	4.4	4.6	5.4	5.3**
Revision	2.3	4.5	4.9	5.1	5.0**
Incidents of self-injury (per week)	1.4	0.8	0.2	0.1	0.2*

* $p < 0.05$; ** $p < 0.01$.
MCMI-3, Millon Clinical Multiaxial Inventory (3rd edition); SCL-R-90, Symptom Checklist–Revised; PTSD-I, Post-Traumatic Stress Disorder–Interview; DIS-Q, Dissociation Questionnaire; TP Ratings, Target Problem Ratings.

self-injury and suicide attempts were recorded for the past two months at pre-therapy and later at three, six and nine months after therapy.

Scores obtained for the 37 clients before entering CAT are shown in Table 11.1, along with scores on the same measures after therapy at three, six and nine months follow-up periods. Element distances on repertory grids are separately described in Table 11.2. The main findings pre-therapy are as follows:

- The personality profiles (MCMI-3) of the survivors demonstrated elevation (scores > 75) on avoidant, dependent, depressive, self-defeating, borderline and paranoid scales.
- The extent of overall dissociation scores (DIS-Q) were higher than those for normal population clients, with particular elevations on scales measuring identity fragmentation/confusion, amnesia and depersonalisation/derealisation.
- At a symptom level (SCL-R-90), survivors reported elevated scores for phobic anxiety, depression, interpersonal sensitivity, paranoid ideation, obsessive-compulsive and psychotic symptoms. The more general Global Severity Index (GSI) for symptoms was noted to be in the clinically significant range for the group.
- The relative endorsement of PTSD symptoms was elevated for re-experiencing, intrusive and avoidance symptoms. Twelve survivors (32.4 %) met criteria for current diagnosis of PTSD.
- As shown in Table 11.2, pre-therapy repertory grids indicated that the survivors equated *self-now* with *self as victim*, *perpetrator* and *person who feels guilty*. *Self as survivor* was construed to be most similar to *ideal self*.

In summary, this group of survivors reported personal histories of chronic, diverse and severe traumatic experiences in childhood, significant revictimisation in adolescence and adulthood with presentations characterised by personality dysfunction, significant psychopathology (including dissociative and PTSD symptoms) and a construct of oneself as similar to the roles of both victim and perpetrator associated with guilt. At a theoretical level, the repertory grid data supports the contention that adult survivors construe their core identity to consist of a close relationship between oneself in the present, the perpetrator of the abuse and being a victim. Most of the survivors in this sample did not construe themselves to be survivors.

Post-therapy changes

All clients received 16–24 sessions of individual CAT, with no one prematurely terminating therapy. Five clients received EMDR (13.5%); 13 completed IRR in addition to CAT (35.1%). Pre-therapy measures were readministered immediately following the final session and after periods of three, six and nine

Table 11.2 Repetory grids of element distances pre- and post-therapy ($N = 37$)

Elements	Self now	Self as victim	Person feels guilty	Perpetrator(s)	Mother	Father	Person should feel guilty	Ideal self	Self as survivor
Self now	–	0.53 (1.47)	0.56 (1.23)	0.21 (1.33)	1.01 (1.21)	1.83 (0.93)	1.56 (0.32)	1.74 (0.82)	1.21 (0.22)
Self as victim		–	0.39 (1.29)	0.11 (1.66)	1.22 (1.04)	1.44 (1.39)	0.22 (1.56)	1.88 (1.70)	0.46 (1.26)
Person feels guilty			–	1.26 (0.11)	1.41 (1.56)	1.30 (1.24)	0.41 (0.21)	1.47 (1.64)	0.43 (1.21)
Perpetrator(s)				–	1.63 (1.41)	1.24 (1.32)	1.23 (0.23)	1.73 (1.64)	1.49 (1.76)
Mother					–	1.24 (1.29)	1.27 (1.64)	0.86 (1.24)	0.94 (0.74)
Father						–	1.61 (1.81)	1.44 (1.27)	1.23 (1.41)
Person should feel guilty							–	1.73 (1.89)	0.66 (0.14)
Ideal self								–	1.29 (0.64)
Self as survivor									–

Mean element distances are calculated where two elements whose distance is less than 1.0 are more similar than that expected by chance and those whose distance is greater than 1.0, less similar. Element distance scores range from 0 to 2. Post-therapy scores are shown in parentheses.

months after therapy (see Table 11.2 for repertory grids). Statistically significant changes were obtained in the following domains:

- Decreases in MCMI-3 personality dimension scores for avoidant, dependent, depressive, self-defeating and borderline scales. The paranoid scale
  remained elevated.
- Decreases in dissociation scores on identity fragmentation/confusion,
  amnesia and depersonalisation/derealisation scales of the DIS-Q were
  noted.
- Decreases on all symptom scales of the SCL-R-90, except paranoid ideation
  and interpersonal sensitivity scales.
- Decreases in PTSD-I scores for re-experiencing, intrusive and avoidant
  symptom scales.
- Incidents of self-injury and suicide attempts diminished as time after CAT
  therapy progressed.
- Improvements in terms of the extent of recognition and revision ratings for
  target problems; this change consolidated after three months.
- Separation (increased element distance) was observed between *self-now*,
  self as victim, *perpetrator* and *person who feels guilty*. *Self as survivor* was
  closer to *ideal self* and *self now*, with *perpetrator* closer to *person who
  should feel guilty*.

The changes observed for repertory grid element distances are similar to those
reported by Pollock (1996), indicating a change within the survivors' constructions of their identities and relationships towards less guilt and perceiving oneself to be an active survivor who is less 'connected' to the original
perpetrator.

Discussion

A single study of treatment outcomes cannot be paraded as an adequate evidence base for the efficiency of the intervention model. Psychotherapy practice is not a competition driven in a managed health care culture. In stating
this, I do not advocate reliance on treatment methods that do not have sufficient evaluative data nor do I concede that CAT for these clients is not a worthy enterprise because clinical data on efficacy is presently limited. As a
preliminary investigation of CAT for a series of adult survivors of childhood
abuse, the outcomes do attest to tentative optimism for the application of
CAT.

It would be premature to claim that CAT is clinically effective for adult survivors (demonstrating beneficial outcomes in routine practice) at this stage
based on the limited data available. Single-case studies and case series evalu-

ations represent viable starting points to investigate clinically innovative psychotherapy techniques. A problem which affects our ability to determine clinical effectiveness is that each survivor's response to traumatic experiences (which also differs in terms of several factors from case to case) is idiosyncratic in developmental trajectory and outcome (see Chapter 1). Hence, each survivor's unique set of complaints and needs from psychotherapy necessitates a flexible, creative and innovative approach rather than a manualised treatment protocol.

Throughout earlier chapters, I have argued against sloppy eclecticism in formulating a client's difficulties. Because CAT is integrative at a theoretical level, this does not mean that it can be charged with not being a strategic, explanatory framework within which a variety of clinical tools can be delivered. For example, a range of techniques such as EMDR, IRR and experiential methods have an impact at differing levels of inference and functioning (cognitive, neurological, emotional, interpersonal domains). The debate about the usefulness of existing and new models will continue and our knowledge of the utility of CAT (and other psychotherapies) will be enhanced by outcome data as it is produced.

One issue worthy of mention is that CAT is relatively user friendly and what is learnt in the consulting room is explicitly meant to be portable outside it. Those receiving CAT, if CAT is the most appropriate mode of helping in the case, grasp and apply the therapeutic tools independently of the need for homework assignments being prescribed by an all-knowing therapist. In the later stages of therapeutic work, the client can initiate, expand and continue the necessary work, learning from improvements, lapses and relapses as time progresses. Like CBT in particular, CAT scaffolds the therapeutic process and socialises the client towards using and enhancing his/her own psychological resources and claiming the changes occurring. This stance is the most empowering for the client and CAT nurtures this perspective from the earliest moments of therapy. If CAT does not directly address certain distressing states of mind, for example heightened anxiety or anger, or sexual dysfunctions, then it does articulate the source and meaning of these difficulties within the client's pathology (e.g., panic related to abandonment fears, rage due to narcissistic injury, guilt and inhibition against forbidden sexual feelings). The context of symptoms is fundamental to understanding their source and achieving their amelioration (Luborsky, 1996). Symptom management methods can diminish subjective distress, but not delineate why the symptoms are evident in the first instance.

There is no clear clinical consensus about treatments of choice for survivors of abuse and, despite the acknowledgement that clinical guidelines and audit standards of practice and benchmarking of outcomes need to be sought in the longer term, CAT is a therapy which is entitled to further research efforts to provide an evidence base for clinical efficacy (how CAT performs in research trials). A therapist's judgement about whether to apply CAT or any other therapy needs to rely upon the therapist's knowledge about research findings, skills and competence in delivering the therapy, the nature of the interaction between therapist and client and the clinical reformulation of the client's difficulties. Tension can exist between a concern about a therapy's meagre evidence base and the desire to avoid a situation were 'premature demand for rigor may discourage clinical curiosity' (Roth *et al.*, 1996, p. 41). The next step for CAT in relation to adult survivors of childhood abuse would be to conduct evaluative studies comparing CAT with other treatment modalities using randomised controlled trials. To improve the help we provide for survivors requires consideration of the interrelationships between clinical practice, theory development, innovative technique and evaluation of clinical efficacy and effectiveness through auditing.

Suggestions for future research

Developing the evidence base for CAT through applied research could be enhanced via the following projects:

1. Comparing CAT for abused adults to other treatment modalities using randomised controlled trials.
2. Investigating to what extent CAT impacts on psychological measures of identity disturbance (e.g., the PSQ) and adequately impacts on the areas inferred by the MSSM.
3. Studies that apply CAT in a group setting and comparisons with individually delivered CAT.
4. Investigating the initial degree of internalisation representing the perpetrator–victim–survivor RRP and changes obtained through CAT. This could be accomplished using measures of transference and repertory grid techniques (e.g., dyad grids).
5. Tracing the patterns of transference within the therapy process to establish which CAT techniques work best towards changing harmful and unhelpful RRPs.
6. Extended applied research studies which investigate changes in PSQ (see Chapter 12) scores after CAT and its relationship to reports of PTSD symptoms and types of traumatic experiences during childhood.

CHAPTER 12

The Personality Structure Questionnaire: a measure of identity integration in CAT

One of the most promising areas of psychotherapy, in which CAT has been shown to be relatively effective, is the treatment and management of personality disorder, particularly borderline personality disorder (BPD; Ryle, 1997). CAT provides a fresh and alternative conceptualisation of personality pathology accounting for the diagnostic phenomena of BPD described in the *Diagnostic and Statistical Manual–4th Edition* (DSM-IV; American Psychiatric Association, 1994) and detailed in psychoanalytic writings (Grinkler, Werble & Drye, 1968; Kernberg, 1975). Identity disturbances are typical features of personality disorder, particularly BPD (Kernberg, 1984), with Dissociative Identity Disorder (DID; DSM-IV, 1994) considered to represent 'the most pronounced form of identity disturbance' (Modestin, Oberson & Erni, 1998, p. 352). A specific emphasis in CAT is made upon targeting problems regarding an individual's identity formation and coherence, experienced as discontinuities in one's sense of self, contradictory changes in moods, confusion and chaotic behaviour. Disturbances in self-experience are accounted for by Ryle's Multiple Self-States Model (MSSM; 1997), as described in Chapter 3 which also directs how psychotherapy should aim to redress these problems.

It is unclear from the MSSM whether the presence of multiple self-states or the fluidity between them is the most important aspect of dysfunctional personality. A specific objective of CAT is to facilitate an improvement within the integrity of the personality indicated by a reduction in the influence of dissociative processes and symptoms (e.g., increasing connectedness, fluidity, appropriate mobilisation of procedures, greater continuity in experience). The *multiple* self-states described may more aptly be described by the rubric of *dissociated* self-states reflecting a lack of integrity within the system of self-states and not fragmentation into partial, disjointed states and multiple identities.

The relationship between DID and BPD remains an area of contention. Kluft (1982) reported a rate of 22% diagnosis of BPD for 70 DID patients and proposes that the link between the two disorders lies in commonalities amongst certain indicators such as impulsivity, identity disturbance, unstable interpersonal relations, marked mood changes, dissociative symptoms and suicidal gestures. Horevitz and Braun (1984) cite 70% of a sample of 33 DID patients to have a concurrent BPD diagnosis and suggest that these disorders are separate and distinct but may coexist. Clary, Burstein and Carpenter (1984) state that, based on psychostructural formulation, all of 11 MPD patients were considered to exhibit BPD. Personality testing confirms the overlap between BPD and DID, along with avoidant, self-defeating, passive–aggressive and schizotypal features in addition (Bjornson, Reagor & Kasten, 1988; Dell, 1998; Ellason, Ross & Fuchs, 1996). Some claim that DID is best conceived of as a superordinate diagnosis (Kluft, 1987) and, furthermore, represents 'an epiphenomenon of a polymorphous BPD' (Ross et al., 1989, p. 416).

Conceptualisations of BPD have also suggested that multiplicity is a distinct feature of the disorder, with greater segregation and dissociation (particularly amnesia) between multiple selves representing the gradation in severity from BPD to DID (Fast, 1974; Searles, 1977). Furthermore, Grotstein (1981) proposes that BPD patients 'experience themselves as split selves but the contradictory nature of the variegated selves is blurred or eclipsed by compromised reality testing which ignores distinctions'. The main differentiation in gradation within the MSSM is that trauma induces multiplicity, with more pronounced separation and demarcation observed due to dissociative processes and symptoms (e.g., amnesia) for BPD to DID.

The PSQ: a measure of identity disturbance in the MSSM

Ryle (1997) proposed that a measure of dissociated personality would be of significant clinical value to enhance estimation of the degree of personality integration throughout the CAT process. Broadbent et al. constructed a self-report measure, termed a 'measure of integration' (the PSQ). Items were generated to reflect the non-DSM-IV features of BPD as conceptualised by the MSSM and refer to identity disturbance per se rather than criteria such as self-injury and impulsive aggression. The items of this short scale are shown in Figure 12.1. The pathological end of the items is indicative of an unstable sense of self, variation in subjective experiences, the presence of differing self-states (items 1–4), changeability in moods (items 5 and 6) and behavioural loss of control (items 7 and 8). The present study reports two empirical studies which examined the reliability, internal structure, validity and clinical utility of the PSQ as a measure of the MSSM as described by Ryle.

It could be questioned to what extent this scale measures either multiplicity and/or dissociation or other aspects of identity disturbances such as mood disturbances. If the PSQ is an adequate tool to assess problems to be targeted during CAT, it is worthy of investigation as to what psychological construct(s) the PSQ actually taps. It is, initially, important to consider the constructs of multiplicity and dissociation in the context of problems conceptualising these phenomena.

1. My sense of myself is always the same.	How I act or feel is constantly changing.
2. The various people in my life see me in much the same way.	The various people in my life have different views.
3. I have a stable and unchanging sense of myself.	I am so different at different times that I wonder who I really am.
4. I have no sense of opposed sides to my nature.	I feel I am split between two (or more) ways of being, sharply differentiated from each other.
5. My mood and sense of self seldom change suddenly.	My mood can change abruptly in ways which make me feel unreal or out of control.
6. My mood changes are always understandable.	I am often confused by my mood changes, which seem either unprovoked or quite out of scale with what provoked them.
7. I never lose control.	I get into states in which I lose control and do harm to myself and/or others.
8. I never regret what I have said or done.	I get into states in which I do and say things which I later deeply regret.

Figure 12.1   PSQ items (Broadbent *et al.*)

Multiplicity, dissociation and identity integration

It must be elucidated how multiplicity and dissociation are conceived to relate to identity pathology and maladaptivity. Identity is formed of both structural aspects and contents. Contents refer to knowledge ('Who am I?') and evaluative ('How do I feel about myself?') components (Altrocchi, 1998; Campbell, *et al.*, 1996). Structural features include facets such as self-complexity (Linville, 1987), clarity (Campbell, 1990), stability (Rosenberg, 1989) and differentiation (Donahue, Robins, Roberts & John, 1993). An integrated personality demonstrates behavioural consistency, inner experience with a sense of continuity over time, self-description and conceptions of significant others which are complex and multifaceted, showing an understanding of positive and negative qualities of oneself and other people. Self-definition is indicated by an ability to delineate one's own temperament, values, convictions, habits and virtues with realistic appreciation (Kernberg, 1984; McWilliams, 1994). Multiple states and dissociation are both structural features of identity and, along with its content, can be targeted within psychotherapy to improve integration and psychological health. Psychotherapy aims to promote the development of these capacities, improving the integrity of the personality (Horevitz & Loewenstein, 1994).

Multiplicity of the self originated in the work of James (1890/1950), who proposed that a variety of alternating states of being are characteristic of normal, well-functioning personalities. Gergen (1971) described multiple conceptions of the self, Mair (1977) referred to a 'community of selves', Markus and Wurf (1987) proposed a multifaceted self-concept and Rowan (1990) described multiplicity as composed of 'subpersonalities'. These theories conceptualise identity as constituted by multiple selves (named *polypsychism, self-pluralism* or *multiplicity*; Rowan & Cooper, 1998) that operate in a personality system which can be more or less integrated, adaptive, fluid, coherent and consistent. At one extreme of this concept, a view is that individuals seek unity (monopsychism) and consistency in personality and this position is related to health (Erikson, 1968).

This assumption is supported by research showing that polypsychism or multiplicity represents maladaptivity and compromised identity (Altrocchi, 1998). Altrocchi and McReynolds (1997) report the development of a self-report scale, which aims to measure multiplicity, named the Brief Self-Pluralism Scale (BSPS). It includes items such as 'People who know me say that my behaviour changes from situation to situation' and 'There are times when I felt like a completely different person from what I was the day before'. Research findings show that individuals who experience greater multiplicity within their personal identity share common features of psychopathology (Altrocchi, McReynolds & House, 1990) whereby polypsychism is associated with self-concept instability, lower self-esteem, less clarity and coherence, negative complexity, greater differentiation, neuroticism and maladjustment.

It is arguable that DID is the most extreme variant of polypsychism, at the pathological end of the spectrum or dimension of pluralism in self-structure. Differences along this dimension of multiplicity can be considered to range from variability, diversity, heterogeneity and instability (polypsychism) to invariability, homogeneity, unity and stability (monopsychism) in self-experience. It is appropriate to conclude that greater polypsychism or multiplicity signifies greater psychopathology generally, the severe end of this continuum denoted by DID.

The change in diagnostic labels from MPD to DID implies a reconfiguration of the conceptualisation of the disorder, mingling notions of polypsychism and dissociative processes and symptoms (Ross, 1997). Dissociation is defined in DSM-III-R (American Psychiatric Association, 1987) as 'a disturbance or alteration of the normal integrated functions of identity, memory and consciousness' revealed as partial or total amnesias, disturbances in self-perception and identity and disruptions to normal consciousness (derealisation and depersonalisation symptoms). It is assumed to occur across many mental disorders (van der Kolk, 1989) and functions as a form of mental avoidance of threatening stimuli or events, particularly during trauma, defending the individual from overwhelming anxiety or pain (Chu & Dill, 1990; Terr, 1981).

Disruptions may occur in behaviour, affect, sensation or knowledge (Braun, 1988) and recurrent reliance upon dissociation during harsh or abusive child-hood environments may culminate in the development of DID with amnesic barriers evident between compartmentalised, separate identities (Kluft, 1984). Although dissociative processes are evidently functioning, multiplicity is inferred in this thesis amidst experiences of confusion, discontinuity, contra-diction and perplexity in self-experience (Mollon, 1999).

Ross (1998), reviewing the debate on multiplicity and DID, reconfigured the continuum of normal (e.g., daydreaming) to pathological dissociation (e.g., fugue states, amnesia) concluding, perhaps differently from previous research findings, that polypsychism may typify a healthy, culture-less personality organisation absent of dissociation and demonstrating adaptive, flexible mul-tiplicity. He infers a wave particle theory to propose that normal multiplicity and DID similarly represent polypsychism. The reconfigured continuum (see Figure 12.2) consists, at one end, of DID ranging through to what he terms pathological pseudo-unity (abnormal polypsychism) which Ross (1998) describes as an unhealthy, culturally moulded, pursuit of monopsychism where 'our part selves are under the totalitarian rule of a disconnected, atheistic, pseudo-masculine, chauvinist, logic-chopping self; one which cannot appreci-ate the subtle, fluid logic of the soul and living things, and which can only repress the human spirit' (p. 195).

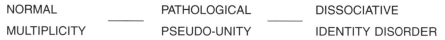

NORMAL ———— PATHOLOGICAL ———— DISSOCIATIVE
MULTIPLICITY PSEUDO-UNITY IDENTITY DISORDER

Figure 12.2   Ross' (1998) reconfigured continuum of dissociation

Ross further states that normal multiplicity would be 'highly desirable' and we need a psychotherapy that moves an individual from pathological pseudo-unity to normal multiplicity. Ross states 'one is either integrated or not – the integrated DID patient seems neither more nor less polypsychic than the average person in our culture' (pp. 192–193). The DID patient exists at the pathological end of this spectrum where 'the difference is in the degree of personification of the ego states, the delusion of literal separateness of the per-sonality states, the conflict, and the degree of information blockage in the system' (p. 193). It may be more easily conceived that an unintegrated per-sonality may demonstrate a similar degree of multiplicity to normal, inte-grated personalities and that the continuum of dissociation most radically affects the integrity of the system.

Psychotherapy of the polypsychic, dissociated patient aims to address the trauma which is likely to have produced a fragmented identity, to increase unity and integration within the self and to promote improved affective and behavioural functioning (Bowers, Brecher-Mauer & Newton, 1971). The targeted problems in CAT for these patients are similar and conceptualised within the MSSM. Some evidence exists that CAT can have a positive therapeutic effect diminishing dissociative symptoms in a case series of seven violent women who were diagnosed with personality disorders and who had experienced a diversity of childhood abuse (Pollock, 1996). Otherwise, outcome findings, which focus on targeting dissociation or identity integrity applying CAT, have not been reported to date.

A number of questions arise from this debate and Ryle's description of the MSSM. Firstly, is the PSQ a psychometrically sound measure of the facets of the MSSM, and how does it relate to the constructs of identity disturbance, multiplicity and dissociation in particular? Secondly, can the PSQ be shown to adequately discriminate between clinical groups representing the gradation of identity disturbance from normal integration to BPD to DID? It is predicted that (a) the PSQ scores will be associated with psychological constructs related to identity disturbance, and (b) a gradation in PSQ scores, multiplicity and dissociative symptoms will be demonstrated when DID patients are compared to BPD patients and normal patients.

The present study reports the preliminary psychometric properties of the PSQ, aims to elucidate the psychological constructs assessed by the PSQ, consider its relevance to the MSSM of CAT, and investigate the relationship between multiplicity and dissociation within BPD and DID.

METHOD

Samples

Several samples were used to investigate the psychometric properties of the PSQ and comparisons are made between data derived by Broadbent *et al.* (samples 1, 2, 3, 5 and 6) and the present study (samples 4, 7 and 8). These samples included the following:

Non-clinical:
1. London general population ($N = 50$)
2. Health authority ($N = 26$)
3. CAT practitioners ($N = 29$)
4. Belfast general population ($N = 50$)

Clinical:
5. CAT clinic ($N = 52$)
6. Borderline personality disorder 1 (Broadbent *et al.*; $N = 24$)
7. Borderline personality disorder 2 (collected by Pollock & Dorrian; $N = 21$)
8. Dissociated identity disorder ($N = 20$)

Samples 1 and 4 (both general population participants) were obtained from the local areas, samples 2 and 3 from health authority employees and practitioners attending a CAT conference respectively. Samples 5 and 6 were obtained by Broadbent *et al.* within clinical settings, the BPD group (BPD1) diagnosed using the Structured Clinical Interview for DSM-IV Axis II Personality Disorders (Gibbon, Spitzer, Williams & Benjamin, 1997). Clinical samples 7 and 8 were drawn from outpatient Psychotherapy Services in Belfast and each participant was diagnosed using the DSM-IV system by the senior clinician. The samples were not matched for gender, age, marital status or other demographic variables.

STUDY 1: NORMATIVE DATA FOR THE PSQ

METHOD

Samples

All available PSQ data for the eight samples were compared to produce normative data for the PSQ.

Procedure

Participants in all of the following studies were asked to complete the PSQ individually and a series of other measures were included depending on the psychometric properties of the PSQ being investigated. Confidentiality and consent were guaranteed for participants.

Normative data for the PSQ

The PSQ scores for all of the samples are separately described in Table 12.1. It is clear that the general population samples (London and Belfast) were comparative to Broadbent *et al.*'s CAT practitioner and health authority samples. The clinical samples scored consistently higher on the PSQ compared to non-clinical samples and PSQ scores for the two BPD samples were observed to be remarkably similar. Broadbent *et al.* obtained no significant differences in terms of age or gender on PSQ scores for non-clinical sample 1 and clinical sample 5. It may be suggested that a PSQ score of >30 warrants further exploration of identity problems using more detailed psychological measurement.

Table 12.1   Normative data for the PSQ

Sample	Sample size (adults)	Mean (SD)
Non-clinical		
1. London General Population	55	20.3 (4.67)
2. Health Authority	26	20.5 (4.07)
3. CAT Practitioners	29	19.7 (3.02)
4. Belfast General Population	50	23.3 (6.14)
Clinical		
5. CAT clinic	52	26.7 (7.14)
6. BPD1 (Broadbent *et al.*)	24	30.4 (5.90)
7. BPD2 (Pollock & Dorrian)	21	31.3 (7.71)
8. DID	20	24.9 (7.63)

BPD, borderline personality disorder; DID, dissociative identity disorder.

STUDY 2: FACTOR ANALYSIS

METHOD

Sample

One hundred adults drawn from the general population in Belfast (mean age = 32.4 years, SD = 10.5) completed the PSQ individually.

Factor analysis

An exploratory factor analysis of PSQ responses was performed using a maximum-likelihood factor extraction. Differences were not observed within the sample in terms of gender, age or marital status. Kaiser–Meyer–Olkin measure of sampling adequacy was 0.80, Bartlett Test of Sphericity = 288.8, $p < 0.001$, indicating that factor analysis was appropriate. A Scree test showed that one single factor accounted for 40.7% of the variance in PSQ scores. A test of fit for a single-factor model indicated this structure to best account for the data (x^2 (20) = 46.6, $p < 0.001$). The factor matrix for the unrotated solution revealed item loadings of PSQI (0.73), PSQ2 (0.60), PSQ3 (0.72), PSQ4 (0.80), PSQ5 (0.77), PSQ6 (0.54), PSQ7 (0.19) and PSQ8 (0.49), accounting for 40.7% of the variance. It is clear that item 7 of the PSQ ('I never lose control ... I get in to states in which I lose control and do harm to myself and/or others') does not load on this single factor (0.19). These findings indicate that, excluding PSQ item 7, the PSQ is a unidimensional measure.

Reliability analysis

A reliability analysis of the same data ($N = 100$) showed that corrected item–total correlations ranged from 0.31 to 0.62, with the removal of PSQ item 7 increasing the alpha coefficient substantially from 0.56 to 0.84. A Cronbach's alpha of 0.59 was obtained for the eight PSQ items. In the study of Broadbent *et al.* using a clinical sample of psychotherapy patients attending a CAT clinic ($N = 52$) the PSQ showed an alpha of 0.77 and with a BPD sample ($N = 24$) an alpha of 0.87 was achieved. The findings suggest that PSQ item 7 should be eliminated to improve the psychometric integrity of the scale.

Test–retest reliability assessed using Broadbent *et al.*'s group of students and CAT practitioners ($N = 29$) after a six-week period indicated that the PSQ was stable across time with a correlation of 0.75.

STUDY 3: CONVERGENT AND DISCRIMINANT VALIDITY OF THE PSQ

The study of Broadbent *et al.* investigated the relationship between the PSQ and general measures of psychopathology, whereas the present authors examined the association of the PSQ to constructs of identity disturbance. Broadbent *et al.* showed that, in the clinical sample of CAT patients, the PSQ correlated 0.46 with depression (Beck Depression Inventory; Beck, *et al.*, 1961), 0.50 with interpersonal difficulties (Inventory of Interpersonal Problems; Horowitz *et al.*, 1988), 0.56 with general psychiatric symptomatology (Brief Symptom Inventory; Derogatis & Melisaratos, 1983) and 0.69 with dissociation (Vanderlinden *et al.*, 1993), the highest correlation observed with the identity confusion and fragmentation scale.

METHOD

Samples

The convergent validity of the PSQ was assessed in the present study using samples 4 (general population of Belfast), 7 (BPD patients) and 8 (DID patients). The three groups differed in terms of gender mix, with more males in the BPD group (62% male versus 47% for the DID group and 45% for the general population). Differences were observed in that the dissociative group of patients were older ($p < 0.01$) than the BPD group. Only four (20%) of the 20 DID patients had concurrent diagnoses of BPD.

Procedure

Participants completed the PSQ and measures assessing identity disturbance as detailed below.

Measures

1. *Dissociation Questionnaire* (DES; Bernstein & Putnam, 1986) is a 28-item measure of dissociative experiences. In line with studies by Waller and Ross (1997), total DES scores were obtained and an eight-item derived scale of pathological dissociation, known as DES-T, was calculated. The DES-T assesses obviously abnormal experiences (e.g., not recognising a friend, fugue states). Responses are rated on a 10 mm analogue format from 0% to 100% rated about what percentage of time the person experiences the symptom. In 16 studies a mean alpha of 0.93 has been reported for the DES, with means for normal samples (7 studies, $N = 1458$) being 11.57 (SD = 10.6; van Ijzendoorn & Schuengel, 1996). The DES-T shows a mean of 5.14 (Waller, Putnam & Carlson, 1996).

2. *Brief Self-Pluralism Scale* (BSPS; Altrocchi *et al.*, 1990) is a 10-item true or false scale, with higher scores reflecting self-pluralism or multiplicity. Low scores indicate stability and a more unitary sense of self. Mean scores for the normal population are 3.78 (SD = 2.8; range 0–10; alpha = 0.86). The BSPS correlated positively with measures of dissociation, ego strength, neuroticism, collage maladjustment and stability of self (Altrocchi, 1990).

3. *Self-Concept Clarity Scale* (SCCS; Campbell, 1990) is a 12-item scale which assesses the extent to which an individual's contents of the self-concept are clearly and confidently defined, internally consistent (alpha of 0.86) and stable over time (test–retest reliability of 0.79). It is scored on a five-point response format from 'disagree strongly' to 'agree strongly'. Mean scores are 42.1 (SD = 8.2; range 12–60). The SCCS is associated with self-esteem and neuroticism and measures a controlled, conscious flexibility of behaviour. Low scores are interpreted as indicative of situational changeability.

4. *Sense of Coherence* (SOC; Antonovsky, 1987) measures three facets of psychological hardiness to stressful circumstances and consists of 29 items with high internal consistency (0.84). These include *meaningfulness* (MEA), which measures an individual's subjective feelings that life makes sense and is worthy of commitment and engagement; *comprehensibility* (COMP) measuring an individual's sense that perceived stimuli make cognitive sense, are clear, ordered and consistent; *manageability* (MAN) measures the extent to which one perceives he/she has adequate resources to deal with environmental challenges. A total SOC score is summed from scores on the three subscales.

5. *Mood Variability Scale* (MVS) is derived from the Affective Lability Scale of Harvey, Greenberg and Seaper (1989). Two subscales were selected which were considered to best reflect the mood items included in the PSQ, named the anger (seven items) and bipolar mood subscales (10 items). The mean score for the anger scale (ANG) was 7.28 (SD = 5.2, range 0–19) and for the bipolar scale (BIP) was 11.34 (SD = 5.6, range 0–26).

RESULTS

Separate correlations for the three groups (to account for the inferential assumptions of the statistical test given the fact that the samples were drawn from different sources) are shown in Tables 12.2, 12.3 and 12.4. It can be seen that consistent patterns are demonstrated for the PSQ scores, which were positively correlated to BSPS, DES total and DES-T, and both ANG and BIPO-LAR mood variability scales. PSQ scores were negatively associated with SCC and SOC total scores and SOC subscales MEA, COMP and MAN. In general terms, the PSQ is related to indices of multiplicity, dissociative processes and mood variability. Measures of psychological health such as self-concept clarity and sense of coherence are inversely related to PSQ scores. The only anomalous observation is seen within the correlations for the DID group in that the PSQ did not show a positive association with the construct of dissociation.

Regression analysis

The data obtained does not clarify exactly what psychological facets the PSQ actually measures. A multiple regression analysis predicting PSQ scores, entering all criterion variables simultaneously, revealed that BSPS scores and the SOC MEAN scores accounted for 65% of the variance in PSQ scores ($F(2,88)$ = 87.7, $p < 0.001$; beta = 0.62). No other criterion variables warranted entry into the analysis. This indicates that the PSQ and a lack of meaningfulness account for the separation between the three samples of participants.

Discriminant analysis

A discriminant function analysis was conducted using the normal, BPD and DID groups (samples 6, 7 and 8). A Box's M of 52.2 ($p < 0.001$) was achieved and a step-wise analysis revealed that pathological dissociation (DES-T), sense of coherence (SOCT), bipolar mood variability (BIPOLAR), PSQ and management (MAN) accounted for 95.6% correct classification for the three groups (canonical $r = 0.90$; x^2 (4) = 62.7, Wilks lambda = 0.48, $p < 0.001$). This finding indicates that the PSQ, in combination with other constructs of identity disturbance, accurately accounts for the separation between normal, BPD and DID participants.

One-way analyses of variance were conducted for PSQ scores and all other variables across groups. Means, standard deviations and significance levels are shown in Table 12.5. Results show that the BPD group scored significantly higher on the PSQ and BSPS, whereas the DID group was elevated on the DES, DES-T and both mood variability (ANG and BIPOLAR) scales. The

Table 12.2 Correlations between PSQ and other variables for Belfast general population ($N = 50$)

	PSQ	DES	DEST	BSPS	SCCS	SOCT	MAN	MEA	COMP	ANG	BIPOLAR
PSQ	–	0.34**	0.27**	0.76***	–0.51***	–0.56***	–0.50***	–0.60***	–0.49***	0.48***	0.29**
DES		–	0.95***	0.34**	–0.53***	–0.68***	–0.68***	–0.55***	–0.66***	0.62***	0.60***
DEST			–	0.24*	–0.50***	–0.66***	–0.66***	–0.54***	–0.64***	0.56***	0.59***
BSPS				–	–0.55***	–0.49***	–0.49***	–0.47***	–0.41***	0.58***	0.28**
SCCS					–	0.65***	0.63***	0.54***	0.64***	–0.61***	–0.43***
SOCT						–	0.94***	0.93***	0.93***	–0.61***	–0.52***
MAN							–	0.93***	0.81***	–0.58***	–0.48***
MEA								–	0.82***	–0.56***	–0.49***
COMP									–	–0.57***	–0.50***
ANG										–	0.63***
BIPOLAR											–

PSQ, Personality Structure Questionnaire; DES, Dissociation Experiences Scale; DEST, Pathological Dissociation; BSPS, Brief Self Pluralism Scale; SCCS, Self Concept Clarity Scale; SOCT, Sense of Coherence Total; SOCMAN, Manageability; SOCMEA, Meaningfulness; SOCCOMP, Comprehension; ANG, Affective Lability Anger Subscale; BIPOLAR, Affective Lability Bipolar Subscale.
* $p < 0.05$; ** $p < 0.01$; *** $p < 0.001$.

Table 12.3 Correlations between PSQ and other variables for borderline personality disorder participants (BPD2; $N = 21$)

	PSQ	DES	DEST	BSPS	SCCS	SOCT	MAN	MEA	COMP	ANG	BIPOLAR
PSQ	—	0.69***	0.53*	0.73***	-0.35	-0.47*	-0.48*	-0.45*	-0.23	-0.31	0.25
DES		—	0.78***	0.55**	-0.23	-0.26	-0.22	-0.18	-0.24	0.10	0.49*
DEST			—	0.35	-0.12	-0.34	-0.24	-0.31	-0.32	-0.15	0.49*
BSPS				—	-0.45*	-0.55**	-0.62**	-0.46*	-0.24	0.21	-0.04
SCCS					—	0.28	0.19	0.27	0.28	-0.53*	-0.10
SOCT						—	0.85***	0.90***	0.75***	0.04	0.17
MAN							—	0.67**	0.34	0.03	0.28
MEA								—	0.69**	0.03	0.07
COMP									—	0.05	-0.00
ANG										—	-0.06
BIPOLAR											—

PSQ, Personality Structure Questionnaire; DES, Dissociation Experiences Scale; DEST, Pathological Dissociation; BSPS, Brief Self Pluralism Scale; SCCS, Self Concept Clarity Scale; SOCT, Sense of Coherence Total; SOCMAN, Manageability; SOCMEA, Meaningfulness; SOCCOMP, Comprehension; ANG, Affective Lability Anger Subscale; BIPOLAR, Affective Lability Bipolar Subscale.
* $p < 0.05$; ** $p < 0.01$; *** $p < 0.001$.

Table 12.4 Correlations between PSQ and other variables for dissociated identity disorder participants (DID; $N = 20$)

	PSQ	DES	DEST	BSPS	SCCS	SOCT	MAN	MEA	COMP	ANG	BIPOLAR
PSQ	–	0.04	–0.15	0.86***	–0.23	–0.58**	–0.52*	–0.67**	–0.34	0.84***	0.46*
DES		–	0.89***	–0.15	–0.20	–0.12	–0.21	0.01	–0.13	0.28	–0.19
DEST			–	–0.34	0.02	0.01	–0.04	0.06	0.02	0.08	–0.25
BSPS				–	–0.11	–0.58**	–053*	–0.67**	–0.33	0.70**	0.55*
SCCS					–	0.04	0.16	–0.10	0.06	–0.17	0.32
SOCT						–	0.94***	0.88***	0.87***	–0.48*	–0.57**
MAN							–	0.76***	0.79***	–0.52*	–0.54*
MEA								–	0.61**	–0.49*	–0.65**
COMP									–	–0.27	–0.31
ANG										–	0.44*
BIPOLAR											–

PSQ, Personality Structure Questionnaire; DES, Dissociation Experiences Scale; DEST, Pathological Dissociation; BSPS, Brief Self Pluralism Scale; SCCS, Self Concept Clarity Scale; SOCT, Sense of Coherence Total; SOCMAN, Manageability; SOCMEA, Meaningfulness; SOCCOMP, Comprehension; ANG, Affective Lability Anger Subscale; BIPOLAR, Affective Lability Bipolar Subscale.
* $p < 0.05$; ** $p < 0.01$; *** $p < 0.001$.

general population sample showed significantly higher scores on measures of identity integrity, including SOC subscales and total score and SCCS and lowest on measures of identity pathology. It is interesting that Wildgoose, Waller, Clarke and Reid (2001) found that personality-disordered patients diagnosed as BPD and non-BPD using the Millon Clinical Multiaxial Inventory–III (Millon *et al.*, 1994) could be discriminated using the PSQ and Vanderlinden's dissociated loss of control scale.

Table 12.5 Comparisons (one-way ANOVAs) between Belfast general population (BGP), borderline personality disorder (BPD2) and dissociative identity disorder (DID) participants

Variable	Group means (SD)			$F(2,88)$ p-value; group diffs
	BGP	BPD2	DID	
PSQ	23.3 (6.14)	31.3 (7.7)	24.9 (7.6)	10.2***; BPD > DID, G
BSPS	3.2 (2.4)	4.9 (2.3)	3.9 (1.7)	4.4**; BPD > GP
DES	18.0 (13.3)	46.8 (21.3)	74.9 (11.9)	104.3***; DID > BPD > GP
DES-T	9.2 (11.6)	37.4 (20.6)	67.5 (12.2)	123.8***; DID > BPD > GP
ANGER	7.2 (5.2)	11.8 (3.9)	15.4 (4.6)	22.1***; DID > BPD, GP
BIPOLAR	11.3 (5.6)	13.2 (5.5)	23.0 (5.8)	30.4***; DID > BPD, GP
SOC COMP	44.8 (8.9)	21.8 (8.0)	24.7 (8.9)	69.2***; GP > BPD, DID
SOC MAN	48.5 (8.1)	26.7 (11.6)	24.1 (11.3)	63.4***; GP > BPD, DID
SOC MEAN	38.4 (6.9)	18.9 (6.6)	23.7 (11.0)	54.4***; GP > BPD, DID
SOC T	131.8 (20.4)	67.4 (22.1)	72.6 (28.2)	83.6***; GP > BPD, DID
SCC S	39.4 (10.1)	25.1 (9.9)	25.1 (9.6)	23.0***; GP > BPD, DID

*** $p < 0.001$; ** $p < 0.01$; * $p < 0.05$ (group differences—Bonferroni test of significance). PSQ, Personality Structure Questionnaire; BSPS, Brief Self-Pluralism Scale; DES, Dissociation Experiences Scale; DES-T, Dissociative Experiences Scale—Pathological; ANGER, Anger Lability subscale; BIPOLAR, Bipolar Lability subscale; SOC COMP, Sense of Coherence Comprehensibility; SOC MAN, Sense of Coherence Manageability; SOC MEAN, Sense of Coherence Meaningfulness; SOC T, Sense of Coherence Total; SCCS, Self-Concept Clarity Scale.

Discussion

The PSQ is a reliable and valid, psychometrically sound, unidimensional measure, which is associated with a number of facets of identity disturbance. With the exception of item 7, which taps a more extreme example of pathological behaviour (i.e., losing control and harming oneself and others), the PSQ correlates as anticipated with constructs reflecting lesser self-concept clarity, sense of coherence (all subscales) and general psychological functioning. A positive relationship was noted for PSQ scores and multiplicity, mood variability and dissociation. It was shown to be consistently higher in clinical samples and contributes to the discrimination between differing diagnostic groups. Clearly, as hypothesised, the PSQ assesses a construct indicative of identity disturbance and not merely a measure of general psychopathology.

It is worthy of note that PSQ scores are most accurately accounted for by multiplicity of the self, conceptualised as variability, changeability and fragmentation. Certainly, the PSQ reflects the multiplicity conveyed by the MSSM and does correlate with dissociative symptoms as measured by the DES and DES-T (pathological dissociation). It is interesting that correlations between the PSQ and DES scales for the DID sample were not observed. A conclusion would be that the PSQ cannot be considered a direct measure of dissociation and should not be used as a substitute for assessments of dissociative processes and symptoms. Multiplicity and dissociation are, therefore, related yet distinct facets of identity disturbance. The regression analysis indicated that PSQ scores reflect fragmentation (multiplicity) in identity and are also related to deficits in sense of coherence and, in particular, the feeling that one's existence, events and the world generally are meaningful and worthy of investment. The BSPS, which is a direct measure of multiplicity, was not observed to contribute to separation between the normal, BPD and DID samples and it cannot be claimed that the PSQ is simply a parallel measure of multiplicity and is redundant.

Comparisons between groups may clarify whether multiplicity and dissociation can be construed to exist along a combined continuum ranging from normality to borderline personality to dissociative identity disorder as suggested by Golynkina and Ryle (1999) and Ryle (1997). Ross' reconfigured continuum also requires consideration. Differences between groups assessed here show that participants from the general population exhibited multiplicity and dissociative symptoms within the normal range. BPD and DID patients differed notably for both constructs. BPD patients showed markedly more multiplicity than DID and general population participants.

Findings regarding dissociation are different for the hypothetical continua of the MSSM and Ross. The extent of dissociative symptoms increased in a graded manner from normality, BPD to DID. Dissociation scores were elevated for both BPD and DID, but were obviously within the pathological range for DID patients. For dissociation, the spectrum from BPD to DID suggested by the MSSM was supported generally by the current data. Summarising the findings, BPD patients demonstrate a dysfunctional degree of fragmentation/multiplicity with dissociative symptoms evident. DID patients do not show more or less multiplicity than the general population, yet their dissociative symptoms are most severe. Dissociation, and not multiplicity, appears to exist along the hypothetical continuum. It is worth mentioning that the DID sample was relatively 'pure' (only 4 of 20 showed co-morbidity with BPD) and it could not be argued that concurrent BPD diagnoses contaminated findings relating to the DID patients

The MSSM of BPD in CAT includes multiple self-states and dissociative symptoms, with the former representing a distinct aspect of the pathology of the disorder, based on the present analysis. The BPD patient can be conceptualised as a *dissociated personality* to a degree. Ryle (1997) has noted that dissociation scores on self-report measures are found repeatedly in BPD patients and he states that 'the relation of such scores to BPD has not been systematically studied to date' (p. 28). It may be proposed that, in line with the diagnostic criteria of DSM-IV, dissociative symptoms are a feature of the disorder but not a central defining aspect. A central aspect of BPD pathology highlighted in the present study is the variability and fragmentation into multiple selves and the accompanying deficits in personality integrity. Mood instability (anger and bipolar variations) were significantly greater for DID than BPD patients. This may be interpreted as reflecting the effects of experiencing pronounced dissociative processes with loss of control over emotions, moods and behaviour. Improving the degree of fragmentation for the BPD patients, as well as diminishing dissociative processes and symptoms, can be considered an important focus for psychotherapeutic efforts.

CAT uses of jointly constructed diagrams of a patient's self-states, accurately describing movement, switches and shifts within and between self-states. Sequences and patterns, which lead to dissociative symptoms (termed procedural loops and symptomatic procedures), are traced to provide the patient with a portable therapeutic tool that guides recognition and eventual revision of harmful patterns enacted towards oneself and others. The patient uses the diagram, termed a Self-States Sequential Diagram (SSSD), to promote self-observation and the capacity to reflect upon one's own patterns of experience, moods and behaviour. Contradictory experiences, chaotic changes in moods from one self-state to another on a frequent and unpredictable basis, cause confusion, a sense of incoherence and distress. Tracking these often radical fluctuations in experience aims to improve the general integrity of the personality, decreasing fragmentation by addressing deficits at levels two and three of the MSSM. Therapeutic work which addresses traumatic memories and images fragmenting an individual's consciousness and sense of stability, is equally important to promote integration (Mollon, 1999). Given the patterns of scores for the BPD patients, diminishing fragmentation and structural variability should be a specific target for CAT.

The PSQ can be considered a reliable and valid measure of the MSSM for BPD based on the implied relevance of multiplicity to the disorder. Its most appropriate use would be as a brief screening tool for identity disturbance in personality-disordered patients. Clinical evaluation of dissociation for BPD patients requires direct assessment and measurement, perhaps using the DES in conjunction with the PSQ to classify the presence and degree of partial or total dissociation within the patient's personality.

Investigating the clinical groups' histories of traumatic experiences and ret-rospective memories of the parental environment could have enhanced the present study. This would permit examination of the potential influence of traumatic development on the degree of multiplicity, identity integrity and dis-sociation. A potentially confounding factor which was not considered is whether trauma is related to multiplicity and whether either the BPD or DID groups demonstrated differential impact in terms of neglect or abuse. The samples reported here were diverse across the two studies and the collection of more substantive demographic data would have enhanced the normative value of the PSQ for clinical use.

CHAPTER 13

MARTIN BAMBER

An independent commentary on CAT for adult survivors of abuse

The CAT model of the conceptualisation and treatment of adult survivors of childhood abuse outlined in this book is adapted from Ryle's (1997) Multiple Self States Model (MSSM) for the treatment of borderline personality disorders. The CAT model described views that 'optimal' personality development necessitates the development of an adaptive and healthy repertoire of reciprocal role procedures (RRPs). However, it is abusive experiences that result in maladaptive RRPs within unhealthy adult-to-child relational units which are at the core of the problems experienced by adult survivors of childhood abuse.

The model, which is described in Chapter 3, is basically a trauma-induced dissociation model of pathology. It assigns prominence to the assessment and treatment of identity disturbance. The model essentially proposes that three levels of disturbance can occur in survivors of childhood abuse, with increasing degrees of dissociation and identity disturbance. The first level involves disruption to the 'content' within a particular self-state, leading to restricted, narrow, limited and extreme relational units. The second level involves the failure to develop the 'metaprocedures' which bind self-states together, resulting in dissociation between separate, discrete self-states. The third level of disturbance results in more extreme deficits in self-reflection, severe dissociation and identity disturbance. The degree of dissociation varies along a 'continuum' of severity. At one end of the continuum are those healthy individuals who are characterised by a coherent, stable, integrated and unchanging identity. At the other extreme are those 'patients' who are characterised by an unstable, inconsistent and fragmented identity, who demonstrate severe and challenging pathology. Chapters 5–8 of this book illustrate in a sequential order the increasingly more extreme presentations of pathology along this continuum. The present chapter aims to consider the following:

1. Whether the model outlined in Chapter 3 meets the requirements of a good working model for treating adult survivors of childhood abuse.
2. What (if anything) the model 'adds' to the conceptualisation (reformulation) and active treatment for adult survivors of abuse.
3. What the unique features of the CAT approach and model are, as applied to adult survivors of childhood abuse.
4. Its relative strengths and weaknesses in treating adult survivors.
5. To what extent the case illustration chapters actually illustrate how to conceptualise and treat adult survivors of childhood abuse.
6. What is required next to enhance an objective appraisal of the model and practice of CAT for adult survivors.

While there is currently no 'treatment of choice' for adult survivors of childhood abuse, there is beginning to be some level of agreement about what constitutes a good working model for the treatment for adult survivors of abuse. It is one that acknowledges the complex interplay of factors and influences involved in cases of abuse. The CAT model of childhood abuse presented in this book attempts to address this complex interplay of factors and influences and incorporate them into the conceptualisation and active treatment of adult survivors. It recognises that pathways between childhood abuse and pathology are rarely if ever linear, and the idea that one can disentangle single influences as being 'causal' is to deny the complexity of the findings in the research literature on the links between childhood abuse and adult pathology.

The CAT model of childhood abuse starts from the premise that abuse is 'necessary' but in itself 'not sufficient' to account for later difficulties in adulthood. It emphasises that there is no preordained route which survivors are bound to take and that abuse should not be seen as 'destiny'. This view is supported by the fact that one third of children abused do not go on to develop any significant psychological problems later in life. Symptoms may continue across time from childhood into adulthood or they may not. They can even change over time within the same individual. The model also argues that each child's response differs idiosyncratically, even when the perpetrator abuses two individuals in much the same way. The model rejects the claim, for example, that sexual abuse results in an 'incest survivor syndrome' which is typical of all cases. This assertion, it is argued, denies the complexity of events and factors which can affect the child's developmental trajectory over time, and fails to account for the wide variety of presentations of adult survivors and also for the 'continuum of severity' in responses shown by survivors.

In the CAT model of childhood abuse presented, it is argued that abusive experiences are expressed through 'adult-to-child' relational units. The extent to which the abusive experience is internalised, in terms of the 'abusing-to-victimised' relational unit, determines the extent to which the perpetrator will define and dictate the victim's personality. The vulnerability of the individual to this type of 'contamination effect' is accounted for well by the CAT model of childhood abuse and is a significant improvement on a number of existing models which fail to address these complexities. The model also identifies that the degree to which the perpetrator directly moulds and shapes the survivor's personality depends upon a number of factors, including environmental and social factors, age at onset of abuse, developmental stage and frequency and severity of abusive experiences.

The family environment in which the abuse occurred is considered very important in the CAT model of abuse. Often these environments inhibit more flexible and adaptive RRPs from developing. However, if there is positive involvement of significant others in the child's life at the time of the abuse, such as extended family, school peers or teachers, good friends or caring professional involvement, then some of the adverse effects can be compensated for. However, they cannot be removed or extracted totally, since the RRPs have already been internalised. New relational units that are formed by subsequent positive experiences of care-giving can compensate to some degree, however. The more frequent and severe the abusive experiences are, the more damaging they are thought to be to personality development (Terr, 1991). The CAT model suggests that where more frequent abuse occurs, it is remembered in a different way from single episodes of abuse. Rather, there is a 'dose effect'. It is not remembered as a series of specific incidents but as a 'summary generic script'. This view is supported by the work of other researchers in the area. It is similar to Stern's (1985) 'Representations of Interactions that have been Generalised' (RIGs) and Bowlby's (1969) 'working models' describing fairly general interpersonal schemata, which have a number of more specific interpersonal schemata embedded within them. They become prototypes, rather than precise representations of specific events.

The model is also capable of explaining 'resilience' in terms of RRP formation. Abuse occurring at an earlier age and developmental stage is more damaging to the personality development of that child than abuse occurring in an older child. This is not intended to minimise the damage caused by abuse in older children but an attempt to explain why older children appear to have greater resilience and coping resources than younger children. In the older child there is a greater likelihood of flexible, adaptive and healthy RRPs having already been formed prior to the abusive experience(s). However, in the younger child, healthy RRPs have never had the chance to develop and the only ones they have to draw upon are the maladaptive, abusive ones. Their perceptions and interactions are distorted from a very early age and they are more likely to follow a more distorted developmental trajectory than the older child. A consequence of this is that the child is likely to develop greater identity disturbance and a more damaged personality. The distinction being made in the CAT model is between 'disintegration' in the older child (or indeed in the adult who has been raped) and 'failure to integrate' adaptive RRPs in the first place in the younger child. Existing social cognitive models of abuse generally propose a violation of 'pre-existing' schemata about oneself, others and the world occurs (disintegration), and fail to address the developmental perspective whereby the child 'fails to integrate' in the first place.

The CAT model presented is thus able to account for the unique and idiosyncratic reactions of survivors. There is recognition that each child possesses different vulnerabilities, displays different reactions and has different coping responses to the experience of abuse. It also acknowledges that the environmental context in which the abuse took place, the reactions of care-givers (either positive and supportive or negative and condemning), the age at onset of the abuse, the child's developmental stage and the frequency, duration and severity of the abuse, all influence the developmental trajectory across time from childhood to adulthood. Its recognition of the complex interplay of these factors and its attempt to incorporate them into the model is one of the particular strengths of the CAT model of abuse.

The CAT model of childhood abuse also identifies three core areas or domains of disturbance, namely affect dysfunction, disturbances of self and interpersonal/social problems which therapy aims to address. Traditional CBT approaches to working with affective disorders have very much focused upon symptom relief as the starting point. However, the earlier confidence and optimism expressed by cognitive therapists have perhaps been a bit premature. This confidence has gradually been replaced by increasing uncertainty, when faced with some of the findings of more recent outcome studies. Even with problems such as depression, once seen as the 'jewel in the crown' of cognitive therapy, there has been a growing dissatisfaction (Bamber, 1997). There has been an increasing realisation that it is not uniquely more effective than other forms of psychological treatment for depression that do not target negative thinking (Williams, 1992), and other forms of therapy such as interpersonal therapy (Sullivan, 1953; Weissman & Markowitz, 1994) are also showing promising results. Too little attention has been paid in the past to the interpersonal 'style' of depressed people and their exchange with the environment that they live in. Cognitive therapists have tended to assume that their patients' cognitions are always distortions in thinking, when in fact they may be a reflection of the depressed person's 'reality' arising from more disturbed communication patterns than those of non-depressed people (e.g., more marital rows or ongoing criticism from one's spouse may precede depression).

The difference between the CAT model of childhood abuse and other models such as the CBT model is that it sees the 'context' in which symptoms exist as crucial in understanding them and achieving their amelioration. It adopts a more 'constructivist' approach, which emphasises the centrality of patients in actively construing and creating their own reality, rather than there being an accurate perception of a physical reality into which the therapist attempts to socialise the patient. A strength of the CAT model is that it does not attempt to treat symptoms in isolation or impose a reality upon the patient but always attempts to place the symptoms into the interpersonal context in which they arose and tries to construct the patient's reality, rather than the therapist's. This is seen as an essential starting point from which to begin to construct, accurately conceptualise and treat the problem that the patient presents with.

Dissociation is central to the CAT model of abuse and pathology. There is an accumulating body of research evidence which supports the notion that dissociation is the key mediating factor between abuse and later pathology (Becker-Lausen, Saunders & Chinsky, 1995; Everill, Waller & Macdonald 1995; Zatzick, Marmer, Weiss & Metzler, 1994). It is also being recognised as a problem in its own right as well as a component of a range of other disorders (Carlson & Putnam, 1993). It can basically be described as 'a failure to integrate that which would normally be integrated'. The 'continuum' of dissociation described in the CAT model has been reported by other researchers in the field such as Putnam (1991), who described a continuum of dissociation from normal 'dissociative tendencies' (which are seen as a healthy aspect of normal functioning), through to pathological dissociation at the other extreme. It has been described as a 'strategy for coping' that can lie anywhere on a continuum from adaptive to maladaptive. The re-emergence of the phenomenon of dissociation (following its being neglected for many years since the original work of Janet in 1898) appears to have been triggered by the greater acknowledgement of the prevalence and psychopathological impact of sexual and physical abuse. The reason for its re-emergence is perhaps because it is increasingly being seen as a construct which can explain the abuse–pathology link. Currently, there is no other comprehensive model (and a lack of theoretically driven treatments) which emphasises a central place for the concept of dissociation. Those models that do exist are essentially descriptive rather than being based in an explanatory psychological theory, for example, psychodynamic models (Fonagy, 1991; Mollon, 1996), and developmental models (Putnam, 1997b; Wolff, 1987; McIntee & Crompton, 1997). The CAT model of abuse thus represents a considerable advance on other existing models in the literature.

While no cognitive-behavioural model of dissociation yet exists in the published literature, Kennedy (1998) and Kennedy and Waller (in press) propose a cognitive-behavioural model of dissociation which involves three levels (of severity) of dissociation, which are able to account for a wide range of dissociative symptoms. Level one dissociation is at the level of automatic processing and pre-conscious scanning. It represents a defensive decoupling of information, which is perceived as threatening. Level two represents a decoupling of the links between schemata within modes (it is interesting to note that

Barnard and Teasdale's, 1991, 'Interacting Cognitive Subsystems' model fits in well at level two even though it was not proposed with dissociation in mind). The third level represents decoupling between modes, which results in more severe identity disturbances. The authors propose that many cognitive-behavioural techniques (e.g. Kennerly, 1996, 2000) target level one dissociation. Some, for example, Linehan's dialectic behaviour therapy (1990) and schema-focused approaches such as Padesky (1994) and Young's schema mode work (Young, 1994a; Young & Behary, 1998), target levels two and three. The present model appears to have level three dissociation as its main focus. As such the CAT model of childhood abuse appears to fill a gap, in that it is able to provide a framework for working with severe dissociation and identity disturbance which is typically found in those with long and severe abuse histories.

What appears striking about models that attempt to work on the more severe levels of dissociation and identity disturbance, whether they be cognitive-behavioural, psychodynamic or CAT, is that they all appear to be conceptually converging and describing something similar, for example, Beck's 'modes' (1996), Young's 'schema modes' (1994a, 1998), Ryle's 'self states' (1997), Mair's (1977) 'community of selves', Teasdale's (1996) 'mind in place' concept, Putnam's (1997) 'discrete behavioural states', Horowitz's (1979) 'states of mind' and Freeman's (1998) 'scripts and lifestyles'. There is a commonality of theme in the various models proposed, even though they use different terminology and language. They also share a common purpose, which is to try and repair the disconnection at different levels. The CAT model of abuse appears to capture this well with its focus upon interpersonal schema-focused therapy.

The CAT model of childhood abuse is also able to account for the amnesia that is commonly reported by adult survivors of abuse using the concept of dissociation. Amnesia may be partial or complete depending upon the degree of dissociation between self-states. The abused individual dissociates him/herself from the 'abused-to-abuser' self-state, resulting in the apparent forgetting of the memories of the abuse. Recovered memories can also be explained as a process occurring in therapy as the therapist and patient work together in repairing the disconnections and activating the schemata associated with the abuse.

A good theoretical model of childhood abuse needs to be able to explain both the 'cognitive' and the 'interpersonal' aspects of a patient's presentation. They are not conceptually or theoretically separable in a working model of abuse but two sides of the 'same coin'. It needs to be able to clarify not only how information is processed but also the ways in which affective, cognitive and behavioural processes develop and interact in an interpersonal context (Safran & Segal, 1996). The CAT model for treating adult survivors of childhood abuse has a number of strengths. Firstly, it recognises that human beings are by nature primarily interpersonal creatures. The CAT model integrates developments in attachment, cognitive, interpersonal and motivational theories. From an evolutionary perspective human beings are thought to be biologically pre-wired to be 'interpersonal' in nature, since to maintain closeness and 'connectedness' between the infant and the primary care-giver has survival value in terms of the security and protection that is provided. The infant learns to behave in ways that maintain interpersonal relatedness and its behaviour is shaped through social learning experiences. Secondly, human beings have unique and idiosyncratic ways in which they construct cognitive representations of their experiences. The model demonstrates a detailed understanding of the patient's characteristic way of 'construing events that is unique and idiosyncratic for each patient. It achieves this by identifying the specific interpersonal patterns that are linked to that particular patient's construal style. Thirdly, it sees interactions with significant others as playing a central role in the emotional development of the child and the importance of integrating these interactions into an overall 'sense of self'. Fourthly, there is an emphasis on 'deep structural change', in which 'interpersonal schemata' are at the core.

The 'dilemma' for many children who are being sexually abused is that the person doing the abusing may also at the same time be the primary care-giver that the child relies upon for 'protection' and closeness. There may be no one else there for the child, so how do they communicate the psychological injury that is being done without at the same time risking losing a vitally needed support? How do they accommodate and internalise both the good and the evil parts of what is essentially one and the same person? The social learning experiences of such children contain the seeds of maladaptive learning of dysfunctional interpersonal schemata and behaviours, leading to pathological development. One scenario is that the child learns that sexually toned behaviour can lead to 'warm' responses from others and learns to act seductively as a way of maintaining interpersonal relatedness. Alternatively, the child may learn to endure unwanted sexual advances in order to maintain the relatedness with the 'care-giver' and the 'protection' that the care-giver provides, leading to different but equally noxious maladaptive interpersonal schemata being created. The CAT model of childhood abuse illustrates this interpersonal dilemma very well.

The CAT model of childhood abuse provides a good framework for explaining revictimisation, which is a common problem for many adult survivors. Human beings not only 'construe' their environment but also construct it. Dyadic communications do not only convey information but also define the relationship between participants. For example, a person who behaves in a domineering way bids to define the relationship with another person in a certain way, namely 'submissively'. However, it requires the other person to accept the reciprocal role and act in a complementary way in order for the cognitive interpersonal cycle to be completed. If the other individual refuses to accept the 'bid' then the reciprocal role relationship cannot be enacted. This process of 'projective identification' (Segal, 1992) presents particular risks for the abused individual, who may have already been subject to a large amount of horror and anxiety and may all too readily reciprocate the domineering, controlling and abusing individual who re-enacts his/her earlier experiences of abuse. The risk is greater for such individuals since much of this process is non-verbal and they may not be consciously aware of what is happening other than a vague feeling of confusion.

Abused individuals live in an interpersonal world defined by the abuser. It consists of restricted patterns (by snags, traps and dilemmas) in which the individual's restricted and inflexible repertoire, negative expectations and contingencies for maintaining them, of limited choices which rarely allows them to encounter interpersonal experiences that are schema disconfirming. As such they are unable to find their own 'exits'. CAT helps them to find those exits they are desperately looking for and is particularly useful in both understanding and preventing future revictimisation. This RRP framework is also useful for helping survivors understand how and why they may be more prone to becoming more abusive to others in later adult life, and also in a minority of cases the violent re-enactment or the intergenerational transmission of childhood abuse. It must be emphasised here that the vast majority of survivors could not contemplate causing anyone else harm or suffering and in fact many are the opposite to such a presentation because they know what it is to suffer. It is also able to account for self-harm, in terms of self-to-self RRPs, or even to reconceptualise acts of self-harm and attempted suicide as interpersonal acts aimed at producing some interpersonal change such as to make another feel sorry, guilty or bad, or an attempt to change the power dynamic in order to make the other fit in and conform to their will. For this to happen, of course, requires the other to reciprocate their part of the script.

The case illustrations presented in Chapters 5–8 of this book outline a therapeutic framework for integrating both relationship and technical factors in a convincing way. They are able to take diverse and idiosyncratic learning histories of individual patients with even very complex problems and work with these at a level of sophistication which goes beyond many other therapeutic approaches. The therapeutic work is conducted with specific and often very idiosyncratic relational units rather than simply using the same 'standardised and cookbook' approach for every patient. The central importance of the 'therapeutic relationship' (Safran & Segal, 1996) is emphasised in these case illustrations, which clearly demonstrate how unhelpful patterns which occur in patients' everyday lives are successfully explored within the therapy session. The value of 'transference' issues in the therapeutic process is also emphasised and there is a recognition of the importance of working with resistance and impasses in therapy as being central to the change process (Blatt & Erich, 1982). The CAT model emphasises the role of 'non-specific' factors in therapy

(Norcross, 1986), such as the therapeutic relationship and the need to understand individuals as part of the interpersonal system in which they are participating. Similarly, useful concepts such as projective identification, transference and countertransference, the focus upon the therapist's and the patient's inner experiences and the importance of working with 'ruptures' in the therapeutic alliance, rather than seeing them only as obstacles to therapeutic progress, are clearly demonstrated in the case illustrations.

The case illustrations show how the CAT approach for working with adult survivors of childhood abuse values survivors' existing coping repertoires, rather than undermining them. They demonstrate the crucial importance of providing support and empowerment to survivors in the context of a collaborative relationship. While the CAT approach offers a particularly structured way of reformulating the patient's problems, the therapist may choose to use a variety of interventions following reformulation (e.g., behavioural, cognitive, psychodynamic, family oriented). It could be argued that this is a case of atheoretical eclecticism. However, they are not randomly delivered without regard for any theoretical underpinnings but are anchored in the theoretical understanding which is offered by the reformulation. CAT for childhood abuse is a time-limited and focused form of therapy which develops its focus relatively quickly and this encourages swift progress. The focus of therapy does not have to be on the abuse itself but rather upon the disturbed interpersonal relationships and self-management issues subsequent to the abuse. This is an important plus in that many survivors find it particularly painful to talk about the details of the abuse itself but are much more willing to talk about their relationship problems.

Understanding RRPs and the separate self-states of the patient can also be very helpful to the therapist in clarifying and containing ruptures or 'impasses' in therapy and also their own reactions and feelings of confusion, especially with more disturbed and chaotic individuals such as those with BPD. Such unpredictable and rapidly changing patients can be challenging even to the most competent of therapists. Many non-CAT therapists may relate only to one end of an RRP and over-identify with either the victim or the abuser role. CAT reformulation and an understanding of the nature of self-states help the therapist to avoid this. At the extreme end of the spectrum of dissociation and identity disturbance there is a 'dearth' of theoretical models informing treatment. The CAT model is very useful to the therapist in attempting to conceptualise such severe cases as BPD and DID. The aim of such therapy is not necessarily to decrease the number of self-states but to promote a co-consciousness and an overseeing self-state which limits the switching between them.

CAT has been applied in a number of innovative ways, including couples work (Ryle, 1990), damaging work environments (Walsh, 1996) and in exploring the dynamics between BPD patients and community mental health teams (Dunn & Parry, 1997; Kerr, 1999). The CAT model has also been adapted to treating adult survivors on group settings (see the relevant chapters of this book). It is argued that the group setting has advantages over individual CAT in that it allows multiple reciprocal role re-enactment and there are multiple transferences of different forms, which allow further opportunities for the therapist to get to know and understand their patients better. Survivors also learn that they are not alone with their problems and not different from others. Also, there are opportunities for sharing experiences and developing trust in others. At the same time, however, there are potential risks that the therapist must be aware of, which can be described in RRP terms. Firstly, there is a risk that some members of the team may experience revictimisation by others in the group by way of reciprocal role re-enactments. Secondly, some of the survivors end up becoming 'helpers' to the more needy and demanding members of the group through a process of 'parentification' (i.e., taking on parent roles in relation to the needy child role). The effectiveness of group interventions has not yet been evaluated and currently there is little agreement on inclusion criteria, optimal duration of therapy, appropriate gender mix or the degree of structure required in such groups, and the high drop-out rate in these groups is something that needs investigating further.

The exploratory piece of small-scale research looking at clinical outcomes carried out in this book (see Chapter 11) acknowledges that CAT for adult survivors is not the 'cure for all ills'. The clinical data on the efficacy of CAT is limited and it would be premature at this stage to make any great claims about its efficacy given the limited amount of data available. At this stage CAT for adult survivors is innovative practice and more rigorous research needs to follow before it could be claimed that CAT is clinically effective for adult survivors of childhood abuse. There may be some methodological problems in attempting to evaluate the effectiveness of the model or design standardised treatment protocols, given that the clinical presentation of each patient is idiosyncratic and unique. At this point in its development a balance needs to be reached (as for all 'new' therapies) between clinical curiosity and innovation and the need for clinical rigour and evidence-based practice. What is required next to enhance an objective appraisal of the model is the setting up of randomised controlled trials comparing CAT with other treatment modalities, using larger sample sizes. A comparison of individual versus group approaches needs to be evaluated and there is scope to investigate the extent to which CAT impacts upon measures of identity disturbance. At the same time it is important that innovation is not stifled.

Final comments

There is currently no one comprehensive therapeutic model of choice for treating adult survivors of childhood abuse which is able to account for the whole spectrum of problems that adult survivors experience. However, the CAT model presented here is able to account for some of the more common problems that such patients present with, such as interpersonal/social problems and revictimisation. Also, most existing models have been found to be inadequate for dealing with some of the more complex problems encountered in treating adult survivors, especially those of a more interpersonal nature and those with more extreme pathology such as severe dissociation and identity disturbance. This, however, is one of the strengths of the CAT model of childhood abuse described in Chapter 3. It is basically a 'trauma-induced dissociation model of pathology', which assigns prominence to the assessment and treatment of identity disturbance. The concept of a 'continuum of dissociation' is given a central role in the model. At the extreme end of the continuum of dissociation and identity disturbance there is a 'dearth' of theoretical models informing treatment. The CAT model is very useful to the therapist in attempting to conceptualise such complex cases with severe pathology (e.g., BPD and DID).

CAT is different from attachment, psychoanalytic and cognitive models in the emphasis it places on RRPs. Particular importance is placed upon internalisation of the 'perpetrator-to-victim' RRP. Abusive experiences which result in maladaptive RRPs within unhealthy adult-to-child relational units are thought to be at the core of the problems experienced by adult survivors of childhood abuse. This way of conceptualising problems has been found to be very useful in explaining the greater occurrence of revictimisation, self-harm and interpersonal relationship problems found in adult survivors. Existing social-cognitive models do not integrate the interpersonal aspect of a patient's presentation and tend to see it as something separable from the cognitive aspects. The CAT model, however, sees them as two sides of the 'same coin' and inseparable. It incorporates both cognitive and interpersonal aspects of the survivor's presentation. Interpersonal problems are usually very much in evidence in the clinical presentations of adult survivors. The CAT model does add to our understanding of the development of later problems in adult survivors of childhood abuse.

The case illustrations presented in Chapters 5–8 of this book clearly demonstrate how unhelpful patterns which occur in patients' everyday lives are successfully explored within the therapy session. The importance of the therapeutic relationship, and the use of the transference relationship used in CAT, help therapists to become aware of their own schemata and how these may erupt in the therapy room. The therapist's own reactions and feelings of confusion, especially with more disturbed and chaotic individuals such as those with BPD, can be more readily understood. This is of crucial importance if one is to avoid harmful interaction patterns or prevent collusion with the patient from developing. Such unpredictable and rapidly changing patients can be challenging even to the most competent of therapists. Understanding

RRPs and the separate self-states of the patient can also be very helpful to the therapist in understanding, clarifying and containing 'ruptures' or 'impasses' in therapy. Many non-CAT therapists may relate only to one end of an RRP and over-identify with either the victim or the abuser RRP. CAT reformulation and an understanding of the nature of self-states help the therapist to avoid this. And there is a recognition of the importance of working with resistance and impasses in therapy as being central to the change process.

The focus of therapy in CAT does not have to be on the abuse itself but rather on the disturbed interpersonal relationships and self-management issues subsequent to the abuse. This is an important 'plus' in that many survivors find it particularly painful to talk about the details of the abuse itself but are much more willing to talk about their relationship problems. The CAT therapist values the survivor's existing coping repertoire, rather than undermining it, and emphasises the crucial importance of providing support and empowerment to survivors.

In terms of the shortcomings of the CAT model, it has little to say about the development and treatment of PTSD. However, there are a number of techniques and methods already in existence and these can be easily incorporated into a CAT framework without losing sight of the survivor's personality functioning. Existing social-cognitive models are essentially information-processing models whose strengths are in their ability to explain clinical and experimental data for PTSD. However, the PTSD concept does not apply to all forms of sexual abuse or all abusive experiences. Such models generally propose a violation of existing schematic beliefs, rather than the failure to develop them in the first place. As such they are not developmental and do not adequately address the developmental trajectory over time in the way that the CAT model of childhood abuse does.

The clinical data on the efficacy of CAT is limited and it would be premature at this stage to make any great claims about its efficacy given the limited amount of data available. At this stage CAT for adult survivors is innovative practice and more rigorous research needs to follow before it could be claimed that CAT is clinically effective for adult survivors of childhood abuse. Also, the effectiveness of group interventions has yet to be properly evaluated.

While the CAT model presented here has its strengths and limitations, like any other method of helping, it does enhance the therapist's 'toolkit' in helping such clients, particularly those with more severe pathology. It does not claim that the CAT approach is the 'Holy Grail' but it does represent a significant advance in helping adult survivors of childhood abuse. The focus upon the therapeutic relationship also provides a framework for integrating both relationship and technical factors in a convincing way. The CAT model presented in this book on the whole provides a good working model for the treatment for adult survivors of abuse. It is one that attempts to address the uniqueness of the individual and the complex interplay of factors and influences, and incorporate them into the conceptualisation and active treatment of adult survivors.

In summary, while the CAT model of adult survivors' adaptation to childhood abuse does demonstrate some unique features and strengths, the most encouraging aspect from surveying emerging models for treating complex cases is that they all appear, regardless of theoretical origins, to be conceptually converging and saying something very similar. There is a commonality of theme in the various models proposed, even though they use different terminology and language. They also share a common purpose, which is to try and repair the disconnection at different levels.

What is evident from research on personality disorders (Beck *et al.*, 1990) is that schemata develop in pairs, each situated at one or other end of a continuum. Non-CAT therapies such as the traditional Beckian model of CBT have tended only to look at one pole of the continuum. For example, in low self-esteem the patient is identified as feeling 'not good enough' or 'inferior'. In childhood abuse, the patient is identified as feeling abused. Although not made explicit, each implies a relationship with another within the context of a relational unit. It seems natural to ask the question 'Inferior to whom?' in the case of the patients who describe themselves as inferior. Similarly, to feel abused, there must have been someone doing the 'abusing'. To feel 'rejected' implies that someone has been doing the 'rejecting'. Existing models generally fail to conceptualise the interpersonal schemata involved as well as the CAT model does, although Young's (1994a) Schema Mode work comes close to doing so. The CAT model of childhood abuse, with its use of the RRP concept as a central part of the model and the use of relational units, adds considerably to the conceptualisation and active treatment of adult survivors.

As stated earlier, the CAT model does not directly address the treatment of PTSD, whereas existing cognitive models have a range of therapeutic tools and techniques which address this aspect of survivors' presentations. Likewise, the CAT approach offers a more developmental perspective than cognitive models and is better geared to addressing more complex problems such as severe dissociation and identity disturbance than existing cognitive models. It is important, therefore, to offer the intervention that is of most benefit to the patient. Given that there are several levels of analysis, treatment requires a multilevel approach and a degree of flexibility from the therapist in terms of the interventions used. An integrative approach that puts the needs of the patient first is thus recommended.

The CAT Psychotherapy File, States Grid and Dissociation Questionnaire

STATES GRID (Golynkina & Ryle, 1999)

Rate each state	5 = applies strongly	4 = applies	3 = +/−	2 = does not apply	1 = does not apply at all

Patient's name:		Therapist's name:		Date/session number:	

Descriptions	States								
	A	B	C	D	E	F	G	H	I
Overwhelmed by feelings									
I feel weak									
I feel happy									
I feel angry									
I feel sad									
I feel guilty									
I feel out of control									
I feel unreal									
Others seem critical									
Others envy me									
Others attack me									
Others admire me									
Others care for me									
I trust others									
I depend on others									
I control others									
I want to hurt others									
Cut off from feelings									

When completing the test I was in state of mind:

Names of different states

A:	D:	G:
B:	E:	H:
C:	F:	I:

THE PSYCHOTHERAPY FILE

An aid to understanding ourselves better

We have all had just one life and what has happened to us, and the sense we made of this, colours the way we see ourselves and others. How we see things is for us how things are, and how we go about our lives seems 'obvious and right'. Sometimes, however, our familiar ways of understanding and acting can be the source of our problems. In order to solve our difficulties we may need to learn to recognise how what we do makes things worse. We can then work out new ways of thinking and acting.

These pages are intended to suggest ways of thinking about what you do; recognising your particular patterns is the first step in learning to gain more control and happiness in your life.

Keeping a diary of your moods and behaviour

Symptoms, bad moods, unwanted thoughts or behaviours that come and go can be better understood and controlled if you learn to notice when they happen and what starts them off.

If you have a particular symptom or problem of this sort, start keeping a diary. The diary should be focused on a particular mood, symptom or behaviour, and should be kept every day if possible. Try to record this sequence:

1. How you were feeling about yourself and others and the world before the problem came on.
2. Any external event, or any thought or image in your mind that was going on when the trouble started, or what seemed to start it off.

3. Once the trouble started, what were the thoughts, images or feelings you experienced.

By noticing and writing down in this way what you do and think at these times, you will learn to recognise and eventually have more control over how you act and think at the time. It is often the case that bad feelings like resentment, depression or physical symptoms are the result of ways of thinking and acting that are unhelpful. Keeping a diary in this way gives you the chance to learn better ways of dealing with things.

It is helpful to keep a daily record for one to two weeks, then to discuss what you have recorded with your therapist or counsellor.

Patterns that do not work, but are hard to break

There are certain ways of thinking and acting that do not achieve what we want, but which are hard to change. Read through the lists on the following pages and mark how far you think they apply to you.

Applies strongly ++   Applies +   Does not apply 0

Traps

Traps are things we cannot escape from. Certain kinds of thinking and acting result in a 'vicious circle' when, however hard we try, things seem to get worse instead of better. Trying to deal with feeling bad about ourselves, we think and act in ways that tend to confirm our badness.

Examples of traps

++	+	0

1. *Fear of hurting others*
   Feeling fearful of hurting others* we keep our feelings inside, or put our own needs aside. This tends to allow other people to ignore or abuse us in various ways, which then leads to our feeling, or being, childishly angry. When we see ourselves behaving like this, it confirms our belief that we shouldn't be aggressive and reinforces our avoidance of standing up for our rights.
   * People often get trapped in this way because they mix up aggression and assertion. Mostly, being assertive—asking for our rights—is perfectly acceptable. People who do not respect our rights as human beings must either be stood up to or avoided.

2. *Depressed thinking*
   Feeling depressed, we are sure we will manage a task or social situation badly. Being depressed, we are probably not as effective as we can be, and the depression leads us to exaggerate how badly we handled things. This makes us feel more depressed about ourselves.

3. *Trying to please*
   Feeling uncertain about ourselves and anxious not to upset others, we try to please by doing what they seem to want. As a result: (1) we end up being taken advantage of by others, which makes us angry, depressed or guilty, from which our uncertainty about ourselves is confirmed; or (2) sometimes we feel out of control because of the need to please, and start hiding away, putting things off, or letting people down, which makes other people angry with us and increases our uncertainty.

4. *Avoidance*
   We feel ineffective and anxious about certain situations, such as crowded streets, open spaces or social gatherings. We try to go back into these situations, but feel even more anxiety. Avoiding them makes us feel better, so we stop trying. However, by constantly avoiding situations our lives are limited and we come to feel increasingly ineffective and anxious.

	++	+	0

5. *Social isolation*

   Feeling underconfident about ourselves and anxious not to upset others, we worry that others will find us boring or stupid, so we don't look at people or respond to friendliness. People then see us as unfriendly, so we become more isolated, from which we are convinced we are boring and stupid—and become more underconfident.

6. *Low self-esteem*

   Feeling worthless we feel that we cannot get what we want because (1) we will be punished, (2) others will reject or abandon us, or (3) anything good we get is bound to go away or turn sour. (4) Sometimes it feels as if we must punish ourselves for being weak. From this we feel that everything is hopeless so we give up trying to do anything which confirms and increases our sense of worthlessness.

Dilemmas (false choices and narrow options)

We often act as we do, even when we are not completely happy with it, because the only other ways we can imagine seem as bad or even worse. Sometimes we assume connections that are not necessarily the case—as in 'If I do x then y will follow'. These false choices can be described as either/or or if/then dilemmas. We often don't realise that we see things like this, but we act as if these were the only possible choices.

Do you act as if any of the following false choices rule your life? Recognising them is the first step to changing them.

Choices about myself

I act as if:

1. Either I keep feelings bottled up or I risk being rejected, hurting others, or making a mess.	++	+	0
2. Either I feel I spoil myself and am greedy or I deny myself things and punish myself and feel miserable.	++	+	0
3. If I try to be perfect, I feel depressed and angry. If I don't try to be perfect, I feel guilty, angry and dissatisfied.	++	+	0
4. If I must then I won't; it is as if when faced with a task I must either (1) gloomily submit, or (2) passively resist. Other people's wishes, or even my own, feel too demanding, so I put things off, avoid them.	++	+	0
5. If I must not then I will; it is as if the only proof of my existence is my resistance. Other people's rules, or even my own, feel too restricting, so I break rules and do things which are harmful to me.	++	+	0
6. If other people aren't expecting me to do things for them or look after them, then I feel anxious, lonely and out of control.	++	+	0
7. If I get what I want I feel childish and guilty; if I don't get what I want I feel frustrated, angry and depressed.	++	+	0
8. Either I keep things (feelings, plans) in perfect order, or I fear a terrible mess.	++	+	0

Choices about how we relate to others

I behave with others as if:

1. Either I'm involved with someone and likely to get hurt or I don't get involved and stay in charge, but remain lonely.	++	+	0
2. Either I stick up for myself and nobody likes me, or I give in and get put on by others and feel cross and hurt.	++	+	0
3. Either I'm a brute or a martyr (secretly blaming the other).	++	+	0
4. (a) With others either I'm safely wrapped up in bliss or in combat; (b) if in combat then I'm either a bully or a victim.	++	+	0

	++	+	0
5. Either I look down on other people, or I feel they look down on me.	++	+	0
6. (c) Either I'm sustained by the admiration of others whom I admire or I feel exposed; (d) if exposed then I feel either contemptuous of others or I feel contemptible.	++	+	0
7. Either I'm involved with others and feel engulfed, taken over or smothered, or I stay safe and uninvolved but feel lonely and isolated.	++	+	0
8. When I'm involved with someone whom I care about then either I have to give in or they have to give in.	++	+	0
9. When I'm involved with someone whom I depend on then either I have to give in or they have to give in.	++	+	0
10. (e) As a woman either I have to do what others want or stand up for my rights and get rejected. (f) As a man either I can't have any feelings or I am an emotional mess.	++	+	0

Snags

Snags are what is happening when we say 'I want to have a better life, or I want to change my behaviour but . . .'. Sometimes this comes from how we or our families thought about us when we were young; such as 'She was always the good child', or 'In our family we never . . .'. Sometimes the snags come from the important people in our lives not wanting us to change, not being able to cope with what our changing means to them. Often the resistance is more indirect, as when a parent, husband or wife becomes ill or depressed when we begin to get better.

In other cases, we seem to 'arrange' to avoid pleasure or success, or if they come we have to pay in some way, by depression, or by spoiling things. Often this is because, as children, we came to feel guilty if things went well for us, or felt that we were envied for good luck or success. Sometimes we have come to feel responsible, unreasonably, for things that went wrong in the family, although we may not be aware that this is so. It is helpful to learn to recognise how this sort of pattern is stopping you getting on with your life, for only then can you learn to accept your right to a better life and begin to claim it.

You may get quite depressed when you begin to realise how often you stop your life being happier and more fulfilled. It is important to remember that it's not being stupid or bad, but rather that:

(a) we do these things because this is the way we learned to manage best when we were younger;

(b) we don't have to keep on doing them now we are learning to recognise them;

(c) by changing our behaviour, we can learn to control not only our own behaviour, but also change the way other people behave to us;

(d) although it may seem that others resist the changes we want for ourselves (for example, our parents, or our partners), we often underestimate them; if we are firm about our right to change, those who care for us will usually accept the change.

Do you recognise that you feel limited in your life:

1. For fear of the response of others: for example, I must sabotage success (a) as if it deprives others, (b) as if others may envy me, or (c) as if there are not enough good things to go around?	++ | +	0
2. By something inside yourself: for example I must sabotage good things as if I don't deserve them?	++ | +	0

Difficult and unstable states of mind

Some people find it difficult to keep control over their behaviour and experiences because things feel very difficult and different at times. Indicate which, if any, of the following apply to you:

1. How I feel about myself and others can be unstable; I can switch from one state of mind to a completely different one.	++ | +	0
2. Some states may be accompanied by intense, extreme and uncontrollable emotions . . .	++ | +	0
3. . . . Others by emotional blankness, feeling unreal, or feeling muddled.	++ | +	0
4. Some states are accompanied by feeling intensely guilty or angry with myself, wanting to hurt myself . . .	++ | +	0
5. . . . Or by feeling that others can't be trusted, are going to let me down, or hurt me . . .	++ | +	0
6. . . . Or by being unreasonably angry or hurtful to others.	++ | +	0
7. Sometimes the only way to cope with some confusing feelings is to blank them off and feel emotionally distant from others.	++ | +	0

Different states

Everybody experiences changes in how they feel about themselves and the world. But for some people these changes are extreme, sometimes sudden and confusing. In such cases there are often a number of states, which recur, and learning to recognise them and shifts between them can be very helpful. Below are a number of descriptions of such stages. Identify those which you experience by ringing the number. *You can delete or add words to the descriptions* and there is space to add any not listed.

1. Zombie. Cut off from feelings, cut off from others, disconnected.
2. Feeling bad but soldiering on, coping.
3. Out-of-control rage.
4. Extra-special. Looking down on others.
5. In control of self, of life, of other people.
6. Cheated by life, by others. Untrusting.
7. Provoking, teasing, seducing, winding-up others.
8. Clinging, fearing abandonment.
9. Frenetically active. Too busy to think or feel.
10. Agitated, confused, anxious.
11. Feeling perfectly cared for, blissfully close to another.
12. Misunderstood, rejected, abandoned.
13. Contemptuously dismissive of myself.
14. Vulnerable, needy, passively helpless, waiting for rescue.
15. Envious, wanting to harm others, put them down, pull them down.
16. Protective, respecting of myself, of others.
17. Hurting myself, hurting others.
18. Resentfully submitting to demands.
19. Hurt, humiliated by others.
20. Secure in myself, able to be close to others.
21. Intensely critical of self, of others.
22. Frightened of others.

DISSOCIATION QUESTIONNAIRE

(DIS-Q; Vanderlinden *et al.*, 1993)

Items for the DIS-Q are reproduced below for the four scales: *identity confusion/fragmentation, amnesia, depersonalisation/derealisation* and *absorption*. A total DIS-Q score is obtained also by summing the scores for the four scales. Each client's scores are compared with those of the normal population and clinical groups to assess the extent to which dissociation is reported.

Each item is rated on a five-point scale, 1 = not at all, 2 = a little bit, 3 = moderately, 4 = quite a bit and 5 = extremely. All scores for the subscales are obtained by dividing the total subscale score by the number of items and can vary between 1 and 5. The mean total DIS-Q score for the 'normal' population (from a sample of 378 people) is 1.5 ($\pm$ 0.4); identity confusion/fragmentation 1.4 ($\pm$ 0.4), loss of control 1.7 ($\pm$ 0.5), amnesia 1.4 ($\pm$ 0.4) and absorption 1.9 ($\pm$ 0.6). Total DIS-Q score for schizophrenia ($N = 31$) is 2.0 (SD = 0.6), eating disorders ($N = 98$) 2.2 (SD = 0.5), obsessive-compulsive disorder ($N = 17$) 1.7 (SD = 0.4), PTSD ($N = 12$) 2.7 (SD = 0.5), dissociative disorders not otherwise specified ($N = 23$) 2.9 (SD = 0.6) and DID ($N = 30$) 3.5 (SD = 0.4).

Identity confusion/fragmentation (25 items)

1. I have the feeling that my body is not mine
2. I have the feeling that I am made up of two (or more) people
3. I have the feeling that my mind is split
4. At times it seems that as if someone inside me decides what I do
5. In particular situations I experience myself as a split personality
6. I have the feeling that I am somebody else
7. I look in the mirror without recognising myself
8. I hear voices in my head telling me what I am doing or making a comment on what I am doing
9. I am determined to do something but my body acts quite differently against my own will
10. I feel a great distance between myself and the things I think and do
11. At times I wonder who I am exactly
12. I have the feeling that other people, other things and the world surrounding me are not real
13. At times it seems I have lost contact with my body
14. I get the feeling that my body has undergone an alteration
15. Sometimes I find myself in a well-known place that appears strange and unknown to me
16. I wish I had more control of myself
17. Sometimes I think or do something against my liking, in a way that does not suit me at all
18. I see myself differently from the way other people see me
19. I do certain things without knowing why
20. I am about to say something but something quite different actually comes out
21. I wonder how I can prevent myself from doing certain things
22. I sometimes see the world through a haze, so that the people and things surrounding me appear remote or vague
23. I regularly have the feeling that everything is unreal
24. I get into situations which I do not want to be in

25. When I am tired, it seems as if a strange power from outside takes possession of me and decides for me what to do

Loss of control (*18 items*)

26. I catch myself day-dreaming
27. I regularly feel the urge to eat something, even when I am not hungry
28. There can be a sudden and complete change in my mood
29. At times I feel as if I am dreaming
30. Sometimes I do things without thinking about them
31. I gorge myself with food without thinking about it
32. I can be listening to someone and suddenly realise that I have not heard part or all of the story
33. At times I get angry without wanting to at all
34. I find it very hard to resist bad habits
35. When eating I do so without thinking
36. At times I feel confused
37. I often do something without thinking about it
38. I can enclose myself in fantasies or day-dreams so much that they seem to be really happening
39. While driving and/or bicycling, I suddenly realise that I cannot remember what happened on the way
40. I stare aimlessly without thinking about anything
41. For no reason, or without wanting to, I burst out laughing or crying
42. I am not sure whether certain memories are real or if I merely dreamed about them
43. I lose every notion of time

Amnesia (*14 items*)

44. I cannot remember some important events in my life, such as my final examinations or wedding day
45. Sometimes I find notes, drawings or annotations that I have made and do not remember having made them
46. At times I cannot remember where I was the day (or days) before
47. I immediately forget what other people tell me
48. Sometimes I suddenly find myself in an unfamiliar place without knowing how I got there
49. Entire blocks of time drop out of my mind and I cannot remember what I did
50. Sometimes I discover that I have done something without remembering anything about it

51. I find new articles among my things that that I cannot remember buying
52. I can be doing something and suddenly be struck by a blackout
53. I cannot remember whether I have really done something or if I merely planned it
54. I sometimes forget where I have put something
55. I am told that I act as if friends or family members were strangers to me
56. I often think about nothing
57. When I watch television I do not notice anything going on around me

Absorption (*6 items*)

58. When eating I am aware of every bite I take
59. I can remember something that happened to me so vividly that it is as though I am reliving it
60. I am aware of each step I take when I walk
61. Things that I find hard to do in some situations I am able to do with the greatest of ease in other situations (e.g., sports, work, social contacts)
62. At times I want to do two things at the same time and find myself arguing about the pros and cons of doing each thing
63. I watch myself closely in everything I do

References

Agazarian, Y. & Peters, R. (1981). *The visible and invisible group*. London: Karnac (Reprinted 1995).

Ainscough, C. & Toon, K. (1993). *Breaking free: Help for survivors of child sexual abuse*. London: Sheldon.

Akhtar, S. (1999). *Inner torment: Living between conflict and fragmentation*. Northvale, NJ: Aronson Press.

Albach, F. & Everaerd, W. (1992). Post-traumatic stress symptoms in victims of childhood incest. *Psychotherapy & Psychosomatics*, **57**, 143–151.

Alexander, P.C. (1992). Application of attachment theory to the study of sexual abuse. *Journal of Consulting and Clinical Psychology*, **60**, 185–195.

Alexander, P.C. Anderson, C.L., Brand, B., Schaeffer, C.M., Grelling, B.Z, & Kretz, L. (1998). Adult attachment and long term effects in survivors of incest. *Child Abuse & Neglect*, **22**, 45–61.

Alexander, P.C. & Lupfer, S.L. (1987). Family characteristics and long-term consequences associated with sexual abuse. *Archives of Sexual Behaviour*, **16**, 235–245.

Alexander, P.C., Moore, S. & Alexander, E.R. (1991). What is transmitted in the intergenerational transmission of violence. *Journal of Marriage and the Family*, **53**, 657–665.

Alexander, P., Neimeyer, R., Follette, V., Moore, M. & Harter, S. (1989). A comparison of group treatments of women sexually abused as children. *Journal of Consulting & Clinical Psychology*, **57**, 479–483.

Alford, B.A. & Beck, A. (1997). *The integrative power of cognitive therapy*. New York: Guilford Press.

Altrocchi, J. (1998). Individual differences in pluralism. In J. Rowan & M. Cooper (Eds), *The plural self: Multiplicity in everyday life*. London: Sage (pp. 168–182).

Altrocchi, J. & McReynolds, P. (1997). The self-pluralism scale: A measure of psychological variability. In S.T. St Jeor (Ed.), *Obesity assessment: Tools, methods, interpretations. A reference case: The Reno Diet–Heart Study*. New York: Chapman & Hall (pp. 420–424).

Altrocchi, J., McReynolds, P. & House, C. (1990). *Self pluralism as a proposed contributing cause of multiple personality disorder.* Poster session at Seventh International Conference on Multiple Personality Disorder and Dissociation, Chicago.

American Psychiatric Association (1987). *Diagnostic and Statistical Manual of Mental Disorders*, 3rd Edition (Revised). Washington, DC: American Psychiatric Association.

American Psychiatric Association (1994). *Diagnostic and Statistical Manual of Mental Disorders*, 4th Edition. Washington, DC: American Psychiatric Association.

Anderson, C.L. & Alexander, P.M. (1996). The relationship between attachment and dissociation in adult survivors of incest. *Dissociation*, **59**, 240–254.

Anderson, S.C. (1993). Anti-stalking laws: Will they curb the erotomanic's obsessive pursuit? *Law & Psychology Review*, **17**, 171–191.

Andrews, B. (1999). *The prevalence and consequences of childhood sexual abuse.* Trauma & Mental Health Conference, London, April.

Antonovsky, A. (1987). *Unravelling the mystery of health: How people manage stress and stay well.* San Francisco: Jossey-Bass.

Armstrong, J.G. & Loewenstein, R.S. (1990). Characteristics of patients with multiple personality and dissociative disorders on testing. *Journal of Nervous & Mental Diseases*, **178**, 448–454.

Arntz, A. & Weertman, A. (1999). Treatment of childhood memories, theory and practice. *Behaviour Research & Therapy*, **37**, 715–742.

Bagley, C., Wood, M. & Young, I.N. (1994). Victim to abuser: Mental health and behavioural sequelae of child sexual abuse in a community survey of young adult males. *Child Abuse & Neglect*, **18**, 683–697.

Bamber, M.R. (1997). An evaluation of three cognitive models of depression. *Clinical Psychology Forum*, **99**, January.

Barnard, P.J. & Teasdale, J.D. (1991). Interacting cognitive subsystems: A systemic approach to cognitive-affective interactional change. *Cognition and Emotion*, **5**, 1–39.

Barnes, B. Ernst, S. & Hyde, K. (1999). *An introduction to group work: A group-analytic perspective.* Basingstoke: Macmillan.

Bartholomew, K. & Horowitz, L.M. (1991). Attachment styles among young adults: A test of a four-category model. *Journal of Personality & Social Psychology*, **61**, 226–244.

Beck, A.T. (1967). *Depression: Clinical, experimental and theoretical aspects.* New York: Harper & Row.

Beck, A.T. (1996). Beyond belief: A theory of modes, personality and psychopathology. Chapter 1 in P.M. Salkovskis (Ed.), *Frontiers of cognitive therapy.* London: Guilford.

Beck, A.T. & Freeman, A. (1990). *Cognitive therapy of personality disorders.* New York: Guilford Press.

Beck, A.T., Schuyler, D. & Herman, I. (1974). Development of suicidal intent scales. In A.T. Beck, C.P. Rosnik & D. Lettier (Eds), *The prediction of suicide*. Bowie, MD: Charles Press (pp. 45–56).

Beck, A., Ward, C.H., Mendelsohn, M., Mock, J. & Erbaugh J.K. (1961). An inventory for measuring depression. *Archives of General Psychiatry*, **4**, 561–567.

Becker-Lausen, E., Saunders, B. & Chinsky, J.M. (1995). Mediation of abusive childhood experiences: Depression, dissociation and negative life outcomes. *American Journal of Orthopsychiatry*, **65**, 560–573.

Beitchman, J., Zucker, K., Hood, J., Da Costa, G. & Akman, D. (1991). A review of the short-term effects of child sexual abuse. *Child Abuse & Neglect*, **15**, 537–566.

Beitchman, J.H., Zucker, K.J., Hood, J.F., Da Costa, G.A., Akman, D. & Cassavia, E. (1992). A review of the long-term effects of child sexual abuse. *Child Abuse & Neglect*, **16**, 101–118.

Bell-Gadsby, J. (1996). *Reclaiming 'herstory': Ericksonian solution-focused therapy for sexual abuse*. London: Greenwood Press.

Bennett, D. (1999a). Readiness of change—the impact of reformulation: A case example of Cognitive Analytic Therapy. *International Journal of Short-term Psychotherapy*, **9**, 83–91.

Bennett, D. (1999b). *Deriving a model of therapist competence from good and poor outcome cases in the psychotherapy for borderline personality disorder*. Unpublished PhD, University of Sheffield.

Bennett, D. & Parry, G. (1998). The accuracy of reformulation in cognitive analytic therapy: A validation study. *Psychotherapy Research*, **8**, 84–103.

Bernard, C. & Hirsch, C. (1985). Borderline personality and victims of incest. *Psychological Reports*, **57**, 715–718.

Bernstein, D.P. & Fink, L. (1998). *Childhood Trauma Questionnaire: A retrospective self-report manual*. San Antonio: Psychological Corporation.

Bernstein, E. & Putnam, F.W. (1986). Development, reliability and validity of a dissociation scale. *Journal of Nervous and Mental Disease*, **174**, 727–735.

Bjornson, L., Reagor, P.A. & Kasten, J.D. (1988). *Multiple personality patterns on standardized psychological tests*. In B.G. Braun (Ed.), Proceedings of the Fifth International Conference on Multiple Personality/Dissociative States. Chicago: Rush Presbyterian St Luke's Medical Center.

Blake, D.D., Weathers, F.W., Nagy, L.N., Kalupek, D.G., Klanminser, G., Chaney, D.S. & Keane, T.M. (1990). A clinician rating scale for assessing current and lifetime PTSD: The CAPS-I. *Behaviour Therapist*, **18**, 187–188.

Blake-White, J. & Kline, C.M. (1985). Treating the dissociative process in adult victims of childhood abuse. *Social Casework,* September, 394–402.

Blatt, S.J. & Erlich, H.S. (1982). Levels of resistance in the therapeutic process. In P.L. Wachter (Ed.), *Resistance: Psychodynamic and behavioural approaches.* New York: Plenum Press.

Boast, N. & Coid, J. (1994). Homosexual erotomania and HIV infection. *British Journal of Psychiatry*, **164**, 842–846.

Bongar, B., Berman, J.L., Maris, R.W., Silverman, M.M., Harris, E.A. & Packman, W.L. (1998). *Risk management with suicidal patients*. New York: Guilford Press.

Boon, S. & Draijer, N. (1993). Multiple personality disorder in the Netherlands: A clinical investigation of 74 patients. *American Journal of Psychiatry*, **150**, 489–494.

Bowers, M.D., Brecher-Mauer, S. & Newton, B.W. (1971). Therapy for multiple personality. *International Journal of Clinical & Experimental Hypnosis*, **19**, 57–65.

Bowlby, J. (1969). *Attachment and loss* (Vol. 1). New York: Basic Books.

Bowlby, J. (1973). *Attachment and loss* (Vol. 2). New York: Basic Books.

Brandt, L.M. (1989). A short-term group therapy model for treatment of adult female survivors of childhood incest. *Group*, **18**, 74–82.

Braun, B.G. (1988). The BASK model of dissociation. *Dissociation*, **1**, 4–23.

Bremner, D. & Marmar, C.R. (1998). *Trauma, memory and dissociation*. American Psychiatric Press: Washington, DC.

Bretherton, I. (1985). *Attachment theory: Retrospect and prospect*. Monograph of the Society for Research in Child Development, 209 (50, No. 1–2). Chicago: University of Chicago Press.

Brewin, C.R. (1988). *Cognitive foundations of clinical psychology*. Hillsdale, NJ: Erlbaum.

Brewin, C.R., Andrews, B. & Gotlib, I.H. (1993). Psychopathology and early experience: An appraisal of retrospective reports. *Psychological Bulletin*, **113**, 82–98.

Brewin, C.R., Dalgleish, T. & Joseph, S. (1996). A dual representation theory of post-traumatic stress disorder. *Psychological Review*, **103**, 670–686.

Briere, J. (1984). *The effects of childhood sexual abuse on later psychological functioning: Defining a 'post-sexual-abuse syndrome'*. Paper presented at the Third National Conference on Sexual Victimization of Children, Washington, DC.

Briere, J. & Conte, J. (1993). Self-reported amnesia for abuse in adults molested as children. *Journal of Traumatic Stress*, **6**, 21–31.

Briere, J. & Elliott, D.M. (1993). Sexual abuse, family environment, and psychological symptoms: On the validity of statistical control. *Journal of Consulting & Clinical Psychology*, **61**, 284–288.

Briere, J., Evans, D.M., Harris, K. & Cotman, A. (1995). The Trauma Symptom Inventory: Reliability and validity in a clinical sample. *Journal of Interpersonal Violence*, **10**, 387–401.

Briere, J. & Zaidi, L.Y. (1989). Sexual abuse histories and sequelae in female psychiatric emergency room patients. *American Journal of Psychiatry*, **146**, 1602–1606.

Brown, P. (1994). Towards a psychobiological model of dissociation and post-traumatic stress disorder. In S.J. Lynn & J.W. Rhue (Eds), *Dissociation, clinical and theoretical perspectives*. (Ch. 5, pp. 94–122). New York: Guilford Press.

Browne, A. & Finkelhor, D. (1985). The traumatic impact of child sexual abuse: A conceptualization. *American Journal of Orthopsychiatry*, **55**, 530–541.

Bryer, J.B., Nelson, B.A., Miller, J.B. & Kroll, P.A. (1987). Childhood sexual and physical abuse as factors in adult psychiatric illness. *American Journal of Psychiatry*, **144**, 1426–1430.

Bucci, W. (1997). *Psychoanalysis and cognitive science*. New York: Guilford.

Buckley, R. & Resnick, P. (1994). *Stalking survey*. Oregan Psychiatric Society, Portland, OR, March 4–5 (unpublished).

Burgess, A.W., Hartmann, C.R. & McCormack, A. (1987). Abused to abuser: Antecedents of socially deviant behaviour. *American Journal of Psychiatry*, **144**, 1431–1436.

Burgess, A.W., Hartmann, C.R., McCormack, A. & Grant, C.A. (1988). Child victim to juvenile victimizer: Treatment implications. *International Journal of Family Psychiatry*, **9**, 403–416.

Butler, S. & Wintram, C. (1991). *Feminist group work*. London: Sage.

Cahill, C., Llewelyn, S.P. and Pearson, C. (1990). The long-term effects of sexual abuse which occurred in childhood: A review. *British Journal of Clinical Psychology*, **30**, 117–130.

Cahill, C., Llewelyn, S.P. & Pearson, C. (1991). Treatment of sexual abuse which occurred in childhood: A review. *British Journal of Clinical Psychology*, **14**, 475–493.

Calhoun, B.M., Giller, E. & Lynn, W. (1991). *Multiple personality disorder: From the inside out*. Lutherville, MD: Sidran.

Calhoun, K.S. & Resick, P.A. (1993). Post traumatic stress disorder. In D. Barlow (Ed.), *Clinical handbook of psychological disorder*. New York: Guilford Press.

Campbell, J.D. (1990). Self-esteem and clarity of the self-concept. *Journal of Personality and Social Psychology*, **59**, 538–549.

Campbell, JD., Trapnell, P.D., Heine, S.J., Katz, I.M., Lavatee, L.F. & Lehman, D.R. (1996). Self-concept clarity: Measurement, personality correlates and cultural boundaries. *Journal of Personality and Social Psychology*, **70**, 141–156.

Carlson, E.B., Furby, L., Armstrong, J. & Schlaes, J. (1997). A conceptual framework for the long-term psychological effects of traumatic childhood abuse. *Child Maltreatment*, **2**, 272–295.

Carlson, E.B. & Putnam, F.W. (1993). An update on the dissociative experiences scale. *Dissociation*, **6**, 16–27.

Carlson, V., Cicchetti, D., Barnett, D. & Braunwald, K. (1989). Finding order in disorganisation: Lessons from research on mistreated infants' attachments to their caregivers. In D. Cicchetti & V. Carlson (Eds), *Child maltreatment: Theory and research on the causes and consequences of child abuse and neglect* (pp. 494–528). New York: Cambridge University Press.

Carr, W. (1994). *Brief encounters*. SPCK: London.

Carver, C., Stalker, C., Stewart, E. & Abraham, B. (1989) The impact of group therapy for adult survivors of childhood sexual abuse. *Canadian Journal of Psychiatry*, **34**, 753–758.

Chewning-Korpach, M. (1995). Sexual re-victimisation: A cautionary note. In M.F. Schwartz & L. Cohn (Eds), *Sexual abuse and eating disorders*. New York: Brunner Mazel.

Chu, J.A. & Dill, D.L. (1990). Dissociative symptoms in relation to childhood physical and sexual abuse. *American Journal of Psychiatry*, **147**(7), 887–892.

Clarke, S. & Llewelyn, S. (1994). Personal constructs of survivors of childhood sexual abuse receiving Cognitive Analytic Therapy. *British Journal of Medical Psychology*, **67**, 273–289.

Clarke, S. & Pearson, C. (in press a). Personal constructs of women survivors of childhood sexual abuse receiving group therapy. *British Journal of Medical Psychology*.

Clarke, S. & Pearson, C. (in press b). Personal constructs of male survivors of childhood sexual abuse receiving Cognitive Analytic Therapy. *British Journal of Medical Psychology*.

Clary, W.F., Burstein, K.J. & Carpenter, J.S. (1984). Multiple personality and borderline personality disorder. *Psychiatric Clinics of North America*, **7**, 89–99.

Classen, C., Field, N.P., Atkinson, A. & Spiegal, D. (1998). Representations of self in women sexually abused in childhood. *Child Abuse & Neglect*, **22**, 999–1004.

Cohen, B.M., Giller, E. & Lynn, W. (1997). *Multiple personality disorder: From the inside out*. Lutherville, MD: Sidran.

Cole, P.M. & Putnam, F.W. (1992). Effect of incest on self and social functioning: A developmental psychopathology perspective. *Journal of Consulting and Clinical Psychology*, **60**, 174–184.

Community Health Sheffield (1999). *Breaking the silence: Working with survivors of childhood sexual abuse*. London: Pavilion.

Coons, P.M. (1984). The differential diagnosis of multiple personality. *Psychiatric Clinics of North America*, **7**, 51–69.

Coons, P.M., Bowman, E.S. & Milstein, V. (1988). Multiple personality disorder: A clinical investigation of 50 cases. *Journal of Nervous & Mental Diseases*, **176**, 519–527.

Corder, B.F. & Whiteside, R. (1996). A survey of psychologists' safety issues and concerns. *American Journal of Forensic Psychology*, **14**, 65–72.

Courtois, C. (1979). The incest experience and its aftermath. *Victimology*, **4**, 337–347.

Courtois, C.A. (1988). *Healing the incest wound: Adult survivors in therapy.* New York: Norton.

Cowmeadow, P. (1994). Deliberate self-harm and cognitive analytic therapy. *International Journal of Short-Term Psychotherapy*, **9**, 135–150.

Crittenden, P.M. (1985). Maltreated infants: Vulnerability and resilience. *Journal of Child Psychology & Psychiatry*, **26**, 85–96.

Dalkin, A. (1997). Male sexual abuse and its relationship with delinquency. *Forensic Update*, February, 32–42.

Davidson, J.R., Kudler, H.S., Saunders, W.B. Erickson, L., Smith, R.D., Stein, R.M., Lipper, S., Hammet, E.B., Mahoney, S.L. & Cavans, J.O. (1993). Predicting response to amitriptyline in post-traumatic stress disorder. *American Journal of Psychiatry*, **150**, 1024–1029.

Davidson, J.R.T. & van der Kolk, B.A. (1994). The psycho pharmacological treatment of post-traumatic stress disorder. In B.A. van der Kolk, A.C. McFarlane & L. Weisaeth (Eds), *Traumatic stress: The effects of overwhelming experience on mind, body and society* (Ch. 23). New York: Guilford Press.

Davidson, L.M. & Baum, A. (1994). Psychophysiological aspects of chronic stress following trauma. In R.T. Ursano, B.G. McCaughey & C.S. Fullerton (Eds), *Individual and community responses to trauma and disaster.* Cambridge: Cambridge University Press.

de Clérambault, G.G. (1942). Les psychoses passionelle. In *Ouevres Psychiatrique.* Paris: Press Unversitaires de France.

Dell, P.F. (1988). Professional skepticism about multiple personality. *Journal of Nervous & Mental Diseases*, **176**, 528–531.

Dell, P. F. (1998). Axis II pathology in outpatients with dissociative identity disorder. *Journal of Nervous & Mental Disease*, **186**, 350–356.

Dembo, R., Williams, L., Worhke, W., Schmeidler, J. & Brown, C.H. (1992). The role of family factors, physical abuse and sexual victimization experiences in high risk youths' alcohol and other drug use and delinquency: A longitudinal model. *Violence & Victims*, **7**, 245–266.

Derogatis, L.R. (1983). *SCL-R-90: Administration, scoring and procedures—Manual II.* Toronto: Clinical Psychometric Research.

Derogatis, L. & Melisaratos, N. (1983). The Brief Symptom Inventory: An introductory report. *Psychological Medicine*, **13**, 595–605.

Dietz, P. (1988). *Threats and attacks against public figures.* Presented at the Annual Meeting of the American Academy of Psychiatry and Law, October 1988, San Francisco.

Dimock, P.T. (1988). Adult males sexually abused as children: Characteristics and implications for treatment. *Journal of Interpersonal Violence*, **3**, 203–221.

Donahue, E.M., Robins, R.W., Roberts, B.W. & John, O.P. (1993). The divided self: Concurrent and longitudinal effects of psychological adjustment and social roles on self-concept differentiation. *Journal of Personality and Social Psychology*, **64**, 834–836.

Donaldson, M.A. & Cordess-Green, S. (1994). *Group treatment of adult incest survivors*. Thousand Oaks, CA: Sage.

Downs, W.R. (1991). Developmental considerations for the effects of childhood sexual abuse. *Journal of Interpersonal Violence*, **8**, 331–345.

Downs, W.R. & Doueck, H.J. (1991). *A three dimensional framework for tracking human behaviour in the environment: The HBSE cube*. Annual Meeting of the Council on Social Work Education, New Orleans, LA.

Draucker, C.B. (1999). The psychotherapeutic needs of women who have been sexually assaulted. *Perspectives in Psychiatric Care*, **35**, 18–28.

Duignan, I. & Mitzman, S.F. (1994). Measuring individual change in patients receiving time-limited cognitive analytic therapy. *International Journal of Short-Term Psychotherapy*, **9**, 151–160.

Dunn, M. (1994). Variations in cognitive analytic therapy technique in the treatment of a severely disturbed patient. *International Journal of Short-Term Psychotherapy*, **9**, 119–134.

Dunn, M. & Parry, G. (1997). A formulated care plan approach for caring for people with borderline personality disorder in a community mental health setting. *Clinical Psychology Forum*, **104**, 19–22.

Dutton, D.G. (1981). Traumatic bonding. *Victimology*, **6**, 139–168.

Dutton, D.G. (1998). *The abusive personality*. New York: Guilford.

Dutton, D. G. & Golant, S.K. (1995). *The batterer*. New York: Basic Books.

Dutton, D.G. & Hart, S.D. (1992). Evidence for long term, specific effects of childhood abuse and neglect on criminal behaviour in man. *International Journal of Offender Therapy & Comparative Criminology*, **36**, 129–137.

Dutton, D.G. & Painter, S.L. (1981). Traumatic bonding: The development of emotional attachments in battered women and other relationships of intermittent abuse. *Victimology*, **6**, 139–168.

Dutton, D.G., Saunders, K., Starzomski, A. & Bartholomew, K. (1994). Intimacy anger and insecure attachment as precursor of abuse in intimate relationships. *Journal of Applied Social Psychology*, **24**, 1367–1386.

Egeland, B. & Sroufe, A. (1981). Developmental sequelae of maltreatment in infancy. *New Directions for Child Development*, **11**, 77–92.

Ehlers, A. & Clark, D.M. (2000). A cognitive model of post-traumatic stress disorder. *Behaviour Research & Therapy*, **38**, 319–345.

Ehlers, A., Clark, D.M., Dunmore, E., Jaycox, L., Meadows, E. and Foa. E.B. (1998). Predicting response to exposure treatment in PTSD: The role of mental defeat and alienation. *Journal of Traumatic Stress*, **11**, 457–471.

Ellason, J.W. & Ross, C.A. (1977). Two-year follow-up of inpatients with dissociative identity disorder. *American Journal of Psychiatry*, **154**, 832–839.

Ellason, J.W., Ross, C.A. & Fuchs, D.I. (1996). Lifetime axis I and axis II comorbidity and childhood trauma history in dissociative identity disorder. *Psychiatry*, **59**, 255–266.

Elliott, D.M. (1997). Traumatic events: Prevalence and delayed recall in the general population. *Journal of Consulting & Clinical Psychology*, **65**, 811–820.

Ellis, P. & Mellsop, G. (1995). De Clérambault's syndrome: A nosological entity? *British Journal of Psychiatry*, **146**, 90–95.

Eltz, M.J., Shirk, S.R. & Sarlin, N. (1995). Alliance formation and treatment outcome amongst maltreated adolescents. *Child Abuse & Neglect*, **19**, 419–431.

Epps, K., Swaffer, J. & Hollin, C.R. (1996). Adolescent firesetters I: Background, findings from an analysis of 47 cases (unpublished).

Erikson, E.H. (1968). *Identity: Youth and crisis*. New York: Norton.

Esquirol, J.E.D. (1965). *Mental maladies: A treatise on insanity*. New York: Hafner.

Evans, D.L., Jeckel, L.L. & Slott, N.E. (1982). Erotomania: A variant of pathological mourning. *Bulletin of the Menninges Clinic*, **46**, 507–520.

Evans, J. & Parry, G. (1996). The impact of reformulation in cognitive analytic therapy with difficult to help clients. *Clinical Psychology & Psychotherapy*, **3**, 109–117.

Everill, J.T., Waller, G. & Macdonald, W. (1995). Dissociation in bulimic and non-eating disordered women. *International Journal of Eating Disorders*, **18**, 1–11.

Exner, J.E. (1991). *The Rorschach: A comprehensive system (Vol. 2). Current research and advanced interpretation*. New York: Wiley.

Falshaw, L., Browne, K.D. & Hollin, C.R. (1996). Victim to offender: A review. *Aggression & Violent Behaviour*, **1**, 389–404.

Fast, I. (1974). Multiple identities in borderline personality organisation. *British Journal of Medical Psychology*, **47**, 291–300.

Favazza, A.R. & Conterio, K. (1989). Female habitual self-mutilators. *Acta Psychiatrica Scandinavica*, **79**, 283–289.

Feeney, J. & Noller, P. (1996). *Adult attachment*. London: Sage.

Feldmann, T.B. (1988). Violence as a disintegration product of the self in post-traumatic stress disorder. *American Journal of Psychotherapy*, **17**, 281–289.

Femina, D.D., Yeager, C.A. & Lewis, D.O. (1990). Child abuse: Adolescent records versus adult recall. *Child Abuse & Neglect*, **14**, 227–231.

Ferdiere, G. (1937). *L'erotomanie, illusion delirante d'être aime*. Paris: G. Douin.

Figley, C. (1997). *The active ingredients of the Power Therapies*. Keynote presentation at The Power Therapies: a conference for the integrative and innovative use of EMDR, TFT, EFT, advanced NLP, and TIR. Lakewood, CO.

Fine, C. (1988). Thoughts on the cognitive perceptual substrates of multiple personality disorder. *Dissociation*, **4**, 5–10.

Fink, L., Bernstein, D., Handelsman, L., Foote, J. & Lovejoy, M. (1995). Initial reliability and validity of the Childhood Trauma Interview: A new multidimensional measure of childhood interpersonal trauma. *American Journal of Psychiatry*, **152**, 1329–1335.

Finkelhor, D. (1987). The trauma of child sexual abuse: Two models. *Journal of Interpersonal Violence*, **2**, 348–366.

Finkelhor, D. (1990). Early and long-term effects of child sexual abuse: An update. *Professional Psychology: Research & Practice*, **5**, 325–330.

Finkelhor, D. (1994). The international epidemiology of child sexual abuse. *Child Abuse & Neglect*, **18**, 409–417.

Finkelhor, D. & Browne, A. (1985) The traumatic impact of child sexual abuse: A review and conceptualisation. *American Journal of Orthopsychiatry*, **55**, 530–541.

Firestone, R.W. & Firestone, L.A. (1996) Firestone Assessment of Self-Destructive Thoughts (FAST). London: Psychological Corporation.

First, M.B., Gibbon, M., Spitzer, R.L., Williams, J.B.W. & Benjamin, L.S. (1997). *Structured Clinical Interview for DSM-IV Personality Disorders (SCID-II)*. Washington, DC: American Psychiatric Press.

First, M.B., Spitzer, R.L., Gibbon, M. & Williams, J.B.W. (1997). *Structured Clinical Interview for DSM-IV Axis I Disorders (SCID-I)*. Washington, DC: American Psychiatric Press.

Fleming, J.M. (1987). Prevalence of childhood sexual abuse in a community sample of Australian women. *Medical Journal of Australia*, **166**, 65–68.

Fleming, J., Mullen, P. & Bammer, G. (1997). A study of potential risk factors for sexual abuse in childhood. *Child Abuse & Neglect*, **21**, 49–58.

Foa, E.B. & Kozak, M.J. (1986). Emotional processing of fear: Exposure to corrective information. *Psychological Bulletin*, **99**, 20–35.

Foa, E.B. & Riggs, D.S. (1993). Post-traumatic stress disorder in rape victims. In J. Oldham, M.B. Riba & A. Tasman (Eds), *American psychiatric press review of psychiatry*. (Vol. 12, pp. 273–303). Washington, DC: American Psychiatric Association.

Foa, E.B., Zinbarg, R. & Rothbaum, B.O. (1992). Uncontrollability and unpredictability in post-traumatic stress disorder: An animal model. *Psychological Bulletin*, **112**, 218–238.

Follette, V.M., Ruzek, J.I. & Abueg, F.R. (1999). *Cognitive behavioural therapy for trauma*. New York: Guilford Press.

Follette, W.C., Naugle, A.C. & Follette, V.M. (1997). MMPI-2 profiles of adult women with child sexual abuse histories: Cluster-analytic findings. *Journal of Consulting & Clinical Psychology*, **65**, 858–866.

Fonagy, P. (1991). Thinking about thinking: Some clinical and theoretical considerations in the treatment of a borderline patient. *International Journal of Psychoanalysis*, **72**, 639–656.

Fosbury, J.A. (1994). Cognitive analytic therapy with poorly controlled insulin dependent diabetic patients. In C. Coles (Ed.), *Psychology and diabetes care.* Chichester: PMH Production.

Foulkes, S.H. (1964). *Therapeutic group analysis.* London: George Allen & Unwin.

Foulkes, S.H. (1975). *Group-analytic psychotherapy.* London: Gordon & Breach.

Francella, F. & Bannister, D. (1977) *A manual for repertory grid technique.* London: Academic Press.

Frederick, C.J. (1986). Post-traumatic stress and child molestation. In A. Burgess & C. Hartmann (Eds), *Sexual exploitation of clients by mental health professionals.* New York: Praeger.

Freedenfeld, R.N. Ornduff, S.R., & Kelsey, R.M. (1995). Object relations and physical abuse: A TAT analysis. *Journal of Personality Assessment,* **64**, 552–568.

Freeman A. (1998). Scripts and lifestyles. Paper presented to the European Conference of Cognitive and Behavioural Therapy, Cork, Ireland. September 1998.

Freud, S. (1896). *Further remarks on the psychoneuroses* (Standard edition, Vol. 7). London: Hogarth.

Freud, S. (1905). *Three essays on sexuality,* (Standard edition, Vol. 7). London: Hogarth.

Freud, S. (1906). *My views on the part played by sexuality in the aetiology of the neuroses* (Standard edition, Vol. 7). London: Hogarth.

Freud, S. (1917). *Introductory lectures on psycho-analysis* (Standard edition, Vol. 11). London: Hogarth.

Freud, S. (1920). *Beyond the pleasure principle.* (Standard edition, Vol. 18). London: Hogarth.

Freud, S. (1926). *Inhibitions, symptoms and anxiety.* (Standard edition, Vol. 20). London: Hogarth.

Freud, S. (1940). *An outline of psycho-analysis.* (Standard edition, Vol. 23). London: Hogarth.

Friedman, M.J. (1991). Biological approaches to the diagnosis and treatment of post-traumatic stress disorder. *Journal of Traumatic Stress,* **4**, 67–91.

Fromuth, M.E. (1986). The relationship of childhood sexual abuse and later psychological adjustment in a sample of college women. *Child Abuse & Neglect,* **10**, 5–15.

Gartner, R.B. (1999). *Betrayed as boys: Psychodynamic treatment of sexually abused men.* New York: Guilford Press.

Garyfallos, G., Adampoulos, M., Saitis, M., Sotirion, M., Zlatanos, D. & Alektorides, P. (1993). Evaluation of cognitive analytic therapy (CAT) outcome. *Neurologia et Psychiatra,* **12**, 121–125.

Gelinas, D.J. (1983). The personality negative effects of incest. *Psychiatry,* **46**, 312–332.

Gergen, K.J. (1971). *The concept of self.* New York: Holt.

Gershunny, B.J. & Thayer, J.F. (1999). Relations among psychological trauma, dissociative phenomena, and trauma-related distress: A review and integration. *Clinical Psychology Review,* **19**, 631–657.

Gibbon, M.B., Spitzer, R.L., Williams, J.B.W. & Benjamin, L.S. (1997). *Users guide to the Structured Clinical Interview for DSM-IV Axis II personality disorders (SCID-II).* Washington, DC: American Psychiatric Press.

Gilbert, P. (1992). *Depression: The evolution of powerlessness.* Hove: Erlbaum.

Gillett, T., Eminson, S.R. & Hassanyeh, F. (1990). Primary and secondary erotomania: Clinical characterstics and follow up. *Acta Psychiatrica Scandinavica,* **82**, 65–69.

Goldberg, A. (1994). Lovesickness. In J.M. Oldham & S. Bone (Eds), *Paranoia: New psychoanalytic perspectives* (pp. 115–132). Madison, WI: International Universities Press.

Goldfried, M.R. & Davison, G.C. (1976). *Clinical behaviour therapy.* New York: Holt, Rinehart & Winston.

Gold-Steinberg, S. & Buttenheim, M.C. (1993) 'Telling one's story' in an incest survivor's group. *International Journal of Group Psychotherapy,* **43**, 173–189.

Golynkina, K. & Ryle, A. (1999). The identification and characteristics of the partially dissociated states of patients with borderline personality disorder. *British Journal of Medical Psychology,* **72**, 429–445.

Gonsiorek, J.C., Bera, W.H. & Le Tourneau, D. (1994). *Male sexual abuse: A trilogy of intervention strategies.* London: Sage.

Goodman, B. & Nowack-Scibelli, D. (1985). Group treatment for women incestuously abused as children. *International Journal of Group Psychotherapy,* **35**, 531–544.

Goodman, G.S., Quas, J.A., Batterman-Faunce, J.M. & Riddlesberger, M.M. (1994). Predictors of accurate and inaccurate memories of traumatic events experienced in childhood. Special issue: The recovered memory/false memory debate. *Consciousness & Cognition,* **3**, 268–194.

Goodwin, J. (1985). Post-traumatic symptoms in incest victims. In S. Eth & R. Pynoos (Eds), *Post-traumatic stress disorder in children* (pp.155–168). Washington, DC: American Psychiatric Association.

Goodwin, J.M. & Talwar, N. (1989). Group psychotherapy for victims of incest. *Psychiatric Clinics of North America,* **12**, 279–293.

Göpfert. M. & Barnes, B. (1994). Psychotherapy and counselling. In B. Green (Ed.), *Psychiatry in general practice* (Vol. 2). London: Kluwer.

Göpfert. M., Webster, J., Pollard, J. & Nelki, J. (1996). Assessing and predicting parenting capacity: A community approach. In M. Göpfert, J. Webster & L. Seeman (Eds), *Parental psychiatric disorder: Distressed parents and their families.* Cambridge: Cambridge University Press.

Gorey, K.M. & Leslie, D.R. (1997). The prevalence of child sexual abuse: Integrative review adjustment for potential response and measurement biases. *Child Abuse & Neglect*, **21**, 391–398.

Grinkler, R.R., Werble, B. & Drye, R. (1968). *The borderline syndrome: A behavioural study of ego functions*. New York: Basic Books.

Grisham, J. (1996). *A time to kill*. Dealerfield: London.

Grotstein, J. (1981). *Splitting and projective identification*. New York: Aronson.

Guidano, V. & Liotti, G. (1985). A constructivist foundation for cognitive therapy. In M.J. Mahoney & A. Freeman (Eds), *Cognition and psychotherapy* (pp. 102–125). New York: Plenum.

Hagan, T. (1999). *A community psychology perspective on working with survivors of childhood sexual abuse: 'Power-mapping' as a therapeutic tool.* Trauma & Mental Health Conference. London: Pavilion Press.

Hagan, T. & Smail, D. (1997a). Power-mapping. I. Background and basic methodology. *Journal of Community & Applied Social Psychology*, **7**, 257–267.

Hagan, T. & Smail, D. (1997b). Power-mapping. II. Practical application: The example of child sexual abuse. *Journal of Community & Applied Social Psychology*, **7**, 269–284.

Haines, J., Williams, C.L., Brain, K.L. & Wilson, G.V. (1995). The psychophysiology of self-mutilation. *Journal of Abnormal Psychology*, **104**, 471–489.

Harmon, R.B., Rosner, R. & Owens, H. (1995). Obsessional harassment and erotomania in a criminal court population. *Journal of Forensic Sciences*, **40**, 188–196.

Hartman, E. (1984). *The nightmare*. New York: Basic Books.

Hartmann, C.R. & Burgess, A.W. (1993). Information processing of trauma. *Child Abuse & Neglect*, **17**, 47–58.

Harvey, P.D., Greenberg, B.R. & Seaper, M.R. (1989). The Affective Lability Scales: Development, reliability and validity. *Journal of Clinical Psychology*, **45**, 786–793.

Hazzard, A., Rogers, J. & Angert, L. (1993). Factors affecting group therapy outcome for adult sexual abuse survivors. *International Journal of Group Psychotherapy*, **43**, 453–468.

Hedges, L. (1999). *Terrifying transferences*. Northvale, NJ: Aronson.

Heide, K.M. (1992). *Why kids kill parents*. Columbus, OH: Ohio State University Press.

Heineman, T.V. (1998). *The abused child: Psychodynamic understanding and treatment*. New York: Guilford Press.

Herman, J.L., Perry, J.C. & van der Kolk, B.A. (1989). Childhood trauma in borderline personality disorder. *American Journal of Psychiatry*, **146**, 490–495.

Herman, J. & Schatzow, E. (1984). Time limited group therapy for women with a history of incest. *International Journal of Group Psychotherapy*, **34**, 605–616.

Herman, J.L. & Schatzow, E. (1987). Recovery and verification of memories of childhood trauma. *Psychoanalytic Psychology*, **4**, 1–14.

Hilgard, E.R. (1994). Neodissociation theory. In S.J. Lynn & J.W. Rhue (Eds), *Dissociation: Clinical and theoretical perspectives*. New York: Guilford Press.

Horevitz, R.P. & Braun, B.G. (1984). Are multiple personalities borderline? Analysis of 33 cases. *Psychiatric Clinics of North America*, **7**, 69–87.

Horevitz, R.P. & Loewenstein, R.J. (1994). The rational treatment of multiple personality disorder. In S.J. Lynn & J. Rhue (Eds), *Dissociation: Clinical and theoretical perspectives* (pp. 289–316). New York: Guilford Press.

Horowitz, I. Rosenberg, S., Baer, Ureno, G. & Villasenor, V.S. (1988). Inventory of Interpersonal Problems: Psychometric properties and clinical applications. *Journal of Consulting & Clinical Psychology*, **56**, 885–892.

Horowitz, M.J. (1979). *States of mind*. New York: Plenum Press.

Horowitz, M.J. (1986). *Stress response syndrome* (2nd edition). New York: Jason Aronson.

Horowitz, M.J. (1997). *Formulation as a basis for planning psychotherapy treatment*. Washington, DC: American Psychiatric Press.

Horowitz, M.J. & Marmar, C. (1985). The therapeutic alliance with difficult patients. In A.J. Frances & R.E. Hales (Eds). *Review of psychiatry*, Vol. 4, (pp. 573–585). Washington, DC: American Psychiatric Press.

Howard, K.I., Kopta, S.M., Krause, M.S. & Orlinsky, D.E. (1986). The dose–effect relationship in psychotherapy. *American Psychologist*, **41**, 159–164.

Hubble, M.A., Duncan, B.L. & Miller, S.D. (1999). *The heart and soul of change: What works in therapy*. Washington, DC: American Psychological Association.

James, W. (1890/1950). *Principles of psychology* (Vol. 2). New York: Henry Holt.

Janet, P. (1889). *L'Automatisme psychologique*. Paris: Alcan.

Janet, P. (1898). *Psychological healing*. New York: Macmillan. Reprinted 1976.

Janoff-Bulman, R. (1989). Assumptive worlds and the stress of traumatic events: Applications of the schema construct. *Social Cognition*, **7**, 113–136.

Janoff-Bulman, R. (1992). *Shattered assumptions: Towards a new psychology of trauma*. New York: Free Press.

Jehu, D., Gazan, M. & Klasson, C. (1988). *Beyond sexual abuse: Therapy with women who were childhood victims*. Chichester: Wiley.

John, S. & Ovsiew, F. (1996). Erotomania in a brain-damaged male. *Journal of Intellectual Disability & Research*, **40**, 279–283.

Josephs, L. (1992). The treatment of an adult survivor of incest: A self psychology perspective. *American Journal of Psychoanalysis*, **52**, 201–212.

Jumper, S.A. (1995). A meta-analysis of the relationship of child sexual abuse to adult psychological adjustment. *Child Abuse & Neglect*, **19**, 715–728.

Kalsched, D. (1996). *The inner world of trauma: Archetypal defences of the personal spirit.* New York: Routledge.

Kaplan, H.S. (1996). Erotic obsession: Relationship to hypoactive sexual desire disorder and paraphilia. *American Journal of Psychiatry*, **153**, 30–41.

Kearney-Cooke, A. & Stregal-Moore, R.H. (1994). Treatment of childhood sexual abuse in anorexia nervosa and bulimia nervosa: A feminist psychodynamic approach. *International Journal of Eating Disorders*, **15**, 305–319.

Kelly, G.A. (1955). *The psychology of personal constructs.* New York: Norton.

Kennedy, F. (1998). Paper presented to the European Conference of Cognitive and Behavioural Therapy, Cork, Ireland, September 1998.

Kennedy F. & Waller G. (unpublished, 2000*). Towards a psychological model of dissociation: Implications for categorisation, treatment and research.*

Kennerly, H. (1996). Cognitive therapy of dissociative symptoms associated with trauma. *British Journal of Clinical Psychology*, **35**, 325–340.

Kennerly, H. (2000). *Overcoming childhood trauma: A self-help guide using cognitive behavioural techniques.* London: Constable & Robinson.

Kernberg, O.F. (1975). *Borderline conditions and pathological narcissism.* New York: Norton.

Kernberg, O.F. (1984). *Severe personality disorders: Psychotherapeutic strategies.* Yale: London.

Kerr, I. (1999). Cognitive analytic therapy for borderline personality disorder in the context of a community mental health team: Individual and organisational psychodynamic implications. *British Journal of Psychotherapy*, **15**, 425–438.

Kienlan, K.K., Birmingham, D.L., Solberg, K.B., O'Regan, J.T. & Meloy, J.R. (1997). A comparative study of psychotic and non-psychotic stalking. *Journal of American Academy of Psychiatry & Law*, **25**, 317–334.

Kiesler, D.J. (1988). *Therapeutic metacommunication: Therapist impact disclosure as feedback in psychotherapy.* Palo Alto, CA: Consulting Psychologists Press.

Kilpatrick, D.G., Amick-McMullan, A., Best, C.L., Burke, M.M. & Saunders, B.E. (1986). *Impact of child sexual abuse: Recent research findings.* In Fourth National Conference on the Sexual Victimization of Children, New Orleans, LA.

Kirschner, C., Kirschner, D.A. & Rappaport, R.L. (1993). *Working with adult incest survivors: The healing journey.* New York: Bruner/Mozel.

Kluft, R.P. (1982). Varieties of hypnotic interventions in the treatment of multiple personality. *American Journal of Clinical Hypnosis*, **4**, 230.

Kluft, R.P. (1984). Multiple personality in childhood. In B.G. Braun, (Ed.), Symposium on Multiple Personality. *Psychiatric Clinics of North America*, **7**, 121–134.

Kluft, R.P. (1987). An update on multiple personality disorder. *Hospital and Community Psychiatry*, **38**, 363–373.

Kluft, R.P. (1991). Clinical presentation of multiple personality disorder. *Psychiatric Clinics of North America*, **14**, 605–629.

Kretschmer, E. (1918). Der Sensitive Beziehungswahn [The sensitive delusion of reference]. Berlin: Springer. In S.R. Hirsch & M. Shephard (1974). *Themes and Variations in European Psychiatry* (pp. 153–195). Bristol: Wright.

Krystal, H. (1968). *Massive psychic trauma*. New York: International Universities Press.

Kundera, M. (1990). *Immortality*. New York: Grove Weidenfield.

Kuyken, W. (1995). The psychological sequelae of childhood sexual abuse: A review of the literature and implications for treatment. *Clinical Psychology and Psychotherapy*, **2**, 108–121.

Lang, P.J. (1985). The cognitive psychophysiology of emotion: Fear and anxiety. In A.H. Tuma & J.D. Maser (Eds), *Anxiety and the anxiety disorders* (pp. 131–170). Hillside, NJ: Erlbaum.

Lange, A., de Beurs, E., Dolan, C., Lachnit, T., Sjollema, S. & Hanewald, G. (1999). Long-term effects of childhood sexual abuse: Objective and subjective characteristics of the abuse and psychopathology in later life. *Journal of Nervous & Mental Diseases*, **187**, 150–158.

Lansky, M.R. & Bley, C.R. (1995). *Post-traumatic nightmares: Psychodynamic explorations*. Hillsdale, NJ: Analytic Press.

Lehman, H.E. (1980). Unusual psychiatric disorders, atypical psychoses and brief reactive psychoses. In H.I. Kaplan, A.M. Freedman & B.J. Saddock, (Eds), *Comprehensive textbook of psychiatry* (3rd edition). Baltimore: Williams & Wilkins.

Leighton, T. (1997). Borderline personality and substance abuse problems. In A. Ryle (Ed.), *Cognitive analytic therapy and borderline personality disorder: The model and the method* (Ch. 10, pp. 128–145). Chichester: Wiley.

Leighton, T. & Ryle, A. (1995). How analytic is CAT? In A. Ryle (Ed), *Cognitive analytic therapy: Developments in theory and practice* (Ch. 8, pp. 139–164). Chichester: Wiley.

Leiman, M.P.N. (1992). The concept of sign in the work of Vygotsky, Winnicott and Bakhtin: Further integration of Object Relations Theory and Activity Theory. *British Journal of Medical Psychology*, **65**, 97–82.

Leiman, M. (1995). Early developments. In A. Ryle (Ed.), *Cognitive analytic therapy: Developments in theory and practice*. Chichester: Wiley.

Lewin, K. (1951a). *Field theory in social science*. Harper & Row: New York.

Lewin, K. (1951b). *Frontiers in group dynamics*. Harper & Row: New York.

Lewis, D.O., Yeager, C.A. Swica, Y., Pincus, J.H. & Lewis, M. (1997). Objective documentation of child abuse and dissociation in 12 murderers with dissociative identity disorder. *American Journal of Psychiatry*, **154**, 1703–1710.

Linehan, M.M. (1990). *Cognitive behavioural treatment of borderline personality disorder*. New York: Guilford Press.

Linehan, M.M. (1993). *Cognitive-behavioural treatment of borderline personality disorder: The dialetics of effective treatment.* New York: Guilford Press.

Linville, P.W. (1987). Self-complexity as a cognitive buffer against stress-related illness and depression. *Journal of Personality & Social Psychology*, **52**, 603–676.

Lion, J.R. (1995). Verbal threats against clinicians. In B.S. Eichelman & A.C. Hartwig (Eds), *Patient violence and the clinician* (pp. 43–52). Washington, DC: American Psychiatric Press.

Lion, J.R. & Herschler, J.A. (1998). The stalking of clinicians by their patients. In J.R. Meloy (Ed.), *The psychology of stalking: Clinical and forensic perspectives* (pp. 163–173). San Diego, CA: Academic Press.

Lipshitz, D.S., Kaplan, M.L. Sarkenn, J., Chorney, P. & Asnis, G.M. (1996). Childhood abuse, adult assault, and dissociation. *Comprehensive Psychiatry*, **37**, 261–266.

Llewelyn, S.P. (1997). Therapeutic approaches for survivors of childhood sexual abuse: A review. *Clinical Psychology and Psychotherapy*, **4**, 32–41.

Loewenstein, R.J. (1991). An office mental status examination for chronic complex dissociative symptoms and dissociative identity disorder. *Psychiatric Clinics of North America*, **14**, 567–604.

Loewenstein, R.J. & Putnam, F.W. (1990). The clinical phenomenology of males with multiple personality disorder. *Dissociation*, **3**, 135–143.

Loftus, E.F. (1993). The reality of repressed memories. *American Psychologist*, **46**, 518–537.

Loftus, E.F., Polonsky, F. & Fullilove, M. (1994). Memories of childhood sexual abuse: Remembering and repressing. *Psychology of Women Quarterly*, **18**, 67–84.

Longo, R. (1982). Sexual learning and experience among adolescent sexual offenders. *International Journal of Offender Therapy and Comparative Criminology*, **26**, 235–241.

Longstreth, G.F., Mason, C., Schreiber, G.I. & Tsao-Wei, D. (1998). Group psychotherapy for women molested in childhood: Psychological and somatic symptoms and medical visits. *International Journal of Group Psychotherapy*, **48**, 533–541.

Luborsky, L. (1996). *The symptom-context method: Symptoms as opportunities in psychotherapy.* Washington, DC: American Psychological Press.

Luborsky, L. & Crits-Christoph, P. (1990). *Understanding transference and the CCRT method.* New York: Basic Books.

MacKenzie, K.R. (1990). *Introduction to time-limited group psychotherapy.* Washington, DC: American Psychiatric Press.

Mahler, M.S., Pine, F. & Bergman, A. (1975). *The psychological birth of the human infant: Symbiosis and individuation.* New York: Basic Books.

Mair, J.M.M. (1977). The community of self. In D. Bannister (Ed.), *New perspectives in personal construct theory* (pp. 125–149). New York: Academic Press.

Maple, N. & Simpson, I. (1995). CAT in groups. In A. Ryle (Ed.), *Cognitive analytic therapy: Developments in theory and practice.* Chichester: Wiley.

Marcus, B.F. (1989). Incest and borderline syndrome: The mediating role of identity. *Psychoanalytic Psychology*, **6**, 199–215.

Maris, R.W., Berman, A.L., Maltsberger, J.T. & Yuflt, R.I. (1992*). Assessment and prediction of suicide.* New York: Guilford Press.

Markus, H. & Wurf, E. (1987). The dynamic self-concept: A social psychological perspective. *Annual Review of Psychology*, **38**, 299–337.

Marziali, E. & Munroe-Blum, H. (1994). *Interpersonal group psychotherapy for borderline personality disorder.* New York: Basic Books.

Marzillier, J. & Butler, G. (1995). CAT in relation to cognitive therapy. In A. Ryle (Ed.), *Cognitive analytic therapy: Developments in theory and practice* (Ch. 7, pp. 121–138). Chichester: Wiley.

Matte-Blanco, I. (1975). *The unconscious as infinite sets.* London: Duckworth.

McCann, D.L. (1992). Post-traumatic stress disorder due to devastating burns overcome by a single session of eye movement desensitization. *Journal of Behaviour Therapy & experimental Psychiatry*, **23**, 319–323.

McCann, I.L. & Pearlman, L.A. (1990*). Psychological trauma and the adult survivor: Theory, therapy and transformation.* New York: Brunner/Mazel.

McCann, I.L., Sakheim, D.K. & Abrahamson, D.J. (1988). Trauma and victimization: A model of psychological adaptation. *The Counselling Psychologist*, **16**, 531–594.

McFarlane, A.C. (1988). The aetiology of post-traumatic stress disorder following a natural disaster. *British Journal of Psychiatry*, **152**, 116–121.

McFarlane, A.C. (1996). Resilience, vulnerability, and the course of post-traumatic reactions. In B. van der Kolk, A.C. McFarlane & L. Weisketh (Eds), *Traumatic stress: The effects of overwhelming stress on mind, body and society* (Ch. 8, pp. 155–181). New York: Guilford.

McIntee, J. & Crompton, I. (1997). The psychological effects of trauma on children. In J. Bates, R. Pugh & N. Thompson (Eds), *Protecting children: Challenges and changes* (pp. 127–142). Aldershot: Arena.

McLeer, S.V., Deblinger, E., Atkins, M.S., Foa, E.B., & Ralphe, D.L. (1988). Post-traumatic stress disorder in sexually abused children. *Journal of the American Academy of Child & Adolescent Psychiatry*, **27**, 650–654.

McWilliams, N. (1994). *Psychoanalytical diagnosis.* New York: Guilford Press.

Meichenbaum, D. (1994). *A clinical handbook/practical therapist manual for assessing and treating adults with post-traumatic stress disorder (PTSD).* Waterloo: Institute Press.

Meissner, W.W. (1980). A note on projective identification. *Journal of the American Psychoanalytic Association*, **28**, 43–67.

Meloy, J.R. (1988). *Violent attachments.* Northvale, NJ : Jason Aronson.

Meloy, J.R. (1989). Unrequited love and the wish to kill: Diagnosis and treatment of borderline erotomania. *Bulletin of the Menninger Clinic*, **53**, 477–492.

Meloy, J.R. (1993). *The psychopathic mind: Origins, dynamics and treatment.* Northvale, NJ: Jason Aronson.

Meloy, J.R. (1996). *Assessment of violence potential.* Workshop presentation, July, Tavistock. London: Specialist Training Services.

Meloy, J.R. (1997). The clinical management of stalking: 'Someone is watching over me . . .'. *American Journal of Psychotherapy*, **51**, 174–184.

Meloy, J.R. (1998). *The psychology of stalking: Clinical and forensic perspectives* (Ch. 1, pp. 2–23). San Diego: Academic Press.

Mennen, F. & Meadow, D. (1992). Process to recovery: In support of long-term groups for sexual abuse survivors. *International Journal of Group Psychotherapy*, **42**, 29–44.

Menninger, K.A. (1935) A psychoanalytic study of the significance of self-mutilation. *Psychoanalytic Quarterly*, **4**, 408–466.

Menzies, R.P.D., Federoff, J.P., Green, C.M. & Isaacson, K. (1995). Prediction of dangerous behaviour in male erotomania. *British Journal of Psychiatry*, **166**, 529–536.

Messer, S.B. & Warren, C.S. (1995). *Models of brief psychodynamic therapy: A comparative approach.* New York: Guilford Press.

Miller, R. (1985). The harassment of forensic psychiatrists outside of court. *Bulletin of the American Academy of Psychiatry & the Law*, **13**, 337–343.

Millon, T., Millon, C. & Davis, R. (1994). *Millon Clinical Mulitaxial Inventory-III Manual.* Minneapolis, MN: National Computer Systems.

Mitzman, S. & Duignan, I. (1993). One man's group: Brief cognitive analytic group therapy and the use of sequential diagrammatic reformulation. *Counselling Psychology Quarterly*, **6**, 183–192.

Modestin, J., Oberson, B. & Erni, T. (1998). Identity disturbance in personality disorders. *Comprehensive Psychiatry*, **39**, 352–357.

Mollon, P. (1993). *The fragile self: The structure of narcissistic disturbance.* London: Whurr.

Mollon, P. (1996). *Multiple selves, multiple voices: Working with trauma, violation and dissociation.* Chichester: Wiley.

Mollon, P. (1999). *A psychoanalytic understanding of the effects of trauma (child sexual abuse) on development.* Paper presented at Trauma and Mental Health Conference, London, April. Pavilion Publishing.

Mueser, K.T., Goodman, L.B., Trumbetta, S.L., Rosenberg, S.D., Osher, F.C. Vidayer, R., Anciello, P. & Foy, D.W. (1998). Trauma and post-traumatic stress disorder in severe mental illness. *Journal of Counselling & Clinical Psychology*, **66**, 493–499.

Mullen, P.C., Martin, J.L., Anderson, J.C., Roman, S.E. & Herbison, G.P. (1993). Childhood sexual abuse and mental health in adult life. *British Journal of Psychiatry*, **163**, 721–733.

Mullen, P., Martin, J., Anderson, J., Roman, S. & Herbison, G. (1994). The effects of child sexual abuse on social interpersonal and sexual function in adult life. *British Journal of Psychiatry*, **165**, 35–47.

Mullen, P.E. & Pathé, M. (1994a). Stalking and the pathologies of love. *Australian & New Zealand Journal of Psychiatry*, **28**, 469–477.

Mullen, P.E. & Pathé, M. (1994b). The pathological extensions of love. *British Journal of Psychiatry*, **165**, 614–623.

Myers, M.F. (1989). Men sexually assaulted as adults and sexually abused as boys. *Archives of Sexual Behaviour*, **18**, 203–215.

Nabokov, V. (1965). *Lolita*. Harmondsworth: Penguin Press.

Nash, M.R., Hulsey, T.L., Sexton, M.C., Harralson, T.L. & Lambert, W. (1993). Long-term sequelae of childhood sexual abuse: Perceived family environment, psychopathology, and dissociation. *Journal of Consulting & Clinical Psychology*, **61**, 276–283.

Neisser, U. (1982). *Memory observed: Remembering in natural contexts*. San Francisco: Freeman.

Neumann, D.A., Houskamp, B.M., Pollock, V.E. & Briere, J. (1996). The long-term sequelae of childhood sexual abuse in women: A meta-analytic review. *Child Maltreatment*, **1**, 6–16.

Ney, P.G., Fung, T. & Wikett, A.R. (1994). The worse combinations of child abuse and neglect. *Child Abuse & Neglect*, **18**, 704–714.

Nicholas, M. & Forrester, A. (1999). Advantages of heterogeneous therapy groups in the psychotherapy of the traumatically abused: Treating the problem as well as the person. *International Journal of Group Psychotherapy*, **49**, 323–342.

Nitsun, M. (1994). *The anti-group*. London: Taylor & Francis.

Norcross, J. C. (1986). Eclectic psychotherapy: An integration and overview. In J. C. Norcross (Ed.), *Handbook of eclectic psychotherapy*. New York: Brunner/Mazel.

Norcross, J.C. & Goldfried, M.R. (1992). *Handbook of psychotherapy integration*. Basic Books: New York.

Northcut, T.B. & Heller, N.R. (1999). *Enhancing psychodynamic therapy with cognitive-behavioural techniques*. Northvale, NJ: Jason Aronson Press.

Ogata, S.N., Silk, K.R., Goodrick, S., Lohr, N.E., Western, D. & Hilt, E.M. (1990). Childhood sexual and physical abuse in adult clients with borderline personality disorder. *American Journal of Psychiatry*, **147**, 1008–1013.

Ogden, J.H. (1983). The concept of internal object relations. *International Journal of Psychoanalysis*, **64**, 227–241.

Ornduff, S.R., Freedenfeld, R.N., Kelsey, R.M. & Critelli, J.W. (1994). Object relations of sexually abused female subjects: A TAT analysis. *Journal of Personality Assessment*, **63**, 223–238.

Ornstein, P.A. & Myers, J.T. (1996). Contextual influences on children's remembering. In K. Pezdek & W.P. Banks (Eds), *The recovered memory/false memory debate* (pp. 211–223). San Diego: Academic Press.

Padesky, C.A. (1994). Schema change process in cognitive therapy. *Clinical Psychology & Psychotherapy*, **1**, 267–278 .

Paris, J. (1993). *Borderline personality disorder: Etiology and treatment.* Washington, DC: American Psychiatric Press.

Parkes, P. (1990). *Rescuing the 'inner child': Therapy for adults sexually abused as children.* London: Souvenir Press.

Parnell, L. (1999). *EMDR in the treatment of adults abused as children.* New York: Norton.

Parry, G. (1999). *Childhood sexual abuse: What does the research tell us?* Trauma and Mental Health Conference, London, April.

Phillips, M.R., West, C.L. & Wang, R. (1996). Erotomanic symptoms in 42 Chinese patients. *British Journal of Psychiatry*, **169**, 501–508.

Piper, W.E., Rosie, J.S., Joyce, A.S. & Azim, H.F. (1996). *Time-limited day treatment for personality disorders: Integration of research and practice in a group program.* Washington, DC: American Psychological Association.

Pistole, D.R. & Ornduff, S.R. (1994). TAT assessment of sexually abused girls: An analysis of manifest content. *Journal of Personality Assessment*, **63**, 211–222.

Pollock, P.H. (1995). A case of spree serial murder with suggested diagnostic opinions. *International Journal of Offender Therapy & Comparative Criminology*, **39**, 258–268.

Pollock, P.H. (1996). Clinical issues in the cognitive analytic therapy of sexually abused women who commit violent offences against their partners. *British Journal of Medical Psychology*, **69**(2), 117–127.

Pollock, P.H. (1997). Cognitive analytic therapy for an offender with borderline personality disorder. In A. Ryle (Ed.). *Cognitive analytic therapy for borderline personality disorder: The model and the method* (Ch. 11). Chichester: Wiley.

Pollock, P.H. (1998a). *Chained by pain: The use of cognitive analytic therapy during chronic pain management programmes* (unpublished).

Pollock, P.H. (1998b). Cognitive analytic therapy for offenders. *Journal of Forensic Psychiatry*, **9**, 629–642.

Pollock, P.H. (1999). *Cognitive analytic therapy for auditory hallucinations during brief psychotic episodes for patients with borderline personality disorder* (unpublished).

Pollock, P.H. (2000). Eye movement desensitisation and reprocessing (EMDR) for Post-Traumatic Stress Disorder (PTSD) following homicide. *Journal of Forensic Psychiatry*, **11**, 176–184.

Pollock, P.H., Broadbent, M., Clarke, S., Dorrian, A.J. & Ryle, A. (2001). The Personality Structure Questionnaire (PSQ): A measure of the multiple self-states model of identity disturbance in cognitive analytic therapy. *Clinical Psychology & Psychotherapy*, **8**, 59–72.

Pollock, P.H. & Kear-Colwell, J.J. (1994). Women who stab: A personal construct analysis of sexual victimisation and offending behaviour. *British Journal of Medical Psychology*, **67**, 13–22.

Pollock, P.H. & Percy, A. (1999). Maternal antenatal attachment style and potential fetal abuse. *Child Abuse & Neglect*, **23**, 1345–1357.

Poole, A.D., de Jongh, A. & Spector, J. (1999). Power therapies: Evidence versus emotion. A reply to Rosen, Lohr, McNally and Herbert. *Behavioural & Cognitive Psychotherapy*, **27**, 3–8.

Pope, K. (1997). Science as careful questioning: Are claims of a false memory syndrome epidemic based on empirical evidence. *American Psychologist*, **52**, 997–1006.

Power, M. & Dalgleish, T. (1997). *Cognition and emotion: From order to disorder.* New York: Erlbaum.

Price, J. (1988). Single sex therapy groups. In M. Aveline & W. Dryden (Eds), *Group therapy in Britain*. Milton Keynes: Open University Press.

Price, M. (1992). The psychoanalysis of an adult survivor of incest: A case study. *American Journal of Psychoanalysis*, **52**, 119–136.

Price, M. (1994). Incest: Transference and countertransference. *Journal of the American Academy of Psychoanalysis*, **22**, 211–219.

Putnam, F.W. (1991). Dissociative disorders in children and adolescents: A developmental perspective. *Psychiatric Clinics of North America*, **34**, 519–531.

Putnam, F.W. (1997a). *Diagnosis and treatment of multiple personality disorder*. New York: Guilford Press.

Putnam, F.W. (1997b). *Dissociation in children and adolescents: A developmental perspective*. New York: Guilford Press.

Putnam, F.W., Guroff, J.J., Silberman, E.K., Barbau, L.R. & Post, R.M. (1986). The phenomenology of multiple personality disorder: A review of 100 recent cases. *Journal of Clinical Psychiatry*, **47**, 285–293.

Putnam, F.W., Post, R.M. & Guroff, J.J. (1986). One hundred cases of multiple personality disorder. *Journal of Clinical Psychiatry*, **47**, 285–293.

Rachman, S. (1980). Emotional processing. *Behaviour Research & Therapy*, **18**, 52–60.

Rayner, E.H. (1995). *Unconscious logic*. London: Routledge.

Resick, P.A. & Schmicke, M.K. (1992). Cognitive processing therapy for sexual assault victims. *Journal of Consulting & Clinical Psychology*, **60**, 748–756.

Resnick, H.S. & Newton, T. (1992). Assessment and treatment of post-traumatic stress disorder in adult survivors of sexual assault. In D.W. Foy (Ed.), *Treating PTSD: Cognitive-behavioural strategies*. New York: Guilford Press.

Ressler, R.K., Burgess, A.W. & Douglas, J.E. (1988). *Sexual homicide: Patterns and motives.* Lexington, MA: Lexington Books.

Richards, D. (1999). The eye movement desensitization and reprocessing debate: Commentary on Rosen *et al.* and Poole *et al. Behavioural & Cognitive Psychotherapy*, **27**, 13–17.

Roberts, L. & Lie, G. (1989). A group approach to the treatment of incest. *Social Work with Groups*, **12**, 77–90.

Rogers, C.M. & Terry, T. (1984). Clinical intervention with boy victims of sexual abuse. In I.R. Stuart & J.G. Greer (Eds), *Victims of sexual aggression: Men, women and children* (pp. 91–103). New York: Van Nostrand Reinhold.

Rogers, M.L. (1995). Factors influencing recall of childhood sexual abuse. *Journal of Traumatic Stress*, **8**, 691–716.

Rosen, G., Lohr, J.M., McNally, R.J. & Herbert, J.D. (1999). Power therapies, miraculous claims and cures that fail. *Behavioural & Cognitive Psychotherapy*, **26**, 99–101.

Rosenberg, M. (1989). *Society and the adolescent self-image* (revised edition). Middletown, CT: Wesleyan University Press.

Rosenstein, D.S. & Horowitz, H.A. (1996). Adolescent attachment and psychopathology. *Journal of Consulting & Clinical Psychology*, **64**, 244–253.

Ross, C.A. (1989). *Multiple personality disorder: Diagnosis, clinical features, and treatment.* New York: Wiley.

Ross, C.A. (1997). *Dissociative identity disorder: Diagnosis, clinical features and treatment of multiple personality* (2nd edition, revised). New York: Wiley.

Ross, C.A. (1998). Subpersonalities and multiple personalities: A dissociative continuum? In J. Rowan & M. Cooper (Eds), *The plural self: Multiplicity in everyday life* (pp. 168–182). London: Sage.

Ross, C.A., Norton, G.R. & Wozney, K. (1989). Multiple personality disorder: An analysis of 236 cases. *Canadian Journal of Psychiatry*, **34**, 413–418.

Roth, A.D. & Fonagy, P. (1996). *What works for whom? A critical review of psychotherapy research.* New York: Guilford Press.

Roth, A., Fonagy, P. & Parry, G. (1996). Psychotherapy research, finding and evidence-based practice. In A. Roth & P. Fonagy (Eds), *What works for whom? A critical review of psychotherapy research* (Ch. 3, pp. 37–56). New York: Guilford Press.

Rothbaum, B.O. & Foa, E.B. (1996). Cognitive-behavioural therapy for post-traumatic stress disorder. In B.A. van der Kolk, A.C. McFarlane & L. Weisaeth (Eds), *Traumatic stress: The effects of overwhelming experience on mind, body, and society* (Ch. 22, pp. 491–509). New York: Guilford Press.

Rothstein, A. (1984). *The narcissistic pursuit of perfection.* New York: International Universities Press.

Rowan, A.B., Foy, D.W., Rodriguez, N. & Ryan, S. (1994). Post-traumatic stress disorder in a clinical sample of adults sexually abused as children. *Child Abuse & Neglect*, **18**, 51–61.

Rowan, J. (1990). *Subpersonalities: The people inside us*. London: Routledge.

Rowan, J. & Cooper, M. (1998). *The plural self: Multiplicity in everyday life*. London: Sage.

Rudden, M., Gilmore, M. & Frances, A. (1980). Erotomania: A separate entity. *American Journal of Psychiatry*, **131**, 1033–1035.

Russell, D. (1986). *The secret trauma: Incest in the lives of girls and women*. New York: Basic Books.

Ryan, G. (1989). Victim to victimizer: Rethinking victim treatment. *Journal of Interpersonal Violence*, **4**, 325–341.

Ryle, A. (1978). A common language for the psychotherapies. *British Journal of Psychiatry*, **132**, 585–594.

Ryle, A. (1979). The focus in brief interpretive psychotherapy: Dilemmas traps and snags as target problem. *British Journal of Psychiatry*, **135**, 46–64.

Ryle, A. (1982) *Psychotherapy: A cognitive integration of theory and practice*. London: Academic Press.

Ryle, A. (1990). *Cognitive analytic therapy: Active participation in change*. Chichester: Wiley.

Ryle, A. (1994a). Consciousness and psychotherapy. *British Journal of Medical Psychology*, **67**, 115–124.

Ryle, A. (1994b). Projective identification: A particular form of reciprocal role procedure. *British Journal of Medical Psychology*, **67**, 107–114.

Ryle, A. (1995a). *Cognitive analytic therapy: Developments in theory and practice*. Chichester: Wiley.

Ryle, A. (1995b). Transference and counter-transference variations in the course of the cognitive analytic therapy of two borderline patients: The relation to the diagrammatic reformulation of self-states. *British Journal of Medical Psychology*, **68**, 109–124.

Ryle, A. (1997). *Cognitive analytic therapy and borderline personality disorder: The model and the method*. Chichester: Wiley.

Ryle, A. & Beard, H. (1993). The integrative effect of reformulation: Cognitive analytic therapy with a patient with borderline personality disorder. *British Journal of Medical Psychology*, **66**, 249–258.

Ryle, A. & Golynkina, G. (2000). Effectiveness of time-limited cognitive analytic therapy of borderline personality disorder: Factors associated with outcome. *British Journal of Medical Psychology*, **73**, 197–210.

Safran, J.D. (1990). Towards a refinement of cognitive therapy in light of interpersonal theory I: Theory. *Clinical Psychology Review*, **10**, 87–105.

Safran, J.D. & Muran, J.C. (2000). *Negotiating the therapeutic alliance: A relational treatment guide*. Guilford: New York.

Safran, J. & Segal, Z. (1996). *Interpersonal process in cognitive therapy*. Northvale, NJ: Jason Aronson.

Salkovskis, P.M. (1995). Demonstrating specific effects in cognitive and behavioural therapy. In M. Aveline & D. Shapiro (Eds), *Research foundations for psychotherapy practice.* Chichester: Wiley.

Salter, A.C. (1994). *Transforming trauma: A guide of understanding and treating adult survivors of sexual abuse.* New York: Sage.

Sanderson, C. (1990). *Counselling adult survivors of sexual abuse.* London: Jessica Kingsley.

Sandler, J. (1976). Countertransference and role responsiveness. *International Review of Psychoanalysis,* 3, 43–47.

Sar, V., Yargic, L.I. & Turkin, H. (1996). Structured interview data on 35 cases of dissociative identity disorder in Turkey. *American Journal of Psychiatry,* **153,** 1329–1333.

Searles, H.F. (1977). Dual and multiple identity processes in borderline ego functioning. In P. Horticollis, (Ed.), *Borderline personality disorder* (pp. 441–455). New York: International Universities Press.

Sedney, M.A. & Brooks, B. (1984). Factors associated with a history of childhood sexual experience in a non-clinical female population. *Journal of the American Academy of Child Psychiatry,* 23, 215–218.

Seeman, M.V. (1978). Delusional loving. *Archives of General Psychiatry,* 35, 1265–1267.

Segal, J. (1989). Erotomania revisited: From Kraepelin to DSM-III-R. *American Journal of Psychiatry,* **146,** 1261–1266.

Segal, J. (1992). *Key figures in psychotherapy: Melanie Klein.* London: Sage.

Seltzer, A. (1994). Multiple personality: A psychiatric misadventure. *Canadian Journal of Psychiatry,* **39,** 422–425.

Shane, M. & Shane, E. (1997). *Intimate attachments: Toward a new self psychology.* New York: Guilford Press.

Shapiro, F. (1989). Eye movement desensitisation: A new treatment for posttraumatic stress disorder. *Journal of Behaviour Therapy & Experimental Psychiatry,* **20,** 211–217.

Shapiro, F. (1995). *Eye movement desensitisation and reprocessing.* New York: Guilford Press.

Shapiro, F. & Forrest, M.S. (1997). *EMDR: The breakthrough therapy for overcoming anxiety, stress and trauma.* New York: Basic Books.

Shearer, S.I., Peters, C.P., Quaytman, M.S. & Ogden, R.L. (1990). Frequency and correlates of childhood sexual and physical abuse histories in adult female borderline inpatients. *American Journal of Psychiatry,* **152,** 1059–1064.

Shearer, S.L. (1994). Dissociative phenomena in women with borderline personality disorder. *American Journal of Psychiatry,* **151,** 1324–1328.

Silva, J.A., Ferrari, M.M. & Leong, G.B. (1998). Erotomania in a case of Fragile X syndrome. *General Hospital Psychiatry,* **20,** 126–127.

Smail, D. (1993). *The origins of unhappiness: A new understanding of emotional distress.* Harper Collins: London.

Smucker, M. & Dancu, C.V. (1999). *Cognitive behavioural treatment for adult survivors of childhood trauma: Imagery rescripting and reprocessing.* Hillsdale, NJ: Jason Aronson Press.

Smucker, M.R., Dancu, C.V., Foa, E.B. & Niederee, J. (1996). *Imagery rescripting: A treatment manual for adult survivors of childhood sexual abuse experiencing PTSD.* Cognitive Therapy Institute of Milwaukee: Milwaukee, WI.

Solomon, Z. & Shalev, A.Y. (1994). Helping victims of military trauma. In J.R. Freedy & S.E. Hobfoll (Eds), *Traumatic stress: From theory to practice.* New York: Plenum.

Sparracelli, S. (1994). Stress, appraisal and coping in child sexual abuse: A theoretical and empirical review. *Psychological Bulletin*, **116**, 340–362.

Spiegel, D. (1999). *Efficacy and cost-effectiveness of psychotherapy.* Washington, DC: American Psychiatric Press.

Spiegel, D. & Cardena, E. (1991). Disintegrated experience: The dissociative disorders revisited. *Journal of Abnormal Psychology*, **100**, 366–378.

Sroufe, L.A. & Fleeson, J. (1986). Attachment and the construction of relationships. In W.W. Hartup & Z. Rubin (Eds), *Clinical implications of attachment* (pp. 18–38). Hillside, NJ: Erlbaum.

Sroufe, L.A. & Rutler, M. (1984). The domain of developmental psychopathology. *Child development*, **55**, 17–29.

Stalker, C.A. & Davies, F. (1995). Attachment organisation and adaptation in sexually abused women. *Canadian Journal of Psychiatry*, **40**, 234–240.

Steinberg, M. (1993). *Interviewer's guide to the Structured Clinical Interview for DSM-IV Dissociative Disorders (SCID-D).* Washington, DC: American Psychiatric Press.

Stern, D.N. (1985). *The interpersonal world of the infant.* New York: Basic Books.

Stewart, H. (1996). *Michael Balint: Object relations, pure and applied.* London: Routledge.

Stone, M.H. (1990*). The fate of borderline patients: Successful outcome and psychiatric practice.* New York: Guilford Press.

Sullivan, H.S. (1953). *The interpersonal theory of psychiatry.* New York: W.W. Norton.

Summit, R.C. (1983). The child abuse accommodation syndrome. *Child Abuse & Neglect*, **7**, 177–183.

Tangney, J.P., Wagner, P. & Gramzow, R. (1992). Proneness to shame, proneness to guilt, and psychopathology. *Journal of Abnormal Psychology*, **101**, 469–478.

Taylor, P., Mahendra, B. & Gunn, J. (1983). Erotomania in males. *Psychological Medicine*, **13**, 645–650.

Teasdale, J.D. (1996). The relationship between cognition and emotion: The mind in place in mood disorders. In D.M. Clark & C.G. Fairburn (Eds), *Science and practice of cognitive behaviour therapy.* Oxford: Oxford University Press.

Teasdale, J.D. & Barnard, P.J. (1993). *Affect, cognition and change: Re-model-ling depressive thought.* Hove: Erlbaum.

Terr, L. (1991). Childhood traumas: An outline and overview. *American Journal of Psychiatry*, **148**, 10–20.

Tessler, M. & Nelson, K. (1996). Making memories: The influence of joint encoding on later recall by young children. In K. Pedzek & W.P. Bauler (Eds), *The recovered memory/false memory debate* (pp. 101–120). San Diego: Academic Press.

Tillman, J.G., Nash, M.R. & Lerner, P.M. (1994). Does trauma cause dissociative pathology? In S.J. Lynn & J.W. Rhue (Eds), *Dissociation, clinical and theoretical perspectives* (Ch. 18, pp. 395–414). New York: Guilford Press.

Tobey, A.E. & Goodman, G.S. (1992). Children's eyewitness memory: Effects of participation and forensic context. *Child Abuse & Neglect*, **16**, 779–796.

Treasure, J., Todd, G., Brolly, M., Tiller, J. & Denman, F. (1994). A randomised trial of cognitive analytical therapy versus educational behavioural therapy for adults anorexia nervosa. *Behaviour Research & Therapy.*

Tsai, M. & Wagner, N. (1978). Therapy groups for women sexually molested as children. *International Journal of Group Psychotherapy*, **34**, 605–616.

Tschudi, F. (1989). *Flexigrid.* Oslo: University of Oslo.

Turner, K., DeRosa, R., Roth, S., Batson, R. & Davidson, J. (1996). A multimodal treatment for incest survivors: Preliminary outcome data. *Clinical Psychology & Psychotherapy*, **3**, 208–219.

Tyson, A. & Goodman, M. (1996). Group treatment of adult women who experienced childhood sexual trauma: Is telling the story enough? *International Journal of Group Psychotherapy*, **46**, 535–542.

van der Kolk, B.A. (1988). The trauma spectrum: The interaction of biological and social events in the genesis of the trauma response. *Journal of Traumatic Stress*, **1**, 273–280.

van der Kolk, B.A. (1989). The compulsion to repeat the trauma. *Psychiatric Clinics of North America*, **12**, 389–411.

van der Kolk, B. (1993). Group therapy with post-traumatic stress disorder. In H. Kaplan & B. Saddock (Eds), *Comprehensive group psychotherapy.* Baltimore: Williams & Wilkins.

van der Kolk, B.A. (1994). The body keeps the score: Approaches to the psychobiology of post-traumatic stress disorder. In B.A. van der Kolk, A.C. McFarlane & L. Weisaeth (Eds), *Traumatic stress: The effects of overwhelming experience on mind, body and society.* New York: Guilford Press.

van der Kolk, B.A. (1996). The complexity of adaptation to trauma: Self-regulation, stimulus discrimination and characterological development. In B.A. van der Kolk, A. McFarlane & L. Weisaeth (Eds), *Traumatic stress: The effects of overwhelming experience on mind, body and society* (pp. 182–213). New York: Guilford Press.

van der Kolk, B.A., Hostetler, A., Herman, N. & Fisher, R.E. (1994). Trauma and the development of borderline personality disorder. *Psychiatric Clinics of North America*, **17**, 715–730.

van der Kolk, B.A., Perry, C. & Herman, J.L. (1991). Childhood origins of self-destructive behaviour. *American Journal of Psychiatry*, **148**, 1665–1671.

van der Kolk, B.A., Roth, S., Pelcovitz, D. & Mandel, F.A. (1993). *Complex post-traumatic stress disorder: Results from the DSM-IV field trials of PTSD*. Cambridge, MA: Harvard Medical School.

van der Kolk, B.A., van der Hart, O. & Marmar, C.R. (1996). In B.A. van der Kolk, A. McFarlane & L. Weisaeth (Eds), *Traumatic stress: The effects of overwhelming experience on mind, body and society*. New York: Guilford Press.

van Ijzendoorn, M.H. & Schuengel, C. (1996). The measurement of dissociation in normal and clinical populations: Meta-analytic validation of the Dissociative Experiences Scale (DES). *Clinical Psychology Review*, **16**, 356–382.

van Reekum, R., Links, P.S. & Boiago, L. (1993). Constitutional factors in borderline personality disorder: Genetics, brain dysfunction and biological markers. In J. Paris (Ed.), *Borderline personality disorder: Etiology and treatment* (pp. 13–38). Washington, DC: American Psychiatric Press.

Vanderlinden, J., Van Dyck, R., Vandereycken. W., Vertommen, H. & van Verkes, R. (1993). The Dissociation Questionnaire (DIS-Q): Development and characteristics of a new self-report scale. *Clinical Psychology and Psychotherapy*, **1**, 21–27.

Wachs, T.D. (1999). *Necessary but not sufficient: The retrospective roles of single and multiple influences on individual development*. Washington, DC: American Psychological Association:

Waller, G. (1991). Sexual abuse as a factor in eating disorders. *British Journal of Psychiatry*, **159**, 664–671.

Waller, G. & Smith, R. (1994). Sexual abuse and psychological disorders: The role of cognitive processes. *Behavioural & Cognitive Psychotherapy*, **22**, 299–314.

Waller, N.G., Putnam, F.W. & Carlson, E.B. (1996). Types of dissociation and dissociative types: A taxometric analysis of dissociative experiences. *Psychological Methods*, **1**, 300–321.

Waller, N.G. & Ross, C.A. (1997). The presence and biometric structure of pathological dissociation in the general: Taxometric and behaviour genetic findings. *Journal of Abnormal Psychology*, **106**, 499–510.

Walsh, S. (1996). Adapting cognitive analytic therapy to make sense of psychologically harmful work environments. *British Journal of Medical Psychology*, **69**, 3–20.

Watson, C.G., Juba, M.P., Manifold, V., Kucala, T. & Anderson, P.E. (1991). The PTSD interview: Rationale, description, reliability and concurrent validity of a DSM-III-based technique. *Journal of Clinical Psychology*, **47**, 179–188.

Welldon, E. (1993). Forensic psychotherapy and group analysis. *Group Analysis*, **26**, 487–502.

Welldon, E. (1996). Group-analytic psychotherapy in an out-patient setting. In C. Cordess & M. Cox (Eds), *Forensic psychotherapy: Crime, psychodynamics and the offender patient*. London: Jessica Kingsley.

Weissman, M.M. & Markowitz, J. (1994). Interpersonal psychotherapy: Current status. *Archives of General Psychiatry*, **51**, 599–606.

Wertsch, J.W. (1985). *Vygotsky and the social formation of mind*. Cambridge, MA: Harvard University Press.

Westbury, E. & Turry, L.H. (1999). The efficacy of group treatment for survivors of childhood abuse. *Child Abuse & Neglect*, **23**, 31–44.

Westen, D. (1991). Clinical assessment of object relations using the TAT. *Journal of Personality Assessment*, **56**, 56–74.

Westen, D., Lohr, N., Silk, K., Gold, L. & Kerber, K. (1990). Object relations and social cognition in borderlines, major depressives, and normals: A TAT analysis. *Psychological Assessment*, **2**, 365–384.

Whitmire, L.E., Harlow, L.L., Quina, K. & Morokoff, P.J. (1998). *Childhood trauma and HIV: Women at risk*. London: Brunner/Mazel.

Wieland, S. (1998). *Techniques and issues in abuse-focused therapy with child and adolescents: Addressing the internal trauma*. London: Sage.

Wilbur, C.B. (1984). Multiple personality and child abuse. *Psychiatric Clinics of North America*, **7**, 3–8.

Wildgoose, A., Waller, G., Clarke, S. & Reid, N. (2001). Psychiatric symptomatology in borderline personality disorder: The mediating role of dissociation and fragmentation. *Journal of Nervous & Mental Disease*, **188**, 757–763.

Williams, J.M.G. (1992). *The psychological treatment of depression* (2nd edition) London: Routledge.

Williams, L.M. (1994). Recall of childhood trauma: A prospective study of women's memories of childhood sexual abuse. *Journal of Consulting & Clinical Psychology*, **62**, 1167–1176.

Wing, J.K., Cooper, J.E. & Sartorious, N. (1974). *The measurement and classification of psychiatric symptoms*. Cambridge, UK: Cambridge University Press.

Wolfe, D.A., Sas, L. & Wekerle, C. (1994). Factors associated with the development of post-traumatic stress disorder among child victims of sexual abuse. *Child Abuse & Neglect*, **18**, 37–50.

Wolff, P.H. (1987). *The development of behavioural states and the expression of emotions in early infancy*. Chicago: University of Chicago Press.

Young, B.H. & Blake, D.D. (1999). *Group treatment for post-traumatic stress disorder: Conceptualisation, themes and processes*. London: Brunner/Mazel.

Young, J.E. (1994a). *Cognitive therapy for personality disorders: A schema-focused approach* (revised edition): Sarasota, FL.

Young, J. (1994b). *Detailed schema strategies.* New York: Cognitive Therapy Center.

Young, J. (1995). *Schema-focused therapy workshop.* New York: Cognitive Therapy Center.

Young, J. & Behary, W.T. (1998). Schema-focused therapy for personality disorders. In N. Tarrier, A. Wells & G. Haddock (Eds), *Treating complex cases: The cognitive behavioural approach* (Ch. 15). Chichester: Wiley.

Young, J.E. & Lindemann, M.D. (1992). An integrative schema-focused model for personality disorder. *Journal of Cognitive Psychotherapy*, **6**, 11–23.

Young, L. (1992). Sexual abuse and the problem of embodiment. *Child Abuse & Neglect*, **16**, 89–100.

Zaidi, L.Y. (1994). Group treatment of adult male inpatients, abused as children. *Journal of Traumatic Stress*, **7**, 718–727.

Zatzick, D.F., Marmer, C.R., Weiss, D.S. & Metzler, T. (1994). Does trauma-linked dissociation vary across ethnic groups? *Journal of Nervous & Mental Disease*, **182**, 576–582.

Zona, M.A., Sharma, K. & Lane, J. (1993). A comparative study of erotomanic and obsessional subjects in a forensic sample. *Journal of Forensic Sciences*, 894–903.

Index